The Cambridge Companion to the violin

The Cambridge Companions to Music

The Cambridge Companion to the Violin

Edited by
ROBIN STOWELL
Professor of Music,
University of Wales College of Cardiff

CAMBRIDGE
UNIVERSITY PRESS

PUBLISHED BY THE PRESS SYNDICATE OF THE UNIVERSITY OF CAMBRIDGE
The Pitt Building, Trumpington Street, Cambridge, United Kingdom

CAMBRIDGE UNIVERSITY PRESS
The Edinburgh Building, Cambrige CB2 2RU, UK   http://www.cup.cam.ac.uk
40 West 20th Street, New York, NY 10011–4211, USA   http://www.cup.org
10 Stamford Road, Oakleigh, Melbourne 3166, Australia
Ruiz de Alarcón 13, 28014 Madrid, Spain

First published 1992
Reprinted 1994, 1995, 1996, 1997, 1998, 1999

Printed in the United Kingdom at the University Press, Cambridge

A catalogue record for this book is available from the British Library

Library of Congress Cataloguing in Publication data
The Cambridge companion to the violin / edited by Robin Stowell.
    p.   cm.
Includes bibliographical references and index.
ISBN 0 521 39033 6 (hardcover). – ISBN 0 521 39923 8 (paperback)
1. Violin. 2. Violin music – History and criticism. I. Stowell,
Robin
ML800.C35 1992 91–34017 CIP
787.2 – dc20

ISBN 0 521 39033 6 hardback
ISBN 0 521 39923 8 paperback

Contents

Illustrations

The contributors

PETER ALLSOP
Peter Allsop is a Lecturer in Music at Exeter University and specialises in Italian seventeenth-century instrumental music. He is the author of *The Italian 'Trio' Sonata* (Oxford University Press, forthcoming) and General Editor of New Orpheus Editions (devoted to the publication of the trio sonata repertory). His study of this subject is a direct result of his lifelong interest in the violin, which he began learning at the age of nine. Over recent years he has concentrated mainly on the Baroque violin.

PETER COOKE
Dr Peter Cooke is the UK's senior ethnomusicologist and teaches at the University of Edinburgh. Apart from being editor-in-chief of the ethnomusicology contributions to *The New Grove Dictionary of Music and Musicians*, he has written extensively on the music of Scotland and is the author of the highly praised study of Shetland fiddle playing, *The Fiddle Tradition of the Shetland Isles* (Cambridge, 1986), in the series Cambridge Studies in Ethnomusicology.

JOHN DILWORTH
John Dilworth graduated from the Newark School of Violin Making in 1979. He has since worked for Charles Beare in the London workshops of J. & A. Beare Ltd as a restorer of violins, violas and cellos. During this time he has made several instruments, including reproductions of classical examples. He also writes for *The Strad* and *Das Musikinstrument*, contributing articles based on practical experience and research into the history of the violin and its makers.

ADRIAN EALES
Having graduated with first-class honours from the University of Wales (Cardiff) in 1976, Adrian Eales initially made his mark as an award-winning violinist. Radio broadcasts followed and subsequently an extensive career with many distinguished orchestras, including principal

positions with the BBC Concert and Royal Philharmonic Pops orchestras. In recent years, freelance activities, especially in the television and recording industries, have complemented his teaching role as Head of Strings at Marlborough College.

MAX HARRISON

Max Harrison for many years wrote classical music criticism for *The Times* and many British and foreign periodicals. He still contributes to some of the latter, and has had books on Scriabin and Brahms published. He has also written much on jazz for magazines in the UK and abroad, and contributed the main jazz entry in *The New Grove Dictionary of Music and Musicians*, since re-published in expanded form in *The New Grove Gospel, Blues and Jazz*. His collection of essays, *A Jazz Retrospect*, has lately appeared in paperback and he is currently at work on vol. II of *The Essential Jazz Records*.

SIMON McVEIGH

Simon McVeigh is a Lecturer in Music at Goldsmith's College, University of London. His Oxford dissertation on eighteenth-century violinists has recently been published, and he is currently completing a book on concert life in London in this period.

BERNARD RICHARDSON

Bernard Richardson is currently a Lecturer in Physics at the University of Wales College of Cardiff. His research activities in musical acoustics stem from a long-standing passion for making and playing musical instruments. He lectures world-wide on the subject.

ROBIN STOWELL

Educated at the University of Cambridge and the Royal Academy of Music, Robin Stowell is currently a Professor of Music at the University of Wales College of Cardiff. He is a practising violinist and Baroque violinist as well as a music editor and author, and has written extensively about the violin and the conventions of performing early music. The author of *Violin Technique and Performance Practice in the Late Eighteenth and Early Nineteenth Centuries*, he has also written articles for numerous music journals and contributed chapters to several collaborative volumes.

ERIC WEN

Eric Wen attended Columbia and Yale Universities, and was awarded a research grant for advanced study at the University of Cambridge. He taught music theory and analysis at the Mannes College of Music, Goldsmith's College (University of London) and the Guildhall School of Music and Drama, and has published a number of articles in the field of

Schenkerian analysis. Eric Wen was editor of *The Strad* (1986–9) and *Musical Times* (1988–90), and is currently director of Biddulph Publications and Recordings.

PAUL ZUKOFSKY

A pupil of Ivan Galamian, Paul Zukofsky is currently Director of the Arnold Schoenberg Institute. He conducts at the Juilliard School, and is founder and Music Director of the Iceland Youth Orchestra. He is a specialist in the performance of contemporary music for the violin and writes with special authority on twentieth-century violin technique.

Preface

The chapters which make up this volume were commissioned from various friends and colleagues, all experts in their fields. The principal objective has been to provide the reader with a compact, composite survey of the history of the violin from its origins to the present day, focusing in particular on the instrument's structure and development, its fundamental acoustical principles, its chief exponents, its technique and teaching principles and its repertory and pedagogical literature, but embracing also its folk traditions and its role in jazz. If we have been successful in stimulating constructive, penetrating thought about the past, present and future of the art of violin playing and its numerous related aspects, our joint purpose will have been realised.

This book is a 'companion', not a 'compendium'. While comprehensiveness would always be our ideal, we have had to acknowledge that achievement of such a goal would require a volume many times the size of this. My contributors and I have therefore had to be selective in our essays and overall scheme, and in our illustrations, music examples and bibliographical references. There are some conscious omissions (for example, useful discussion of such treacherous areas as specific and improvised ornamentation is impossible in the limited space available, hence their one brief mention in Chapter 7); but if there are significant areas which we have inadvertently overlooked we very much regret our negligence. As editor, I must take full responsibility for the volume's overall proportions and various subdivisions, which were devised to comply with the understandable limitations of length imposed by the publisher.

Inevitably, therefore, the Cambridge Companion to the Violin employs the telescope rather than the microscope, revealing principally the central issues of our subject and their broad outlines while occasionally pinpointing the finer detail of particularly significant aspects. Although this finer detail may not always fill out and qualify simplified accounts of complex matters, my sincere hope is that the fifteen chapters have touched upon, if not fully embraced, nearly every aspect of the violin's history from its origins to the present day.

We have written for all who have an interest in the violin – 'amateurs' as well as students and professional musicians. Although some technical knowledge has been assumed of our readers, those unversed in 'musical mechanics' will find help to hand in the explanatory glossary of technical terms, included at the end of the volume on pp. 261–6. There is an appendix listing the principal pedagogical literature of the instrument and a select bibliography, and numerous illustrative plates and musical examples have been included to enhance the text and contribute to a balanced publication, thus avoiding the 'coffee-table book' formula of so many recent volumes on the subject. Dates of birth and death of certain significant figures in the violin's history are sometimes included in the text to clarify historical perspective, but such details are provided in the index as points of reference in respect of most personalities cited.

It is a pleasure to acknowledge the help given so willingly and by so many in the preparation of this book. I am indebted to my contributors one and all for their co-operative attitude, promptness of response to various problems and queries and for giving readily of their expertise in their various fields. The University of Wales College of Cardiff has also been generous in its help, granting me a short period of study leave in order to bring this volume to completion, and I am indebted to my wife and family and many friends and colleagues who have assisted and encouraged me during the course of this project. Last, but far from least, I must extend my sincere thanks to Penny Souster and her team at Cambridge University Press, and especially Lucy Carolan, for their helpful advice and firm but unobtrusive encouragement in bringing the book to press.

Robin Stowell

Acknowledgements

Acknowledgement for kind permission to reproduce illustrations and music examples is due to the following:

Illustrations

Ashmolean Museum, Oxford: Figs. 9, 10, 11
J. & A. Beare Ltd: Figs. 3b, 3c, 13, 15b, 18, 20
Michael Franke (Wiesbaden): Figs. 14, 15a
Mr R. Hargrave: Figs. 1, 2, 4
Max Jones Files: Fig. 45
National Gallery, London: Fig. 6
Dr G. W. Roberts: Fig. 27c
The Shrine to Music Museum, Vermillion, South Dakota: Fig. 7
Thanks are also due to Dr C. M. Hutchins for the loan of the plate used in Figure 27 and to Mr G. P. Walker for his assistance in the production of Figure 27b.

Music examples

Music from *Beginners Please* by Sheila Nelson. Reproduced by kind permission of Thames Television plc (Ex. 2)
© Copyright 1948 by Boosey & Co. Ltd (Exx. 2 and 5b)
By permission of Schott and Co. Ltd London (Exx. 5c and 36)
© Copyright for all countries 1967 by J. & W. Chester/Edition Wilhelm Hansen London Ltd, with the exception of Poland, Albania, Bulgaria, Czechoslovakia, Rumania, Hungary, Union of Soviet Socialist Republics, Cuba, Chinese People's Republic, Vietnam and North Korea where the Copyright is held by Polski Wydawnictwo Muzyczne, Cracow, Poland. All rights reserved.

Special thanks are also due to Tony Russell for locating some of the discographical information included in Chapter 15.

Abbreviations, fingering and notation

amp vn	amplified violin
bc	basso continuo
ch orch	chamber orchestra
fl	flute
hpd	harpsichord
kb	keyboard
orch	orchestra
perc	percussion
pf	pianoforte
rec	recorder
str	strings
va	viola
va da gamba	viola da gamba
vc	violoncello
vn	violin
vn picc	violino piccolo
ww	woodwind

Violin fingerings are indicated in the usual manner:

0	open string
1	the index finger (not the thumb as in keyboard fingering) and so on

Pitch registers are indicated by the following letter scheme:

Under this scheme the notes to which the violin is normally tuned are represented as g, d^1, a^1 and e^2.

1 The violin and bow – origins and development

JOHN DILWORTH

The violin: introduction and terminology

The violin is an endlessly fascinating instrument, both historically and artistically. A performer's instrument may be four hundred years old, but it will not differ significantly from one made yesterday. That the frail-looking violin has endured shows the perfection of its design, both as an expressive instrument of music and as a beautiful object in itself.

The violin is a mechanically simple but acoustically complex instrument. The four tapered tuning pegs for adjusting the G, D, A and E strings are made usually from rosewood or boxwood for durability, and project laterally from the backward curving pegbox (see Fig. 1). This latter ends in the scroll, a baroque adornment which is a characteristic feature of the violin family. The backward slope of the pegbox tensions the strings across the ebony nut, which is grooved to locate and raise them just above the surface of the ebony fingerboard, against which the strings are stopped by the fingers of the left hand. The fingerboard is glued to the neck, which is carved in one piece with the pegbox and scroll from maple (*acer pseudoplatanus*). It has a curved top in cross-section, and increases in width from the nut end to permit wider string spacing across the bridge, allowing easier movement for the bow. The neck joins the body of the violin at the root, whilst the fingerboard extends further above the body. The framework of the violin body is the rib structure, assembled from six thin maple ribs bent to shape by dry heat, and reinforced at the joints by interior blocks – one in each of the four outward curving corners, one at the lower end of the instrument, and the top-block, into which the neck root is fitted with a tapered mortice (prior to the nineteenth century, the neck was glued to the outside of the ribs, and secured with nails through the top-block). The six ribs correspond to the six main curves in the violin outline, the upper bouts, inward-curving middle or 'C' bouts, and wide lower bouts, on treble and bass sides. To ensure a strong glue-joint between the extremely thin ribs and the table and back of the violin, strips of pine or willow, the linings, are glued

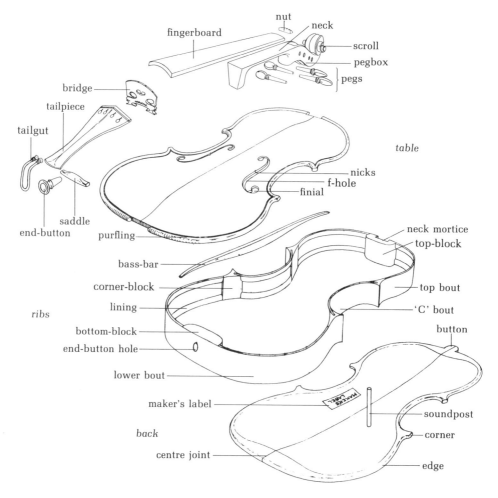

Fig. 1   An 'exploded' view of a violin

along the inside edges of the ribs. The traditional technique is to assemble the rib structure around a shallow hardwood mould.

The back of the violin is made from one or two matched pieces of maple, onto which the outline of the violin is drawn and sawn out (see Fig. 2). the arching, the outward swell, is then carved. The inner surface is also carved out to give a finished thickness in the centre of a violin back of about 5 mm, reduced around the edges to about 2.5 mm. The height and shape of the arching, combined with the finished thickness, are fundamental factors in determining the tonal quality of the instrument. Fig. 3a illustrates a two-piece back cut 'on the quarter'. Note the joint up the centre of the instrument and the horizontal 'figure', matching on both sides. Fig. 3b shows an example of a one-piece back cut 'on the quarter'; there is no centre joint, and the horizontal 'figure' runs continuously across. The horizontal 'figure' is less apparent in Fig. 3c, which shows a one-piece back cut 'on the

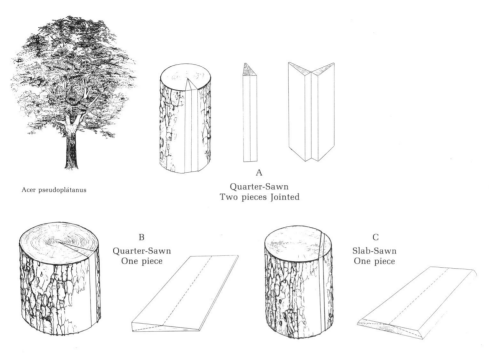

Acer pseudoplátanus

A
Quarter-Sawn
Two pieces Jointed

B
Quarter-Sawn
One piece

C
Slab-Sawn
One piece

Fig. 2   Cutting the back of the violin: three different methods

Fig. 3   The backs of three violins: (a) the 'Vieuxtemps' Guarneri (see also Fig. 12); (b) a violin by Antonio Stradivari, Cremona, 1691 ('The Hilton'); and (c) a violin by Nicolo Amati, Cremona, 1656

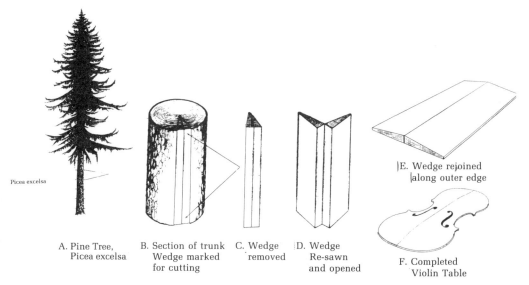

Picea excelsa

|E. Wedge rejoined
|along outer edge

A. Pine Tree,   B. Section of trunk C. Wedge :D. Wedge
    Picea excelsa   Wedge marked   removed   Re-sawn
                 for cutting   and opened

F. Completed
Violin Table

Fig. 4   Cutting the table of the violin

slab'; the 'contour' markings of the wood grain are particularly notable in this example.

The table is made in a similar way (see Fig. 4), but using spruce (*picea abies*, *picea excelsa* or *picea alba*), carefully chosen for fine even grain, and the finished thickness is usually 3 mm throughout. Just inside the edge of the front and back is a narrow inlay, the purfling. This comprises three separate strands of wood, the outer two of pearwood stained black, the inner strand of poplar, the whole less than 1.5 mm thick. As well as being decorative, the purfling inhibits the development of cracks around the edges, which are especially vulnerable since they project outside the fragile ribs by a margin of about 2 mm. On the back, this overhanging margin incorporates the button, which strengthens the neck joint.

The table, or front, of the violin is pierced by two soundholes, known as f-holes from their shape, which consist of round finials at each end of a curving body. The bridge, whose location on the instrument is indicated by the small nicks cut in the middle of each f-hole, is held on the violin by the pressure of the strings alone, and its precise position is critical for tonal quality. The bridge itself is cut from a thin sliver of maple, which is further reduced in mass by cutting intricate shapes known as the 'heart' and 'ears', and the two small 'feet' which actually stand on the violin table. The top curve of the bridge matches that of the fingerboard and enables the bow to play one string at a time without fouling the adjacent strings. Inside the violin just behind the outside edge of the bridge foot on the treble side is the soundpost (see Fig. 26, p. 41). This is a spruce or pine rod which is precisely fitted to the interior contours and lightly wedged in place to resist the downward pressure of the strings. Its position and 'tightness' is carefully regulated by the violin maker to produce the best possible tone. Beneath the bass foot of the bridge is fitted the bass-bar (see Fig. 26, p. 41), a supporting strut of spruce or pine, which runs from top to bottom of the inside of the table for most of its length. The exact dimensions of the bass-bar affect tone-quality, and are matched to each individual instrument by the maker or repairer.

The strings, having passed over the bridge, are secured to the ebony or boxwood tailpiece, which itself is fastened to the violin by a loop of gut or nylon, the tailgut, which runs over a saddle of ebony let in to the bottom edge of the table, and round the end-button, a small hardwood peg fitted into the lower block.

The species of timber chosen by different makers will differ only very slightly. Spruce and pine are softwoods, and their structure is simple, light and rigid, essentially a bundle of long hollow tubes which transmit vibrations more readily along than across the grain. Balkan maple is the favoured material for backs, but most local varieties have been used, chosen usually for the decorative cross-grain pattern known as 'curl' or 'flame'. Maple is a hardwood, having a complex structure of interlocking cells, and so is denser and harder than spruce or pine. The adhesive used throughout the construction has always been animal glue, which can easily be redissolved when repairs are necessary (the table is usually fixed with slightly weaker glue to facilitate removal).

The violin is covered with a protective varnish, the quality of which is more than merely an indicator of the quality of the instrument. The classical Italian makers appear to have used different formulations for the ground coat, which seals and protects the wood and does much to bring out its natural beauty, and the top coats, which were tinted with rich red, yellow and golden-brown colours. Different combinations of oils and resins give different degrees of hardness and flexibility; furthermore, a well-judged varnish allows the violin to speak with its full voice for many years, whilst a poor one can stifle it. Recent research suggests that walnut or linseed oil may have been an important constituent of the finest old Italian varnish, later supplanted by recipes based on shellac and alcohol.[1]

Origins and antecedents

Tracing the origins of the violin is not easy. Instruments played with a bow appear in European carvings and illustrations from around 900 AD, but interpretation is difficult, and the names given for them in texts vary and overlap. Broadly speaking, however, they fall into four categories: the rebec, the medieval and Renaissance fiddle, the lira da braccio and the viol.

The rebec was adopted, like the lute it resembles, from Moorish culture. Its half-pear-shaped body was originally carved and hollowed from a single block of wood, with a vellum soundboard. The medieval fiddle, appearing in the twelfth century, was constructed from flat boards

Fig. 5   Angel playing a rebec: cupola of Saronno Cathedral painted by Gaudenzio Ferrari (1535). Note the curved pegbox and lateral pegs, similar to the violin.

for the top, back and sides, a more flexible system of construction which was adapted to many forms from the simplest rectangular box to complex Gothic patterns (the name 'fiddle' persists as a familiar term for the violin but no longer has any technical meaning). It is generally depicted with a spade-shaped pegbox with upright pegs and three to five strings lying over a flat fingerboard and bridge (Fig. 6). Only the top string could thus be separately bowed for the melody, whilst the others provided a droning accompaniment. The playing position restricted the movement of the left hand, which also supported the instrument against the chest or shoulder. Similar types are still found in Eastern European folk music, and the rebec is familiar in North Africa and Turkey.

Medieval and Renaissance bowed instruments are almost indistinguishable from their plucked counterparts, but specialised refinements appeared during the fifteenth and sixteenth centuries. Around 1490, the viol came to Italy from Spain, a large, flat-topped instrument with a low bridge, but played in an upright position, resting on the player's lap or between the knees. Already well advanced and prestigious in Italy at that time, however, was the lira da braccio, the most significant antecedent of the violin (Fig. 7). A development of the fiddle, it is shown in very early illustrations being played in virtually the modern violinist's position; it had seven strings, two of which ran beside the neck and were played as drones.

Fig. 6   Hans Memling (c.1430–95): 'The Virgin and Child with Saints and Donors' (detail of central panel). A beautifully clear and detailed depiction of a five-stringed fiddle. Notice the vertical pegs in the flat pegbox and the flat fingerboard (with frets) and bridge.

Fig. 7   Lira da braccio by Francesco Linarol, Venice, 1563. Length of body: 505 mm

As early as 1508, the first depictions of violins appeared in Italian art,[2] but the main surviving examples of this crucial period are Venetian viols. In these can be traced the origins of the arched top and the bass-bar. To enable the large viol to sound individual strings, a high, curved bridge was needed, and to support the extra pressure this exerted on the instrument, the top was originally bent, then later carved into a strong, arched shape. Transverse bars provided internal stability to bent tops, but carved tops were left with a thicker central spine, which evolved into the bass-bar.[3] Although it is tempting to see these as forerunners of the violin, developments probably occurred simultaneously in all three types, viol, lira and violin (along with its relatives, the viola and cello). By the end of the sixteenth century the lira shared all the characteristics of the violin, save the stringing and pegbox, but the viol developed separately. Viol and lira continued in use in Italy until the early seventeenth century, although the viol persisted in Northern Europe, and especially in England, as the premier bowed instrument for the greater part of the next century. All these instruments frequently appear together in angelic bands in paintings of the late Renaissance, and a fine example, which includes the violin family, is in the cupola of Saronno

Fig. 8 Angel playing a violin: cupola of Saronno Cathedral painted by Gaudenzio Ferrari (1535). This represents one of the earliest known depictions of the instrument.

cathedral, painted by Gaudenzio Ferrari in 1535 (Fig. 8). The earliest surviving violins date from 1564,[4] and come from the same area of Northern Italy, covering Lombardy and the Veneto.

Almost every European country has made its claim to the invention of the violin, but no one can seriously challenge the pre-eminence of Italy in its history. All the greatest makers, with perhaps one exception, originated from Cremona, Brescia or Venice. Lute and viol makers flourished in Northern Italy in the early sixteenth century, encouraged by the richness of Venetian commerce and courtly entertainment. *Luthier* (or lute maker) came to mean maker of all stringed instruments, and a diverse and beautiful profusion emerged from their workshops, of which the violin was but one, and ultimately the most successful.

Development

The earliest violins are identified in illustrations by their carved backs, f-holes, and lateral pegs in a curved pegbox. The shaped back gave greater depth of sound, and produced a more flexible acoustical system which responded to adjustment and development. From the three-stringed instruments seen in paintings of the early sixteenth century, the first improvement was the addition of the fourth string, tuned to e^2, giving the definitive tuning of g–d^1–a^1–e^2. Patterns and dimensions were

Fig. 9   Violin by Andrea Amati, Cremona, 1564. The earliest known violin
to have survived, it was part of a set of thirty-eight instruments made
for Charles IX of France, and decorated on back and sides with his
coat of arms. Length of body: 342 mm

fairly fluid amongst makers in the sixteenth century, but the superb work
of Andrea Amati in Cremona established a settled standard. The technique of contemporary Brescian makers was closely allied to viol
making, for which they were renowned, but the design and construction
methods used by Andrea Amati for his earliest surviving violin (dated
1564) were original and unique, becoming the blueprint for violin
makers ever since (Fig. 9). He defined the classical form of the scroll and
the single row of purfling around the gently channelled edges of the
body. The channelling of the edges was in itself an important innovation
which changed the character of the arching, and therefore the tone-
quality.

The accepted modern form of the violin (excepting the shape of the
neck) was in place by 1710, largely owing to the work of Antonio
Stradivari. He reduced the height of the table and back, thereby producing a more powerful sound. Extraneous painted, inlaid and jewelled
decoration gradually fell out of fashion as the performance demands on
the instruments became greater, and the aesthetic perfection of the
violin's shape and proportion made them redundant. Dimensions

became standardised by musicians' need for consistency in technique, and makers had to exercise their imagination within narrower constraints.

Other significant changes were brought about by improvements in string making in the seventeenth century. Instrument making had been hampered by the limitations of strings made from strands of twisted sheep gut. Thick bass strings made in this way were stiff and unresponsive. From around 1560, however, more flexible 'rope-twist' strings made from two strands twisted together became popular, and these improved the clarity of the G and D strings. One hundred years later, 'overspun' strings were developed, making the G string thinner and more flexible by wrapping a small gut core with metal wire, and thereby improving matters still further. During the eighteenth century overspun strings replaced the twisted gut G and D. Furthermore, the neck and fingerboard were given a steeper backward slope, giving the strings a sharper angle over the bridge and increasing the resultant downward pressure on the front of the instrument.

These developments made the sound of the violin much more penetrating and enabled soloists to compete with the larger orchestras of the period. Although not necessarily the initiators of the idea, the Mantegazza brothers of Milan were, by 1790, busy refitting necks in old instruments to bring them up to the new standards. There are nowadays few violins made before that date which retain their original necks, but it should be noted that the original scroll and pegbox were retained during neck replacement.

Gradually the fingerboard was lengthened to accommodate playing in the higher positions, and the neck was made thinner to facilitate the movement of the left hand. However, the high tension required on the thin gut E strings made them unreliable, and it was not until the early years of this century that the use of steel E strings solved this problem. In modern times, silver- and aluminium-wound G, D and A strings with a synthetic core have also raised standards of consistency and power. All-metal strings are also in use, providing great volume of sound, but these require more precise tuning owing to the less elastic nature of metal, and a special tailpiece with integral screw adjusters is usually fitted.

Principal centres of violin making and their chief representatives

Cremona and Brescia

Andrea Amati (b. before 1505; d.1577) was the first recorded maker in Cremona, the greatest centre of violin making, and the first of four generations of *luthiers* who spanned the entire period of Cremona's

Fig. 10   Violin by Nicolo Amati, Cremona, 1649 ('The Alard'), one of the
finest examples of his work. Length of body: 351 mm

dominance of the craft. His work is marked by great elegance and an awareness of geometrical principles in design. His modelling is of the greatest delicacy, from the regular winds of the scroll to the tips of the f-holes. Andrea and all his family were consummate craftsmen. He was succeeded by two sons, Antonius (b.1540) and Hieronymus (1561–1630). They continued using their father's glorious golden-brown varnish, which was perhaps the greatest possession of the Cremonese makers in general, but gave his pattern a more substantial appearance. The f-holes were altered by making the circular finials smaller, and the tips, or 'wings', wider.

Nicolo Amati (1596–1684) was the son of Hieronymus and perhaps the greatest of the dynasty. His 'grand' pattern incorporated all the developments of his father and added some of his own (see Fig. 10). These instruments are today the most sought-after products of the Amati workshop, since his larger model has greater sound potential. He continued the process of strengthening the appearance of the instrument and experimented with new arching shapes.

Plague decimated Cremona in 1630, and Nicolo, with no immediate heirs, took on apprentices, including Francesco Rugeri (1620–c.1695) and G. B. Rogeri (active 1670–1705); but by far the most famous follower of Nicolo Amati was Antonio Stradivari (1644–1737). His earliest work dates from 1666 and already shows great originality. His craftsmanship was impeccable, and hardly faltered throughout his seventy-year career, allowing him to concentrate all his energies on a steady refinement of design.

Taking as a starting point the violins of Nicolo Amati, Stradivari gradually imbued the already graceful style with a noble aspect, a majestic quality to match the profound sonority he achieved. His most important innovations were the flatter and more powerful archings he evolved, and his new system of thicknessing. The most striking difference in appearance is the 'C' bout, which is straighter and stronger than the deeply incurving form of Amati. The f-holes are longer and less curved, and the scroll more substantial. Stradivari also changed the varnish, introducing a stronger red pigment, which gives the best surviving instruments a seemingly bottomless depth of colour. Stradivari proved his woodworking skills with a series of instruments inlaid with ebony and ivory filigree, but devoted himself to purity of line in later work. Experimentation with form resulted in the elongated 'long pattern' instruments of the 1690s and culminated in the broader model of his 'Golden Period' of 1700–20. This produced, amongst many masterpieces, the 'Messiah' violin of 1716, possibly the most prized instrument in the world because of its near-perfect state of preservation (Fig. 11). His later instruments, made with the increasing assistance of his sons Omobono and Francesco right up until his death, continued to develop in strength of character and depth of sound, but to some eyes and ears, lack the brilliance of his 'Golden Period'.

Beside the Amatis and Stradivaris, the best known makers of Cremona were the Guarneri family. Andrea (1626–98), a pupil of Nicolo Amati, inherited his mentor's concern for good design, but not his preoccupation with flawless craftsmanship. He produced delightful instruments whose asymmetries and tool-scarred surfaces show great personality. He sometimes chose rather a small model for his violins and gave them a steep, pinched arching, which is strong but not sufficiently flexible to provide a great sound.

His son, Giuseppe Guarneri (1666–c.1739), followed in his rough-hewn style, but improved the arching and therefore the sound quality. He also began to use a deep red-brown varnish not unlike that of his contemporary, Stradivari.

Giuseppe had two sons, Pietro (1695–1762) and Giuseppe 'del Gesù' (1698–1744).[5] Pietro left Cremona for Venice, but Giuseppe 'del Gesù' stayed in Cremona and is recognised by players today as the only rival to Stradivari. Whilst his earlier efforts show continuity with his father's work, by 1734 his instruments grew more confident and then wilder as he worked freely (see Fig. 12). Always under control, however, was his

Fig. 11   Violin by Antonio Stradivari, Cremona, 1716 ('Le Messie'), probably the most celebrated violin in the world. Length of body: 355 mm

understanding of the requirements of good tone. He cut the f-holes freely, not always elegantly, but always full of life. His scrolls are sometimes little more than a caricature of the prim designs of his predecessors, but they gain in personality. He varnished his instruments with equal verve, using copious amounts of lustrous red pigment which still retains its glow today.

The last great maker of Cremona, and the last to use its beautiful varnish, was Carlo Bergonzi (1683–1747). He achieved a satisfying synthesis of the styles of Stradivari and Guarneri. With carefully carved scrolls, elegant edge-work and purfling and finely cut f-holes, he used strong, flat archings inspired by the best work of del Gesù.

Although no maker has since reached the heights of Stradivari and Guarneri, Cremona still remains an influential centre. Its International School of Violin Making has trained many of today's leading makers.

The first rival to Cremona as a centre for violin making was Brescia. Only a short distance from Cremona, it nevertheless had a distinctive style of work in the sixteenth century. Gasparo da Salò (1540–1609) was its first known violin maker.[6] His violins are rare but distinctive (see Fig. 13), with an unrefined finish that anticipates del Gesù by one

Fig. 12   Violin by Giuseppe Guarneri 'del Gesù', Cremona, 1741 (known as 'The Vieuxtemps')

hundred years. The archings are often extremely high, but full, with the wood worked sufficiently thin to allow flexibility and a robust sound. Gasparo used a fine varnish (usually a deeper brown than Amati) and very extended f-holes, with the unusual feature of equal-sized finials at top and bottom of the 'f'. His purfling, although crudely laid in, is sometimes doubled, or led into decorative traceries on the back.

Gasparo was succeeded in Brescia by his pupil Giovanni Paolo Maggini (c.1581–c.1632), whose whose early work is almost indistinguishable from that of his master. However, Maggini seems to have become aware of the high level of craftsmanship in Cremona, and set himself to emulate it, perhaps bearing in mind that Brescian violins at the time fetched only a quarter of the price of Cremonese. Although he retained the general appearance of the Gasparo model, he lowered the arching, and started to work more neatly, carving the scrolls with care. He persisted with the double rows of purfling, although this can be a structural weakness. He produced both a small and a large model, the latter being almost unmanageable for modern players, but having great sonority.

Fig. 13   Violin by Gasparo da Salò, Brescia, c.1580

Other Italian centres

Although the violin was quickly adopted in France and the Netherlands, and imported Italian instruments were imitated by the Médards in France and Jacobs in Holland during the seventeenth century, violin making in Italy did not spread beyond Cremona and Brescia until about 1690. The third important centre was Venice, and its first renowned violin maker was Matteo Gofriller (c.1659–1742). The Venetian style practised by Gofriller is largely distinguished by the use of a deep red varnish, which usually has a crackled and wrinkled finish. There is some resemblance between the violins of Gofriller and those of Andrea Guarneri, and a deep trench around the edge sometimes renders the arching a little weak. His undersized and casually worked scrolls have great character.

Domenico Montagnana (c.1687–1750) is known as the 'mighty Venetian' because of his superlative cellos. His violins, though variable, can touch the sublime, with dramatic coverings of curdled ruby-red varnish over extravagantly wrought f-holes and scrolls, and produce first-rate tonal results.

Pietro Guarneri, the brother of del Gesù, worked in Venice from c.1718 to 1762, making instruments with a flamboyant blend of Cremonese and Venetian ideas.

Sanctus Seraphin (1699–c.1760) was the next master of the Venetian school. He developed an individual style, employing the highest standards of craftsmanship, comparable with the Amatis in Cremona. The design of his scroll, however, is quite distinctive, with a very deep pegbox and small, tightly wound volute.

The other cities of Italy occupy a lower rung of the ladder. Milan was very productive, and the earliest makers very fine, but later rushed and cheaper-quality work led to decadence. Giovanni Grancino (active 1685–1726) took his inspiration from the Amatis and worked in a looser but attractive style. At first he used a luscious golden-yellow varnish, but later adopted a thinner brown recipe. He made his scrolls large and deeply carved, the f-holes sweepingly elegant, and the corners particularly delicate. The arching is sometimes pinched, but the sound is generally excellent.

Carlo Giuseppe Testore (active 1690–1720) was a pupil of Grancino, and his excellent work is often indistinguishable from his teacher's. His son Carlo Antonio (active 1720–60), though not untalented, was not inspired to fine work. He used thin, yellow varnish, seldom bothered to purfle the back, merely scratching on a double line, and often left the carving of the scroll incomplete on the back of the pegbox. His younger brother, Paolo Antonio, and his son Pietro worked in successively cruder styles, but their instruments are still sought after for their fine tone. Carlo Ferdinando Landolfi (active c.1750–75) was a slightly more attentive craftsman, who produced a wide range of instruments.

Neapolitan makers produced abundant numbers of instruments, from the finest to the mediocre, from c.1700 onwards. Their instruments are still sought after for tonal quality and often provide the backbone of an orchestral string section. Particularly significant among these makers were members of the Gagliano family, of whom the earliest was Alessandro (active 1700–35). Most of his comparatively rare violins are of the finest wood, and made with great flair. His workmanship was not of the best – he set the f-holes too low on the body and his scrolls are weak – but the design is graceful and the arching strong and low.

His two sons, Nicolo and Gennaro (both active c.1740–80), pursued a more orthodox path, losing some of their father's flair as well as his gorgeous varnish. They adopted largely Cremonese models, Nicolo using a Stradivari pattern, but Gennaro made very convincing copies of other masters as well, including Amati and Bergonzi. Of Nicolo's sons, Ferdinando and Giuseppe (both active c.1770–c.1800) employed a cheaper quality of varnish, which was hard, thin and glassy, and subsequent members of the family, Giovanni, Nicolo (ii), Antonio (ii) and Raffaele continued the decline in quality, but not quantity, of the family's work.

In Mantua, close to Cremona, worked Pietro Guarneri (1655–1720), the elder son of Andrea. Although not prolific, he was by far the neatest craftsman of the family, and a strong influence on subsequent Mantuan makers such as Camilli (c.1704–54) and Balestrieri (active 1750–80).

David Tecchler (before 1700 – after 1747) and one of his pupils, M. Platner (active 1720–50), in Rome and G. B. Gabbrielli (active 1740–70) and the Carcassi brothers (active 1750–80) in Florence were the best of the many makers who followed the Tyrolean pattern of Jacob Stainer, which has not proved so durable as the Cremonese.

Amongst the first and most successful makers of Turin was Giofredo Cappa (1644–1717). An early disciple of Nicolo Amati, he developed his model with swooping f-holes set slightly low on the body. It is his fine brown varnish which most invites comparison with the Cremonese.

Giovanni Battista Guadagnini (c.1711–86) spent the last years of his life in Turin under the patronage of an influential enthusiast of the violin, Count Cozio di Salabue. A highly important maker, he was born in Piacenza, close to Cremona. Working there, and later in Milan and Parma, he evolved an individual and powerful style, his instruments giving first-class tone-quality. Many features of his work are generally consistent, such as the oval-shaped lower finials of the f-holes, but his varnish, often of the best quality, changed from town to town.

The next makers of significance in Turin belong to the nineteenth century. J. F. Pressenda (1777–1854) and his pupil, Giuseppe Rocca (1807–65), were the greatest copyists of Stradivari of their time, and the tonal results they achieved make their instruments highly sought after. They both worked accurately, but with a recognisable style of their own.

Europe outside Italy

Beyond Italy, many fine makers originated from the Tyrol and Bavaria but settled in other cities and adopted French, English or Italian nationality. The town of Füssen was a centre for lute making as early as the fifteenth century, and its craftsmen set out across Europe as journeymen. The greatest maker of the region, however, was Jacob Stainer of Absam (1617–83). He developed a style that is now recognised as uniquely German, followed by German makers over many generations and taken up elsewhere during the mid eighteenth century. During this period, Stainer's high-built violins, with small, gracefully curled f-holes (Fig. 14) were judged to be the epitome of the craft, and the silvery but modest tone ideal for the music of the period, but as orchestras later grew more powerful the sound of Stainer's instruments proved inadequate. His craftsmanship and taste were impeccable, allowing him to experiment with forms and decoration. He occasionally carved a lion's head in place of a scroll, and his varnish was equal to that of the Amatis.

Northern Europe did not become an influential centre for violin making until the late eighteenth century. Nicolas Lupot (1758–1824) and François Pique (1758–1822) worked in Paris and made fine violins based

Fig. 14   Violin in original condition by Jacob Stainer, Absam, 1679, one of
the few seventeenth-century violins to have survived without
'modernisation'

on Stradivari but with their own character and fine red and orange
varnish. Together with Pressenda, they re-established the Cremonese
model as the ideal.

The best known of all Parisian makers is Jean-Baptiste Vuillaume
(1798–1875). Following the work of Lupot and Pique, he copied the great
Italian masters with great ingenuity and was highly successful as a violin
maker, inventor, bow maker and businessman. His copies of those
Stradivari and Guarneri instruments which he collected and sold in his
shop were of clinical accuracy right down to the worn varnish. Such
patination and apparent 'wear' made Vuillaume's instruments particularly attractive to the player. Since the nineteenth century problems
have been caused by instruments made as imitations or downright fakes.
After one hundred years of genuine wear, a Vuillaume can be mistaken
for a Stradivari; furthermore, the work in London of John Lott (c.1800–71)
and, in the current century, the Voller brothers, who produced many
very clever fakes, has sown confusion amongst experts.

Violin trading was perhaps first made respectable by the expertise of
Count Cozio di Salabue (1755–1840), who did much to pass on his

carefully acquired knowledge in the form of diaries and by his patronage of makers. Much of his collection, including the 'Messiah' Stradivari (Fig. 11), passed to the legendary Luigi Tarisio (1790–1854), a passionate collector of violins, who rescued many other masterpieces from oblivion in the Italian countryside. Although he sold some to dealers in Paris, notably Vuillaume, he kept the best for himself, and when he died in apparent poverty, Vuillaume found in Tarisio's Milan attic 24 violins by Stradivari, and 120 by other great makers. This discovery was instrumental in raising the standard of violin making and appreciation in Paris.

With the growing popularity of the violin, the art of violin making took on the trappings of commerce and industry. In eighteenth-century London, many craftsmen were virtually anonymous; their names are known to us only through signatures hidden inside their violins, which were labelled and branded by the shopkeeper. Even the distinguished Sicilian-born maker Vincenzo Panormo, who arrived in London around 1790, rarely labelled his own instruments. Work became more imitative than creative, and much was lost in the process.

In the closed communities of mountainous Bavaria and Saxony, it had long been the practice for whole villages to sustain themselves through specialised woodworking crafts, and in the nineteenth century towns such as Mittenwald, Markneukirchen and Schönbach (now Luby in Czechoslovakia), virtually became violin-making factories. Although individual makers pursued distinguished careers, notably the Klotz family in Mittenwald, many instruments were made through cottage-industry methods. Different workers specialised in scrolls, fronts, backs, assembly and varnishing, and completed instruments were sent abroad, often to be labelled by dealers as their own work. Similar practices were established in Mirecourt, in the Vosges Mountains of France, and machinery was soon developed for mechanical carving and even for pressing arched fronts and backs from flat plates of wood. These instruments are tonally inferior, and of little beauty, but they have been useful in providing student instruments at an affordable price. Many great makers served their apprenticeships in such places, and Mittenwald and Mirecourt have now been established as the state violin-making schools of Germany and France, inspiring similar establishments in Britain and America. With the school at Cremona also, there has been a renaissance of violin making in recent years which has helped restore the supply of handmade instruments, previously overwhelmed by the factory products of nineteenth-century Europe, and, more recently, China.

Fine makers active today include Carl Becker, David Burgess and David Gusset in America, Wilfred Saunders, William Luff and Rowland Ross in England, F. Bissolotti and G. B. Morassi in Italy, Joachim Schade in Germany, and Premsyl Spidlen in Czechoslovakia. There are also fine craftsmen now working in Japan as a result of the phenomenal popularity there of Western classical music.

The restoration of old violins, which are in increasing demand despite the flood of new instruments, has become a sophisticated craft of its own. It was pioneered by W. E. Hill (1817–95) in London in the 1840s, and has been continued to the present by his successors, the firm of W. E. Hill & Sons. The influential genius of recent years has been S. F. Sacconi, born in Rome but best known for his work in the shop of Rembert Wurlitzer in New York. One of his students, Charles Beare, now head of the family firm of J. & A. Beare Ltd in London, is recognised as one of the leading authorities on old instruments.

The Baroque and 'modern' violin

One of the factors in the current renaissance of violin making is the interest in 'authentic' instruments for performances of Baroque music. Since so few have survived, it has been necessary to make reproductions and conduct detailed research into old methods of construction and playing set-up. These have changed significantly in the four hundred years of the violin's history. The most obvious change in tone comes from the different strings of modern instruments, but the main outward difference between the Baroque and modern instrument is the neck. Violins were originally made with the neck angled only slightly downward, if at all, the fingerboard having a wedge shape in order to follow the rise of the strings up to the bridge (see Figs. 15a and 15b). The fingerboard was made of softwood veneered with ebony, to lessen the weight, and was wider at the nut, but shorter in overall length. The neck was generally thicker, and some 5–10 mm shorter, but there was considerable variation between makers, and conflicting evidence has been collected about precise dimensions.

The bridge of a Baroque violin is quite similar to a modern one, but has a flatter curve (see Fig. 16). The tailpiece is much lighter, usually maple, sometimes veneered with ebony, but thinner and flatter. Many seventeenth-century paintings appear to show violins with the bridge set very far back, but none of the surviving instruments from the period reveals any evidence of this practice.

Internally, there were originally one or more nails in the top-block, securing the neck to the instrument. Of greater significance to the sound quality, however, is the size of the bass-bar. Stradivari's bass-bars were between 20 and 35 mm shorter and about 6 mm lower than their modern counterparts. Soundposts were also smaller in diameter. Baroque instruments are also lighter in weight and under less tension, and their sound is lighter and freer, responding to the lighter pressure of the smaller bows of the period.

The chin rest, an innovation attributed to Louis Spohr (1784–1859), is a carved wooden (usually ebony or boxwood) block clamped to the lower ribs of the instrument. It has developed from a small crescent shape,

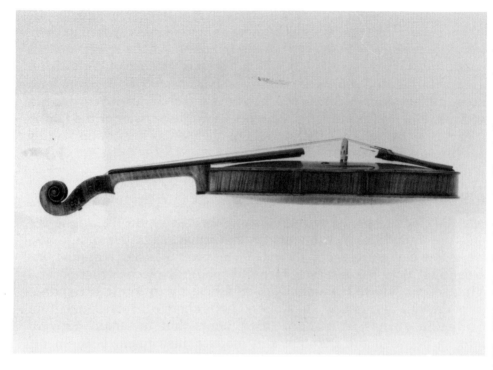

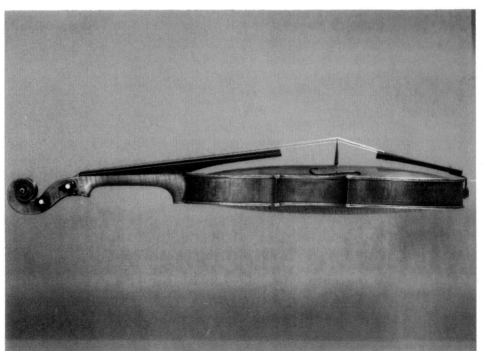

Fig. 15   Side view of (a) Stainer violin (see also Fig. 14) and (b) 'The Hilton' Stradivari (see also Fig. 3). Compare the shorter, straighter (with no discernible backward slant) and thicker neck and wedge-shaped fingerboard of the Stainer instrument with the 'modernised' neck and fingerboard (tilted back sharply from the plane of the ribs) of the Stradivari.

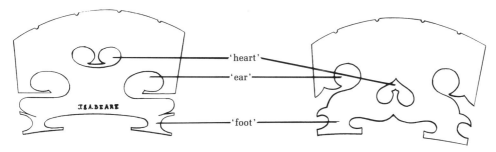

Fig. 16   Violin bridges: modern (left) and 'Baroque'

originally placed directly over the tailpiece, to more complex forms (positioned to the left of the tailpiece) which lift the chin clear of the violin. A shoulder rest is nowadays also commonly used. This is an inverted bridge shape which is clipped to the lower bouts of the back, lifting the instrument away from contact with the shoulder.

The mute, in use since the seventeenth century, is basically a weight which can be attached to the bridge, inhibiting its vibration and producing a stifled sound for specific musical effects (or, if it is particularly heavy, for quiet practice). Violins nowadays are generally fitted with a fine-tuner, a small screw adjuster fixed to the tailpiece for tuning the metal E string. Metal strings are too sensitive to be tuned satisfactorily by the pegs alone.

Measurements

Note: Measurements given are for a Stradivari violin of the 'Golden Period' in modern playing order

Length of back	355mm
Width of top bouts	168mm
Width of middle bouts	113mm
Width of lower bouts	219mm
Depth of ribs	32mm at endpin, tapering to 30mm at neck
Length of stop (distance from top edge of belly to bridge position)	195mm
Length of neck	130mm
Length of fingerboard	270mm
Height of bridge	41mm

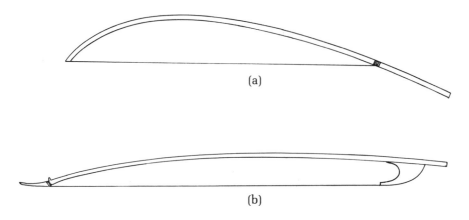

(a)

(b)

Fig. 17   Types of medieval (above) and Renaissance bows

The bow: history and development

The bow has a far longer history than the violin, but the development of the violin made new demands on the existing bow of the sixteenth century. Although many different forms appeared before 1500, the bow was often depicted as a simply curved stick with a skein of horsehair fixed from a point some way in from one end, which was used as the handle, to the opposite tip (Fig. 17a). The hair was in permanent tension from the deep curve of the stick, which also gave the bow a high centre of gravity above the string, making it difficult to control. The curve was made much flatter during the sixteenth century, with the addition of the frog (named after a similarly shaped part of a horse's hoof), a large wedge which kept the hair clear of the stick at the handle (Fig. 17b).

Early bow makers remained anonymous, and it is not clear whether violin makers also made bows for their own instruments; this is not the case today. The major innovations in bow making in the Baroque are associated with musicians rather than craftsmen. The type of bow named after Corelli (1653–1713) has a longer and straighter stick, and a down turned tip to raise the stick away from the hair, matching the frog. The tip evolved elegant shapes, referred to as the 'pike's head' or 'swan-bill' (see Fig. 18c). The 'clip-in' frog (Fig. 19) allowed the tension on the hair to be relaxed, prolonging the life of the hair and the stick. The hair was fixed to the stick at each end, and the frog provided the tension when wedged in place. The screw adjustment mechanism, with the hair fastened into the frog, was anonymously developed around 1700 and was eventually universally adopted.

Tartini (1692–1770) promoted the introduction of a deeper, more modern shape of tip (c.1730), and Cramer (1746–99) later introduced the incurved, or concave stick. This last development, made possible by the previous changes to the tip and frog and the use of stronger varieties of

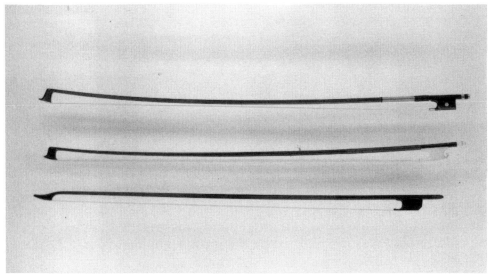

Fig. 18   Three bows of different periods: (a) modern type with pernambuco
stick and ebony screw-adjusting frog (top); (b) transitional type with
'hatchet' head and 'open' ivory, screw-adjusting frog, Italian c.1780
(middle); (c) 'Corelli' type, fluted snakewood bow with 'clip-in' frog,
Italian c.1700 (bottom)

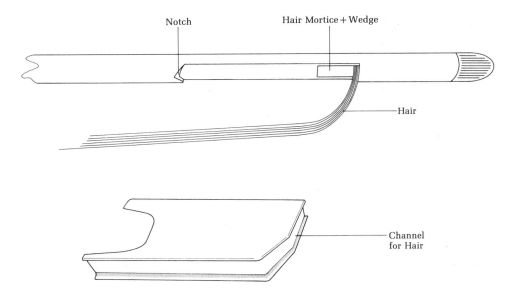

Fig. 19   Diagram of a 'clip-in' bow frog

wood, is the most crucial and provides the essential playing qualities of
the modern bow. The Cramer bow is a transitional type, with a squat
'hatchet' or tall 'battleaxe' head and an 'open' frog (without a slide to
cover the hair along the bottom face), often ornately carved (Fig. 18b).
Much experimentation went on in England and France to decide the
optimum size of the head and curve of the stick, and the playing length

(a)   (b)

Fig. 20   (a) Head and (b) frog of a bow by François Tourte. Notice the facets
on the stick, the ivory face, the silver ferrule and the mother-of-pearl
slide.

and the width of the band of hair gradually increased. The final form of
the violin bow was determined by the great French craftsman François
Tourte (1747–1835).

Tourte, the 'Stradivari of the bow', possessed not only the ingenuity to
bring the bow to perfection but also the skill to make bows of unsurpassed quality, which are still sought after by players and emulated by
makers. Although it cannot be shown that he invented any of the features
of the modern bow, he was the first to employ them all effectively. He
refined the shape of the head, and equipped the frog, carved from ebony,
with the slide and 'D-ring' or ferrule to keep the hair in a uniform ribbon
(Figs. 20a and 20b). He also perfected the incurved shape of the stick to
produce an ideal balance and weight, using pernambuco wood.

Materials and manufacture

Pernambuco (*echinata caesalpina*) is the only acceptable material for a
good modern bow, because of its strength and resilience. It is an
Amazonian timber, named after the port from which it was first exported.
The 'Corelli' bow of the seventeenth century was generally made from
snakewood (*brosimum aubleti*), a heavier Amazonian variety, with a
speckled snakeskin-like grain. The introduction of South American
timbers to Europe in the sixteenth century made possible the changes in
bow making, since only these woods have the suppleness and strength
needed in a long, straight bow.

The stick is first sawn out straight, with the rough head at one end, and
bent to the correct curve with dry heat. It is then finished with planes and
files to the required tapering diameter. This work is very highly skilled,
and the maker's appreciation of the strength of the wood determines the
final shaping, and the strength, weight and balance of the bow, all of
which fall within very close tolerances. To make the bow easier to
control, the tip must be reasonably light, yet responsive to the player.
Therefore the stick is made thinner, and the curve, or spring, progressively deeper towards the head. In the finished bow, the stick will

normally be closest to the hair approximately two thirds of its length towards the head. Bows are made either with an octagonally faceted or round cross-section, and snakewood bows of the Corelli period were often fluted along their length for lightness. When the stick has been shaped, the head can be carved and given its protective face of ivory lined with ebony, and a mortice is cut in to receive the hair and its retaining wedge, usually cut from limewood. In the other end, a mortice is cut in the stick to accept the screw eye, and a hole drilled lengthwise for the screw and adjuster.

The frog is carved from a block of ebony. The top surface is carefully fitted to the stick and provided with a silver shoe to protect the thin edges (see Fig. 21). A groove is cut in the lower face to receive the mother-of-pearl slide which covers the hair-mortice. The front is shaped to take a silver 'D-ring' and a silver back-plate is fitted. The sides are usually decorated with a mother-of-pearl dot. The brass screw eye is threaded into the top face, and the silver screw adjuster, often with ebony and mother-of-pearl decoration, is set on a threaded steel shaft.

The finished bow is oiled or french polished, and the handle is given a lapping of leather, thread, silver wire, or whalebone. The maker shows his individual style in his choice of decorative materials and devices; gold is quite often substituted for silver, and frogs have been made of ivory and tortoiseshell.

Only white horsehair of sufficient length is usable, which comes now mainly from China and Siberia; about 180 hairs are needed for each bow. The hair is in effect only the carrier for the rosin (pine-tree resin), a naturally sticky substance which is essential to the cyclic slip-stick motion involved in the excitation of the string.[7] Beneath the 'D-ring' is the willow-wood spreader wedge which keeps the hair in a flat ribbon. By applying the edge of the ribbon to the string, only a few hairs come into contact with the string, and the adhesion is diminished; this gives a *pianissimo* sound. The full width of hair on the string, however, provides maximum grip and full volume. The hair may become greasy and individual strands break with use. Thus, bows have to be re-haired regularly, a skilled job which Vuillaume tried to eliminate with his 'self-hairing' bow, where a previously prepared hank of hair slotted into the specially adapted head and frog; however, his idea never caught on.

With the increasing difficulty in obtaining the fine natural materials used in bow making, and the recent emphasis on conservation, there has been a search for substitutes. The ingenious Vuillaume developed a hollow steel bow, which despite good playing characteristics was just as vulnerable to bending and dents as a wooden stick is to cracks. Carbon fibre and other modern synthetics are being used with some success, and W. E. Hill & Sons adopted a synthetic tortoiseshell for frogs; however, traditional materials remain unequalled.

The dimensions of the bow changed considerably during its develop-

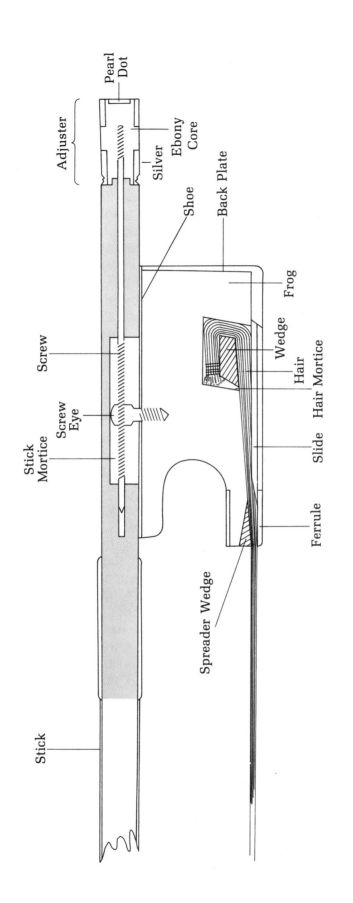

Fig. 21   Cross-section of the frog of a modern bow

ment, becoming longer to fulfil the more legato ideals of the mid to late eighteenth century onwards, and heavier to draw a fuller sound. Since Tourte, the overall length has been settled at around 74 cm and the weight ideally at 60 gm.

Famous makers

Little is known about early bow makers. An English reference (c.1670) mentions a violin by a named maker with a 'stockman's bowe', implying that the bow was an accessory supplied by another tradesman. A bow with the brand of Tononi, the eighteenth-century Venetian violin maker, is extant as well as many bows with eighteenth-century English brands. It was common practice, however, for violin makers to stamp the work supplied by others. The collection of Stradivari tools and templates in the Civic Museum in Cremona does contain patterns for bow frogs, but of the bows attributed to his hand, only two fluted snakewood bows in the collection of W. E. Hill & Sons have any real claim to authenticity.

The Cramer bow and other transitional types are the first to be attributed to specialist bow makers. In Paris, François Tourte's father, Louis (c.1740–80), and Jacques Lafleur (1757–1832) both made bows with incurved sticks and elegant ivory frogs, and adopted various head shapes. In London, Edward Dodd (1705–1810) has been credited with many transitional bow-types in England, but his son John (1752–1839), whose bows evolved in tandem with those of François Tourte in Paris, is historically more important. However, John Dodd's work takes second place to that of the great Frenchman because of his less consistent craftsmanship.

The French school has dominated bow making, just as Italy has dominated violin making, and many of the world's more renowned makers of today base their work on the French tradition. Most of the great French bow makers come from the town of Mirecourt: Maline (1793–c.1855); Adam (1795–1865) and his son known as 'Grand Adam' (1823–69); Maire (1800–78); Simon (1808–82); Peccatte (1810–74); Henry (1823–70); Voirin (1833–85); Lamy (1850–1919); and Sartory (1871–1946). Most of these craftsmen moved to Paris, where Tourte, Pajeot (1791–1849), a pupil of Lafleur, and Vuillaume had workshops. Vuillaume employed many of the finest, notably Persois (active 1823–43), Peccatte, Simon and Voirin.

Among the respected German makers are Kittel, who worked in St Petersburg 1839–70, Bausch (1805–71) and Nürnberger (1854–1931). The name of Bausch, however, has passed on to huge numbers of factory-produced bows. In England, Dodd, was succeeded in importance by James Tubbs (1835–1921) and Samuel Allen (1848–1905) and later by the firm of W. E. Hill & Sons, who developed their bow workshops under William Retford (1875–1970) and others. They have employed and trained many of the finest British bow makers of the current century.

2　The physics of the violin

BERNARD RICHARDSON

Introduction

A study of the physics of the violin gives a fascinating insight into how the instrument converts the player's intricate motions into musical sounds. Practising musicians are often blissfully unaware of the ways in which their instruments function, but a basic understanding of the mechanics involved can be of great benefit when teaching, selecting instruments or dealing with minor problems. It also brings a little more objectivity to a subject otherwise clouded with myth, mystique and superstition.

The twentieth century has witnessed a great increase in the scientific evaluation and development of a wide range of musical instruments. Occasionally, investigations are designed specifically to improve the performance of instruments or to achieve greater control during their manufacture. Some of these studies have been successful. More usually, they are carried out purely for the sake of curiosity – a desire to seek a rational explanation of an observed phenomenon. The researcher now has a wide range of powerful analytical techniques at his disposal. For example, he can use sensitive electronic instrumentation, high-speed computers and even lasers to probe the tiny vibrations of the violin. Although these physical studies have demonstrated the basic action of the violin and unravelled a few of its 'mysteries', they are still far from answering those tantalising questions relating to the finer details of violin tone. Once we begin to involve the *subjective* evaluation of instruments, we may raise many psychological questions concerning the relationship between the instrument and the player and also about the perception of music. An instrument must provide a perfect vehicle for musical expression. It must 'feel' right and respond to the nuances of the player. The sound quality must appeal to both the player and the audience in a wide variety of acoustical environments, and it must have a tonal range suitable for the performance of different styles of music. It must also be visually attractive. These are not purely physical aspects of the instrument. To make substantial further progress in our *objective* understanding of the finest instruments requires the combined efforts of physical scientists, psychologists, musicians and makers.

The acoustical function of the violin[1]

Sound is produced when a vibrating surface interacts with the surrounding air. As the surface moves backwards and forwards, it decreases and increases the local air pressure. These pressure variations travel rapidly away from the source as sound waves, which spread out filling the space around the listener. The primary source of vibrations in a violin is the bowed or plucked string, but it produces virtually no sound on its own because its surface area is too small to drive the air. The body of the violin is designed to act as a mediator between the string and the air. The vibrating string creates a time-varying force at the bridge which causes the whole body to vibrate in sympathy. The sound we hear comes from the tiny vibrations induced in the wooden structure. Amplification is achieved mechanically through resonance of the violin body, and the large, lightweight plates (the table and back) making up the instrument form efficient sound radiators, not unlike the cones of loudspeakers.

The driving force created by the string can be measured with a transducer on the bridge. The force of interest is not the considerable static down-loading of the strings (typically about 10 kg weight) but the small, rapid variations caused by the vibrating string as it swings to and fro. The form of the force signal depends on the method of excitation. A bowed string always produces a 'saw-tooth' waveform, as shown in Fig. 22a. This results from a cyclic slip-stick motion created by the frictional forces which exist between the string and the bow. The motion involves periods where the bow and the string move together slowly (sticking) and periods in which the string slips rapidly in the opposite direction. The rosin provides the friction which drives this process and must be present on both the string and the bow hair for correct action.

A waveform of the sound radiated by a violin is shown in Fig. 22b. This appears to have little in common with the force signal, though close inspection shows that both waves have the same period (the repeat time of the waveform). The shape and perceived tone-quality of the waveform are related to its harmonic content. This can be determined from the spectrum, which shows the relative amplitudes of the individual harmonics making up the signal. The spectrum of the sound wave shows that although the body responds to all harmonics, it does not do so equally, radiating some more efficiently than others. This spectral transformation, or filtering effect, is a function of the construction of the instrument and varies considerably from one violin to another, giving each instrument a unique tone.

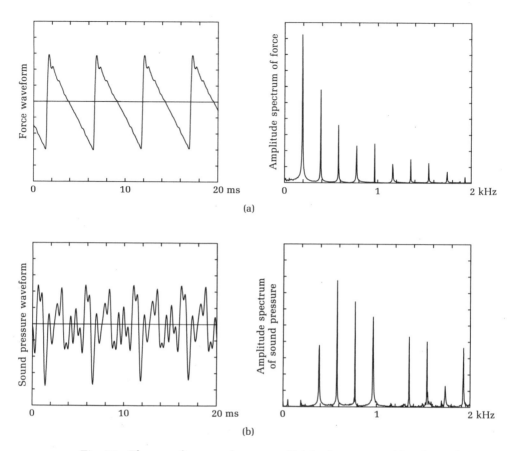

Fig. 22   The waveforms and spectra of (a) the force exerted by a bowed string
at the bridge, and (b) the sound radiated by the violin playing the
same note (open G string). The two waveforms have the same period
(0.005 seconds or 5 ms), but the spectra show that they have
different harmonic content.

String vibrations and the player

A casual observation of the vibrations of a bowed string fails to reveal the
complexity of its motion. 'Snapshots' taken at different times show that
the string is bent into two straight sections (Fig. 23a). The 'kink' between
these sections travels at a uniform rate around a cyclic path plotting out
the envelope of the motion. The envelope is all we see of the string's
motion without special equipment. When the kink is on the far side of
the bow, the string 'sticks' and moves slowly with the bow, but when it
lies between the bow and bridge, the string slips quickly in the opposite
direction. This slip-stick cycle is repeated over and over. The time taken
for the kink to complete one cycle is the period of the motion and governs
the perceived pitch of the sound it produces; the longer the period, the
lower the pitch. The inverse of the period gives the number of cycles per

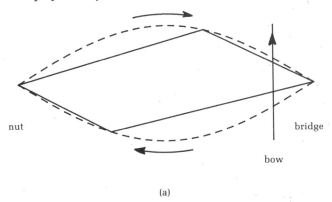

(a)

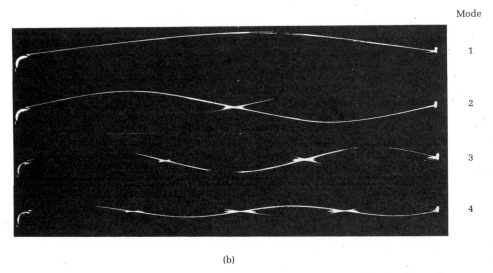

(b)

Fig. 23   (a) Schematic representation of the motion of a bowed string arrested at two different times during its cycle. The kink in the string draws out the envelope of the vibration (dotted line). The displacement of the string at any arbitrary instant can be synthesised by adding, in the correct proportions, the simple string displacements shown in (b). The latter are photographs of a real string vibrating in its individual modes of vibration. The string now flaps up and down between the extremities of its motion, always retaining the same mode shape.

second or the *frequency* of the oscillations, measured in Hz (Hertz) or kHz (thousands of Hertz).

It is instructive to view the motion of the string in an alternative way, as a summation of more basic vibrations of the string. The first four modes of vibration of a string are shown in Fig. 23b. These 'simple' vibrations can be used to synthesise more complex motions, such as those produced by bowing or plucking, by adding modal vibrations of appropriate amplitudes (this is the information we see in the spectrum of the string vibrations). The frequency of the motion of the string in its

Ex. 1   The first eight harmonics of the harmonic series based on C. The
approximate frequency associated with each note is shown below the
stave.

Harmonic   1   2   3   4   5   6   7   8

Frequency (Hz)   65   131 196 262 329 392 466 523

fundamental mode (mode 1) is the same as the frequency of the
bowed-string vibrations. The frequencies of higher modes are harmonically related to the fundamental frequency; that is, they are integer
multiples of the fundamental. Played individually as a sequence, sounds
corresponding to these frequencies form the harmonic series (Ex. 1). The
technical use of the term 'harmonic' is no accident. The blending
properties of sounds whose frequencies are related by low-order integers
form the very basis of musical harmony and are what give rise to the
harmonious sounds of stringed instruments. In the violin, the action of
the bow is to excite all the string's modes simultaneously, locking them
together into a single harmonic entity.

Each of the higher modes of vibration has one or more stationary or
nodal points at rational positions along the string. The player exploits
these nodal points to play harmonics (in the musical sense). Normally,
all modes can co-exist, but if new boundary conditions are imposed on
the string, some modes can be eliminated to alter its pitch. Suppose, for
example, that the player touches the string at its mid point, then only
those modes which have nodes at this point will sound. These are the
even-numbered modes; when sounded together they create a new
harmonic series based on a note one octave higher. The pitch of the
sound thus rises by an octave.

The pitch of a string is governed by its vibrating length, mass and
tension. A 6 per cent change in the length produces a pitch change of one
semitone. Because of this geometric relationship, notes get 'closer'
together in higher positions. Increases in tension give a higher pitch,
while increases in mass give a lower pitch. For practical reasons, tension
and mass must be traded off against each other. To maintain reasonable
consistency in tension across the four strings, the mass must increase on
the lower strings, each being roughly double that of its neighbour.
High-mass strings are normally made by overwinding heavy wire on a
flexible core, since thick plain strings have a high bending stiffness
which reduces harmonicity of the higher modes. This leads to poor
sound in plucked or struck strings (it is a particular problem in the higher
notes of pianos). In the bowed string, where the bow excites strictly
harmonic frequencies, inharmonicity has a significant effect on the

spectral content of the sounds. High-tension strings give greater sound output, but materials must have sufficient breaking strain to bear the higher tension. Technological innovations have introduced materials with higher breaking strains, allowing the use of heavier, more powerful strings (the most obvious example being the change from gut to steel). The materials and construction used in the manufacture of strings affect their dynamics, altering the harmonic content of the vibrations and the rate at which vibrations are set up and die away, all of which influence the sound-quality of the instrument.

For steady bowing, the player must carefully control the bow's speed and its down-bearing force on the string (the 'bow pressure'). The bow's speed does not affect the period of the string's vibrations, but it does control the amplitude (loudness). For stable oscillations the bow force must lie between a maximum and minimum value, each dependent upon the proximity of the bow to the bridge and the bow's speed. If the bow force is too low, the string tends to slip two or three times per cycle, producing whistles or accentuating certain string harmonics and giving a 'ghostly' sound. At the other extreme, the tone becomes raucous or 'gritty' – the sort of sound which gives *sforzando* playing its biting edge. The bow hair now holds on to the kink for too long, releasing it at imprecise times, which is heard both as a noise component in the sound and a flattening of the pitch of the string. This latter effect is most noticeable near the bridge, where higher bow force is necessary for steady playing. Similar random fluctuations are present in all steady bowing, and although not harmonious, this noise is an accepted and essential part of the violin sound.

Music is, of course, not dominated by 'steady' playing but by starting and stopping and changing notes. The stable vibrations discussed above are the result of bending waves on the string travelling backwards and forwards, reflected from the two end stops and interacting with the bow. These waves take time to establish themselves. This transient part of the note can be an unpredictable period for the violinist. Instruments which 'speak' easily are those in which stable oscillations are set up quickly and uniformly. Factors which affect the transient are the mobility of the bridge, the physical characteristics of the player's left-hand fingertips, the construction of the strings and the bow control. Changes of strings or modifications to the bridge and soundpost can often help to improve troublesome notes on an instrument.

Plucking the string sets up fundamentally different types of vibration, in which the driving force measured at the bridge looks more rectangular. The precise shape of the waveform depends on the excitation point on the string, having significantly greater high-frequency content for plucking positions near the bridge. Similar effects also occur in the bowed string but to a much lesser extent. Because energy is not continually supplied to the plucked string, its vibrations begin to decay immediately. The decay rates of each harmonic are not the same but depend on how efficiently the energy at that frequency is transmitted to the air by the body or absorbed by the finger in a stopped string.

Body vibrations

For a given set of strings, player and playing conditions, the form of the force at the bridge would be virtually the same irrespective of the instrument on which the strings were mounted. The same cannot be said for the sounds produced by different instruments. Although the body responds to each of the harmonic motions of the vibrating string, it does not respond equally, and it alters the proportion of the harmonics in the radiated sound. It thus 'colours' the sound. The variable response is produced by mechanical resonances of the body. In other words, it has modes of vibrations, just like the string. The difference is, however, that the vibrations are now spread over the entire body, and because of the complexity of the violin's shape and structure, the frequencies at which they occur are no longer harmonically related.

Fig. 24 shows a response curve made on a good-quality violin. It was produced by electronically driving the instrument with an oscillating force of constant amplitude in the frequency range 100 Hz to 20 kHz. This represents a range which starts one octave below the bottom note of the violin and extends to the upper limit of human hearing. The curve shows the amplitude of the velocity (speed) of the motion induced in the body, or its mobility, as seen by the strings. The main response occurs in the range 300 Hz to 5 kHz, in which the relative mobility varies over a range of about 100:1. Each of the peaks on the curve represents a resonance of the instrument. String harmonics which coincide with these peaks are strongly present in the radiated sound. At each resonance frequency, the centre frequency of each peak, the instrument vibrates predominantly in one of its modes of vibration. Off resonance, the body vibrates in a combination of its modes. The strength, or height, of each resonance peak is governed partly by the proximity of the bridge to nodes of the body vibrations (see Fig. 25) and also by the damping of the mode, which is a measure of the energy radiated as sound or converted into heat by the body. A different response curve is obtained for every possible combination of driving and observation points. Other forms of response curves showing the sound radiation as a function of frequency tend to be more complex because of the directional character of the radiation from many of the modes.

Every instrument will produce a unique set of response curves, and for this reason they can be regarded as the instrument's 'fingerprint'. There are, however, some common features among them. The overall shapes of the curves, though variable, have a pattern which identifies them as belonging to a violin rather than a viola or cello. With experience it is

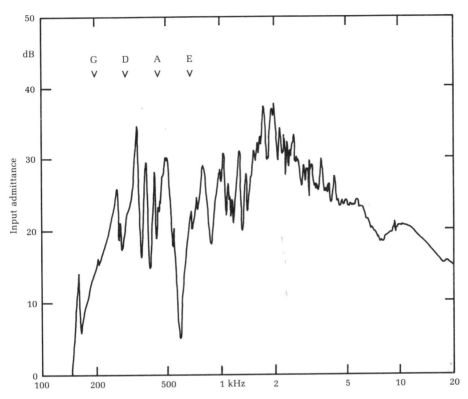

Fig. 24   A violin response curve showing the input admittance (velocity amplitude per unit driving force) of the body as a function of frequency. The vertical scale is expressed in decibels (dB). A change of 20 dB represents a tenfold increase in the amplitude of the body's motion.

possible to distinguish between good and bad instruments. The overall shape is sometimes referred to as a formant, a term derived from the analysis of speech and vowel sounds. Thus the curve can give an indication of the general sound quality, whether it is 'nasal' or has an 'ee' or 'u' sound. Good violins tend to have strong resonances which lie near to the frequencies of the open D and A strings (293 Hz and 440 Hz respectively). Like other aspects of the instrument's acoustics, this resonance placement is not necessarily an optimum design, but it is where from experience one *expects* to find strong resonances.[2] Undoubtedly the placement of many of the higher resonances is equally important but these modes are not so readily controlled by the maker.

The large variations in mobility across the playing range might be expected to produce an instrument with wildly fluctuating loudness. This is not the case, however. Fig. 24 was obtained by driving the violin with a signal equivalent to a single harmonic of the string (a signal known as a sine-wave). The saw-tooth waveform generated by the bowed string includes higher harmonics, and a good instrument is engineered such that at least one of the note's principal harmonics (one of the lower two or three) is strongly present in the sound emitted by the violin. For example, the fundamental component of the open G string (196 Hz) always falls in a region of weak response of the body and is virtually absent in the spectrum of the radiated sound (see Fig. 22b, in which even the second harmonic is rather poorly represented). Lack of fundamental does not alter the pitch of the note because the higher harmonics are still present, but the note tends to sound less 'full' than notes a few semitones higher when the first resonance of the body is able to give it support. Because of the complexities of the response curves, no two notes on the same instrument have the same harmonic content. Even the small modulations in frequency induced by vibrato vary the harmonic content, adding greatly to the richness of the overall sound. Surprisingly, listeners have little difficulty in associating sounds with a particular instrument, even when it is part of a larger ensemble. The perception of instrument tone does not merely involve the analysis of the steady-state part of the note. There are important perceptual clues in the transient parts of notes which are characteristic of an individual instrument and help the listener to identify the origin of the sound.

Fig. 25 shows a small selection of some of the modes of vibration of a violin. These particular modes are strong radiators of sound, both to the player and beyond. The low-frequency modes involve motion of the whole violin body and there is strong co-operation between the wooden plates and the air inside the cavity. At the first strong resonance, usually to be found around the second position on the G string, the net motion is that the whole body swells and contracts. Fig. 25a shows the motion of the table. The main activity occurs roughly along the line of the bass-bar, and the right-hand rib is also in motion. A node sweeps down the full length of the plate traversing the soundpost and treble foot of the bridge. The back exhibits similar motion at this frequency. Sound is created not only by the motion of the two plates but also by the air being squeezed resonantly in and out of the f-holes. The frequency of this mode is controlled to a large extent by the volume of the air cavity and the area of the f-holes. This is the same sort of resonance which can be produced by blowing across the top of a wine bottle, but in the violin the walls are flexible and the air motion is excited by vibrations of the walls. The coupling between the plates and air cavity extends the response of the instrument at low frequencies, without which the bottom octave would be weak. When the driving frequency is raised to about that of the open A string, the body exhibits similar motion except that the two plates tend to swing in the same direction so that the body as a whole bends like a thick sandwich and both ribs vibrate actively. An interesting observation is the degree of asymmetry of these two modes, primarily caused by the presence of the soundpost and bass-bar. At progressively higher frequencies the modes become more complex, breaking into a number of smaller

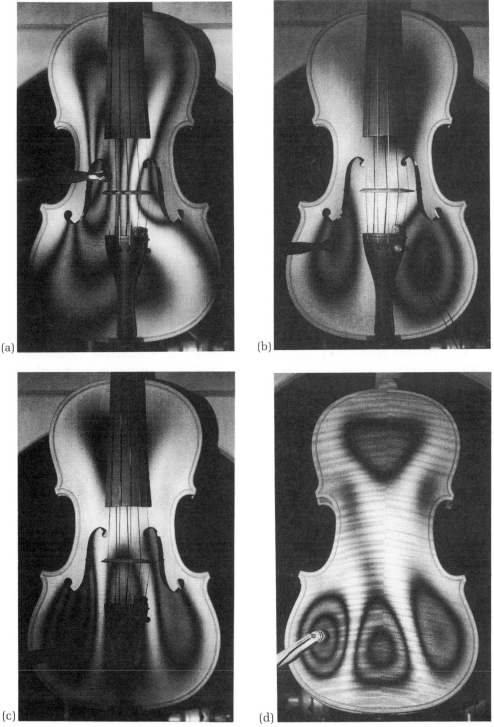

Fig. 25 Modes of vibration of a violin body visualised by means of an optical technique called holographic interferometry. The light and dark bands overlying the images are 'contour maps' of the vibration amplitude (the brightest bands are nodal lines – see also Fig. 27). Mode frequencies in this violin were (a) 272 Hz, (b) 755 Hz, (c) 1255 Hz and (d) 1288 Hz.

vibrating regions separated by nodal lines, not unlike two-dimensional versions of string modes. In Fig. 25b the motion in the lower bout has separated into two regions, resulting in a rocking motion about a nodal line which now runs almost up the centre of the plate. Fig. 25c shows the next mode, in which the vibrations have separated into three regions. The two outer regions now swing in the opposite direction to the patch under the tailpiece. Note how the f-holes relieve the bending in the central area of the plate giving greater flexibility to the bridge region. This progression continues with division occurring both along and across the plates. The higher modes are generally confined to one or other of the plates.[3] A similar set of motions exist on the back (e.g. Fig. 25d), though equivalent modes tend to occur at slightly different frequencies. The vibrations of the back plate are excited primarily by energy which flows from the bridge and table via the ribs. The majority of the sound we hear is produced directly by these flexures of the plates or of the instrument as a whole.

There are other categories of low-frequency body motion which involve simple bending or twisting of the body, neck and fingerboard. These tend to be poor radiators, though they can colour the sound heard locally by the player and may, via feedback, influence the overall performance of the instrument. Neck vibrations can also influence the player through tactile response.[4] In effect, there is virtually no part of the instrument which is not involved in sound production on the violin.

The precise features of the modes shown in Fig. 25 are, of course, unique to that instrument. There is, however, considerable similarity of mode shapes and their hierarchy among violins. The differences lie in the subtle variations of the positions of nodal lines relative to the bridge and the frequencies and damping of the modes. As in the string, the modes of vibration are created by waves, which now spread out and flow around the entire body, becoming partially reflected and transmitted at any boundaries, such as the intersection between the ribs and belly. These waves travel fastest along the length of the instrument because the wood is stiffest in this direction. The waves themselves are not influenced directly by details of the grain pattern of the wood. Instead, the wave propagation is governed by the general mass and stiffness distribution of the plates and by the instrument's dimensions. The stiffness distribution is very sensitive to the particular arching of the plate and the material properties of the wood. The sound quality of an instrument is thus closely linked to its construction.

The bridge and soundpost

The bridge and soundpost play a particularly important role in the lower playing range of the violin. For obvious practical reasons, the player must bow the strings of a violin from side to side. Unfortunately, the

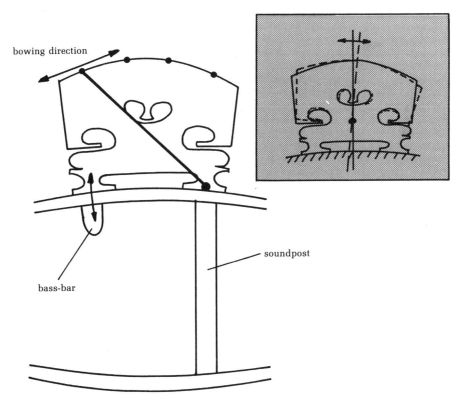

Fig. 26 At low frequencies, the violin bridge acts like a lever, with the
soundpost acting as a fulcrum, converting the sideways motion of
the string into an up-and-down motion at the plate. Note the
different mechanical advantage of each string. At higher frequencies
(inset) the bridge can no longer be considered to be rigid and
exhibits resonances of its own.

body is least responsive to forces exerted in this direction, being most
readily excited by forces perpendicular to the plate. What the soundpost
does, at low frequencies at least, is to induce a node in the vicinity of the
bridge foot, creating a fulcrum at that point. This can be seen in all the
body modes in Fig. 25. The bridge, which is virtually rigid at these
frequencies, then acts like a lever, swinging about this fulcrum, converting the sideways motion of the bowed string into an up-and-down
motion at the other bridge foot (Fig. 26). At mid-range frequencies, the
table and back co-operate more readily and allow the soundpost to move
up and down, destroying the nodal line near the bridge foot. The lever
action of the bridge then breaks down. Above 2 kHz, the bridge itself
begins to exhibit strong resonances, which help to boost the sound power
radiated by the instrument. The broad peak seen at 2 kHz in Fig. 24 is
caused by a bridge resonance. As in the case of the body, the density and
stiffness of the wood and the precise way in which it is cut and shaped
determine the resonance frequencies.

Because the bridge and soundpost are easy to manipulate, they can be used to fine-tune the sound or playing qualities of the completed instrument. From the previous discussion, it is clear that changes to the internal position of the soundpost will affect the mechanical action of the violin as a whole. Bridge resonances can also be adjusted, being particularly sensitive to wood removal from between the 'ears' or from the 'legs'. The drastic effects of the mute can also be understood. First, it adds mass to the instrument at the driving point, making it harder to drive and reducing the sound output. Secondly, it substantially lowers the resonance frequencies of the bridge, altering the filtering effect of the bridge–body structure.

The body has thus far been described very much as the servant of the string. This is true except at strong resonances of the body. The motion at the bridge then becomes very large, and the string no longer has a node at this point, which upsets the usual vibrations and can lead to intolerant or troublesome notes. In the extreme it creates a cyclic stutter known as a wolf-note, common in cellos but also found occasionally in violins. Wolf-notes can be subdued by using lower-tension strings or using an 'eliminator', which tunes some other part of the structure to the same frequency as the wolf, absorbing energy and helping to keep the bowed string under control.

Construction and tone

The violin combines the best in fine engineering, visual artistry and sound-quality. The arched plates provide maximum strength for the body to bear the considerable down-bearing force of the strings, whilst retaining sufficient flexibility to allow the instrument to vibrate in response to the bowed string. The instrument's shape is functional, but its functionality is never allowed to interfere with its perfect classical form. The design is not rigidly fixed, but invites an individualistic approach by the maker, so that the violin has undergone a continual, subtle development to cater for the specific needs of the day.[5]

It may seem strange that in our advanced technological age we cannot emulate the sound of the instruments of past masters. From an acoustical point of view, copying implies reproducing the vibrational modes of an instrument. Size-for-size copies do not work because the frequencies, shapes and damping of the body modes are determined not only by the dimensions and construction of the instrument but also by the mechanical properties of the wood. Mechanical properties vary considerably from sample to sample because of differences in growth or because of the way the timber is cut. The very best wood is split from the tree, ensuring that the wood fibres run parallel to the surface of the plate and that the wood is quartered, i.e. the grain runs vertically through the plate. These two conditions ensure maximum stiffness both along and across the grain. Even small deviations from the quarter can substantially reduce the cross-grain stiffness of the wood, which then has to be compensated for by an increase in the plate's thickness or arching with a consequential reduction in sound power. The influence of long-term changes in the mechanical properties of wood is an additional, unknown factor. In an effort to maintain consistency or to achieve a predetermined tone-quality, the maker has to modify the dimensions and design of an instrument to compensate for differences in the quality of the wood. All but the very best of makers perform this task with a high degree of uncertainty.

Quality control by the maker starts at the earliest stages in construction. The choice of wood is made carefully according to empirical and traditional rules. The table is made from spruce or pine. This type of wood combines great strength and stiffness with low density, which are important structurally and acoustically. Low internal friction in the material ensures that energy losses within the plate itself are minimised. The back and ribs are made from maple, which is a less obvious choice (and is undoubtedly selected more for appearance than acoustical reasons). The maker's work then proceeds with the carving of the plates. These are the most important vibrating parts of the instrument. Good makers can tell when they are correctly dimensioned and rely little on modifications to the near-finished instrument. They are able to respond to the 'feel' of the plates and adjust them through experience.

A common method for testing plates is tap toning. The plates are thinned gradually until they produce certain notes when held and tapped at special places. The maker is actually making measurements of the modes of vibration of the free plates. Ideally, the plate is held at a node and tapped at an antinode (a point of maximum vibration), thereby isolating an individual mode. The well-defined pitch produced by the plate then corresponds to the resonance frequency of that mode. The duration of the sound gives an indication of the damping. With practice five or six modes can be isolated in this way.

It is not clear how the maker uses information about the free-plate modes. Through experience, each maker develops his own set of empirical tuning rules for the free plates, which is one of the reasons why propagating his art is so difficult. But since the best makers produce consistently good instruments, it seems reasonable to conclude that there are *measurable* properties of the free plates which give some indication of the quality of the finished instrument.

The first serious scientific work to determine tuning rules for violin plates was undertaken in the nineteenth century by Félix Savart (1791–1841). He was fortunate in being able to test plates removed from many fine instruments (including Stradivari and Guarneri violins), loaned to him by the great French luthier J.B. Vuillaume. He concluded that in good instruments the most dominant tap-tone of the free back plate (now

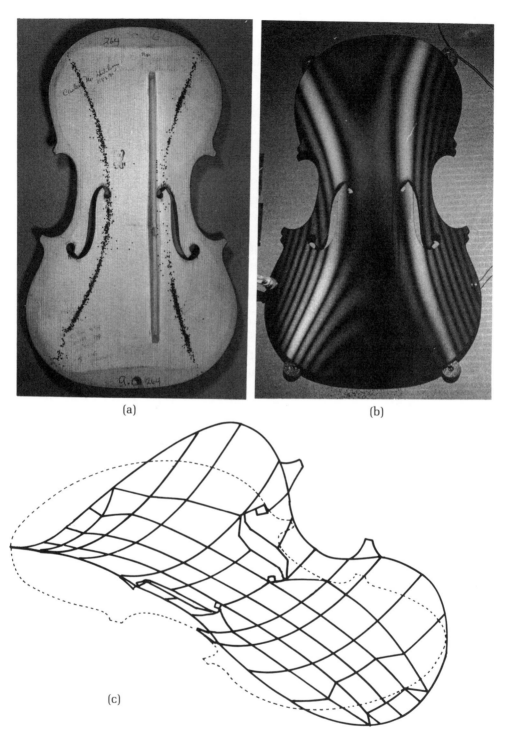

(a)

(b)

(c)

Fig. 27   The second mode of vibration of a free violin plate visualised by (a)
a Chladni pattern; (b) holographic interferometry; and (c) numerical
calculations. The black lines in (a) show the positions of the nodal
lines. The light and dark bands in (b) are equivalent to contour lines
showing the bending across the plate (the two bright bands are the
nodal lines). (c) Computer-generated plot showing the bending of the
plate during its vibration cycle. The dotted line shows the outline of
the stationary plate. The motion is grossly exaggerated.

known to be the fifth mode) was always a semitone to a tone higher in pitch than in the free table. More recently, Carleen Hutchins has developed tuning rules for free violin plates which help her to achieve consistency in the quality of finished instruments.[6] Besides tuning the frequencies of a number of modes, she adjusts the plates to obtain particular nodal configurations. The positions of the nodes are identified by means of Chladni patterns (Fig. 27a). The plate is excited electronically at one of its resonance frequencies, by suspending it over a loudspeaker for example. It is then dusted uniformly with sand or coloured aluminium flake, which bounces off the vibrating parts and collects along the nodal lines. Chladni patterns are one of the most vivid demonstrations of the vibrations of violin plates. They can highlight asymmetries in the vibrations, which often occur because of inconsistencies in thickness, arching, or material properties. Manipulating the frequencies *and* the shape of *several* modes is extremely difficult. The technique is so sensitive that the plates are tuned after varnishing to account for the small but significant changes which the surface coatings induce in the stiffness and mass distributions of the plate. It is clear from Hutchins's descriptions that these methods do not make the maker's task any easier – they simply define the goals more objectively.

Free-plate tuning alone is not sufficient to produce a good violin. The problem is that the modes of vibration of the free plates bear little relation to the modes of the finished instrument; the rib structure, the neck and the internal air cavity are also important in determining the dynamical properties of the completed body. Modifications to seemingly unimportant components such as the top-, bottom- or corner-blocks or the linings can be expected to induce perceptual changes in the tone quality of an instrument. Plate-tuning rules work for individual makers because they tend to build the rest of the instrument in a consistent way. Recent work in computer modelling of violin vibrations is helping to cast light on this otherwise intractable problem.

The relationships between the construction of musical instruments and their tone qualities will remain an extremely difficult problem at the forefront of physics and psychology; this is, of course, one of the attractions of the problem to all concerned with the violin. The physical differences between the 'best' instruments are undoubtedly extremely small, but nevertheless clearly perceived by the accomplished player. Thus although physical studies have created an accurate picture of the mechanical function of the violin, in itself a most valuable contribution, the only true test for quality is to play on the instrument.

3 The violinists of the Baroque and Classical periods

SIMON McVEIGH

During the seventeenth and eighteenth centuries the violin underwent an astonishing transformation of role. A lowly dance instrument at the beginning of the period, it had by 1800 become a dominant force in Western musical culture. Virtuoso violinists were fêted at court and public concert alike, and only singers were more highly rewarded. While none could perhaps be placed among the very front rank of composers, many violinists were important creative figures, including Heinrich von Biber, Arcangelo Corelli, Antonio Vivaldi and Giovanni Battista Viotti. Indeed the instrument's capabilities influenced the course of musical style itself, to the extent that singers in the early eighteenth century were expected to be able to rival the figurations of violin music. The period also saw the establishment of the string basis of the orchestra, and violinists such as Jean-Baptiste Lully and Johann Stamitz played a major part in the refinement of orchestral discipline. In addition the violin was accepted during the eighteenth century as an accomplishment for gentlemen amateurs.

These developments were closely tied in with those of musical life in general. Early-seventeenth-century Italy was a hotbed of experiment, culminating in the operatic masterpieces of Monteverdi. The violin was the only instrument fully able to match the voice in the new aesthetic, which favoured a subjective and strongly projected individuality, expressed in a dramatic 'affective' idiom, with exuberant virtuosity and ornamentation. Both violinists and style spread through Austria and Germany, but the new Italian manner was rejected in seventeenth-century France, and only guardedly accepted in England. After a period of consolidation in Italy, culminating in the pivotal figure of Corelli, the eighteenth century witnessed a new wave of Italian virtuoso influence throughout Europe. Around the mid century a distinct German school was associated with the dynamic orchestral idioms of the early Classical period, focused on the Mannheim orchestra under Stamitz. Paris not only succumbed to the soloistic idiom, but became a cosmopolitan centre for violin playing in the second half of the century, the influence

46

of Viotti eventually leading to the foundation of the modern French school of violin playing in the 1790s.

Changes in the status of the violinist can be perceived in the late eighteenth century. Increasing specialisation resulted in an emphasis on soloistic display, which was often (with the notable exception of Viotti) allied to a decline in compositional aspiration. Some preferred to concentrate instead on orchestral leading, even as the violinist's supremacy as orchestral director was being challenged by keyboard players, a dichotomy only resolved in the nineteenth century by the acceptance of the baton-wielding conductor.

Dance-bands and court orchestras

The history of violin playing in the sixteenth century remains rather shadowy, despite the archival researches of David Boyden and others. While the viol was a favoured instrument of gentlemen's recreation, the violin was primarily a professional instrument: its sharply-etched tone and lively manner recommended it for dance-music and dinner entertainment. But it also played a part in extravagant court spectacles such as the famous Florentine *intermedi* for the 1589 wedding festivities of Ferdinando de' Medici. More surprisingly, perhaps, there is evidence that the violin was also used in sixteenth-century Italian church music.

Around 1555 an Italian dance-band was introduced at the French court, headed by one of the first named violinists – Baltazarini, or Balthasar de Beaujoyeux. He achieved considerable influence at court, and was largely responsible for the celebrated *Circé ou le balet comique de la royne* of 1581. The score, published the following year, includes dances for five-part strings, the first printed music to specify the violin. Such an ensemble became particularly associated with French court entertainment. Its official status was confirmed in 1626 by the establishment of the 'Vingt-quatre Violons du Roi' (a five-part string orchestra with three viola lines). French music in the second half of the seventeenth century was dominated by another Italian violinist and dancer, Jean-Baptiste Lully (1632–87). By 1656 he had taken over the smaller 'Petits Violons', with which he developed a new precision and a crisp style of string playing, using short French bows in a highly rhythmic fashion. This was the first permanent, well-disciplined string orchestra – but it was not the venue for violinistic experiment, and it was several decades before the violin was allowed to develop as a solo instrument in France.

England, too, retained a conservative stance. Though the violin was known there in the sixteenth century, the viol retained its status well into the next century. In 1676, Thomas Mace, evidently fighting a rearguard action, decried the 'High-Priz'd Noise' of a string orchestra, 'which is rather fit to make a Mans *Ears Glow*, and fill his *Brains full of Frisks*, &c.

than to *Season, and Sober his Mind'.*[1] By this time, however, Charles II had already instituted his own 'Twenty-Four Violins' on the French model, and violins had been introduced at the Chapel Royal. Furthermore, as will be seen, the English proved more susceptible than the French to the seductions of Italianate virtuosity.

Virtuoso violinists in seventeenth-century Italy

By the time of Mace, Italian violinists had developed a soloistic technique far beyond anything expected in France or England. The earliest virtuosi were mostly associated with North Italian cities: it can be no coincidence that Monteverdi's opera *L'Orfeo*, produced at Mantua in 1607, includes a violin duet of intricate filigree brilliance as a symbol of Orpheus' musical prowess. Still more idiomatic are the interweaving motives and iridescent figuration of the violin parts in his Vespers collection, published in Venice in 1610. A string-player himself, Monteverdi continued to exploit string effects: measured *tremolo* and pizzicato are vividly used to depict the battle scenes in *Il combattimento di Tancredi e Clorinda* (1624).

One of the first violin virtuosi, Biagio Marini (c.1587–1663), served under Monteverdi at St Mark's, Venice, from 1615. Others, such as Carlo Farina (c.1600–c.1640), Salamone Rossi (1570–1630) and Giovanni Battista Buonamente (d.1642), were associated with the Mantuan court in the early years of the seventeenth century. All of these, and most sensationally Marco Uccellini (c.1603–80) at Modena, developed the resources of the violin remarkably quickly. Much of their music is avowedly experimental, often improvisatory, showing a liberated delight in novel instrumental effect for its own sake. But it would be a mistake to judge these pioneer Italians on the basis of the farmyard effects of Farina's notorious *Capriccio stravagante* (1627). The preoccupation with technical experiment was part of the current search for the widest range of expression, as on the opera stage. Significantly one of the idioms transferred to the violin was the intense and declamatory style of current recitative.

Violinists were already finding employment at major cathedrals and courts throughout Italy. With the opening of the first public opera-house in Venice in 1637, a new source of income opened up, though the extravagant ensemble of *L'Orfeo* was forsaken for smaller pit-bands (perhaps only a pair of violins with accompanying continuo). Italian violinists were also in demand outside their own country.

The new style in Germany and England

The virtuoso ideal spread rapidly to the courts of Austria and Germany. Marini spent much of his life north of the Alps, while Buonamente was in Vienna at least from 1626 to 1629. Farina took up a post in 1625 at the Dresden court, working alongside Heinrich Schütz (who had himself studied in Italy). It was not long before local violinists achieved equal or even higher standards of virtuosity, notably Johann Heinrich Schmelzer (c.1620–80) in Vienna, Heinrich von Biber (1644–1704) in Salzburg, and (mainly in Dresden) Johann Jakob Walther (c.1650–1717) and Johann Paul von Westhoff (1656–1705). Schmelzer was described in 1660, with unusually frank qualification, as 'nearly the finest violinist in Europe', while a decade later Biber was said to be a 'formidable virtuoso' by the violin maker Stainer. The Austro-Germans took over and extended considerably the technical achievements of the early Italian school. In particular they made a speciality of double and multiple stops, enabling the performance of polyphonic music that looks forward to that of Bach. They have been subject to some of the same criticisms as the early Italian school, especially an over-reliance on technical effects and pictorial representation. But these they raised to a new artistic plane, by virtue of a more serious approach to structure and a more deeply felt musical expression (Italianate affective recitative can here be profoundly moving). Biber in particular transformed the programmatic concept in his 'Mystery' (or 'Rosary') sonatas (c.1675). The evidence of Biber's music suggests that he combined a brilliant technique and command of double stopping with an expressive intensity unmatched in the seventeenth century. Apart from the possible influence on Bach, however, the Austro-German school had no direct artistic progeny; they represent rather a late flowering of an early Baroque ideal.

England witnessed two revelatory visits by foreign violinists. Around 1655 the German-born Thomas Baltzar (c.1630–63) arrived from Sweden. Anthony Wood was astonished when Baltzar played up to the end of the fingerboard and back 'and all with alacrity and in very good tune'.[2] Towards the end of the century the Italian style made headway in England, with the arrival soon after 1670 of Nicola Matteis, 'that stupendious Violin ... whom certainly never mortal man Exceeded on that Instrument: he had a stroak so sweete, & made it speake like the Voice of a man; & when he pleased, like a Consort of severall Instruments.'[3] Purcell espoused the cause in his 1683 trio sonatas, written in 'just imitation of the most fam'd Italian Masters', by contrast with 'the levity, and balladry of our neighbours' across the Channel.

Bologna and Corelli

In mid-century Italy something of a reaction set in against the extravagances of the early virtuosi. Bologna proved an important centre, with the basilica of San Petronio providing a focus for the development of instrumental music. In addition, the Accademia Filarmonica encouraged a serious approach to instrumental composition by its cultivation of contrapuntal writing (Corelli himself came into a famous dispute with the academicians over a passage of alleged consecutive fifths). A more sober-minded attitude towards the violin ensued, and composers such as Cazzati and G. B. Vitali (himself a string player) eschewed the technical emphasis of Uccellini at nearby Modena and Parma. Undoubtedly the most prominent violinist of the Bologna school was Giuseppe Torelli (1658–1709), known to us mainly for his pioneering violin concertos, but an even more important figure studied there: Arcangelo Corelli (1653–1713). Though he spent most of his life in Rome, Corelli proudly recalled his upbringing by describing himself as 'il Bolognese' on title-pages.

We have contradictory views of his performance. Some thought his playing restrained to the point of mildness (as in Mainwaring's famous anecdote of Handel seizing Corelli's violin out of his hands). On the other hand, there is the following graphic description:

> I never met with any man that suffered his passions to hurry him away so much whilst he was playing on the violin as the famous Arcangelo Corelli, whose eyes will sometimes turn as red as fire; his countenance will be distorted, his eyeballs roll as in an agony, and he gives in so much to what he is doing that he doth not look like the same man.[4]

An important feature of his playing was the improvised ornamentation of those slow movements that appear so bald on the printed page (some embellished versions attributed to Corelli were printed in 1710, but their authorship was disputed almost as soon as they appeared).

Corelli represents a curious figure in the history of the violin. He was scarcely one of the great virtuosi of his day; he travelled little; his compositions were few and comparatively limited in scope. But his influence was immeasurable. Those few compositions, neatly packaged in four sets of trio sonatas, one of solo sonatas, and one (posthumously published) of concerti grossi, spread across Europe as the epitome of 'classical' Baroque composition. They were devoured by the English: the very first day that his concertos arrived in London, a bookseller interrupted a concert to show them to Henry Needler (an amateur violinist), whereupon 'the books were immediately laid out, and he and the rest of the performers played the whole twelve concertos through, without rising from their seats'.[5] Corelli was also widely respected as a leader, known for his discipline in ensuring uniform bowing.

Equally important, his teaching initiated the first major school of violin playing, the violinistic descendants of which can loosely be traced down to the present day. Among Corelli's students were Francesco Geminiani (1687–1762) and Giovanni Battista Somis (1686–1763), possibly also Francesco Maria Veracini (1690–1768) and Pietro Locatelli (1695–1764). No violinist can have escaped his influence – the early music of Antonio Vivaldi (1678–1741) and Giuseppe Tartini (1692–1770) betrays a strong debt to Corelli. In unspoken homage to his teacher (and no doubt to make a tidy profit), Geminiani arranged many of Corelli's trio sonatas as concerti grossi, while Veracini paid him the more doubtful compliment of rewriting and updating the Op. 5 sonatas. Many of these violinists were directly responsible for spreading Corelli's influence throughout Europe, as will be seen. However, none was content simply to replicate Corelli's playing, for there were early developments in violin playing, as there were in musical language.

Italian violin playing after Corelli

The decades after Corelli's death saw the conscious cultivation of the image of the virtuoso with such remarks as Veracini's 'there is but *one* God, and *one Veracini*' and Pugnani's 'with a violin in my hand I am Caesar'. Musically this was reflected in the invention of the violin concerto as a vehicle for soloistic display, in which development Vivaldi played a leading role. More fundamentally, violinists sought new types of musical expression, new heights of virtuosity, and a new range of sonority.

Expression, the ability to 'touch the heart', became a touchstone for true violinistic greatness, especially as musical taste moved into the age of sensibility. Even Geminiani and Veracini, perhaps closest to Corelli's aesthetic and technical means, were not immune. At first those English who revered the simplicity and purity of Corelli found Veracini's music 'too wild and flighty'.[6] But they were won round by Geminiani, who began to indicate subtle expressive nuances in his publications by means of dynamic shadings. He also drew on the art of refined ornamentation for similar ends: one section of his violin treatise (1751) explains 'all the Ornaments of Expression, necessary to the playing in a good Taste'. John Hawkins highlighted these qualities in Geminiani's playing: 'All the graces and elegancies of melody, all the powers that can engage attention, or that render the passions of the hearer subservient to the will of the artist, were united in his performance.'[7]

Tartini took the violin into a *galant* phase. Though best known now for the powerful and technically demanding 'Devil's Trill' Sonata (unpublished during his lifetime), Tartini in fact developed a highly expressive style of playing, noted for its cantabile manner, sensitive ornamentation and a certain pre-Romantic pathos (reflected in the poetic mottoes at the head of many of his works). These were qualities inherited and exaggerated by his favourite student, Pietro Nardini (1722–93), who deliberately disdained technical display in favour of a 'delicate, judicious, and highly finished' style.[8] The late-eighteenth-century German aesthetician C. F. D. Schubart left a romanticised description of Nardini:

The tenderness of his playing is beyond description: every comma seems to be a declaration of love. His ability to touch the heart was quite extraordinary. Ice-cold princes and ladies were seen to cry when he performed an Adagio; often his own tears would fall on the violin as he played ... His bowstroke was slow and solemn; yet, unlike Tartini, he did not tear the notes out by the roots, but only kissed their tips. He detached them very slowly, and each note seemed like a drop of blood flowing from his tender soul.[9]

Nardini was clearly a player of unmatched sensitivity: nevertheless an expressive cantabile combined with elegant phrasing and ornamentation were regarded throughout the century as Italian characteristics.

After the comparatively restrained technical demands of Corelli's music, the quest for virtuoso brilliance was resumed. At its best, this was still part of the search for expression, for example in the widening range of bowing demands; and it could be contained satisfactorily within the secure tonal bounds of the concerto. But there was always the possibility of abuse. Critics repeatedly censured violinists for appealing to shallow public taste, in empty displays of execution and unmeaning ornamentation at the expense of genuine musical feeling. Even Vivaldi was regarded in this light by J. F. A. von Uffenbach, visiting Venice in 1715:

He added a cadenza that really frightened me, for such playing has not been heard before and can never be equalled: he brought his fingers no more than a straw's breadth from the bridge, leaving no room for the bow – and that on all four strings with imitations and incredible speed. With this he astonished everyone, but I cannot say that it delighted me, for it was more skilfully executed than it was pleasant to hear.[10]

But Vivaldi was easily outshone by Locatelli, whose playing reached unprecedented technical heights, to judge from the demands of his collection of concertos and caprices entitled *L'arte del violino* (1733). Some reports of his playing stress the demonic way in which he attacked the violin, and his trance-like appearance when performing. These attributes have led to comparisons with Nicolò Paganini, who avowedly built his technical achievements on those of Locatelli. The association has not always been meant kindly, but much of Locatelli's music is quite different from *L'arte* and of sufficient quality to allay doubts about his musicality.

Much less secure is the position of that other great showman, Antonio Lolli (c.1725–1802), regarded by many as the transcendent technician of the century. Giovanni Battista Rangoni, in a pamphlet comparing Nardini, Lolli and Pugnani, argued that Lolli's pyrotechnics, flitting from one extreme of the range to the other, were inevitably detrimental to musical expression.[11] The English, who prided themselves on their rejection of shallow musical stunts imported from the continent, thought him a charlatan:

LOLLI, as far outshone by Cramer and Giardini in the superior excellencies of the violin, *taste* and *pathos*, as he outdoes them in excentric oddity, trick, and voluble execution, is esteemed at the highest rate in some foreign countries ... But not in Italy, nor, to the credit of our musical judgement, in England![12]

One consequence of these technical developments was the distancing of the professional player from the amateur market – even Tartini's sonatas Op. 1 were regarded as too difficult for most amateurs (which did not, however, prevent the most demanding music from reaching print).[13]

A third concern of the eighteenth century was the cultivation of tone. In a general sense this was often seen as an ingredient of expression, liable to be found wanting in such performers as Lolli. Nardini was constantly praised: Leopold Mozart wrote that 'it would be impossible to hear a finer player for beauty, purity, evenness of tone and singing quality'.[14] But others consciously sought a larger sound, in line with the development of bigger orchestras and concert-halls. Somis, possessed of 'the most majestic bowstroke in Europe', was noted for his ability to sustain a single bow; and his Piedmont school prided itself on its sonorous tone-quality. Felice Giardini (1716–96), for example, had 'a tone so sweet, and at the same time so powerful, that he appeared to me to be performing on strings so large, I really thought his fingers must have been blistered by the necessary pressure he gave them'.[15] Gaetano Pugnani (1731–98) also preferred thicker strings; he inherited Somis's commanding style of bowing, which he in turn transmitted to Giovanni Battista Viotti (1755–1824), thus providing a direct link with the early-nineteenth-century French school.

Italian violinists – profession and lifestyle

Many Italian violinists sought the patronage of the wealthy, a patronage which could take many different forms. Corelli, in Rome by 1675, was fortunate in the protection of three prominent patrons of the arts – Christina (former Queen of Sweden), Cardinal Pamphili and (from 1690) Cardinal Ottoboni. He would mostly have been heard at small concerts or 'academies' such as those on Monday evenings at Ottoboni's palace, attended by Rome's cultural elite. But he also led very large orchestras on special occasions, such as the 150 strings at an opulent entertainment laid on by Christina in 1687. At some such occasion around 1682 Georg Muffat heard concertos by Corelli 'beautifully performed with the utmost accuracy by a great number of instrumental players'.[16] To judge from his correspondence, Ottoboni treated Corelli more as a friend than as an employee. This charmed existence allowed Corelli the time to refine his compositions to perfection before publication (in this period of rapidly expanding markets they were quickly available from Rome to Amsterdam and London). He was accorded that signal honour, rare for the mere violinist, of the approval of the literary and artistic community, symbolised by his admission in 1706 to the Accademia dei Arcadi.

Violinists continued in demand at courts throughout Italy and German-speaking countries. Somis was principal violinist of the Turin *cappella*, responsible for leading concerts and church music, and later the famous opera orchestra.[17] His most celebrated student, Pugnani, was also associated with the court throughout his life, rising from the back desk of the second violins (at the age of ten) to leader in 1770 (rather belatedly it might be thought). Other Italians found their way to courts north of the Alps: Nardini, for example, was principal violinist at the Stuttgart court in the early 1760s, before returning to a prestigious post at the ducal court of Florence. But the average émigré could scarcely entertain such aspirations. Thus Luigi Tomasini (for whom Haydn wrote at least one of his concertos) began his employment at the Esterházy court as a *valet-de-chambre*; later as leader of the court orchestra he was only modestly paid, remaining essentially a liveried servant with strict conditions of service.

Another form of secure employment was a teaching post. In 1703 Vivaldi was appointed *maestro di violino* at the Ospedale della Pietà, a Venetian orphanage for girls which gave strong emphasis to musical education, and whose chapel music attracted large congregations. Vivaldi's duties included instrumental teaching, the provision of new concertos, and the training of the orchestra, which evidently achieved a surprisingly high standard. But his relationship with the Pietà was not a smooth one, as will be seen.

Tartini, too, made a profession out of teaching. While remaining first violinist at the cathedral of San Antonio in Padua, he founded a school of violin instruction in 1727 or 1728 (sometimes known as the 'School of Nations'). This should not be thought of as a conservatoire in a modern sense, but it is clear that Tartini developed a serious training programme for young violinists: nine or so students were enrolled for a ten-month year, at least two of whom he taught for no fee, though even with only four or five students he 'felt like the most worried man on earth'.[18] Some of his ideas are expounded in his *Regole per arrivare a saper ben suonar il violino* (transmitted by a student, and posthumously published as *Traité des agrémens*). More informal but equally revealing is a letter of 1760 to Maddalena Sirmen, née Lombardini (the first woman violinist of European fame). Around seventy of his students, from all over Europe, have been identified: many of the compositions of this school, together with ornamentations of Tartini slow movements, are in a collection at the University of California, Berkeley.

Few Italian violinists were content with the relatively narrow confines and low profile of court life, and the freedom to travel was sometimes written into a contract. Pugnani, for example, made regular forays into the public arenas of Northern Europe, playing at concerts in Paris in 1754, writing operas for London in 1769 and 1773. It was on an extended European concert tour with Viotti that the latter left for Paris in 1782, with momentous consequences for the history of the violin. Vivaldi, too, was notoriously lax about his teaching duties. Already in the 1710s he was devoting much of his attention to opera, and a rising chorus of complaint resulted in the loss of his teaching post in 1716. However, he retained some connection with the Pietà throughout his life, even when his operas and violin playing took him all over Italy and as far north as Amsterdam. Thus in 1723 he was invited to contribute two new concertos every month, which he might send by post, and to direct rehearsals when in Venice.

Others sacrificed the security of a court post for the enticing prospects offered by the capitals of Northern Europe. Locatelli settled in 1729 in Amsterdam – where he spurned professional performance in favour of concerts with the wealthy bourgeoisie. He likewise taught only amateurs, preferring to pass on his violinistic achievement through the purely musical *L'arte del violino*. He also contributed to Amsterdam's thriving music-publishing industry, in which he was remarkable for bringing out much of his music at his own expense.

English money lured many of Europe's finest violinists to London at some time during the century. Opportunities here for the enterprising were unrivalled: as Johann Mattheson wrote from Germany in 1713, 'he who at the present time wants to make a profit out of music betakes himself to England'.[19] Roger North quipped that England had 'dispeopled Italy of viollins', and the situation had changed little seventy years later: 'Many foreign singers, fidlers, and dancers, are extravagantly paid; and, if they are the least frugal, they are enabled to retire to their own country, where they may live in affluence, enriched by English money.'[20]

By far the most famous Italian to settle in London in the first half of the century was Geminiani, who arrived in 1714. After initial success, however, he was seldom heard in public, but 'his compositions, scholars, and the presents he received from the great, whenever he could be prevailed upon to play at their houses, were his chief support'.[21] Among these students was Matthew Dubourg, who led the first performance of *Messiah* in Dublin in 1742. Geminiani's teaching methods are explained in the *Art of Playing on the Violin* (1751), a valuable source, though its brief and enigmatic explanations of certain technical matters must have been as perplexing to the gentleman violinist then as they are to us today.

Perhaps Geminiani's reticence was caused by the 'unsteady manner' that Burney found in his leading of an orchestra in 1749. He never played in Handel's orchestra, which was led instead by two other students of Corelli – Pietro Castrucci (whose brother is thought to have been the 'enraged musician' of Hogarth's print) and Giovanni Stefano Carbonelli. But in general violin playing in London seems to have languished, for Giardini's modern style of playing caused a sensation there in 1751. His playing 'threw into the utmost astonishment the whole company, who had never been accustomed to hear better performers than *Festing*, *Brown*, and *Collet!*'; and at his public debut the applause was 'so loud, long, and furious, as nothing but that bestowed on Garrick had ever equalled'.[22] Giardini transformed the playing of the Italian opera orchestra, and took a major role in London's concert and operatic life for the next thirty years.

With the growth of international travel during the eighteenth century, some Italian violinists moved towards the more volatile lifestyle of the travelling virtuoso. These international stars were considerably reliant on public support (and the consequent whims of fashion); it was a highly competitive world, as the continual comparisons make clear:

The Connoisseurs in Italy have dubbed Signor Lolli Prince of the Fiddlers; after him they place Nardini, Pugnani, and Crammer; but should they hear Mr. La Motte, they would undoubtedly judge him equal if not to Lolli, at least to the others. We do not forget the Merit of Signor Giardini, who among us is deemed a very eminent Fiddler; but we mean only to relate the Opinion of the Professors of Music all over Italy.[23]

Violinists might organise their own concerts (like today's pianists, they were second only to singers in public esteem). But they still courted patronage, whether or not this involved a recognised title or post. Such a lifestyle was precarious: if there were great riches to be gained, there were also great risks (especially as many dabbled in risky operatic ventures). And violinists like everyone else were subject to political upheavals: Viotti felt compelled to leave Paris for London in 1792, being associated with Marie Antoinette – only to be deported from England in 1798, suspected of being a Jacobin activist.

Several Italians did not settle in one particular place. Veracini, for example, though he did retain some ties with Florence, toured Europe during the 1710s, took a court post at Dresden from 1717 to 1722, and was resident in London on three separate occasions. Giornovichi and Viotti had strikingly similar careers, involving some years in Eastern Europe, a decade in Paris (the 1770s and 1780s respectively), and recourse to London in the 1790s. But the archetypal travelling virtuoso must be Lolli, whose life was a typically fluid mixture of court posts and independent concert touring. He held positions at Stuttgart (1758–74) and St Petersburg (1774–83), but was granted numerous extended leaves of absence, enabling him to give concerts in Vienna, Paris, Germany, Italy, Poland and Scandinavia. One such leave expanded to over two years, to the distinct annoyance of the Russian court. In 1785 he was in London, and thereafter seems to have continued to tour Europe without any permanent post.

Germany and Austria in the eighteenth century

Although many German courts were under the influence of French culture, and imitated Versailles in taste and decoration, Italian music retained the strong hold it had built up during the seventeenth century. Johann Georg Pisendel (1687–1755), for example, was taught the violin by Torelli at Ansbach, before joining the Dresden court orchestra in 1712; four years later he was in Venice, where he studied with Vivaldi. He returned to Dresden with a collection of Vivaldi's music, thus contributing to its rapid dissemination during this decade. (Bach in Weimar was already familiar with the concertos entitled *L'estro armonico*, two of which he arranged for organ.) There is an unsubstantiated tradition that, on a visit to Dresden in 1717, Bach may have heard Pisendel play an unaccompanied violin sonata, and even that Bach may have intended his own set for Pisendel. Among Pisendel's students was Franz Benda (1709–86), the most prominent violinist at the Berlin court of Frederick the Great. Though the unvarying taste and routine of the King had a stultifying effect on some, Benda and C. P. E. Bach 'dared to have a style of their own', in the opinion of Charles Burney, who was impressed by the pathos of Benda's Adagio playing.[24]

As North German courts drew back financially after the Seven Years War, the artistic focus moved southwards. Especially prominent was the Mannheim court, where the orchestra achieved a European reputation under the direction of Johann Stamitz (1717–57). The Bohemian violinist was renowned for his role in developing a vivid and energetic style of string playing in tune with the emerging symphonic idiom. He was succeeded by Christian Cannabich (1731–98), whose exceptional qualities as a leader inspired 'the love and awe of those under him', according to Mozart.[25] Stamitz's son Carl (1745–1801) was also a violinist, but he was more celebrated as the first international soloist on the viola.

For the first time German and Bohemian violinists began to exert a major influence outside the German-speaking countries. Stamitz himself visited Paris in 1754–5 with success. In London, where concerts began to focus on the Austro-German symphonic repertory, the Italian domination began to crumble. The Mannheimer Wilhelm Cramer (1746–99) was invited to London in 1772 specifically to lead the orchestra of the Bach–Abel concerts; he founded the excellent orchestra of the Professional Concert in 1785. Johann Peter Salomon (1745–1815), said to have been a student of Benda, moved to London in 1782 and was responsible for Haydn's arrival there in 1791. Cramer in particular was noted for the fire and spirit of his playing, which eventually usurped Giardini's graceful Italianate cantabile. Both Cramer and Salomon, though acknowledged virtuosi, increasingly specialised in orchestral leading, in which Cramer was unsurpassed. Salomon excelled in chamber music (a popular feature of London's concerts), and was the inspiration for Haydn's brilliant concert quartets of Op. 71 and Op. 74.

In 1756, Leopold Mozart published his celebrated *Versuch einer gründlichen Violinschule*, not in Salzburg but in the South German city of Augsburg. Somewhat indebted to material by Tartini (then unpublished), it represents by far the most comprehensive violin treatise of its time, and it continued to be highly influential with a third edition appearing in 1787. Mozart *fils* was himself trained as a violinist (his concertos were probably intended for himself, not for Antonio Brunetti as once thought), but he maintained a firm stance against his father's ambitions in this regard. In later life he preferred to play the viola, as on the famous occasion witnessed by Michael Kelly, when

Haydn, Dittersdorf, Mozart and Vanhal played for an informal quartet party.[26]

France in the eighteenth century

Most complex was the situation in France, where resistance to the Italian violin school and its genres persisted well into the eighteenth century. Indeed the violin itself was still under suspicion in 1740, when Hubert Le Blanc published a defence of the bass viol 'contre les entreprises du violon et les prétentions du violoncel'. Partly this was a matter of national pride (the violin was as much a symbol of foreign intervention as was Italian opera). Partly it was a question of musical taste, for both the mechanical fireworks and the emotional intensity of the Italian Baroque were out of line with the French aesthetic.

However, the bastions were to fall (as they did not in the opera-house). The early decades of the century saw a spate of sonata composition by violinists associated with the French court, such as François Duval, Jean-Féry Rebel and Jean Baptiste Senaillé. Links between France and the Turin court were encouraged when the Prince of Carignan moved to the French capital in 1718, and several of Somis's students settled in Paris, with its flourishing concert life and publishing markets. Somis himself played in 1733 at the Concert Spirituel, the prestigious series of concerts on religious holidays. In addition the private concerts of La Pouplinière (from 1731 to 1762) popularised Italian instrumental music.

Even more significantly, several Frenchmen studied with Somis in Turin. The most important of these was undoubtedly Jean-Marie Leclair (1697–1764), the foremost French violinist of the first half of the century. To judge from his sonatas, Leclair's playing formed a remarkable blend of Italian expression with Gallic charm. Some found the precision of his playing somewhat cold, though one contemporary attributed this to 'an excess of taste rather than a want of boldness and freedom'.[27] He was especially renowned for his accurate playing of double stops; indeed, these, rather than the high figuration of the Italians, provide the principal technical demand of his music.

Leclair, though highly esteemed, seems to have been less than skilful in political manipulation, and he never achieved the court favour accorded to another Somis student. The Italian Jean-Pierre Guignon (1702–74), originally Ghignone, was introduced in 1725 at the newly established Concert Spirituel. The foreign influx had provoked the inevitable rivalry, and the occasion was set up as a competition with the Frenchman Jean-Jacques-Baptiste Anet (1676–1755), curiously enough a student of Corelli. Witnesses recorded an honourable draw, but it was Guignon who went on to attain the greater prestige: in 1741 Louis XV was even persuaded to revive the dormant position of *roi des violons* for him.

Despite Guignon's success it remained inadvisable to overemphasise

an Italian connection. André-Noël Pagin (b.1721), prominent at the
Concert Spirituel from 1747 to 1750, played the music of his teacher
Tartini almost exclusively (he also edited several sets of his sonatas). But
according to his own testimony he was hissed 'for daring to play in the
Italian style, and this was the reason of his quitting the profession'.[28] No
doubt he suffered also from comparison with Pierre Gaviniès (1728–
1800), a French violinist of the highest class and a major figure in Paris
throughout the second half of the century. Possibly a student of Leclair,
Gaviniès was a popular performer at the Concert Spirituel in the years
around 1750 with his concertos in the incipient Classical style. In 1762
he was appointed leader, as part of a revitalisation of the orchestra, and
eleven years later he became co-director with Gossec and Leduc.

The orchestra of the Concert Spirituel, which had been formed to
accompany French motets, was somewhat slow to reflect modern practices suitable for Classical symphonies: only with the reforms of 1762
was the audible beating of time abandoned. In 1777 the leadership
passed to yet another student of Tartini, Pierre Lahoussaye (1735–1818),
but Mozart found the orchestra still insecure:

I was very anxious at the rehearsal, for I have never heard anything worse in all my life;
you cannot imagine how they twice bumbled and scraped through the symphony ...
[I was] determined that if it went as badly as at the rehearsal, I should certainly go up to
the orchestra, take the violin from the hands of Lahoussaye, the leader, and direct it
myself![29]

In the end, however, the 'Paris' symphony scored a resounding success,
its arresting opening ably showing off the legendary attack of the
orchestra's *premier coup d'archet* (literally 'first bowstroke'). Paris also
supported another concert series, the Concert des Amateurs. Founded in
1769 by Gossec for the performance of modern symphonic repertory, its
standards were much higher. The large orchestra was led by the extrovert
Chevalier de Saint-Georges, part West Indian, who was as well known for
his fencing as for his musical talents. The series was succeeded in the
1780s by the Concert de la Loge Olympique, for which Haydn composed
his six 'Paris' symphonies.

In the course of only a few decades Paris had become established as a
cosmopolitan centre for European violin playing. The often forward-
looking *Principes du violon* by L'abbé *le fils* was published there in 1761.
Opportunities for concert performance were rivalled only by those in
London, and there was an even more thriving publishing industry:
indeed the majority of the most difficult violin concertos were published
here. Paris was certainly perceived as the focus of violinistic virtuosity
– witness Cramer's amazement at rank-and-file violinists at the Concert
Spirituel 'flourishing the most difficult passages up to the top of the
finger-board'.[30] One of the consequences of this international confluence
was a breakdown of the national schools, at least temporarily.

The foremost Parisian violinist of the 1770s was Giovanni Mane

Giornovichi (c.1740–1804), perhaps the outstanding violinist of the mid Classical era. Even his country of birth is unclear (he was also known as Jarnowick), though he seems to have studied in Italy, possibly with Lolli. Whatever his origins, Giornovichi's playing seems to typify the musical life of Paris during this decade. He combined a brilliant if facile virtuosity with a polished and elegant manner; for slow movements he favoured the graceful romance and for finales the piquant rondo. Equally characteristically, the same decade saw the sudden rise of the agreeable and colourful *symphonie concertante*, a genre which was cultivated with a frenzy of enthusiasm.

But this undemanding musical *milieu* was not to last. Viotti's first performance at the Concert Spirituel on 17 March 1782 caused a sensation. Virtually single-handedly Viotti was to change the course of violin playing during the 1780s. His excellent technique was taken for granted (and he was no doubt exceeded in violinistic trickery by Lamotte and Lolli). What struck audiences was the grand and forceful manner of his bowing (derived from Pugnani), and his rich expressive tone – both enhanced by his preference for a Stradivari violin and the new bow developed by Tourte. He particularly exploited the sonorous qualities of the lowest string and the soaring aspirations of the highest; and he was renowned for the noble cantabile of his Adagio playing. Even virtuosity was used less for decorative display, with signs of a more assertive rhetoric and bravura. Altogether Viotti attempted a more serious approach to the whole concept of violin performance, reflected in the number of minor-key concertos he published. In this his playing was in accord with the bolder drama of current French operatic taste (as represented by his friend Cherubini) and also with Haydn's symphonic style.

After sweeping all opposition before him for two seasons, Viotti unexpectedly abandoned the public platform. Instead, he played at select private concerts, including those of Queen Marie Antoinette; he also gave concerts at his own lodgings, to which admittance was highly prized. Towards the end of the decade he became involved in opera management, with some success, before circumstances forced his departure for England in 1792. In London Viotti moderated the virtuoso element of his concertos, but he maintained the expressive intensity and bold imagination, pleasing those harsh critics who had so consistently complained about the empty display of his predecessors:

It is impossible to speak of [Viotti's] performance in common terms, and therefore we may be pardoned the rhapsody. His execution is not more astonishing by its difficulty, than it is delightful by its passion. He not only strikes the senses with wonder, but he touches the heart with emotion.[31]

One critic ventured a direct comparison. By contrast with the 'always delightful, finished and elegant' playing of Giornovichi, he found Viotti 'original and sublime – he reaches at unattempted grandeur'.[32] This unmistakably Romantic image assuredly looks towards the next century.

4   The nineteenth-century bravura tradition

ROBIN STOWELL

At the beginning of the nineteenth century the derivative French classical school of violin playing was pre-eminent, based at the Conservatoire de Musique in Paris (established in 1795). The parent Italian violin school had largely run its course, but it was an Italian, Viotti, who had largely been responsible for laying the foundations of the highly systematised French approach to violin playing and teaching, and his methods were disseminated widely through his own performances and teaching. With the extension of the French school into Belgium in the 1840s and the influence of violinist-composers such as Spohr in Germany, the stage was set for the full flush of Romanticism to blossom in the form of the itinerant virtuoso, 'one of the essential and corroding institutions in music history'[1] responsible for both the development and the debasement of the violin art.

France and Belgium

By the beginning of the nineteenth century Viotti had retired almost entirely from music in order to devote his attentions to his London wine business, the eventual failure of which left him with substantial debts; Gaviniès, Leclair's successor as leader of the French violin school, had left his legacy of distinguished pupils (e.g. Baudron, Capron, Guénin, Leduc and Paisible), some of whom had come under his wing while he was violin professor at the Paris Conservatoire; and Michel Woldemar (1750–1815) was encouraging the cultivation of more virtuosic techniques after the 'school' of his mentor Lolli. Although Viotti performed in public for less than ten years, the qualities of his playing dominated an entire generation of violinists. His technical brilliance, the breadth, beauty and power of his tone and the overall expressive characteristics of his performances captured the imagination of his listeners. Paul Alday, Cartier, Duranowski, Vacher, Labarre, Libon, Robberechts, F. W. Pixis and Rode were among his pupils, and both Kreutzer and Baillot have been regarded as disciples. Certainly, the principles of his performing style were embodied in the two major French treatises of the early nineteenth century adopted by the Paris Conservatoire – *Méthode de violon* (1803) by Baillot, Rode and Kreutzer, and Baillot's more detailed *L'Art du violon* (1834).

Pierre Rode (1774–1830) was Viotti's most renowned pupil and the most finished member of the French school. At the age of twenty-one, he was appointed professor of violin at the newly founded Conservatoire in Paris, and he combined this pedagogical interest with an active career as a touring virtuoso. He was solo violinist to the Tsar at St Petersburg (1804–8) and lived for some years in Berlin (1814–19) before returning to his native Bordeaux.

Rodolphe Kreutzer's (1766–1831) early musical instruction from his father was furthered by violin studies with Anton Stamitz. Fired by the playing of Viotti, he became a leading virtuoso, but his solo career was foreshortened when he broke his arm (1810). He took up conducting, became *maître de la chapelle du roi* (1815) and served as assistant, and later (1817) principal conductor at the Opéra. He was music director at the Opéra (1824–6) and became a *chevalier de la légion d'honneur* in 1824. He was professor of violin at the Paris Conservatoire[2] from its foundation until 1826, when his health went into decline. Notable among his pupils were his brother Auguste, Artôt, Lafont, Massart and the Italian Pietro Rovelli.

Unlike Rode and Kreutzer, Pierre Baillot (1771–1842) was essentially a musical amateur who turned professional only after he had reached maturity. His early violin teachers included Polidori, Sainte-Marie and Pollani. His career wavered between working in the ministry of finance, military service and orchestral playing in the Théâtre Feydeau before his successful performance of a Viotti concerto in Paris led to his appointment as a violin professor at the Conservatoire. In 1802, he joined Napoleon's private orchestra, made a successful tour of Russia (1805–8) and later achieved particular acclaim as a chamber musician. He also led both the Paris Opéra orchestra (1821–31) and the Chapelle Royale orchestra (from 1825). Among Baillot's more significant pupils were Jacques-Féréol Mazas (1782–1849), a touring virtuoso and highly respected pedagogue, and Jean Baptiste Charles Dancla (1817–1907), who returned to the Conservatoire as professor of violin in 1892. François Habeneck (1781–1849), perhaps best remembered for introducing Beethoven's music to French audiences and continuing to promote it in his various roles as director of the Conservatoire students' orchestra, the Concert Spirituel (from 1818 onwards) and the Société des Concerts du Conservatoire, also attended Baillot's class at the Conservatoire, where he won a *premier prix* for the violin in 1804. He was a violin professor at the Conservatoire (1806–16 and 1825–48), and he also served as conductor of the Paris Opéra during one of its most successful periods.

One of Habeneck's foremost pupils was Edouard Lalo (1823–92), who specialised initially in the chamber sphere and became a founder member (in 1855, initially as violist) of the Armingaud Quartet, which enjoyed a particular reputation for its performances of Beethoven. Among other prominent Habeneck pupils were Hubert Léonard (1819–90) and Jean-Delphin Alard (1815–88), the latter renowned as a soloist, orchestral player and as Baillot's successor at the Paris Conservatoire (1843–75), where Sarasate was his most celebrated pupil.

The Belgian school of violin playing, founded by Charles Auguste de Bériot (1802–70) in the early 1840s, was very much an offshoot of the French school, combining the brilliance of Paganini's influence with the traditions established by Viotti, Baillot, Rode and Kreutzer. De Bériot received instruction from Viotti's pupil Robberechts and advice from Viotti himself before completing his studies with Baillot. He did not take easily to the disciplines of a conventional training and developed various eccentricities of performing style modelled after Paganini, gaining considerable acclaim both on his Parisian debut and at the Philharmonic Society in London (1826). His appointment as solo violinist to King William I of the Netherlands was cut short by the revolution of 1830 and he spent much of the following decade on concert tours to many of the world's foremost musical capitals. He was principal violin professor at the Brussels Conservatoire from 1843 to 1852, eventually resigning his post because of failing eyesight.

De Bériot's most celebrated pupil, Henri Vieuxtemps (1820–81; see Fig. 28) was a child prodigy who soon achieved a worldwide reputation as a virtuoso, undertaking tours in Europe and America. Most responsible for the essential characteristics of the Belgian school, he spent five years (1846–51) in Russia as violin professor at the St Petersburg Conservatoire, contributing much to the development of the Russian violin school. In 1871 he accepted an appointment as violin professor at the Brussels Conservatoire, including Ysaÿe among his numerous pupils, but deteriorating health forced him to resign his post in 1879.

Another de Bériot disciple who is believed also to have studied with Vieuxtemps and Wieniawski was Emile Sauret (1852–1920). Much travelled as a virtuoso, Sauret eventually settled in London (1890–1903), and he succeeded Prosper Sainton as professor at the Royal Academy of Music. After a sojourn in Chicago and further concert commitments in Europe, he returned to London to take up an appointment as professor at Trinity College of Music (1908).

Hubert Léonard (1819–90), one of the numerous disciples of François Prume at the Brussels Conservatoire and of Habeneck in Paris, became one of Vieuxtemps's closest friends. He did much to perpetuate the ideals of the Franco-Belgian violin school, succeeding de Bériot as violin professor at the Brussels Conservatoire in 1853. He moved to Paris in 1866 and established himself there as a virtuoso and composer, and

Fig. 28   Henri Vieuxtemps (1820–81)

especially as a teacher and chamber musician, championing the music of Brahms as well as that of composers such as Saint-Saëns, Fauré, Lalo and d'Indy.

Among other prominent Belgian figures were Rodolphe Massart, Ovide Musin, Armand Parent, Leopold Charlier, Mathieu Crickboom and the renowned pedagogue Lambert Massart (1811–92), whose numerous pupils included Wieniawski, César Thomson, Fritz Kreisler and four other distinguished teachers who succeeded him at the Paris Conservatoire – the two Frenchmen Lefort and Berthelier, and the two Belgians Martin Marsick and Guillaume Rémy. Thomson was unrivalled for some time as a soloist and he became renowned as a pedagogue at the Conservatoires of Liège (1882–97), Brussels (1898–1914) and later in Paris and the USA. Marsick included Carl Flesch and Jacques Thibaud among his pupils at the Paris Conservatoire.

The Belgian school's most significant late-nineteenth-century 'product' was Eugène Ysaÿe (1858–1931). After training at the Conservatoires of Liège (with Heynberg and R. Massart) and Brussels (with Wieniawski) and later with Vieuxtemps in Paris, Ysaÿe led the Bilse orchestra in Berlin (1879–82) before embarking on concert tours of Russia and Scandinavia with Anton Rubinstein. He settled in Paris in 1883–6, contributing much to the popularity of the violin works of composers such as Fauré, d'Indy, Saint-Saëns, Chausson and Franck and receiving many dedications. He was violin professor at the Brussels Conservatoire (1886–98) and further encouraged the progress of contemporary French and Belgian music by establishing the 'Concerts Ysaÿe', in which he appeared as conductor and violinist. Meanwhile, he made a considerable reputation in Europe and the USA. Acknowledging his waning powers as a soloist, he eventually increased his conducting schedules, and he directed the Cincinnati Symphony Orchestra (between 1918 and 1922) with considerable success.

Italy

Although his violinistic and musical backgrounds were embedded firmly in the Italian classicism of Viotti and his predecessors, Nicolò Paganini (1782–1840) became one of the most significant figures in the history of virtuosity. He received instruction from Antonio Cervetto, Giacomo Costa and possibly Alessandro Rolla, but influences such as the performance of the Polish violinist Duranowski (a pupil of Viotti) in Genoa (1794), the virtuosic violin concertos of his fellow countrymen Antonio Lolli and Giornovichi, and his discovery of Locatelli's *L'arte del violino* (1733) caprices had a far more potent effect on his technique and performing style. This latter was analysed by the Frankfurt-based violinist and conductor Karl Guhr in his *Ueber Paganinis Kunst* ... (1829). Without this study, knowledge of Paganini's technique, manner of performance and some of his compositions would be slight, since Paganini guarded his works and executive skills with the utmost secrecy.

After a few acclaimed early solo performances and a conventional appointment in Lucca (initially as leader of the national orchestra and later in the service of Napoleon's sister, Princess Elisa Baciocchi), Paganini embarked on a career as a touring virtuoso in 1810. He conquered Milan and other Italian cultural centres with his performances and compositions to gain national prominence and extended his touring net to the rest of Europe (from 1828) with a gruelling concert schedule. Returning to Italy in 1834, he settled in Parma and served the Grand Duchess Marie-Louise for a short period, resigning his post in 1836 to resume his concert touring in France. His association with the 'Casino Paganini' in Paris (1837–8) was disastrous and left him with considerable losses, but his financial situation was still sufficiently healthy to enable him to present Berlioz with a generous gift of 20,000 francs in December 1838. His own health, however, deteriorated rapidly, and his concert career was near its end. Paganini's virtuosic achievements represent the summit of technical artistry in violin playing in the early nineteenth century. His performances aroused an enthusiasm suggestive of sorcery at work, and his genius in extending the technical and expressive boundaries of the violin prompted executants of many different instruments to emulate him, notably the pianist-composers Liszt and, to a lesser degree, Schumann and Chopin, the cellist Franchomme and violinist-composers such as de Bériot, Vieuxtemps, Ernst, Bull, Lipiński, and Paganini's only known pupil, Camillo Sivori.

Sivori (1815–94) was brought up in the Paganini mould, studying for two years with Paganini's former teacher Giacomo Costa and later with Agostino Dellepiane, before receiving instruction from the maestro himself in 1824. Making his debut at the age of twelve, he embarked on the first of his many concert tours to the musical capitals of the world, one of his major tours beginning in 1841 and lasting some eighteen months. He settled in Paris from c.1863, but made frequent visits to England, Germany and Italy.

Also much encouraged by Paganini was Antonio Bazzini (1818–97), a violin pupil of Camisani. Moving to Germany (1841–5), he counted Schumann and Mendelssohn among his many admirers. After a touring concert life, punctuated with periods of more settled teaching, Bazzini returned to Brescia and devoted himself to composition. Among his pupils at the Milan Conservatoire was Giacomo Puccini. More classically trained in the French tradition were Teresa (1827–1904) and Maria (1832–48) Milanollo, who completed their violin studies with de Bériot before embarking on numerous extended European concert tours (1842–8).

Germany

German musical taste was influenced most substantially by Louis Spohr in the first half of the nineteenth century, and much of his artistic credo was perpetuated by his numerous pupils; among them was Ferdinand David (1810–73), who in turn guided Joseph Joachim (1831–1907) in the early part of his career. Spohr was himself a pupil of, among others, Franz Eck of Mannheim. However, he came to admire the playing of Rode and imitated him in certain respects; in this way he linked the German school to the French school, particularly to Rode's teacher Viotti. Spohr's tours as a virtuoso were punctuated with other engagements, ranging from the post of *Konzertmeister* at Gotha (1805–12) and *Kapellmeister* at Kassel (from 1822) to various conducting engagements (Vienna, Frankfurt), and composition commissions. Apart from David, Spohr's most prominent violin pupils included Léon de Saint-Lubin, Hubert Ries, Bernhard Molique and August Wilhelmj.

David became a close friend of Mendelssohn while serving as a violinist in the Königstadt Theatre in Berlin (1826–9). After a six-year period as a chamber musician for Karl von Liphart in Dorpat, he moved to Leipzig (1836) to lead the Gewandhaus Orchestra under Mendelssohn, and he quickly established himself there as a player, composer, teacher and conductor, making only occasional trips to perform abroad. He became a violin professor at the newly-established Leipzig Conservatoire in 1843 and, in addition to Joachim, included among his pupils Wilhelmj, F. Hermann, A. Hilf and Wilhelm von Wasielewski. However, he is perhaps best known for advising Mendelssohn on the solo writing in his Violin Concerto in E minor Op. 64. His *Hohe Schule des Violinspiels*, a collection of violin sonatas and other works by composers of the two previous centuries, was also a highly significant work for its time, despite the enormous editorial liberties contained therein.

Mendelssohn's influence on succeeding generations was made more potent through the achievements of his protégé, and David's 'pupil', Joseph Joachim (Fig. 29). Of Hungarian descent, Joachim was to become the inspirer of many of the great violin concertos of the second half of the nineteenth century, and his championing of Beethoven's Violin Concerto, for which he wrote some remarkable cadenzas, was instrumental in establishing the work in the repertory. After the formative years in Leipzig under the guidance of Mendelssohn and David, Joachim accepted Liszt's invitation (1850) to become concertmaster at Weimar. He resigned two years later to become royal music director at Hanover. From there, he strengthened his friendship with Schumann, established a long association with Brahms which was to be of enormous benefit both to that composer and to music generally, and gradually gained international recognition. He resigned the Hanover post in 1865 and gained his final appointment, as director and violin professor at the newly

Fig. 29   Joseph Joachim (1831–1907)

formed Hochschule für Ausübende Tonkunst in Berlin, in 1868. He created a distinct Berlin violin school (for example, one of the leading German violinists at the turn of the century, Willy Burmester, was among his numerous pupils there) and made an enormous contribution to the growth of the city as a cultural centre, particularly in the fields of orchestral and chamber music. The celebrated Joachim Quartet, formed by Joachim in 1869 with colleagues from the Hochschule (although there were many changes in personnel during the ensemble's existence), gave an annual series of concerts in Berlin and made many tours abroad to great acclaim. Like David, Joachim freely gave advice to other composers who consulted him about problems of string writing and dedicated works to him. Among these were Schumann, Dvořák, Bruch, Niels Gade and Brahms.

One of the most celebrated of David's pupils (1861–4) at Leipzig was Wilhelmj (1845–1908), who later continued his composition studies in Frankfurt with Joachim Raff. He commenced concert tours in Europe in 1865 and was particularly well received in England. By 1876, he was concertmaster for Wagner in Bayreuth and he also persuaded Wagner to accompany him to London (1877) to conduct at the Albert Hall, Wilhelmj himself acting as concertmaster. In the following year Wilhelmj embarked on a four-year world tour, success in this venture contrasting with failure in his next, the establishment of a violin school in collaboration with Rudolf Niemann in Wiesbaden. Wilhelmj's next major step was to settle in London (1894), where he was appointed principal violin professor at the Guildhall School of Music.

Poland

Most significant of the Polish violinist-composers of the period were Feliks Janiewicz (1762–1848), August Durand (Duranowski) (c.1770–1834), Karol Lipiński (1790–1861) and Henryk Wieniawski (1835–80). Janiewicz left his native country in 1785 and made lengthy sojourns in Vienna, various Italian cities and Paris before coming to Britain in 1792, eventually settling in Edinburgh (c.1815). A pupil of Viotti, Durand toured widely as a soloist in Europe but eventually settled in Strasbourg as concertmaster of the theatre orchestra.

After a fairly inauspicious start to his violin training with his classically orientated father, Lipiński heeded the advice of Spohr, resigning his post as violinist and conductor of a theatre orchestra in Lvov in order to further his technical skills. While pursuing a solo career, he became influenced by Paganini, meeting the maestro in Padua (1818) and performing with him on two occasions. They regarded each other with mutual respect and performed together again over a decade later in Warsaw during the coronation of Nicholas I of Russia as King of Poland (1829). Lipiński eventually renounced a solo

Fig. 30 Henryk Wieniawski (1835–80)

touring career in favour of an appointment as royal concertmaster in Dresden (1839–61).

Wieniawski (Fig. 30) was a child prodigy on the violin and became a violin student at the Paris Conservatoire in 1843, transferring to Massart's class a year later. Completing his violin studies in 1848 (although he returned to study composition in 1849–50), Wieniawski embarked on a successful career as a travelling virtuoso violinist, incorporating many of his own compositions into his varied repertory. Persuaded by Anton Rubinstein, he settled in St Petersburg (1860–72), and his activities as soloist, leader, chamber musician and teacher (he served as the first violin professor at the newly established Conservatoire, 1862–8) contributed towards both the improvement of musical conditions in Russia and the development of a national violin school. Apart from a short spell (1875–7) as violin professor (succeeding Vieuxtemps) at the Brussels Conservatoire, he spent the rest of his years touring the world as a concert artist until deteriorating health intervened.

Hungary

Hungary's musical culture in the nineteenth century was developed to a great extent by foreign visitors, the inadequate facilities for musical training and the limited musical opportunities prompting many talented native musicians (e.g. Joseph Boehm, Joachim, Goldmark, Reményi, Hubay, Auer and Nachez) to emigrate in their youth. Jenö Hubay (1858–1937) was one who returned. Trained initially by his father and then by Joachim in Berlin, he befriended Vieuxtemps whilst in Paris (1878) and benefited greatly from his advice. He did much valuable work in editing and, in some cases, completing Vieuxtemps's posthumous works in the 1880s. In 1882 he was appointed violin professor at the Brussels Conservatoire but returned to Budapest four years later to succeed his father as violin professor at the Budapest Academy, serving as director of that institution from 1919 to 1934. His pupils there included Joseph Szigeti, Franz von Vecsey, Jelly d'Arányi, Zoltan Székely and Sándor Végh.

Exiled from Hungary in 1848, Joseph Boehm's pupil Ede Reményi (1828–98) also returned briefly to his native country after obtaining an amnesty (1860), but he spent most of his career in the USA and London (where he was solo violinist to Queen Victoria, 1854–9), as well as making solo appearances in other major European centres.

Austria

Austria (and Vienna in particular) was well in the forefront of musical activities in the nineteenth century. To conquer Vienna was the prime objective of most virtuosi, and the Viennese public did much to cultivate the appreciation of chamber music. Ignaz Schuppanzigh (1776–1830) and his string quartet (from 1808 onwards this comprised Schuppanzigh, Sina, Weiss and Linke) introduced the quartets of Beethoven and Schubert to Viennese audiences, who, thanks also to Schuppanzigh, developed a taste for the type of salon music which was later to become even more popular with the likes of Johann Schrammel and Fritz Kreisler.

Schuppanzigh also encouraged violinists such as Joseph Mayseder (1789–1863),[3] who was later appointed leader of the Hoftheater orchestra in Vienna (1810), soloist at the Hofkapelle (1816), soloist to the emperor (1835) and musical director of the Hofkapelle (1836). The teacher of the salon violinist Miska Hauser, Mayseder's only musical journey was to Paris (1820) where he met, among others, Habeneck and Kreutzer; but the main link between Vienna and the pre-eminent French violin school was the Hungarian violinist and teacher Joseph Boehm (1795–1876), whose advanced studies with Rode proved extremely influential. He became professor of violin at the newly established Vienna Conservatoire (1819–48), played in the imperial orchestra (1821–68), and was a frequent soloist and quartet performer at the height of his powers. His pupils included such eminent performers as Ernst, Joachim and Reményi and the renowned pedagogues Georg Hellmesberger and Jakob Dont (1815–88).

Georg Hellmesberger (1800–73) was appointed assistant to Boehm at the Vienna Conservatoire in 1821, being made a titular professor five years later and an active professor in 1833, a post he held until he retired in 1867. Hellmesberger helped to establish a Viennese school of violin playing in the early nineteenth century, gradually replacing Boehm and Mayseder as the leading violinist in the capital. He succeeded Schuppanzigh as concertmaster at the Hofoper in 1830 and soon after became a member of the Hofkapelle. He was also a founder and conductor of the Philharmonic Concerts (1842) and included Joachim, Hauser, Auer and his sons Joseph (i) and Georg (ii) among his pupils.

Joseph Hellmesberger (i) (1828–93) became a Viennese musician of considerable influence, becoming artistic director and conductor of the Gesellschaft der Musikfreunde concerts (1851–9) and giving them a sound professional basis for their continued future. He was also violin professor and director of the Conservatoire, concertmaster at the Hofoper (from 1860), director of the *Singverein* of the Gesellschaft der Musikfreunde (temporarily in 1879), and *Hofkapellmeister* (from 1877). As founder and leader of the Hellmesberger Quartet (from 1849 to 1891), he played a vital role in the dissemination of the chamber-music repertory in the capital. His son Joseph (ii) (1855–1907), also a violin professor at the Conservatoire (from c.1878), assumed the leadership of the Quartet on his father's retirement in 1891, but he was to gain greater renown as a conductor, succeeding Mahler in conducting the Philharmonic Concerts (1901–3).

The Moravian-born violinist Heinrich Wilhelm Ernst (1814–65) was one of the notable virtuoso products of Boehm's 'school' at the Vienna Conservatoire, but his extraordinary virtuosity was due more to the influence of Paganini's technique and performing style. Paganini's appearance in Vienna in 1828 made such an impression on him that he followed the maestro on tour the following year. After three years of intensive further study, Ernst fulfilled a dream, appearing with Paganini in Marseilles (1837), and he then embarked on extensive concert tours, becoming a regular visitor to London and settling there in 1850.

No section on nineteenth-century Austrian violinists would be complete without mention of the violinist, conductor and composer Franz Clement (1780–1842), for whom Beethoven wrote his Violin Concerto Op. 61; and the Hungarian composer Károly Goldmark (1830–1915) may more conveniently be considered as an adopted Viennese, studying the violin in the Austrian capital first with Jansa and later at the Conservatoire with Boehm, and living there for most of his life.

Bohemia

Bohemia was once a separate kingdom in the Holy Roman Empire, with Prague as its capital. Although many Bohemian composers had left their fatherland to seek worthwhile posts elsewhere in Europe, there was already a strong tradition of violin playing, particularly in Prague, when Friedrich Wilhelm Pixis (1785–1842) moved there from Vienna to become violin professor at the Conservatoire (and conductor of the theatre orchestra). Pixis spread the gospel of his 'finishing' teacher Viotti and included among his pupils Josef Slavík, Rudolf Dreyschock, Moritz Mildner (1812–65) and Johann Kalliwoda (1801–66). Kalliwoda, who worked most of his life in the service of the Prince of Fürstenberg in Donaueschingen, was a highly respected violinist and a prolific composer in various genres. Mildner succeeded Pixis at the Prague Conservatoire and counted among his numerous pupils Ferdinand Laub and Antonin Bennewitz (1833–1926).

Bennewitz, another esteemed violin professor at the Prague Conservatoire, taught František Ondříček (1857–1922).[4] Ondříček toured widely as a virtuoso, and to considerable acclaim, but he is chiefly remembered as the violinist who premiered Dvořák's Violin Concerto in Prague (1883). Towards the end of the century he settled in Vienna, later teaching at the Conservatoire (1909–12), but he returned to his pedagogical duties in Prague after World War I (1919–22). Another student of Bennewitz, Dvořák's son-in-law (and composition pupil) Josef Suk (1874–1935), came to the fore as a member of (second violinist until 1933) the famous Czech String Quartet, formed in 1891 by pupils of the chamber-music coach Hanuš Wihan at the Prague Conservatoire. Furthermore, Bennewitz's pupil Otakar Ševčík (1852–1934) was an eminent violinist and teacher, becoming an esteemed concertmaster in Vienna and Salzburg and a distinguished violin professor, first in Kiev (1875–92) and later in Prague and Vienna. Notable among his disciples are Jan Kubelík, Kocián, Pawel Kochánski and Wolfgang Schneiderhan, many of whom were raised on his systematic training method.

Another Bohemian who, like Ondříček, spent much of his career in Vienna was Leopold Jansa (1795–1875), who succeeded Schuppanzigh as first violinist of the Schuppanzigh Quartet. Jansa also spent some years in London but returned to Vienna in 1870. Among his more notable pupils were Wilma Neruda (later to become Lady Hallé by her second marriage) and Eduard Rappoldi.

Scandinavia

Perhaps the most influential violinist of the Scandinavian countries in the nineteenth century was the Norwegian Ole Bull (1810–80), who was nurtured in the French tradition by J. H. Poulsen and M. Ludholm, pupils of Viotti and Baillot respectively. He also took a deep interest in the techniques of the peasant fiddlers of his native country and experimented with a Hardanger fiddle, the Norwegian peasant violin with sympathetic strings, giving a performance of his own *Souvenirs de Norvège* in Paris (1833) on that instrument. Inspired by meeting Ernst and by hearing Paganini in Paris, Bull toured widely as a concert violinist, describing himself as 'artiste norvégien' and putting Norway indelibly on the cultural map of Europe. He did much to make his compatriots aware of their national heritage of folk music and was involved in several schemes throughout his career designed to give his country prominent status in the world's culture; for example, he was instrumental in establishing a Norwegian national theatre in Bergen (1849–50). He eventually allowed Norwegian folk techniques to influence his own playing style by adopting the flatter bridge of the Hardanger fiddle and employing a longer, heavier bow of different shape. Held in an unorthodox manner, this bow-type, together with the set-up of his violin, enabled him to play polyphonic music with ease, which explains his Quartet for solo violin, composed in an effort to outshine Paganini's popular Duo.

Johan Svendsen's (1840–1911) first orchestral experience as a violinist was in the orchestra of the Norwegian Theatre established by Bull. He later undertook advanced violin (under Ferdinand David) and composition studies at the Leipzig Conservatoire with the intention of becoming a concert violinist, but a problem with the fingers of his left hand caused him to concentrate rather more on composing and conducting. His reputation as a conductor soon became second to none in Scandinavia and in 1883 he was appointed conductor of the Royal Opera in Copenhagen, the most prestigious musical post in Denmark. Another

Norwegian graduate from the Leipzig Conservatoire was Christian Sinding (1856–1941), whose composition studies soon predominated over his violin lessons with Schradieck. At the end of the century, the Swedish violinist of French birth Henri Marteau (1874–1934), a pupil of Léonard, was regarded as one of the greatest violinists of his time.

Russia

The influence of the French school of violin playing reached Russia by the beginning of the nineteenth century, thanks largely to the visits of Baillot (1802) and Rode (1804–8), the latter remaining in the country for approximately five years as solo violinist to the Tsar in St Petersburg. But apart from the impetus provided by such foreign musicians and the efforts of such a fine native violinist as Ivan Khandoshkin (1747–1804), early-nineteenth-century Russian music was organised essentially on an amateur level and was firmly rooted in opera and song. The main catalyst in eradicating the 'mischievous amateurishness' in Russian musical circles and encouraging the cause of his country's instrumental music was the pianist-composer Anton Rubinstein, who headed a major initiative to reorganise musical life there along European lines. Rubinstein was instrumental in establishing both the Russian Musical Society (1859), whose concerts he conducted, and the Conservatoire in St Petersburg (1862), which he directed until 1867 (and again from 1887), appointing Wieniawski as that institution's first principal violin professor.

Wieniawski's successor in 1868 was the Hungarian Leopold (von) Auer (1845–1930), a pupil of Ridley Kohne in Budapest, Jakob Dont in Vienna and finally Joseph Joachim in Hanover. When Auer (Fig. 31) quit his post (1917), he moved eventually to New York, where he proved considerably influential as a pedagogue. But his greatest achievement was in establishing an outstanding Russian 'school' of violin playing, with Mischa Elman, Efrem Zimbalist, Jascha Heifetz and Miron Poliakin among his more notable pupils. His various transcriptions and arrangements for violin are competent but unmemorable, but his editions of the more classical violin repertory and his books on violin playing and interpretation[5] have been widely used. Although he has often been regarded as Wieniawski's inferior as an executant, his influence as a performer was considerable. From 1868 to 1906 he led the string quartet of the Russian Musical Society, introducing the quartets of Tchaikovsky, Borodin, Glazunov and Rimsky-Korsakov to Russian audiences as well as championing the music of Brahms, Schumann and others. He also conducted the society's orchestra in 1883 and from 1887 to 1892. Amongst his duties as court violinist was to play the solos at the Imperial Ballet, a tradition which Tchaikovsky in particular exploited to great effect, most memorably in the solos for *Swan Lake*. Auer was also the

Fig. 31   Leopold (von) Auer (1845–1930)

Fig. 32   Pablo de Sarasate (1844–1908)

inspiration behind Tchaikovsky's *Sérénade mélancolique* Op. 26 (1875), and the intended dedicatee of his Violin Concerto, but, for reasons best known to him, he declined to premiere them. Tchaikovsky re-dedicated the concerto to the Russian-Jewish violinist Adolph Brodsky (1851–1929), who gave the first performance in 1881. Brodsky later led both the New York Symphony Orchestra (1890–4) and the Hallé Orchestra (1895–6), and he succeeded Sir Charles Hallé as principal of the Royal Manchester College of Music.

Spain

Apart from Viotti's pupil Philippe Libon (1775–1838), who held positions as court violinist at Lisbon (1796), Madrid (1798) and Paris (1800–38), the colourful personality Pablo de Sarasate y Navascuéz (1844–1908; Fig. 32) dominated amongst native Spanish violinists. He was already of advanced standard when he attended the Paris Conservatoire (1856) to study with Alard. Three years later he set out on the first of many tours which won for him critical acclaim in the Americas as well as in Europe. He was a tremendous inspiration to numerous composers (notably Bruch, Saint-Saëns, Lalo, Wieniawski and Dvořák), who wrote concertos or other works specifically for him.

Great Britain

Although the so-called British musical renaissance was well advanced by the mid nineteenth century, few violinists of international merit emanated from these shores during the period. Perhaps most significant were Henry Blagrove (1811–72), and Alfred (1837–76) and Henry (1839–1905) Holmes.

5   The twentieth century

ERIC WEN

At the turn of the century Joachim and Sarasate, two of the most prominent exponents of nineteenth-century violin playing, were still active. Highly regarded throughout their careers, the two figures represented opposite ideals: Joachim was the serious musician who probed the musical essence of a composition, and Sarasate the elegant violinist who played with a sleek but somewhat glib virtuosity. Renowned for the depth and spiritual quality of his interpretations, Joachim was venerated as the greatest interpreter of the German masterworks. He had first performed the Beethoven concerto as a thirteen-year-old under the baton of Mendelssohn and, as leader of the distinguished Joachim Quartet, did much to bring the Beethoven quartets to the public's attention. As a close friend of Brahms, Joachim not only championed many of the composer's works, but also inspired and advised Brahms, notably in the writing of his Violin Concerto. By contrast, Beethoven and Brahms were composers for whom Sarasate had little affinity. The violinist Albert Spalding recalled that 'he played Beethoven with the perfumed polish of a courtier who doesn't quite believe what he is saying to Majesty'.[1] As for the Brahms concerto, Sarasate unashamedly refused to perform the work, explaining, 'Why should I stand there while the oboe has the only proper melody in the whole piece?'[2] It would be unfair, however, to dismiss Sarasate's achievement on the basis of his musical tastes. He was a unique personality, and had sufficient musical qualities to inspire a wide variety of composers to write works for him.

Standing apart from Joachim and Sarasate was Ysaÿe (Fig. 33), and it was his influence which was to predominate in the twentieth century. A student of Vieuxtemps and Wieniawski, Ysaÿe had a direct link with the grand romantic tradition of violin playing. He was also friendly with the most distinguished composers of his age, many of whom dedicated their works to him. Ysaÿe was a gargantuan personality whose playing was characterised by enormous sweep and panache. In some ways he can be regarded as a synthesis of the two extremes represented by Joachim and Sarasate. Combining a virtuoso technique with a rich musical imagina-

Fig. 33   Eugène Ysaÿe (1858–1931)

Fig. 34   Fritz Kreisler (1875–1962)

tion, he had the ability to convey a range of musical expression through his unique tone. By creating a new ideal in violin sound, Ysaÿe initiated the modern style of string playing. In the words of the Hungarian violinist Joseph Szigeti, who discerned this new quality upon hearing Ysaÿe, Kreisler and Elman for the first time in Berlin in 1905, this sound was characterised by 'sensuous beauty, coloristic [*sic*] finesse and dramatic contrasts'.[3]

Mischa Elman (1891–1967), the first of Leopold Auer's many brilliant students, was only fourteen years old and already a seasoned performer when Szigeti first heard him. He and Franz von Vecsey, two years Elman's junior, were the sensational child prodigies of the time, but it was Elman with his luscious sound who ultimately gained the public's favour. Elman played with great spontaneity and abandon, and his interpretations were characterised by his uniquely personal rubato. In later years this rhythmic freedom had a tendency towards exaggeration, and his reputation suffered as a result. Elman maintained a loyal following throughout his career, however, and continued performing up until his death.

Fritz Kreisler (1875–1962; Fig. 34) was thirty years old in 1905 and, although Elman's senior by sixteen years, had been no less remarkable as a child prodigy. Following his graduation from the Vienna and Paris Conservatoires at the ages of ten and twelve respectively, Kreisler made an extended tour of the United States in 1888. Upon his return to Vienna the following year, he laid aside the violin to pursue his academic studies. At twenty-one, after attending medical school for two years and serving briefly in the Austrian army, he resumed his career as a violinist. During this time two other figures – the highly communicative Bronislaw Huberman (1882–1947), who had performed the Brahms concerto at the age of twelve in the presence of the composer, and the technically polished Jan Kubelík (1880–1940), dubbed 'Paganini revidivus' by his adoring audiences – were regarded by the Viennese public as the premier violinists of the day. Kreisler's rise to prominence was steady, however, and by the end of the century's first decade he became the undisputed 'king of violinists'. Carl Flesch ascribed Kreisler's relatively late acceptance by the general public to his novel technique (a rhythmically incisive bow arm and a consistently vibrant left hand), but as early as 1901 Ysaÿe had predicted: 'I have arrived at the top ... but Kreisler is on the ascendant, and in a short time he will be the greater artist'.[4] Kreisler had a unique combination of intensity and relaxation in his playing; despite the focused energy and articulation of his technique, there was always a naturalness and ease in his interpretations. Kreisler's supremacy prevailed until the mid 1930s, and his pervasive influence is confirmed by Flesch, who wrote that Kreisler 'divined in advance and satisfied the specific type of emotional expression demanded by our age'.[5]

Fig. 35   Jascha Heifetz (1901–87) aged seventeen

Among the other violinists who gained prominence during the period before the First World War were Carl Flesch, George Enescu and Jacques Thibaud. Despite their different backgrounds, all three studied at the Paris Conservatoire with Martin Marsick. The Hungarian-born Flesch (1873–1944) made his mark as one of the century's leading pedagogues, while the Romanian-born Enescu (1881–1955),[6] a violinist of great imagination and fantasy, was also a superb pianist, conductor and composer. Jacques Thibaud (1880–1953), the leading French violinist of the century, was particularly admired by Ysaÿe and Kreisler. His playing was characterised by an enchanting mixture of sensuality and tenderness, and his sonata performances with the pianist Alfred Cortot (as well as trios together with Pablo Casals) were especially distinguished. One of the most eloquent violinists of the century, Thibaud died tragically in a plane crash en route to a performance in Indo-China.

By the First World War the most prominent violinists began to rival the great singers in popularity. A violin recital by a major artist was regarded as a special event, and these concerts often took place in large venues which could accommodate huge audiences (e.g. the Royal Albert Hall in London and the Hippodrome in New York). In an age preceding radio and television it was only natural that live concerts should inspire this interest. One of the most celebrated violin recitals of this century was the American debut of the sixteen-year-old Jascha Heifetz (1901–87) in New York's Carnegie Hall on 27 October 1917. Heifetz (Fig. 35) was a remarkable prodigy; at the age of eleven he had performed the Tchaikovsky concerto with Artur Nikisch and the Berlin Philharmonic. He tossed off the most difficult passages with a nonchalant ease, and his name became synonymous with violinistic perfection. His sheer mastery of the instrument brought a new level of technical awareness which consequently altered the course of violin playing in this century. In addition to the razor-sharp finish of his technique, there was a smouldering passion beneath the sheen and polish of his playing. Soon after Heifetz's formidable American debut, a critic remarked 'Kreisler is king, Heifetz the prophet, and all the rest, violinists!' If the playing of Kreisler was like the cosy warmth of a log fire, that of Heifetz was like the luminous white heat of a laser. Despite their differences the two violinists, who incidentally shared the same birthday, represented the two ideals of violin playing in the twentieth century. Yehudi Menuhin's recollection that his 'greatest desire as a child was to play the violin as well as Heifetz, and to communicate as Kreisler did'[7] echoed the wish of many generations of budding violinists.

Although Kreisler and Heifetz were the dominant figures, the period between the two world wars has been dubbed the 'golden age of violin playing' owing to the many distinctive violin personalities who were active at the time. There was a proliferation of individual talents from virtually every country, and interest in the violin was pervasive. Adolf

Fig. 36   Joseph Szigeti (1892–1973)

Busch (1891–1952) and Georg Kulenkampff (1898–1948) were the principal violinists of Germany, and, in addition to Huberman, Eastern Europe had produced Pawel Kochánski (1887–1934), Erica Morini (b.1904) and Váša Příhoda (1900–60). Auer's many outstanding pupils included Efrem Zimbalist, Toscha Seidel, Mischa Piastro, Kathleen Parlow and Eddy Brown, and Carl Flesch had taught such superb talents as Max Rostal, Szymon Goldberg, Henri Temianka, Ida Haendel, Josef Wolfstal and Ricardo Odnoposoff. Two students of Ysaÿe, Alfred Dubois and Mathieu Crickboom, carried on the Franco-Belgian tradition, and Manuel Quiroga and Juan Manén were two remarkable virtuosi from Spain. The leading violinists of England, Italy and America were Albert Sammons, Arrigo Serato and Albert Spalding.

One of the most distinguished figures to emerge during this period was Joseph Szigeti (1892–1973). A student of Jenö Hubay, Szigeti (Fig. 36)

Fig. 37   Yehudi Menuhin (b.1916) aged eleven

made a number of recordings as a young prodigy in the first decade of this century. Unlike Hubay's other prodigy, Vecsey, whose career had faded after his early success, Szigeti's reputation grew gradually. He lived for several years in London and Geneva (where he taught at the Conservatoire), and by the late 1920s he was recognised as a violinist of paramount importance. Equipped with a virtuoso technique, Szigeti combined a natural musicianship with a penetrating intellect. His purity of intonation was especially notable, and the depth of his interpretations remains unequalled.

The 'golden age' of violinists coincided with the development of the recording process, and, fortunately for posterity, most of the well-known performers of the period have been aurally documented. The phonograph was widely disseminated after the First World War, and brought music to a much wider audience than ever before. The popularity of short pieces in violin recitals was related to the 78 rpm record; the three- to four-minute duration of these miniatures fitted perfectly within the time limits of a single side. Not only did these violin pieces adapt to the length of a recording, but the violinists themselves developed a concentration of expression which could show off their special qualities within the time given.

In the late 1920s the American-born Yehudi Menuhin (b.1916) began his career as one of the most remarkable violin prodigies of all time. In addition to his technical prowess on the instrument, Menuhin (Fig. 37) displayed a poetry of musical expression which was unimaginable in a child. A student of Persinger, Busch and, most of all, Enescu, Menuhin made his debut in Berlin on 12 April 1929 performing concertos by Bach, Beethoven and Brahms. At this memorable concert Albert Einstein exclaimed 'Now I know there is a God in heaven!'[8] Three other outstanding American prodigies, Ruggiero Ricci, Oscar Shumsky and Guila Bustabo, also made their first appearances during these years, but it was Menuhin who made the strongest impression.

Several years later another remarkably individual young talent, Ginette Neveu (1919–49), emerged. The elemental force of Neveu's playing was wholly original, and she was destined for a major career before her tragic death in a plane crash. Neveu had sprung to fame upon winning first prize at the 1935 Wieniawski Violin Competition (David Oistrakh and Henri Temianka were the second and third prize-winners). This event, created to honour the centenary of the great Polish violinist's birth, signalled the beginning of a new musical institution: the major international violin competition. Although competitions had existed for many years, this was the first one staged as an open event on an international scale. Following the Second World War international music competitions have flourished, and today there are violin competitions named after composers (Tchaikovsky, Sibelius, Busoni), performers (Paganini, Thibaud, Kreisler, Flesch, Enescu) and cities (Geneva, Munich, Montreal and Beijing). Two years after the first Wieniawski Competition, the Ysaÿe (now Queen Elisabeth of Belgium) Competition was established. This event, won by David Oistrakh, was a Soviet triumph, as five of the top six prizes were awarded to Russians. The determination and rigorous training of violinists in the Soviet Union (taught primarily by Stoliarsky in Odessa and Yampolsky in Moscow) had now proved to be a new force in violin playing.

In the decade preceding the Second World War a number of violinists began to turn their attention to the repertoire of the twentieth century. Louis Krasner had commissioned and performed the Berg concerto in the mid 1930s, and in 1940 he premiered Schoenberg's Concerto. Samuel Dushkin worked closely with Stravinsky, and commissioned the composer's Violin Concerto as well as several other chamber works. Prokofiev's two violin concertos were championed by Szigeti and Heifetz respectively, and the composer received much support from David Oistrakh in the composition of his two violin sonatas. The Hungarian violinists Zoltán Székely and Szigeti featured many compositions by their compatriot Bartók in their respective repertories.

Although there had been a number of successful women violinists such as Maud Powell, Isolde Menges, Marie Hall, Celia Hansen, Renée Chemet and Jelly d'Arányi in the early part of the century, the years

during and following the Second World War witnessed a notable rise in
the number of female soloists. Of these, Gioconda de Vito, Ida Haendel,
Camilla Wicks, Johanna Martzy and Guila Bustabo were among the most
successful. Two extremely gifted violinists of the war years were Josef
Hassid and Ossy Renardy. With their tragic early deaths (at the ages of
twenty-seven and thirty-three respectively) the violin world was
deprived of two of its most promising talents.

Following the Second World War, Zino Francescatti (1902–91) and
Nathan Milstein (b.1903), both in their prime, rose to the international
prominence they had long deserved. A direct descendant of Paganini,
Francescatti was taught exclusively by his father, who studied with
Paganini's only pupil, Camillo Sivori. Francescatti's iridescent tone and
grand virtuoso style combined to form one of the most brilliant violin
sounds of this century. Milstein took lessons with Stoliarsky and, for a
short time, with Auer, but from the age of thirteen onwards he was
virtually self-taught. He executed his immaculate technique with pris-
tine clarity, and always performed with suave elegance.

In the third quarter of the century, a new wave of Soviet-trained
violinists made successful international careers. David Oistrakh
(1908–74) was Russia's leading violinist, but he did not give many
concerts abroad until the 1950s (his American debut did not take place
until 1955). Oistrakh's powerful technique and warm burnished tone
endeared him to audiences throughout the world, and he was a gifted
conductor as well as an inspiring teacher. The other younger Soviet
violinists who emerged during this period were Leonid Kogan, Igor
Bezrodny and Oistrakh's talented son, Igor. Among the violinists from
Europe to establish important solo careers were Arthur Grumiaux,
Christian Ferras, Josef Suk and Franco Gulli. Two other highly individual personalities of this time were Tossy Spivakovsky and Ivry Gitlis.
Perhaps the most outstanding European violinist to emerge in the 1950s
was Henryk Szeryng (1918–88). A student of Flesch in Berlin until the
age of thirteen Szeryng lived in Paris before settling in Mexico during the
Second World War. For years his primary activity was teaching, and
it was only after his compatriot the Polish pianist Artur Rubinstein
encouraged him that he decided to return to the concert stage. Szeryng's
playing was characterised by a creamy smoothness and an infallible
technical control.

Although all the leading violinists had traditionally been trained in
Europe, the United States emerged as one of the great centres of violin
playing in the twentieth century. The wave of immigrants from Europe
and Russia had a deep effect on American culture, and by the middle of
the century a number of important solo violinists had been produced in
the United States. Isaac Stern (b.1921), the leading American violinist of
the second half of the century, was born in the Ukraine, and, after the
family moved to San Francisco, was taught by Naum Blinder, another

Russian émigré who had studied with Adolph Brodsky. An authoritative figure, Stern is a violinist of tremendous energy and force. He is a persuasive communicator, and, in addition to his violinistic gifts, is an influential personality who has been a champion of many philanthropic causes. Another American violinist who rose to prominence in the 1950s was Ruggiero Ricci (b.1918). Although his career had waned after his successful years as a child prodigy, his return to the concert platform following the Second World War was met with great enthusiasm. Despite his reputation as a Paganini specialist, Ricci has a vast and varied repertoire.

Two renowned centres of violin teaching in the United States have been the Juilliard School (formerly the Institute of Musical Art) in New York and the Curtis Institute of Music in Philadelphia, founded in 1905 and 1924 respectively. Franz Kneisel established the international reputation of the Institute of Musical Art by producing such excellent violinists as Sascha Jacobsen, Louis Kaufman, Jacques Gordon, William Kroll and Joseph Fuchs, and both Auer and Zimbalist, who taught at the Curtis Institute, numbered Oscar Shumsky, Benno Rabinoff, Aaron Rosand, Eudice Shapiro, Joseph Silverstein and Shmuel Ashkenasi among their successes.[9]

In the years following the Second World War Demetrius Dounis emerged as another influential teacher. A physiologist who played the mandolin, he concentrated on the physical aspects of violin playing. By the middle of the century the most important violin pedagogue in the United States was Ivan Galamian (1903–81). Born in Iran, Galamian studied with Konstantin Mostras in Moscow and the renowned quartet leader Lucien Capet in Paris before settling in New York in 1937. He was on the faculty of both the Curtis Institute and Juilliard School, and had his strongest influence in the three decades after the Second World War. His immense roster of superb violin students included Paul Makanowitsky, David Nadien, Jaime Laredo, Berl Senofsky, Arnold Steinhardt, Erick Friedman, Michael Rabin, Paul Zukofsky, Itzhak Perlman, Pinchas Zukerman, Kyung Wha Chung and Dong Suk Kang.

By the late twentieth century the general technical standards of the average player had reached a uniformly high level internationally. A certain codification of violin technique, however, set a standard in sound production which lacked variety. The concentration on left-hand technique led to an increase in digital facility, but also an overemphasis on vibrato at the expense of shadings in the bow. Recital programming also underwent a major change. In 1928 Flesch had recommended the inclusion of at least one piece of chamber music (i.e. a sonata) in a recital;[10] half a century later most violin concerts with piano consisted exclusively of duo-sonata works. In the 1950s concertos with piano accompaniment were no longer featured, and the number of short violin pieces included in recital programmes had severely diminished. One factor in the declining popularity of these miniatures was the displacement of the 78 rpm disc by the LP ('long playing') record. Another consequence of the LP era was that recordings were no longer mastered directly from a performance, but put on tape which had the potential to be edited finely. By the 1970s the 'perfectionism' and 'sonic fidelity' of recordings had irrevocably affected violin playing. The aesthetic transformation of violin playing before and after the Second World War can be likened to the replacement of flickering gas lamps by even electric light; the individual and sometimes wayward approach had now been replaced by one of consistent but occasionally charmless accuracy.

As we begin the final decade of the century several violinists have already established themselves as major figures. Two of the most prominent are the American-trained Israelis Itzhak Perlman (b.1945) and Pinchas Zukerman (b.1948). The honey-toned Perlman communicates an infectious joy in his playing, and Zukerman displays a rare poetic sensitivity beneath his cavalier manner. Two other younger Israelis, Shlomo Mintz and Gil Shaham, display great potential. A number of young Soviets such as Vladimir Spivakov and Viktoria Mullova have also had success, but the most individual personality is Gidon Kremer (b.1947), whose pointed, clinical style has strong expressive capabilities.

While many of the major violinists in this century have been of Jewish origin, the past fifteen years have witnessed a flood of superb Oriental talents. Kyung Wha Chung is perhaps the most well known, but Cho-Liang Lin, Dong Suk Kang, Mayumi Fujikawa and Midori have exceptional qualities. Europe has also produced its share of fine violinists such as Salvatore Accardo of Italy, Pierre Amoyal and Augustin Dumay of France, and two young Germans, Anne-Sophie Mutter and Frank Peter Zimmermann. A number of promising American violinists have been trained by Dorothy DeLay and Josef Gingold in recent years, and there are reports of a new generation of Soviet violin stars nurtured in Siberia.

As the emphasis in twentieth-century violin playing has shifted from the expression of one's individual personality to accuracy and fidelity to the score, there has been an interest in the past few years in the 'authentic' performance of seventeenth-, eighteenth- and early-nineteenth-century music. Characterised by a non-legato, strongly articulated style, the 'authenticity' movement can be seen to be a reaction against the smooth but occasionally bland approach prevalent in much of today's string playing. Some of its performers, however, emphasise surface gesture at the expense of emotional depth, and it remains to be seen whether this 'authentic' approach will produce any truly great artists.

The increase in competitions and growth of the recording industry have also had a strong influence on violin playing in recent years. Although they have occasioned a high general standard, there has been a de-personalisation of musical expression. Competitions have also had the effect of narrowing the concert repertory through their insistence on the same 'set pieces'. The carefully constructed interpretations of edited recordings have replaced the spontaneity of live events, and it is ironic that the invention which documented so many varied personalities in the 'golden age' of violin playing has now created a normalised ideal which strives for the illusory concept of the 'definitive' performance. Finally, as distinctions between different solo players have become more subtle, the visual dimension of the concert has increased in importance. Not only is this related to the pervasiveness of the visual media (especially television), but it has been encouraged by managements intent on building the public image of their artists.

6   The fundamentals of violin playing and teaching

ADRIAN EALES

Preamble

As the twentieth century draws to a close, violinists are faced with a bewildering range of teaching and playing styles. Teaching rarely achieves the elevated status of the performing career except in the USA and, more notably, in the traditions of Eastern Europe. As a profession it lacks the formal training and benefits derived from systematic apprenticeship. Moreover, many players resort to violin teaching as a supplement to their main income – with the result that their lessons are invariably unstructured and idiosyncratic.

Written information on the violin fares little better. The authoritative texts of Flesch and Galamian are remarkably thorough; here the beneficiary is the specialist embarking on a solo career, not the teacher, for whom little is on offer. Subsequent authors have continued this trend, though contemporary ideas are even more acutely polarised. The books of Gerle and Jacoby champion a scientific and analytical exposé of skills, while the works of Havas, Menuhin and Polnauer represent the more abstract approach, where general concepts such as *Gestalt* philosophy are preferred to detailed investigation. By contrast, although the Rolland and Suzuki methods are appreciably different from each other, they are both geared to the beginner and pioneer teaching *en masse*, involving extensive use of modern audio and visual equipment.

Serious gaps therefore exist not only for the general student of intermediate standard and modest aspiration but also for today's player and teacher, who is offered little perspective on a wide range of issues and techniques. While this chapter cannot profess to be comprehensive, it does seek to redress the balance. Its agenda, a judicious mix of new and traditional ideas, emphasises topics which are generally neglected, and makes only brief reference to those which can be easily gleaned from the main publications.

The teacher

Observation

Awareness is the heart of good teaching. Observations should begin immediately your pupil arrives, since breathing patterns, facial expressions, speed and type of walk, and your conversation together will give you information about your pupil and some clues as to how the lesson may develop. You will need to move from time to time to ensure that you can see all aspects of your pupil's playing. It is worth remembering, for example, that you will get the best view of thumb, left shoulder and shifting movements by sitting to the left of your pupil and looking up. When accompanying, that legendary upright piano should not be left against the wall; if you are unable to look over the keyboard, then install a large mirror above. Your vision must never be impaired!

Communication

Successful communication is a high priority, so decide whether the student responds more quickly to explanation or demonstration. Strategically, it is best to keep to yourself any disappointment or frustration you might feel, for pupils are human and respond best to praise and positive comment. Choosing the most appropriate style is of paramount importance; like master puppeteers, we must 'play' the appropriate character – bossy, sympathetic, funny, discreet, humble, scolding, arrogant, praising – the choice is endless. It is perhaps surprising that the words we use account for only 7 per cent of what we communicate to another person; 35 per cent is achieved by our tone of voice, while the lion's share (55 per cent) results from our physiology and body-language. Indeed, a degree of empathy with a pupil's speech patterns, rate of breathing, posture and movement, for instance, may help you to 'come across' to each individual in a unique and subtle way.

Challenge

During the lesson try to introduce musically penetrating questions. These can challenge your pupils to think for themselves during the week. Pupils' answers also provide feedback for the teacher, and they often demonstrate that rather less has been understood than might have been expected. If a pupil has a lot of problems it is better to be patient, structuring new ideas throughout the term rather than risking an overkill of change and criticism in a single lesson. When introducing new material try the first and last few minutes of the lesson for best effect.

Flexibility – the young student

The average six-year-old can only concentrate for about ten minutes. The timing and structure of lessons is therefore vitally important and should be tailored to each pupil's age and musical competence. Short lessons with plenty of variety ought to be considered. Using different areas of the music room for various activities such as singing, reading, theory and playing by ear is an option. An individual lesson of fifteen minutes may also be adequate if combined with group lessons.

Group teaching can be fun. It reduces inhibition and, significantly, may encourage critical listening. When no ensemble experience is available, playing duets (e.g. Pleyel's Op. 8) with your pupil is an excellent substitute.

Keeping a record

A notebook is a good visual record of work covered, and it can re-express new topics from the lesson. New material should be thoroughly explained before the lesson ends, possibly with a parent present to guarantee correct practice at home. For the beginner you may wish to follow a syllabus. This may introduce most skills in the first twelve months and need not neglect third position and off-the-string bowing. In succeeding years you can then choose a repertory to define and apply the techniques. At this early stage be precise in your instructions, exact in your requirements and establish stringent standards of accuracy. At the same time respect the value of humour and entertainment in lessons. Lengthy explanations are best avoided. Imagery is a powerful resource for the teaching of rhythm and bowstrokes (Ex. 2). Finally, over-complicated fingering and a proliferation of high positions (notoriously

Ex. 2   The use of imagery as a resource for the teaching of rhythm and bow-strokes (from S. Nelson, *Beginners Please*)

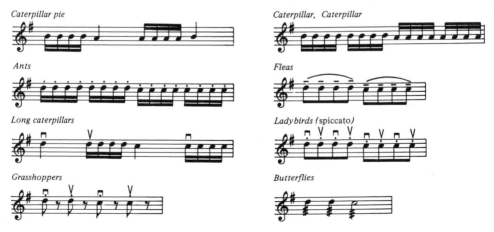

favoured by editors), when simplified, will enable elementary pupils to concentrate on phrasing, tone, rhythm and other performance criteria which are frequently neglected.

Further practical hints

Constant revision of topics is recommended. If lessons are divided into small sections – for example fifteen minutes, with small breaks between – pupils normally benefit, because their concentration peaks after a break. By reviewing previous work during the break maximum progress is made.

When playing together, consider muting your instrument to allow the student's tone and intonation to dominate. Periodically, you will need to play your pupil's violin to assess its potential.

Never position yourself where you are unable to see your pupil's face. Periodic use of a high stool is worth considering, for it not only reduces your fatigue but you can create a more relaxed atmosphere.

Language is important. Words such as 'pressure' and 'stretch' can be replaced by 'weight' and 'spread'. Use words like 'experiment' and 'play' in favour of expressions such as 'hard practice'. Repertory is also a key factor in successful teaching. Pieces which are too difficult for a pupil may impede many musical aspects, including bowing fluency, expression, rhythm, performance tempo and memory. New pieces will need to be clearly bowed and carefully fingered.

Vibrato is best introduced after precise intonation is well developed and when students can understand the importance of variety and context. However, traditional teaching unwisely delays the study of chromatics, octaves and bowing patterns and frequently ignores the benefits of piano accompaniment. The ability to accompany at the piano is a vital asset for the teacher and should be used extensively, especially if it is absent from the home environment.

For the advanced pupil, when concentrating on musicality, style, communication and presentation, you will need to use a large teaching room, ideally the performance venue itself.

The shy pupil is particularly in need of role-play and imagery. To try to overcome that dull performance, why not challenge your student to 'visualise' his playing? Would the gestures and body-language be sufficient to make the expression and dynamic obvious, even without the sound?

Assessment

A 'pupil profile' (see Fig. 38 for an example) is most effective for monitoring progress when used once or twice each term. Developments in education, especially in the GCSE examination, suggest that the

NAME _____ TERM _____ INSTRUMENT _____

Teacher's Comments

Pupil's Comments

....

....

....

	VERY CAPABLE	CAPABLE	NEEDING HELP	NEEDING CONSIDERABLE HELP
INTELLIGENT PRACTICE				
VIRTUOSITY				
ACCURACY				
SIGHT READING				
BOWING AND BOW STROKES				
DYNAMIC AND PITCH RANGE				
POSTURE, SITTING INCLUDED				
VIBRATO RANGE				
MEMORY OF WHOLE MOVEMENTS				
ORCHESTRAL AND CHAMBER MUSIC				
CONTROL IN PERFORMANCE				
TONE COLOURS				
IMPROVISATION				
STYLE AND INTERPRETATION				

	ALWAYS	SOMETIMES	SELDOM
ORGANISING MUSIC AND INSTRUMENT			
PUNCTUALITY TO LESSONS AND REHEARSALS			
WORKING TO MAXIMUM ABILITY			

EFFORT

EXCEPTIONALLY GOOD	
WORKING WELL	
NOT ENOUGH EFFORT	

SIGNATURE: _____

SIGNATURE: _____

Fig. 38   A specimen 'pupil profile' for an advanced violinist

Ex. 3 (a)

(b)

profile should involve evaluation of some skills which are not usually associated with violin study. Certainly, you will need to think about your pupil's progress and ability beyond the narrow confines of any single lesson if you are to make a sound assessment. The profile illustrated is for an advanced violinist. The skills column can be adjusted to the individual pupil's ability. Profiles are particularly useful in LEA teaching (pupil self-assessment is stressed in the National Curriculum guidelines);[1] they are also thorough, flexible and quick to process for all teachers.

In conclusion

Good rapport is important in all teaching, but it is absolutely vital in the one-to-one situation. Strive for a feeling of partnership in which the pupil experiences some freedom, choice and responsibility; a long-term relationship of mutual trust should then develop. Avoid unnecessary comparisons with other pupils, for these merely erode the feeling of individuality. Taking a personal interest is as simple as asking the occasional question about life outside the musical arena.

Diagnostic skill is another essential teaching requirement. You must detect the cause of inferior playing and always provide the individual solution. Resourcefulness and simplicity is often the key to success. Consider, for instance, the value of duets such as those in Ex. 3, which train awareness of other parts when your student is invited to dictate or play the complementary line from memory. Such imagination and inventiveness are essential where progress is slow, and constant reappraisal of the style and content of lessons may be necessary. At all costs avoid an idiosyncratic approach which lacks perspective – for example, one which censures playing as inferior because it does not conform to your personal expectations. As Yehudi Menuhin has reminded us, 'Someone who has been accustomed to playing well all his life, who has great talent from childhood onwards, may rely mainly on instinct and intuition. He may never have had to analyse and eradicate defects of technique, and so has never discovered intellectually the basic principles.'[2]

The student

Practice

'When one encounters a passage like the one which Beethoven marked *beklemmt* in the Cavatina of the quartet Op. 130 with its ineffably poignant expression, one realises that not even the Four Thousand Bowing Exercises of the estimable and industrious Ševčík have prepared one for those *parlando* up-bows.'[3] Szigeti's warning here highlights two important shortcomings in traditional practice patterns: the danger of separating technique from music, and the false complacency derived from a study routine of unthinking repetition. Although this view is shared by many eminent teachers, unpleasant and negative associations for 'practice' still prevail – enthusiasm is limited only to the most highly motivated students. Simply defined, good practice involves playing intelligently and responding to aural, visual and other physical stimuli in such a way that the good is stored and the inferior rejected or modified – in other words, changing incompetence to conscious competence and eventually unconscious competence. Despite Robert Gerle's recent publication,[4] the average student's practice is poor, with little 'quality' guidance from the teacher. Why, then, do we not record our practice for discussion and analysis later?

The following suggestions are offered for consideration in respect of practice:

1 Structure each session.
2 Don't neglect practising in tempo.
3 For the persistent problem – 'missing' a shift, for instance – consider making the mistake deliberately. To miss a 'target' you must know where it is; once you gain control you can choose whether to 'make it' or not! If this does not work, diversionary tactics (i.e. concentrating on some other aspect of playing) are a last resort.[5]

4 Allocate equal time to bowing.

5 Work with the left hand alone to sharpen articulation and rhythm.

6 Practise difficult sections in context.

7 Experiment continually with fingerings and bowings and select the simplest solutions.

8 Keep a healthy balance between *whole learning* and *part learning*.

9 Cover as many skills as possible in each session.

10 Numerous shorter practices are preferable to longer periods throughout a week's work.

11 A positive attitude is important. Breaking new ground and making discoveries can and should be exciting.

Sight-reading[6]

There is little doubt that fear of this test plagues most violinists. Sight-reading is of immense importance and reflects natural talent. Poor literacy often exposes an ignorance of theory, as well as deficiencies in rhythm and dexterity. Although the slow reader will improve through good teaching and practice, some weaknesses may prove unassailable. As with conducting, the essential skills of anticipation (not just reading ahead) and quick response are essential for fluency. At all levels it is wise to note the following before starting: (a) key- and time-signatures; (b) tempo marking; (c) dynamic range; (d) expression marks. The golden rule is to perform musically, without being distracted by minor blemishes in your performance of the test-piece.

The most significant individual technique to enhance reading speed is illustrated in Ex. 4, where each group of six notes can be read as a chord. Advanced performers can derive great benefit from *restez* playing (i.e. maintaining a position and avoiding multiple shifts), which is greatly

Ex. 4 Reading groups of notes as members of a chord (from R. Kreutzer, *42[40] Etudes ou caprices*, No. 8)

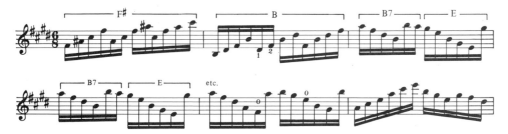

Fig. 39   A model posture for playing when seated

neglected despite its usefulness in complicated passage-work. Finally, on no account take the short cut of playing fingerings without full knowledge of the individual pitch and context of each note; this is the main contributor to inferior literacy.

Posture

The most enthusiastic attention to posture appears in the teaching publications of Havas, Rolland and Menuhin.[7] Conceptual and highly personal in style, their books all emphasise balance, motion and relaxation. Menuhin, for example, includes lengthy chapters on yoga, stretching and breathing, involving prolific exercises before the violin is used.[8] A more analytical approach is offered by Robert Jacoby, who allows no preamble within a page entitled 'General Physical Considerations'.[9]

Whichever approach is adopted, the object is surely to reflect one's natural posture, free of the myriad distortions associated with uncorrected playing. Third-person involvement or the use of audio-visual equipment is invaluable because distortions are deeply rooted and bad habits subconscious. The most frequent include facial contortions, rapid high breathing, twisted spine, stiff neck and an exaggeratedly high left shoulder. Stiffness in any joint is detrimental to the transmission of messages from brain to fingers and vice versa. The following description of Heifetz illustrates how free and relaxed he appeared: 'I thought that if I stood too close to him and breathed hard, I would blow the violin and bow right out of his hands.'[10]

Orchestral and chamber musicians face a further hazard – the curved plastic chair! Here serious thought needs to be given to sitting forward with both feet placed firmly on the floor, the right leg confined to improve E string access in the upper half (see Fig. 39). During a long rehearsal, poor blood circulation behind each knee can be caused by the unnecessary moulded ridge at the front of some chairs. The use of a cushion supporting the lower back may be expedient.

Rhythmic accuracy

Although few dispute the importance of rhythm in music teaching, it is remarkably neglected. For example, the Suzuki method, in which rhythm patterns are reproduced mechanically by ear, makes no attempt to develop disciplined counting. The word 'rhythm' does not appear in eight volumes! Ex. 5 illustrates some of the most common rhythmic difficulties encountered. Accuracy can be monitored by using a metronome. A tendency to rush, anticipate, or count rests inaccurately may be revealed.

Ex. 5 (a) Total mix of time values and rests made more complex by grace notes (from J. F. Mazas, *75 Etudes mélodiques et progressives pour violon* Op. 36: Book 1 *Etudes spéciales*, No. 29)
(b) Changing time signatures and syncopation (from B. Britten, *Saint Nicholas* Op. 42, 2nd movement)
(c) Syncopation, ostinato and pizzicato, a formidable combination (from C. Orff, *Carmina Burana*)

Pitch accuracy

Playing in tune is universally prized. It can be severely affected by poor left-hand flexibility, a lazy ear, and practice which allows mistakes to pass uncorrected. While octave and chromatic practice is valuable, the most important feature of intonation is the combination of advance hearing and a 'feel' for the location, distance and context of each pitch. In contradiction to popular belief, fast scale practice can actually be destructive to this process – the harmonic sequence is too predictable and the custom of maintaining the same fingerings uncritical. Blind repetition sometimes results.

Ex. 6   (a) i and ii: from E. Elgar, Concert Overture: 'Cockaigne' Op. 40

Ex. 6a includes two typically unorthodox scale-like passages from the orchestral repertory which are far more demanding than the average scale. No amount of virtuoso scale work (tenths, octaves, sixths, thirds etc.) will help intonation in Ex. 6b. Extra vigilance is required when performing in a resonant acoustic. Swift correction becomes difficult; the sound not only escapes quickly but fast-moving semiquavers can sometimes merge, creating quasi-chordal effects – the smallest imperfection magnified!

Ex. 6   (b) from W. A. Mozart, String Quartet in A major, K464, fourth movement

Where intonation is intelligently related to key, harmonic structure, or even other instruments in an ensemble, the added projection is a further dividend. As Mark Johnson (Vermeer Quartet) remarks, 'I have memories of certain chords so perfectly in tune that they made this entire room ring; [they] will never happen again in quite the same way in either rehearsal or performance.'[11]

Tone

Although never an end in itself, tonal beauty is a highly personal aspect of primary importance. Projection and quality of sound are more desirable than volume. In the recording studio the sensitivity of microphones reduces the need for herculean dynamics; while in the concert-hall a conductor's lack of sensitivity may cause any instrument to be 'drowned'. Technically, violin sonority is influenced by both left and right functions. Vibrato aside, the left-hand influences are less obvious. Strong finger-pressure can create a hard, glassy tone; when combined with fingertips dropped from high above the strings, clear articulation can be produced. Conversely, less pressure with the finger pads normally leads to a mellow timbre. Rolland devotes one-third of his original thesis (1959) to the physical factors of tone-quality.[12] Superlative descriptions are given regarding technical problems such as proximity to fingerboard, bow speed, bow hair, bow distribution, vibrato, bow weight and finger articulation, as well as instruments and accessories. The pressure differential resulting from varying string thicknesses, gravitational weight and bow speed are also explored. Naturally, such information is of limited value without a vigilant attitude on the part of the player, who must constantly select the good and reject the bad. The Mazas study shown in Ex. 7 enables the player to explore many of these technical aspects, while Ex. 10 requires more imagination, the inner ear selecting from a whole world of different tone-colours and timbres. As Charles Libove has remarked, 'I feel that the quality of sound should carry with it something of the ambience, the drama of the music. Sound cannot be indiscriminately applied, like a specific colour of paint, to everything that has notes. It must "bespeak" the feeling.'[13]

Ex. 7   from J. F. Mazas, *75 Etudes mélodiques et progressives pour violon,* Op. 36: Book 1, *Etudes spéciales,* No. 1

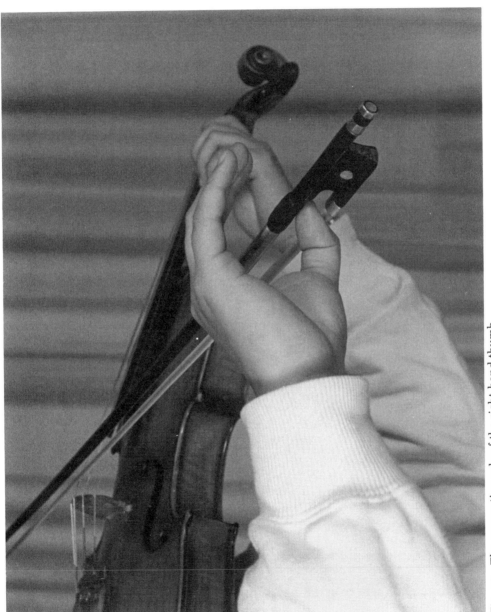

Fig. 40 The supporting role of the right-hand thumb

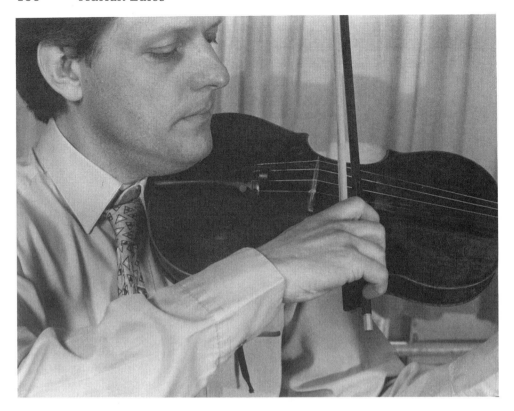

Fig. 41   The optimum position of the right-hand fingers

Bowing and bowstrokes

Considering the volume of available information on this subject, it is surprising that writers fail to recommend the selection of a bow of proportions appropriate to the physical characteristics of the individual.[14] The following comments endeavour to offer practical and general guidelines on bowing, avoiding the abstract wherever possible.

Thumb, little finger and gravity

The supporting role of the thumb is commonly neglected. In fact, it is possible to play in the upper half with no fingers on the bow (see Fig. 40)! Similarly undervalued, the little finger sits most naturally on the inner edge of the stick in the lower half (see Fig. 41). Maximum involvement of the fingers is illustrated by Ex. 8a, in which the strings should be crossed avoiding major arm or wrist movements. At the heel, curved fingers and flexible knuckle-joints are also crucial in controlling the amount of weight which is allowed to 'sink' into the string.

Ex. 8   (a)

Wrist, fingers and knuckles

Flexibility in all joints is a prerequisite of fluent bowing; without it Ex. 8b would be impossible to play smoothly and quickly:

Ex. 8   (b) from F. Fiorillo, *Etudes pour le violon formant 36 caprices* Op. 3
          No. 36

A general facility can also be developed by the following simple hand-rotation exercises, which should be practised minimising arm movements:

Ex. 8   (c)

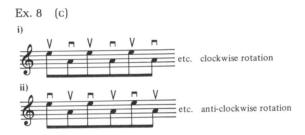

Shoulder and elbow

Equally crucial is the alignment of elbow and forearm. A player whose elbow is lower than the forearm and bow normally produces a hard, 'dead' sound. Conversely, a high elbow-position produces a *flautando* tone, which, though appropriate in some ensemble playing, may lack projection for solos. A possible solution is to vary the elbow position according to context. Triple stopping, for instance, can benefit from a marginally lower position (see Fig. 42). Furthermore, the right shoulder frequently remains hunched, and it is therefore worth comparing both shoulders in horizontal profile when playing in the lower half (Fig. 43).

Bow change

Although descriptions of that elusive smooth bow change vary in most contemporary sources, it must be realised that to effect a change of direction the bow slows down almost to the point of stopping. Subtle movements from the knuckles act rather like shock absorbers, the bow continuing its movement while the arm changes direction. Describing an arc at the extremes will also enhance the legato effect.[15]

Fig. 42   A slightly lower position of the elbow to accommodate triple stopping

Bow distribution

It is imperative to develop a technique which not only uses the extremes of the bow but also varies the speed of each stroke. The following exercise (Ex. 8d) will improve efficiency in this area and can be combined easily with scale practice:

Ex. 8   (d) Numbers refer to beats. No audible change of dynamic or articulation between bows should occur.

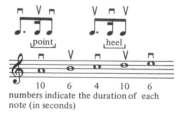

Finally, Ex. 8(e) illustrates how simple movements are deceptive. Played at the point with the bow remaining on the string, it requires supreme control to start and stop the bow clearly and consistently:

Ex. 8   (e) from E. Elgar, 'Enigma' Variations, Var. 10 (rehearsal figure 38)

Fig. 43   The optimum 'horizontal' profile of the shoulders when playing in
the lower half of the bow

Bowstrokes

In addition to the virtuosic associations of *saltato*, up-bow- and 'flying'-
staccato, *ricochet* and 'Viotti' bowings, all violinists require a bowing
vocabulary which includes *détaché*, *portato*, *spiccato*, *martelé*, *sautillé*
and, most importantly, legato. However, while it is easy to produce
exhaustive descriptions and bowing lists, these do little for the player
who lacks the imagination or experience to select the appropriate stroke
for the context. In this respect the concept must be clearly established;
only then will such details as bowstroke fall into place. The teaching
methods of Galamian and Jacoby are invaluable for their inclusion of

copious musical examples. Galamian invokes the inspired analogy of consonant and vowel sounds to differentiate between soft and hard articulation. On-the-string playing, smooth starts and legato are akin to the vowel; off-the-string strokes and accents relate to the consonant. The characteristics of each venue are also part of the equation. While a recording studio may require a sustained 'vowel' style, an articulation of the 'consonant' type is more appropriate in a large, resonant concert-hall. Other variables to consider are volume and tempo. When playing off the string, for example, the sound can differ according to the angle of descent and lift-off, the height of 'drop' and 'bounce' and the length of stroke.

Vibrato

Although vibrato was originally employed sparingly as an ornament, it has become almost mandatory in modern times,[16] violinists being expected to produce large and fast oscillations without a break. Leslie Sheppard considers the device an illusion of the ear and shows that it is 'heard much less in extent than actually performed'.[17] When using vibrato, violinists should aim for economy of finger movement with maximum effect. Mobility in the first joint of each finger is crucial, for static and steep finger alignments frequently impede the energy generated by the larger hand movement. A style in which an incessant 'wobble' is executed by wrist or finger alone with no variety of speed or inflection is also undesirable and thwarts many a fine player. Vibrato, like many nuances, must be used with discretion and good taste, matching with the style and period of the music wherever possible.

The performer

Control in performance

The subject of nerves and performance stress is neglected by most teachers, but research has revealed that 97 per cent of orchestral players experience apprehension before a concert and 60 per cent regularly take alcohol or beta-blockers to reduce tension.[18] Havas's *Stage Fright*, which mainly re-states her well-known body-balance theories, does not cover all aspects of the problem. The following additional advice would be beneficial:

1 Thorough preparation is essential. The slightest imperfection is exaggerated in public; technical proficiency is therefore a prerequisite of secure performance.
2 Legato playing in slow tempo will suffer from an accelerated heartbeat. Avoid high chest breathing and ensure good exhalation occurs. Check your 'at rest' pulse-rate and strive to achieve this in performance.

3 Flexibility of fingering, bowing, articulation and even dynamics in the dress rehearsal is important. Curiously, large shifts which work perfectly well at speed are hazardous and are best avoided with a slow-moving bow.

4 Don't underestimate slow-moving and simple passages; paradoxically, they hold more potential for disaster.

5 Avoid 'shock' by simulating concert conditions. Consider, for example, practising with one string out of tune, or preparing an orchestral solo in a seated position and wearing formal evening dress.

6 Play in public as much as possible.

7 A feeling of well-being and energy from 7.30 p.m. onwards (or whatever time the concert commences) requires pacing through the day and moderate food intake. *Do not* eat a large meal before a performance.

8 Guard at all costs against the wandering mind and self-consciousness. Focusing the mind somewhere will help you remain calm. There is an 'inner game' to play – and win!

9 Do not brood over mistakes. While performing, it is better to be unconcerned with results and to repress the desire to succeed at all costs. Trying too hard may be destructive by increasing tension. Above all, it is the achievement of peace of mind that will go hand-in-hand with success. Possible approaches to this goal are described below respectively by Norbert Brainin and Yehudi Menuhin:

'If I communicate with a crowd I have to be secluded and alone. I pretend I am the only person left in the world, and then I play for myself, and I play for God.'[19]

'An artist's presence is more strongly felt the more he is concentrated, centred and disregarding the audience.'[20]

Memory

Although traditionally neglected, the development of memorising skills is of vital importance. The new Advanced Certificate examination of the Associated Board (1990) is innovative in allowing credit to be given for playing from memory. Following Flesch's contribution to the subject, however, only Gerle has written anything of substance, identifying five aspects of memory: sensory; factual; episodic; skilled; and semantic.[21] More importantly, he proposes the following ten steps towards improved memorising:

1 Read the music without the instrument to hand. Observe and be aware of the musical content from the outset.

2 Decide upon bowings and fingerings, still without the instrument to hand.

3 Start slow practice with the instrument. Register in your mind all impressions, information, connections.
4 Try playing in tempo in the early stages with instrument.
5 Practise intensely the difficult parts, but don't neglect the easy ones.
6 Divide the work into shorter segments for better retention.
7 Re-connect shorter segments and fit them into the contexts of form and interpretation. Put facts which are not needed into the back of the mind.
8 Practise performing, with accompaniment, still with music (if needed).
9 Play the entire work through in your mind, without instrument or music. Recall vividly everything which pertains to actual performance.
10 Play from memory a complete 'concert' performance.

Valuable general advice is also offered: Gerle suggests, for example, that frequent rest periods will enhance concentration and retention. He also elaborates on the immense benefit of anticipation. Although the Suzuki method demands playing without the music from the very start, it does not include any factual or semantic learning.

Virtuosity and more advanced practice

Although Ruggiero Ricci's *Left Hand Violin Technique* provides much virtuosic practice material with commentary, the following highly selective comments may also prove helpful.

Chords (double stopping)
It is always preferable to construct the interval by first playing the lower finger rather than the lower note (Ex. 9a). In Ex. 9b, though both notes are stopped, precise intonation can be more critically assessed by sounding only one with the bow:

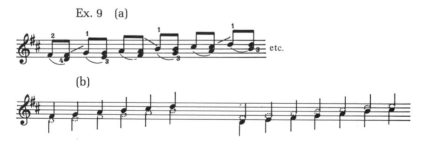

Ex. 9 (a)

(b)

Concentration on the release rather than placing the fingers (Ex. 9c) enhances stamina and strength by developing the frequently neglected extensor muscles:

Ex. 9 (c)

When shifting in scale passages, it is essential to identify the tone–semitone differential between successive chords; more effort is required for the finger moving a tone, the semitone finger usually being drawn naturally into position (Ex. 9d). For tenths, players with small hands will benefit by adopting a hand position as illustrated in Fig. 44, where the thumb adopts a more central position and the first finger extends backwards replacing the usual fourth-finger stretch.

Ex. 9 (d)

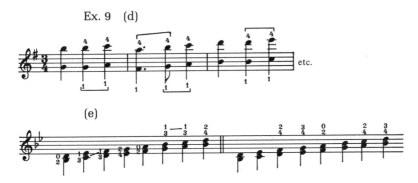

(e)

In Ex. 9e the customary finger pattern $\frac{12-12}{34-34}$ is replaced, showing that fingerings can be selected according to the physical characteristics and size of the hand.

Speed, fluency and co-ordination

Anticipation of string-crossing and a chordal approach which includes horizontal as well as vertical movement are the main contributors to fluency (See Ex. 4 on p. 99). An astute choice of fingering based on the criterion of simplicity for speed usually requires sequential finger patterns, minimal shifting or shifts carried out on main beats.

A lack of mobility in the left shoulder joint is a common impediment to virtuosity. Fig. 43 illustrates a 'model' playing posture and particularly emphasises the optimum shoulder position. Interestingly, Menuhin, who focuses at length on the destructive nature of the 'clamped' shoulder, advocates no shoulder rest.[22]

In conclusion, it must always be remembered that however sophisticated the technique, mastery of the instrument will not be achieved without critical listening and stringent 'quality control'.

Fig. 44   The optimum position of the left hand for the execution of tenths,
particularly by players with small hands

Style and interpretation

Empathy with a composer's style and period is an entirely honourable
objective. Having established the date of a composition, the player can
glean valuable details on performance practice by consulting standard

Ex. 10   The fingering indicated exploits the uniform vocal timbre of one
string and invites *portamento* (from R. Schumann, Intermezzo,
'F. A. E. Sonata').

texts. The interpretation is then idiomatic without being too subjective, and the performance comprises a healthy blend of analysis and instinct. A degree of musical fantasy is also valuable, for without fervour the audience is usually unmoved.[23] A score with limited markings (e.g. Ex. 10) will require more interpretative imagination than the music of composers like Debussy and Bartók, most of whose requirements are annotated.

Ultimately, it is depth of character, multiplicity of interests and the translating of life's experiences into music which create an inspired performer. Mechanical perfection, bigger tone, faster speeds, and the stereotype performance, clinically planned and executed, should not be the prime objectives. As Felix Andrievsky has commented, 'Occasionally one hears an artist who is not playing perfectly, but I would not change them for these who are faultless but who can't reach my heart.'[24] In the acting profession preliminary character and context research allows space for creativity and instinct, and so with the musician discipline and technique enable him to take risks in performance that he would not otherwise attempt.

Improvisation

Improvisation is an essential element in popular music and is a recognised performing skill in the GCSE examination. From the blues onwards, fiddle playing has mirrored the texture and range of the voice. Light music of this type developed its own style, featuring the 'gliss', the 'flare', the 'whip', 'raspy wails' and the 'shimmer' combined with harmonics and many varieties of vibrato, but it always followed the original harmony and structure.

Ex. 11a shows the blues scale, which avoids the second and sixth notes of the scale, and a more ingenious scale combining chromatic and whole tones:

Ex. 11   (a)

Rhythmic variation of a melody is the simplest improvisatory technique (Ex. 11b):

Ex. 11   (b)

Original

Varied

Extra notes are added to this rhythmic variation in Ex. 11c, but the melody remains clearly identifiable:

Ex. 11   (c)

The final 'hot' version (Ex. 11d) allows the imagination to run freely, disregarding the time, though the fundamental harmonies still determine the rhythmic figures:

Ex. 11   (d)

Hot
Version

Editing and bowing parts

The avoidance of string-crossing in legato, selecting a string or position according to the appropriate sonority, bow articulation and choice of edition comprise a few of the numerous details for consideration here. Whilst the standard texts on violin playing provide a wealth of information on fingering, no teaching method actively encourages students to make such decisions, however simple. In the Suzuki books, for instance, every bar of their exclusively Baroque–Classical repertory is ponderously edited.

Since the detailed bowing of parts is integral to both chamber music and orchestral playing, the following simple recommendations are made. The down-bow, being easier to follow, suits difficult rhythmic entries; clarity for high registration; marking the bar-line in extended ostinato and syncopated passages; precise ensemble where rehearsal time is short. The up-bow, lighter and smoother in articulation, is more effective for *subito pianissimo* in the upper half; discreet entries; the start of crescendos.

Clarity and ensemble
Rhythmic accuracy and articulation are best achieved in the lower half of the bow. Ex. 12a is a prime example:

Ex. 12   (a) from J. S. Bach, Brandenburg Concerto No. 4, first movement

Phrasing
Retain original phrase marking where possible, but be prepared to use more bow when the acoustic is 'dry' and the players few.

Dotted rhythms
Although separate bows are stylish for dotted rhythms in works of the Baroque, Classical and early Romantic eras, they can be difficult for a large group to co-ordinate. Orchestral players will certainly expect 'linked' bowings.

Looking ahead
There are many occasions where working back from a 'bowing priority' is essential. For example, Ex. 12b will need to start down-bow in preparation for the 'priority' pizzicato in bar 2:

Ex. 12   (b)

Tremolo is another case where the upper half should be sought in advance to avoid an undesired accent.

Character
Character determines style. The dramatic choreography resulting from a down-bow re-take, for instance, is ideal where the score is full of indications such as *sul G, con forza, sforzando,* etc.

Orchestral playing and chamber music

Although chamber music – where significantly fewer job opportunities exist – is coached extensively at specialist music schools and colleges and benefits from a wealth of articles in leading journals,[25] musicians and administrators alike throughout the profession agree that our orchestral training is inadequate. This view emerges consistently in André Previn's *Orchestra*, and is also shared by the Gulbenkian Enquiry of 1978. Many violinists, though adequate at audition, are unable to meet the personal demands of professional life and also lack the musical and technical sensitivity to ensemble required by our finest orchestras.[26]

Playing in a large ensemble requires:

1 Rhythm: personal accuracy is assumed; *ensemble rhythm* requires playing in a synchronised manner with the section.
2 Listening: the ability to assimilate your colleagues' playing in dynamics, technique, intonation and style is paramount, so that the section as a whole can relate to other sections.
3 Dynamics: as a result of duplication, dynamic range is immense, especially in *pp*, where the individual sound drops so low it may become inaudible. Consider the opening of Mahler's First Symphony.
4 Articulation: a myriad of gradations from on- to off-the-string occur. Playing in a large section requires a combination of close-to-the-string strokes for co-ordination and biting articulation for clarity.
5 Virtuosity and stamina: a first violinist needs a certain brilliance and fluency of execution, especially in extended '8va' passages. Second violin parts challenge string crossing and accuracy in passages of accompaniment, which are often clumsily written for the instrument.
6 Literacy: read all bowing marks thoroughly; no discrepancy is tolerated!
7 Style: although principal players may play flamboyantly, rank-and-file members are usually expected to play discreetly, taking no decisions and making no mistakes. Discipline and conformity are essential.
8 Pizzicato: speed in excess of 232 notes per minute and a large dynamic range are common requirements.

9 Sight-reading: rehearsal time is at a premium for the standard British orchestra contract, which stipulates more concerts each week than its continental counterpart. As a result, British musicians have a reputation for speed and excellence in sight-reading.

10 Vision: visual awareness of the conductor, the bow distribution of the section, and especially of the principal is more possible than one might suppose, for movement can be interpreted without direct line of sight.

11 Musicianship: sensitivity and discrimination between melodic and accompanying material is an important asset in all ensemble music and must not be underestimated.

12 Concentration: sitting at the rear of the section requires greater concentration and anticipation. Proximity to loud brass and percussion sections provides a further distraction.

Ex. 13   from E. Elgar, 'Enigma' Variations, Var. 2

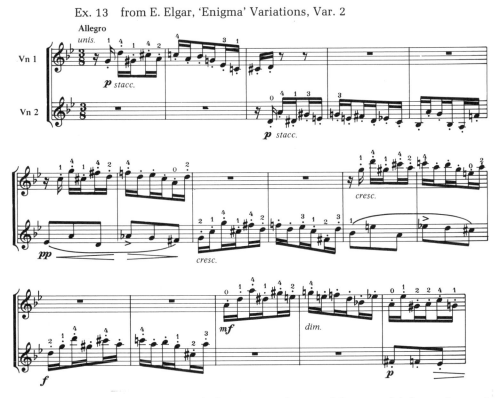

Ex. 13 focuses on some of the particular problems which orchestral violinists are required to overcome. Prepare for the contingency of tempos varying from between dotted crotchet = 60–84, according to conductor. Delivering each phrase at precisely the right moment demands supreme rhythmic and technical control. The individual dots and staccato indications suggest a *sautillé* bowstroke, the amount of bounce depending on tempo, dynamic and the qualities of your bow. Fluency requires economy of movement – the suggested fingering, which reduces impediments from clumsy string crossing, would be useful for the faster speed. To avoid delay, the first up-bow semiquaver needs to start from the string, 'flicked' not 'dropped'. Listening for the antiphonal phrase will help to co-ordinate bars 3, 6 and 10, but stay with your section, even if the phrases do not appear to coincide. Pay attention to the down beat at each bar-line. If this does not synchronise with what you hear, be sure once again to follow the principal and remain with your section. Finally, it is crucial to know your part. Total concentration is required to absorb and filter all this information whilst you play.

Auditions and trials

Auditions may last as little as ten minutes. Audition panels may vary from a minimum membership of three to a maximum of a dozen, depending on the importance of the position, but usually comprise at least the section principal, the orchestral manager and an external assessor. Standard requirements may include the performance of two short contrasting pieces of your own choice, sight-reading and playing some prepared orchestral excerpts. Successful candidates are normally short-listed for a 'trial', which offers work-experience in the vacant post for a minimum of a week. Clearly your aim is to display orchestral assurance together with a professionalism characterised by punctuality, smartness and sociability. Whatever the vacant position, prepare yourself for the possibility of playing on the front desk for a short spell.

The audition may be unaccompanied – which may seem quite a 'culture shock' if you are unprepared for it! When an accompanist is provided, however, take the opportunity to display your sensitivity to ensemble and balance. Ultimately an orchestral career is tough and demanding; it is therefore important to appear mature and composed. Summon the confidence to look at your adjudicators; don't be evasive – it is perfectly acceptable to address them when invited. You must also expect to be stopped frequently, owing to pressure of time. It is quite rare for auditionees to play both prepared pieces to the end, and it may well be a positive indication of your playing if you are allowed to continue uninterrupted.

Applicants for a rank-and-file orchestral post would be well advised to familiarise themselves with the following repertoire, for playing at sight extracts from these works is a common requirement: overtures by Mozart, Weber, Smetana and Wagner; the symphonic works of Dvořák and Brahms; Mozart's Symphonies Nos. 39, 40 and 41; Richard Strauss's *Don Juan*; Bartók's Divertimento. The following works include important violin solos which are most frequently expected of applicants for principal positions: J. S. Bach's *St Matthew Passion* and Mass in B minor; Beethoven's *Missa solemnis*; Brahms's First Symphony; Tchaikovsky's

Swan Lake; Rimsky-Korsakov's *Capriccio espagnol* and *Sheherazade*; Richard Strauss's *Ein Heldenleben* and *Le Bourgeois Gentilhomme*.

Finally, whatever the occasion, the importance of visual interest in your performance cannot be overestimated. Good body-language and a confident stage-manner are vital for success in communicating to your audience.

7   Technique and performing practice

ROBIN STOWELL

Violin treatises through the years have consistently emphasised the importance of a comfortable and natural bearing when holding the instrument, but it was not until the early nineteenth century that there was any general agreement on the precise position to be adopted. The nineteenth-century violinist's goal was a noble and relaxed posture, with head upright, feet normally in line but slightly apart, and body-weight distributed with a slight bias towards the left side. The seated position involved bending the right wrist and elbow rather more, turning the right leg slightly inwards (to avoid contact between knee and bow when bowing at the point on the upper strings) and supporting the left leg (and hence the body-weight) on a footstool, thereby enabling the trunk to remain erect. Flesch (1923) considers the position of the feet extremely important, discussing three possible positions: the joined-together, rectangular leg position in which the feet are close together; the acutangular leg position, in which the feet are separated, with either right or left foot advanced and the body-weight on the rear foot (this resembles the recommendations of Suzuki, but the advanced left foot takes the body-weight); and his preferred 'spread leg' position, which offers the greatest stability and freedom. Galamian is more flexible of attitude, claiming that 'How to stand or to sit should not be the object of exact prescriptions other than that the player should feel at ease.'[1] However, he does insist that exaggerated body movement should be avoided when playing.

During its history the violin has been held at the breast, at the shoulder and at the neck. Differing degrees of support were recommended for these positions; furthermore, the chin could be placed to either side of the tailpiece. Some methods required the chin to steady the instrument, normally on its E-string side, while others required the left hand to lend support to the violin, which sat flat on the collar-bone. L'abbé *le fils* recommended resting the chin on the violin to the left of the tailpiece, thus implying the chin-braced grip that had formerly been employed only to stabilise the instrument during shifts.[2] This method did not immediately gain universal approval – even Spohr's chin rest (invented c.1820) was originally positioned directly over the tailpiece; but it eventually became the most commonly employed (e.g. by Baillot (1834); Habeneck (c.1835) and other leading theorists), affording firmer support for the instrument and enabling it to be held horizontally at shoulder height and directly in front of the player at almost 90°. Optimum freedom of left-hand movement and flexibility of bowing were thereby gained. If playing while seated, the player generally lowered the scroll to facilitate straight bowing.

Some performers employed a shoulder pad to increase security and comfort and to avoid raising the left shoulder. Baillot was one of the first writers to recommend use of a shoulder pad[3] and such supports between the shoulder and the violin gradually became general in the nineteenth and early twentieth centuries. Many violinists nowadays have reacted against this trend, claiming that the advantage of complete freedom of the left hand is outweighed by the disadvantages of such a rigid violin hold, especially the extra body tensions induced, the neck-sores incurred by many and the shoulder pad's adverse effect on the violin tone.

During the early nineteenth century the left hand was gradually relieved of its semi-supporting role and the common right-arm position (closer to the player's side than formerly) required the instrument to be inclined more to the right for optimum bowing facility on the lowest string. Baillot prescribes an angle of 45°, Spohr 25°–30°. Flesch, Suzuki and numerous other teachers nowadays opt for the violin to be held parallel to the floor.

Baroque and Classical violinists generally positioned the elbow well under the middle of the instrument, much closer to the body than nowadays. The wrist was turned inwards to avoid contact between the palm and the violin neck, which was not allowed to sink into the hollow between the thumb and index finger. The thumb, occasionally employed in multiple stopping, generally assumed a position 'opposite the A natural on the G string';[4] or, for greater freedom of action and facility in extensions and shifting, it was placed 'more forward towards the second and third fingers than backward towards the first without projecting too far over the fingerboard'.[5]

Ex. 14   The so-called 'Geminiani grip'

Although its merits were opposed by some writers (e.g. Courvoisier, 1899), the so-called 'Geminiani grip' (Ex. 14) remained the most common guide to correct elbow, hand, wrist and finger placement (in first position) until well into the current century, the hand and fingers generally forming a curve with the fingers well over the strings. Each knuckle was bent so that the top joints of the fingers could fall straight down on to the strings from the same height. During the nineteenth century players strove for easy elbow manoeuvrability and flexibility of the hand position to cope with new technical demands. Many opted for a more advanced position of the thumb for greater mobility and facility in extensions, more often than not avoiding formal shifts between positions. Some of Paganini's fingerings, for example, rendered the recognition of a definite concept of positions practically impossible (Ex. 15).

Ex. 15   from C. Guhr, *Ueber Paganinis Kunst die Violine zu spielen*, p. 43.

Unnecessary finger activity was avoided. According to Leopold Mozart,[6] necessity, convenience and elegance were the reasons for using positions other than the first. Modern half and second positions assumed greater importance from c.1750 onwards, from which time most advanced violin treatises incorporated position-work up to at least seventh position (some extended to eleventh position and beyond in supplementary study material). With the shorter fingerboard (pre-c.1800), excessively high position-work was not unanimously sanctioned because clarity of finger-stopping was difficult to achieve, but the lengthening of the fingerboard ensured the exploitation of the entire range of hand positions on string instruments (Baillot records the violin range as four and a half octaves).

Until at least the end of the eighteenth century, shifts were generally made when the punctuation of the music allowed: on the beat or on repeated notes (Ex. 16a), by the phrase in sequences (Ex. 16b), after an open string (Ex. 16c), on a rest or pause between staccato notes or after a dotted figure where the bow was generally lifted off the string (Ex. 16d). If possible one position was chosen to accommodate an entire phrase, and extensions and contractions were often used (but harmonics rarely so) to avoid or facilitate shifts (Ex. 16e). With the gradual adoption of the more stable chin-braced grip, shifting proved less precarious. Baroque and Classical theories regarding where to shift were relaxed somewhat and emphasis placed rather more on the odd-numbered positions. Cultivation of the semitone shift facilitated achievement of the prevalent legato ideal.

The mechanics of shifting are sparsely documented in most treatises, but the role of the thumb in following the fingers (as opposed to the modern ideal of the hand moving more as a unit) was consistently emphasised. Upward shifts tended to increase the instrument's stability

(a) from L. Mozart, Versuch ..., p. 155

(b) from L. Mozart, Versuch ..., p. 168

half position   * whole position   * half

(c) from L. Mozart, Versuch ..., p. 155

(d) from L. Mozart, Versuch ..., p. 156

(e) from L. Mozart, Versuch ..., p. 181

against the player's neck, but downward shifts, particularly without a chin-braced grip, generally required the left hand to crawl back 'caterpillar fashion' from the high positions. Like Leopold Mozart, most eighteenth-century writers advocated small upward shifts, using adjacent fingers (23–23 or 12–12), rather than the bold leaps prescribed by Geminiani, Tessarini and Corrette (Ex. 17), though this naturally depended on matters of tempo and speed. Galeazzi excepted, large leaps

Ex. 17

Ex. 18   from L'abbé le fils, Suite de jolis airs de différents auteurs variés
pour un violon seul

L'abbé's fingering

Modern fingering? [4

(4321–4321) were favoured in descending passages, irrespective of speed.

There is conflicting evidence regarding the incidence of *portamento* in shifting. The systems described above rendered its use largely unnecessary; indeed, some eighteenth-century writers reject it outright.[7] Nevertheless, other contemporary sources, supported by certain notated fingerings (Ex. 18), suggest that *portamento* was employed by some players, especially in solo contexts, either as part of the shift mechanism or as an expressive device.[8] In the following century, Baillot acknowledges the interrelationship between fingering, the player's hand position and musical intentions. He distinguishes between sure fingering, fingering for small hands and expressive fingering relevant to selected composers. The last category includes Kreutzer's frequent shifts on all strings for brilliance of effect, and Rode's more uniform tonal characteristics, incorporating *ports de voix*.[9] Baillot's discussion of *ports de voix* and expressive fingering[10] provides clues to the mechanics of shifting. Anticipatory notes (unsounded) indicate the method of shifting, the stopped finger sliding forwards (or backwards) in order to be substituted by another finger. Spohr endorses this,[11] especially for rapid shifts involving leaps from a low to a high position in slurred bowing (Ex. 19a) (without *glissando* effect), and gives a further example of a fast shift

Ex. 19   (a) from L. Spohr, Violin Concerto No. 10 in A Op. 62, 2nd movement

(b) from P. Rode, Violin Concerto No. 7, 2nd movement, quoted in L. Spohr, *Violinschule*, p. 209

(c) from P. Rode, Violin Concerto No. 7, 2nd movement, quoted in L. Spohr, *Violinschule*, p. 209

(Ex. 19b) in which the highest note is a harmonic. Stopping the bow momentarily during the shift also helped to make shifting inaudible (Ex. 19c), as many writers desired.

Nevertheless, Habeneck and Baillot allow the tasteful introduction of *portamento*,[12] especially in slow movements and sustained melodies when a passage ascends or descends by step. In these cases they advise that the *portamento* should be accompanied respectively by a crescendo or diminuendo. De Bériot[13] uses signs to indicate three types of *port de voix*: *vif*, *doux* and *traîné* (Exx. 20a, 20b, and 20c).

Ex. 20   (a) *vif* (lively). Employed for notes drawn with grace or pushed with energy (from C. A. de Bériot, *Méthode . . .*, Eng. tr. p. 237)

(b) *doux* (sweet). Employed for affectionate expression (from C. A. de Bériot, *Méthode . . .*, Eng. tr. p. 237)

(c) *traîné* (drawn out). Plaintive or sorrowful expression (from C. A. de Bériot, *Méthode . . .*, Eng. tr. p. 237 – extracted from Halévy's *La Juive*)

(d) from N. Paganini, Variations on Rossini's *Moses*, Var. 1

(e) from N. Paganini, *24 Caprices* No. 21

Paganini regularly employed *glissando* with great effect, both for showmanship (Ex. 20d) and for cantabile execution of double stopping (Ex. 20e). Exploitation of the *glissando* and *portamento* as an 'emotional connection of two tones'[14] (invariably in slurred bowing and with upward shifts) to articulate melodic shape and emphasise structurally important notes became so prevalent in the late nineteenth century that succeeding generations reacted strongly against it. Flesch criticises the excessive use of *portamento* by late-nineteenth- and early-twentieth-century violinists, the false accents it creates and the fact that it was invariably employed too slowly and merely for the player's convenience in shifting rather than for expressive ends. He considers Joachim's crescendo during a *portamento* 'offensive'[15] and distinguishes between three *portamento* types: a straightforward slide on one and the same finger (Ex. 21a); the 'B-*portamento*', in which the beginning finger slides to an intermediary note (Ex. 21b); and the 'L-*portamento*', in which the last finger slides from an intermediate note (Ex. 21c). Flesch reports that the straightforward slide and the B-*portamento* were commonly employed in the early years of the twentieth century, but the L-*portamento* was rarely used until the 1930s, when, however, it was still the least common of the three. Broadly speaking, the execution of *portamenti* became 'generally faster, less frequent and less prominent'.[16] Auer, for example, objects to *portamenti* being executed 'in a languishing manner, and used continually',[17] and he advises that they 'should be employed only when the melody is descending, save for very exceptional cases of ascending melody'.[18]

Ex. 21   (a) slide finger

(b) the 'B-*portamento*'

(c) the 'L-*portamento*'

Only from about the middle of the eighteenth century were the benefits of scale practice fully acknowledged in the cultivation of accurate intonation, finger independence, elasticity and agility, together with strong finger action for tonal clarity and many bowing disciplines. Notable nineteenth-century developments include the introduction of the fingered octave technique (first discussed by Baillot),[19] which gradually found favour because of its greater clarity, accuracy and less frequent displacements of the hand (Ex. 22), and Spohr's fingering system for three-octave diatonic scales, in which the root position of a four-note chord of the key of a scale effectively determines the finger-position for the start of that scale.[20] Spohr thus begins all scales with the second finger, except, of course, those commencing on g, ab and a.

Ex. 22 from Habeneck l'aîné's *Fantaisie Pastorale*, quoted in P. Baillot, *L'Art du violon*, p. 152

keep the same fingering

There were two principal approaches to the fingering of chromatic scales. One, advocated by Geminiani (1751), employed one finger for each note (with open strings where necessary); the other was a 'slide' fingering of the type advocated by Leopold Mozart (1756). Leopold's recommendation (Ex. 23a), adopted by many of his immediate successors, involves different fingerings for chromatic scales written in sharps from those written in flats. Geminiani's fingering was largely ignored in formal scale contexts by his contemporaries and his successors in the nineteenth century – the 'slide' fingering was preferred – but its principle was acknowledged in isolated passage-work (Ex. 23b) and it has achieved more positive recognition in the current century, on account of its greater evenness, articulation and clarity.

Ex. 23 (a) and (b) from L. Mozart, *Versuch ...*, pp. 66–7

Although open strings were sometimes necessarily employed in the execution of shifts, *bariolage*, double and multiple stopping, *scordatura* and suchlike, they were invariably avoided (at least from the early eighteenth century onwards) when stopped notes were technically viable. This was particularly the case in descending scale passages involving more than one string (especially in slurred bowing), in trills (except in double trills where there was no alternative), appoggiaturas and other such ornaments and in most melodic or expressive contexts. Such limitations in open string usage appear to have become more desirable as plain gut was gradually displaced by other materials in string making, and as performers began (particularly from c.1750 onwards) more seriously to cultivate uniformity of tone-colour within the phrase. Sequences were played wherever possible with matching fingerings, bowing articulations and string changes, and the higher positions were increasingly exploited for reasons of timbre and expression. Baillot (1834) demonstrates how the timbre of every instrument, and each of the four strings, can be modified in imitation of other instruments, and differences in string timbre were veiled wherever appropriate.[21] *Una corda* playing was particularly encouraged by the late-eighteenth-century French violin school. Likewise, Spohr (1832) advocates the exploitation of the higher positions for expressive and tonal purposes,[22] and *una corda* playing reached its zenith with the extravaganzas on the G string by Paganini.

Contrary to modern practice most seventeenth- and eighteenth-century violinists adopted a modified type of meantone temperament in order to accommodate particularly to keyboard instruments of the period. They generally considered a sharpened note a 'comma' (i.e. about 22 cents) lower in pitch than the flattened form of the note a tone higher (i.e. a D♯ was lower than an E♭). Around the turn of the nineteenth century, this whole practice was reversed and preference was eventually given to tuning sharpened notes higher than the flattened form of the note a tone higher, making diatonic 'semitones' (e.g. D–E♭) smaller than chromatic ones (e.g. D–D♯) and inflecting notes such as the leading note and the seventh of the dominant-seventh chord according to their implied harmonic resolutions. It appears that this change of fashion was related directly to the sharp third of equal temperament and assisted in fulfilling the desire for greater brilliance of sonority.

Vibrato, discussed as early as the sixteenth century by theorists such as Ganassi and Agricola, has passed in and out of fashion during the violin's history. Despite Geminiani's exceptional recommendation of what was essentially a continuous vibrato in the approved modern fashion,[23] vibrato was generally used selectively and sparingly up to the early twentieth century as an expressive ornament linked inextricably with the inflections of the bow. It was employed particularly on long sustained or final notes in a phrase, at a speed and intensity appropriate to the music's dynamic, tempo and character; it also served to emphasise certain notes, to articulate melodic shape or to assist in the cultivation of cantabile playing. It doubtless had a more striking effect than the continuous variety practised today, even though the vibrato movement of the Baroque and Classical periods, executed with the fingers and wrist but not with the lower arm, was necessarily somewhat narrower, tighter and less intense, owing to the types of violin hold then in vogue. The gradual adoption of the more stable chin-braced grip towards the end of the eighteenth century freed the left hand to cultivate a more fluid vibrato movement.

Leopold Mozart (1756) distinguishes three types of vibrato: slow, accelerating and fast. Spohr (1832) writes of four kinds: fast, for sharply accentuated notes; slow, for sustained notes in impassioned melodies; accelerating, for crescendos; and decelerating, for decrescendos. He demonstrates their selective application (Ex. 24a)[24] and, like Baillot (1834), emphasises that deviation from the true pitch of the note should be scarcely perceptible to the ear. Baillot expands the vibrato concept to include three types of 'undulated sounds': a wavering effect caused by variation of pressure on the stick, the normal left-hand vibrato, and a combination of the two. He recommends that notes should be begun and terminated without vibrato to achieve accuracy of intonation. He provides some examples of Viotti's vibrato usage, some of which link the use of vibrato with the 'swell' effect (Ex. 24b).[25] Joachim and Auer, among others, recommended selective use of vibrato,[26] while Ysaÿe's use of the device, though more perceptible, was still restricted to long notes. According to Flesch,[27] it was Kreisler who re-introduced a continuous vibrato, and he and Heifetz (a pupil of Auer!) were probably its foremost advocates. By the late 1920s Kreisler's uninterrupted vibrato had captured the imagination of most of his contemporaries, though not without a little controversy, and vibrato was considered more a constituent of a pleasing tone than an embellishment. Most theorists advocate a combination of finger, hand and arm movements for optimum vibrato production, but Rolland includes the shoulder as well.

Ex. 24 (a) from L. Spohr, *Violinschule*, pp. 175–6

(b) from G. B. Viotti's Violin Concerto No. 19, quoted in P. Baillot, *L'Art du Violon*, p. 138

Although natural harmonics were exploited well before the Classical period, particularly in France (e.g. by Mondonville),[28] their unanimous acceptance was slow owing to their 'inferior' tone quality.[29] The brief yet progressive survey by L'abbé *le fils* incorporates a minuet written entirely in harmonics (both natural and artificial),[30] but it required virtuosi such as Jakob Scheller and Paganini to arouse public interest in harmonics and the techniques involved in their mastery. Paganini's introduction of artificial harmonics in double stopping was innovatory. Chromatic slides, single trills, trills in double stopping and double trills, all in harmonics, together with some interesting pseudo-harmonic effects, were included in his repertory, and he extended the range of the G string to cover at least three octaves.

The earliest known use of right-hand pizzicato in violin music is found in Monteverdi's *Combattimento di Tancredi e Clorinda* (1624), where the player is required to 'pluck the strings with two fingers'. The use of one finger, normally the index finger, became the norm, but the right-hand thumb was sometimes employed for a special effect, the instrument being held across the body and under the right arm, guitar-fashion. The thumb's fleshy pad proved ideal for sonorous arpeggiation of chords or for soft passages. Farina's *Capriccio stravagante* (1627) throws up an early example of this method. Berlioz recommends plucking with the second finger and even suggests using the thumb and the first three fingers as plucking agents for variety in certain rapid pizzicato passages (Ex. 25).[31] Interestingly, the invention of 'snap' pizzicato, often attributed to Bartók in the current century, actually dates back to Biber, who uses the effect to represent gunshot in *Battalia*. However, Bartók's pizzicato *sul ponticello* indication and Elgar's orchestral 'pizzicato *tremolo*' (Violin Concerto Op. 61) appear to have no precedent, and the pizzicato effect with the fingernail is another invention of the current century. Left-hand pizzicato, rarely used in the early eighteenth century, gradually became more popular and reached its zenith with Paganini and his successors, who sometimes combined it with right-hand pizzicato or used it simultaneously with bowed notes.

Ex. 25   from H. Berlioz, *Grande Traité d'instrumentation* ..., tr. Clarke, p. 21.

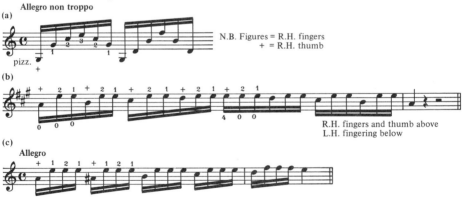

Scordatura has also been in and out of fashion, but it was particularly popular with violinists between c.1600 and c.1750. Marini's use of the device in his Op. 8 No. 2 (1629) was imitated by Biber (for example, in his 'Mystery' sonatas) and many others – e.g. Uccellini, Bononcini, Lonati, Vivaldi, Tartini, Castrucci, Lolli, Barbella, Campagnoli and Nardini in Italy; Abel, Arnold, Fischer, Kindermann, Pachelbel, Schmelzer, Strungk and von Westhoff in Germany; and Corrette, Le Maire, Tremais and Bertheaume in France. Walther, on the other hand, despised its use.[32] Composers were attracted to the new colours, timbres and the increased sonority or brilliance offered by different tunings of the instrument and the consequent tension changes of the relevant strings. Furthermore, *scordatura* could provide new harmonic possibilities, extend the range of the instrument (for example, by lowering the G string), help in imitating other instruments, or facilitate the execution of whole compositions or certain technical passages, especially those involving wide intervals, intricate string-crossing or double stopping, which might otherwise be impossible. The particular tuning employed was generally indicated at the beginning of each composition or movement, accompanied, in most cases, by a form of tablature indicating a key-signature for each string.[33] With this tablature the violin was treated as a transposing instrument, the music being notated according to the disposition of the fingers and not according to sound. This method of notation inevitably required the violinist to observe three fundamental rules in performance: to use first position wherever possible, to use open strings wherever possible unless otherwise indicated, and to apply accidentals only to the register indicated.

Scordatura gradually lost popularity during the nineteenth century, although it never became obsolete, the numerous disadvantages of the device outweighing the advantages. Mazas, Spohr, de Bériot, Prume and Winter were among those composers who employed it, but Paganini was undoubtedly its most prolific exponent, using it to simplify his music, to add tonal brilliance and to reproduce, on open strings, harmonics which would normally have to be stopped. Two notable twentieth-century examples of the device appear in Bartók's *Contrasts* and Mahler's Fourth Symphony (scherzo).

Interest in the expressive potential of the bow, 'the soul of the instrument it touches',[34] increased markedly during the eighteenth century. Vital to the fulfilment of such ideals was a natural and flexible bow hold. The close relationship between the manner of holding the violin and the bow hold suggests that the right elbow was positioned close to but detached from the body in a natural, unconstrained manner below the level of the bowstick.[35] During the nineteenth century, the elbow took up a position closer to the body than formerly, necessitating a characteristically high, supple wrist position, especially when bowing at the heel. The trend in more recent times has been to strike a compromise between these two elbow positions (above) and to 'flatten out' the wrist at the frog.

Many factors influenced the bow grip adopted by players: national style, musical demands, personal taste, the size of the hand and fingers, and the balance (and hence the type) of the bow itself. In the early Baroque period, the thumb was placed typically on the hair near the frog. Italian violinists introduced a thumb position on the under-side of the stick, but the thumb-on-hair 'French grip' persisted in France into the eighteenth century.[36] The standardisation of bow construction prompted a corresponding, if gradual, standardisation of bow holds. The prevailing cantabile ideals and the increasing popularity of the sonata and concerto in France in the mid eighteenth century led to the demise of the thumb-under-hair 'French' grip in favour of the greater subtleties of tone production offered by the Italian method. Furthermore, L'abbé *le fils* implies that the hand was placed at the frog and not, as Geminiani, Corrette and Leopold Mozart had advised, slightly above it (c.3–7 cm). The normal bow grip of nineteenth-century violinists involved placing the thumb at the frog, although some players (e.g. Mazas, Bruni, Paganini and Dancla) employed the old 'Italian' grip for optimum balance with the hand rounded naturally and the thumb a short distance from the frog, even with Tourte bows.

Contrary to the practice of violinists of the late nineteenth and current centuries, performers of earlier times kept the thumb fairly straight on the bow – Baillot (1834) explicitly states: 'Avoid bending the thumb'[37] – allowing a secure grip without stiffness in the hand, fingers or wrist. Opinion varied regarding the thumb position, but normal practice was to place it opposite the second finger,[38] although positions between the index and second fingers, or between the second and third fingers, were also used.[39] These thumb positions naturally affected the contact point of the index finger on the bow. The so-called 'German' grip (recommended also by Suzuki) has a contact point at the first joint of the index finger; the 'Franco-Belgian' between the first and second joints but nearer the second, with the thumb approximately opposite the second finger or between the second and third fingers; the 'Russian' (advocated by Flesch) at the second joint. Rolland relates his method of holding the bow to the exigencies of the music, allowing the bow hold to be modified during its course.

Up to about the end of the eighteenth century players generally separated the index finger slightly from the others for the control of volume, by applying or releasing pressure as required. The second and third fingers, naturally rounded, merely rested on the stick, while the fourth finger aided balance when bowing in the lower half. The nineteenth-century fashion was to avoid separation of the index finger from the others on the stick and to encourage a combination of thumb, index finger (on or near the middle of the second joint) and wrist-joint pressure on the bow.[40] This differs little from current common practice, although some violinists nowadays also apply third-finger pressure to the bow, creating Isaac Stern's 'circle of pressure' with the thumb, as well as a greater degree of turning inwards (pronation) of the hand.

Corrette, Herrando and L'abbé *le fils*'s recommendation that the stick should be inclined slightly towards the fingerboard was endorsed by most of their successors, although some (e.g. Leopold Mozart) discouraged this practice, ostensibly because of its detrimental effect on tone quality. However, the degree of inclination was modified to suit the instrument, the string thickness and the desired musical effect.

The fundamental short bowstroke of the Baroque and Classical periods was executed by only the wrist and forearm, but the upper arm was also brought into play for longer strokes; this upper-arm movement naturally was directed upwards and downwards but was never lateral. A low elbow and suppleness of the wrist and fingers were thus of paramount importance[41] (although no mention was made of how much the wrist should turn in towards the body). This was particularly important in the execution of smooth bow changes and string-crossing, for the natural stroke of most pre-Tourte bows was of an articulated, non-legato character (especially in the upper third). Leopold Mozart (1756) writes of 'a small, even if barely audible, softness' at the beginning and end of each stroke, a reference to the typical delayed attack (through only gradual take-up of hair) of pre-Tourte bows, their lightness at the tip and their balance point (closer to the hand). The player could vary the degree of articulation and modify the stroke by the application of nuances appropriate to the length of the note, tempo and the character of the music, as well as by the regulation of bow speed, pressure and the point of contact (Leopold Mozart was the first to pinpoint the relationship between bow speed and volume).

Unlike modern staccato, the eighteenth-century staccato stroke[42] involved a 'breath' or articulation between notes somewhat greater than the articulation of the typical separate stroke. This articulation was invariably conveyed by lifting the bow from the string after each stroke, especially in slow tempos, and implied the use of a dry, detached stroke in the lower part of the bow, with some feeling of accent although not comparable to the sharp attack of the modern staccato. In fast movements the bow necessarily remained on the string in the upper half, producing an effect similar to modern *spiccato*.

Few pre-Tourte bows were suited to such accented bowings as *martelé* or such effects as *sforzando*; these were used only rarely in the modern sense during the nineteenth century. However, such 'bounding' strokes as *sautillé*, *spiccato* and 'flying staccato' were occasionally employed in bravura passages. True legato bowing was achieved only by slurring. The capacity of the slur was enlarged substantially and slurred bowings (whether or not so notated) were increasingly exploited during the Classical period as a means of emulating the qualities of the human voice, especially in slow movements. The execution of slurred staccato, confused somewhat by the variety and ambiguity of notation, was necessarily governed by the music's tempo and character. Dots above or under the notes in slow movements normally indicated an on-the-string execution rather like a *portato*; strokes above or under the notes were more common in faster tempos and generally indicated playing in 'lifted' style, brief passages being executed in either up- or down-bow but longer

Ex. 26   from L'abbé *le fils, Principes* ..., p. 54

segue

Ex. 27   (a) from M. Woldemar, *Grande Méthode* ..., p. 48

(b) from A. Bailleux, *Méthode raisonnée* ..., p. 11

passages normally being taken in the up-bow (Ex. 26). The so-called 'Viotti' bowing (Ex. 27a), the slurred *tremolo* and the *portato* strokes are all related to the slurred staccato. However, the slurred *tremolo* (Ex. 27b), involving repeated notes on the same string under one slur, was played either staccato (normally indicated by dots or strokes under a slur) or legato (implied by a slur alone). The expressive *portato* stroke, its articulations generally indicated by dots or lines above or under the slur, was mainly confined to slower tempos. *Bariolage*, the alternation of notes on adjacent strings (of which one is usually open) in either separate or, more usually, slurred bowing (Ex. 28a), and *ondeggiando* (Ex. 28b),

Ex. 28   (a) from L'abbé *le fils, Principes* ..., p. 79

(b) from P. Gaviniès, *24 Matinées* ..., No. 12

similar to the slurred *bariolage* but with a potential range over more than two strings, were also part of the pre-Tourte bow's typical repertory.

These bowstrokes represent merely a point of departure for the appreciation of an expanding and developing eighteenth-century technique, as some transitional bows were capable of all but matching the repertory of the Tourte model. The advent of the Tourte bow shifted the emphasis away from the articulated strokes, subtle nuances and delayed attack of most mid-eighteenth-century models to a more sonorous cantabile style, with the added capability of a more or less immediate attack, *sforzando* effects and accented bowings (e.g. *saccadé* and *fouetté*) and various 'bounding' strokes (*spiccato, sautillé, ricochet* etc.). The full modern vocabulary of bowstrokes began to emerge, the French school again giving the lead. Baillot's survey,[43] unique in the way it integrates bow speed and articulation, forms the most extensive catalogue of violin bowings from the first half of the nineteenth century. Baillot classifies bowstrokes in two basic categories according to speed: slow or fast (a classification few modern players would endorse). He also admits a 'composite' stroke which adopts elements of slow and fast strokes simultaneously. The fundamental fast strokes were the *détachés*, which could be 'muted' (*mats*) – on-the-string strokes articulated by wrist and forearm (*grand détaché, martelé,* staccato); 'elastic' (*élastiques*) – mostly off-the-string strokes exploiting the resilience of the stick (*détaché léger, perlé, sautillé, staccato à ricochet,* 'flying staccato'); or 'dragged' (*traînés*) – composite, on-the-string strokes (*détaché plus ou moins appuyé, détaché flûté*). The lifted bowstroke played a less prominent role, Ex. 29a being executed generally with the bow on the string, its movement checked momentarily (usually for no more than a demisemiquaver's duration) between the notes and the second note sounded through gentle wrist movement (Ex. 29b). *Bariolage* and the 'Viotti' and 'Kreutzer' bowings still remained in the repertory of slurred strokes, and other specialised bowings such as *tremolo, col legno, sul ponticello* and *sulla tastiera* were increasingly employed.

Ex. 29 (a) from F. Habeneck, *Méthode ...,* p. 68

(b) from F. Habeneck, *Méthode ...,* p. 68

Bowing indications and articulations were more thoroughly annotated in the late eighteenth and the nineteenth centuries, ostensibly to avoid ambiguity of interpretation. However, inconsistent use of signs, notably of the dot and wedge (a dot generally required an on-the-string and the wedge an off-the-string articulation, but not without exception), imposed extra responsibility on performers to interpret the music faithfully. With the general trend towards enlarging the capacity of the slur, bow apportionment and a general appreciation of the inter-dependence of bow speed, pressure and contact point (together with their combined effect on tonal quality and volume) became paramount for convincing execution. Habeneck (c.1835) illustrates how irregular bow apportionment relates to bow speed and the desired effect (Ex. 30).[44]

Ex. 30   from F. Habeneck, Méthode . . ., pp. 100–2

Despite the absence of detailed expressive markings in much Baroque and early Classical music,[45] such were the expressive intentions of the violinists of those times that inflected bowing was fundamental to their art.[46] Except for genuine echo effects, the often very basic dynamic indications (simply *forte* and *piano*) call not for sudden, 'terraced' changes from dynamic extremes, but for a more graduated and expansive approach to expression. The *messa di voce* commonly adorned long notes, often with vibrato, and the so-called 'divisions' (the four types of nuanced bowings – crescendo, diminuendo, *messa di voce* and double

messa di voce – categorised by Leopold Mozart[47] for the cultivation of
tonal purity, variety of expression and mastery of bowing) were retained
by many early-nineteenth-century writers and applied to Tourte-model
bows. However, although de Bériot includes them in his method, he
emphasises that expression must embrace a whole phrase, and he
deplores the practice of swelling the sound towards the middle of each
stroke.[48] Significantly, the term 'bow division' took on a different
meaning in the nineteenth century, referring to the actual division of the
bow into parts (middle, upper third etc.) for the classification and
technical description of bowstrokes.

Phrasing, generally considered analogous to punctuation marks in
language or breathing in singing, was increasingly discussed in
eighteenth-century literature, although few composers notated it in their
works.[49] Nuances were applied (whether notated or not) to establish the
'peaks' and general contours of phrases, as well as their expressive
content, and were also freely employed to highlight certain dissonances,
ornaments, chromatic notes, cadences (especially interrupted cadences),
roulades and suchlike. Although nuances were indicated in rather more
detail in the nineteenth century, writers still found it necessary to
provide some ground rules for their application. Habeneck (c.1835), for
example, recommends that long notes should be 'spun out'; ascending
phrases should crescendo; descending phrases should decrescendo;[50]
any note foreign to the harmony placed on the strong beat of the bar or on
the strong part of the beat must be emphasised if it is of any length; any
modified note foreign to the scale of the prevalent key must be emphasised.[51] Baillot's survey of phrasing concentrates particularly on the
technique of 'phrasing off', making a diminuendo on or just before the
last note of a phrase.[52]

Bow apportionment according to tempo, the number of notes per
stroke and their respective dynamics, values and accentuation, assumed
greater significance during the eighteenth century, when musicians
observed the three categories of accent used in everyday speech –
'grammatic', 'rhetorical' and 'pathetic' – in their performances. Grammatic accents were those that occurred regularly at the beats of a bar.
They were not all given equal length and emphasis. The 'good' notes
(*note buone*) received most stress according to their position in the bar.
Thus, the first beat of a 4/4 bar generally received the most emphasis, the
second less, the third more than the second but less than the first, and the
fourth less again. Metres such as 2/2 and 2/4 involved one major stress
(on the first beat), while in triple metres, the first time-unit was the 'good'
and the second and third were the 'bad'.[53] This conscious 'weighting' of
the beats of a bar was accommodated in string playing by the traditional
rule of down-bow, which required notes of greatest emphasis to be
played with the stronger down-bow. This long-standing principle had its
origins in the theoretical writings of Riccardo and Francesco Rognoni,

Zanetti, and others.[54] It was a vital constituent of Baroque bowing, particularly in seventeenth-century France. Muffat (1698) gives a detailed exposé of the bowing principles of Lully and his followers, Ex. 31 showing perhaps the most distinctive of the Lullists' methods of complying with the down-bow rule. Geminiani (1751), however, despised 'that wretched Rule of drawing the Bow down at the first Note of every Bar';[55] both he and Tartini (1771) preferred to encourage more equal accentuation in the up- and down-strokes. Nevertheless, the rule of down-bow lies behind the instructions of Leopold Mozart and Herrando as well as appearing in numerous eighteenth-century French and British treatises. It has remained a guiding force in bowing to this day.

Ex. 31   from G Muffat, 'Premiers observations de l'auteur sur la manière de jouer les airs de balets à la françoise selon la méthode de feu Monsieur de Lully', in *Florilegium secundum* (Passau, 1698)

'Rhetorical' and 'pathetic' accents were distinguished from 'grammatic' accents not only by the more pronounced manner in which they were executed but also by the fact that they were not restricted to any part of the bar. For example, a note that is longer, or markedly higher or lower than its predecessor, and dissonant notes are all common instances when emphasis through prolongation of that note beyond its written length generally provided a flexible, musicianly solution.

Traditionally, the performer's role consists in conveying faithfully, yet personally, the composer's intentions according to the music's mood(s), character(s) and style(s). The eighteenth century witnessed the culmination of the 'doctrine of the affections', the ultimate aim of which was the musical expression of specific human emotions, characterised by certain musical devices which are to some extent standardised and identifiable. Descriptive words at the beginning of a piece, movement or section suggested broadly its mood and approximate tempo – from Grave, Leopold Mozart (1756) infers 'sadly and earnestly, hence very slow indeed', whilst Allegro suggests 'a gay, but not hurried tempo'. Tempo, metre, rhythm, dynamic variations, harmony, melody and tonality[56] were among the eighteenth-century composer's principal means for the creation of such a language of the emotions.

About fifty years on, Baillot, Rode and Kreutzer (1803) classify sound-quality, movement, style, taste, genius of execution and precision as the chief expressive means.[57] Precision involved rigorous time-keeping, allowing at the same time for some freedom of expressive effect within the 'outlines' of the pulse. The principal means of this freedom was *tempo rubato*, a species of ornament with a definite structural function. It has been applied to four different expressive techniques: a natural flexibility of the prescribed rhythm within a constant tempo, after which the ensemble between melody and accompaniment was restored; the modification of dynamics and/or the displacement of natural accents (resulting, for example, in unaccented 'strong' beats of the bar); the expansion of the bar(s) to incorporate more notes than the time signature theoretically allows and a flexible, yet rhythmically controlled perform-ance of these passages; or flexibility of tempo by arbitrary, unwritten accelerandos or ritardandos. 'Often a beautiful disorder is an artistic effect', remarks Baillot,[58] and such tempo flexibility invariably extended over a whole movement to articulate motivic and melodic structure.

Performing directions were more copiously and explicitly annotated from the late eighteenth century onwards, and the introduction of gerund forms into verbal indications[59] possibly implies an increasing vogue for more gradual modifications of tempo and expression, or at least a desire to systematise such gradations. But this did not make the performer's initiative redundant in the task of producing a faithful, expressive and convincing performance. The nineteenth-century theory that every melodic idea had an optimum tempo[60] encouraged performers to cultivate tempo differentiation within movements, articulating the structure by creating pockets of tempo, thematic and harmonic stability (for example, the two subject groups of a conventional sonata-form movement) and instability (development sections or developmental codas may incorporate tempo fluctuation to heighten tension).[61] Liszt lends his support to this idea (1870): 'time and rhythm must be adapted to and identified with the melody, the harmony, the accent and the poetry'.[62]

A flexible approach to dotted rhythms was characteristic of the eighteenth-century style (particularly in France),[63] the dotted note invariably being lengthened and its complementary note shortened and played in lifted style.[64] This tendency persisted in the nineteenth and early twentieth centuries, but more literal interpretation of dotted figures was encouraged from about 1930 onwards.

Polyphony was notated ambiguously in such a way that it was often impossible to perform multiple stopping exactly as the music implied.[65] The aim was to clarify both the musical progression and the melodic and harmonic functions of the voice parts rather than provide precise prescriptions as to note durations. Chords were generally spread either upwards or downwards (usually according to the register of the main melody note to be sustained), or played as arpeggios. Rapid upward spreading was the more common practice; this was generally taken in the down-bow (even successions of chords, which involved re-taking the bow). Most players evidently held the lowest note a little (some went as far as holding it for almost its full value), presumably to emphasise the harmonic progression, before sounding the other chord members in a rapid cross-string movement. However, the fact that Leblanc prescribes a series of three-note chords in his Sonata in E♭ (c.1767) to be played in a down-bow with all three strings struck simultaneously shows that other options were open to the performer.[66]

The less yielding qualities of the Tourte bow resulted in differing approaches to multiple stopping. Three strings could be played either simultaneously, by pressing on the middle string in a down-bow at the frog (but only in *forte*), or 'broken'. Four-note chords were also 'broken', perhaps $2+2$,[67] commencing either before or on the beat, $3+1$ or $2+1+1$. A down-bow was normally employed, even for consecutive chords, but arpeggiation of chordal progressions was less common than formerly. Open strings were generally sounded (where possible) in multiple stopping for greater sonority, and the left-hand thumb was sometimes brought into play for certain chord shapes.

Finally, a brief word about ornamentation, arguably one of the most treacherous aspects of historical performance practice! While it is impracticable to present here a definitive interpretation of so-called 'essential' ornaments (i.e. those indicated by some sort of written sign – primarily the appoggiatura, mordent, trill and turn), performers should make themselves aware not only of the variety of ornaments documented in, for example, eighteenth-century instrumental instruction books, but also of the wide range of valid interpretations of those ornaments according to national theory, musical context, and even individual practice.[68] They should also recognise the desirability of introducing free improvisation (principally in the form of melodic variation, the decoration of fermatas and the extemporisation of cadenzas) in their performances of much 'early' music (particularly that of Italian origins) in their quest to re-create that ever-elusive quality of 'authenticity'.[69] Interestingly, C. P. E. Bach deliberately refrains from detailed discussion of such improvised ornamentation, arguing chiefly that its implementation is too variable to classify.[70] Given the limits of the present volume, who am I to disagree with him?!

8 Aspects of contemporary technique (with comments about Cage, Feldman, Scelsi and Babbitt)

PAUL ZUKOFSKY

The twentieth century presents string players with two sets of (somewhat related) technical problems: the variety of timbral and dynamic demands made upon the bow arm; and the intervallic demands made upon our left hand/arm. There are other concerns that make the music of this century difficult for many (i.e. complex metric and rhythmic structures, and general questions of form and musical content), but these concerns affect all musicians, not just string players.

As regards the first problem, the assumption is usually made that the demands *per se* are new; unique; different. This assumption is at least partially false. It is the *rate* at which the demands *change* that is new, not the demands themselves.

As regards the left hand/arm, these problems result from the intervallic and harmonic choices used by composers in the music of this century, and string players have simply disregarded anything in their preparatory studies that might make this music less of a physical cipher to them. Indeed, the training material and thought processes behind today's teaching have generally continued as if the compositional milestones and solutions of this century had never happened.

The primary timbral demands made today upon our bow arm (other than normal bowing – which still constitutes the majority of what we do) are: pizzicato; playing on the bridge (Ital. = *sul ponticello*; Fr. = *sur le chevalet*; Ger. = *am Steg*); playing on the fingerboard (*sul tasto*; *sur la touche*; *am Griffbrett*); playing on or with the wood of the bow, either struck or drawn (*col legno*); and (occasionally) playing behind, or on the 'wrong' side of the bridge. Cases where one is required to 'jump' strings while still preserving a melodic line are usually more of a musical or perceptual problem, as opposed to a timbral or production one. All of the above demands are of course combined with constantly varying loudness levels which we refer to as dynamics.

Most of these demands are not new. Monteverdi specified the use of pizzicatos (and tremolos). Haydn used playing on the bridge and on the fingerboard. Playing with the wood, or behind the bridge, are not inventions of this century. Indeed, if truth be told, one moment after the start of the first orchestral rehearsal that ever was, some disgruntled string player did all of the above simultaneously, long before any composer dreamed of asking for it.

What distinguishes this century's usage, and creates the problem for us, is how brief the durations are between changes from one type of right-arm use to another. For example, the second movement of Haydn's Symphony No. 97 (written in 1792) has a concatenated forty-three(!)-bar passage marked *al ponticello* followed by *vicino al ponticello*. If (for argument's sake) one accepts Czerny's metronome marking (crotchet = 112, which at least in some circles is a very brisk Adagio ma non troppo), those forty-three bars of 4/4 have a total duration somewhat longer than 1.5 minutes (43 × 4/112).

As a counter-example, compare bars 15–17 of the solo violin part of Luigi Nono's *Varianti* (1957). In the space of eleven crotchets lasting barely ten seconds there are twelve pitches, each one of which has a specific right-arm indication, viz:

1 bowed *flautando*
2 bowed *sul ponticello*
3 bowed *sul ponticello flautando*
4 pizzicato
5 bowed normal
6 pizzicato *sul ponticello*
7 bowed *sul ponticello*
8 bowed *sul ponticello flautando*
9 bowed normal
10 bowed normal
11 bowed *sul ponticello*
12 bowed normal

Note that this progression of changes involves three dimension, i.e. bow vs. pizzicato (hand-grip change), normal bow position vs. *ponticello* (horizontal-plane change), and normal bow pressure vs. *flautando* (vertical-plane change) as opposed to the single horizontal dimension change of the Haydn (normal bow position vs. *ponticello*).

These two examples may represent extremes but are hardly isolated instances. As the rate of change for dynamics has also increased dramatically with this century's music, and as the number of possible dynamic/ timbral combinations is large, it becomes increasingly difficult to control the bow, forcing us to create new approaches to the bow arm.

As regards left hand/arm problems something as basic as Geminiani's suggestion of practising *all* the intervals within the octave[1] has still not been taken seriously after only 239 years! The practice of all the intervals is not only beneficial as regards training the ear, but also serves to 'balance' the hand, in that the physical inverse of an octave (first finger on lower string, fourth finger on upper string) is a second (first finger on upper string, fourth finger on lower); the physical inverse of a third is a seventh; and that of a sixth is a fourth. We can hardly expect to feel comfortable with the pitch and intervallic concerns of today's music when we have neither the aural nor physical cosiness that the habitual practising of traditional interval scales (thirds, sixths, octaves and tenths) provides for diatonic music. Incorporating all the other intervals in our daily practice routine would be an enormous step forward in our ability to be of service to today's music.

Another left-hand area where our knowledge tends to be wanting is harmonics. Few violinists approach them systematically, yet today's music frequently requires them for timbral and structural reasons, and they are useful as substitute fingerings in certain extreme passages.[2]

As a result of our not keeping up with their musical demands, many recent composers have either avoided writing for strings or have kept their demands within fairly traditional confines. Of those composers whose thought-processes and demands have most influenced how I think about the violin,[3] and who have made large and new contributions to our craft (all of whose music I care more or less deeply about and with some of whom I have often collaborated), I can mention John Cage, Morton Feldman, Giacinto Scelsi and Milton Babbitt.

I credit Cage with three ideas, at least two of which are of primary importance for violinists, the third being potentially of great use to composers as well as violinists.

The first of these ideas is the concept of a 'gamut' of sounds. By this Cage means (for string players) the assignment of a specific string for a specific pitch, so that each time that pitch occurs at the same octave, it is always played on the same preassigned string.[4] The concept of a 'gamut' is one that Cage has used generally,[5] but its general application to violin fingerings opens possibilities of delineating structural lines, or colouring a work sonically, that traditional position-maintaining fingerings simply do not allow.

The next of Cage's ideas – and one of great usefulness – is the incorporation of chance into music. The specific application that I am thinking of (and one that I am proud to have had a hand in inventing) concerns the use of chance to determine bowings and fingerings.[6] Chance cannot be relied upon to provide a practical and expedient fingering or bowing, nor should that be its function. What it does do, and does without fail, is open a window on possibilities that one never thinks of because of one's training – training having the simultaneous advantage/disadvantage of making certain responses autonomic, while at the same time reducing one's need, and sometimes ability, to think.

The third idea is the result of the compositional process used in Cage's *Freeman Etudes* – a 'Chord Catalogue', consisting of all the chord-ranges used in the work. The catalogue will serve two purposes. On the most simplistic level it will be a reference for the possible and not quite so possible, thereby serving (through extrapolation) as a guide to both composers and violinists. Of far greater interest (at least to me) is that it could serve as the basis for a mapping of left arm–hand–finger configurations in three-dimensional space. These configurations are not as self-evident as one might think because of the confounding of the decreasing geometry of string lengths (ascending one string, the first octave uses one half the total string length; the second octave one quarter of the length; the third one eighth; and so on *ad infinitum*, although that is of no practical use to us) and the rounded body of the instrument, both of which make it impossible to maintain the same angles between arm, hand and finger throughout the complete fingerboard length.

Morton Feldman's later music,[7] which explores small variations in various domains (pitch, duration, register, timbres, attacks and decays) over long periods of time, forces us once again to think seriously about intonation systems. This is not the place to discuss specifically how such systems might operate in music since Schoenberg, i.e. in music based on a concept of twelve equal tones. Suffice it to say that while it is theoretically possible for string players to adopt an equal temperament system for such music, it is not clear that they can, or do, do so;[8] and certainly, a true equal temperament prevents us from using what might be called an 'opinionated' intonation, i.e. a colouring device that allows us to indicate where we think we are going 'harmonically'.[9] Feldman utilised a system where, for example, an e♭ is played sharper than a d♯, or to generalise, for any enharmonic pair, the higher pitch label always implies the higher pitch. In short, Feldman returned us to a world where double sharps and double flats have real and individual physical, musical and emotional meaning, as opposed to equal microtones, which simply present finer slices of equal temperament.[10]

One cannot discuss vibrato as it might be thought of today without confronting the music of Giacinto Scelsi. Scelsi explored the phenomena of wavering single-note surfaces, creating a palette that included acoustic beating, tremolos (both slurred and reciprocating bowing), microtonal trills, different vibratos, and in certain cases, *scordatura*, using tunings that enabled him to combine all of the above on one instrument.[11] His ideas and works ought to affect every aspect of our thoughts on vibrato, as opposed to what today passes for 'slow, medium and fast' vibratos. It should be pointed out that there is a large amount of string music written in this century that requires no vibrato.[12] Some of this is a reaction to the excesses of an older style. Some of it is due to compositional concerns which wish to emphasise steady-state pitch precision. For whatever reasons, the twentieth century explodes the concept of vibrato as we tend to think about it (when and if we do think about it, as opposed to using it like ketchup).[13]

The relevance of Milton Babbitt's use of dynamics to our control of the bow with respect to speed, pressure and distribution combinations cannot be overstated. Some of our problems arise from his use of a quantised, as opposed to analogue, representation of dynamics; i.e. Babbitt will use a different dynamic on each note rather than a global symbol such as a crescendo. Some of our problems arise from not grasping that the dynamics are indications that the metric stress (relative to the bar) has shifted, the general metric rule being to play *what* the durational patterns are, as opposed to emphasising *where* they are relative to pro forma barlines. The concepts we must employ when bowing Babbitt's music completely contradict the stasis that is our norm, i.e. do the same thing for a very long time. Once, however, having opened the door, one suddenly finds oneself using portions of this approach very effectively in older virtuosic music.

There are of course today's equivalents to yesterday's tricks, i.e. Xenakis's use of *glissandi*,[14] or Penderecki's use of playing behind the bridge could be thought of as similar in manner to the 'flying staccato'. There are also idiosyncratic usages, such as Stravinsky's instruction 'glissez avec toute la longueur de l'archet',[15] or Schoenberg's insistence on the most abstruse (when not outré) harmonics, but to my mind, none of these provide a basis for technical thought, or have opened my eyes violinistically, as did the works of Cage, Feldman, Scelsi and Babbitt.

9 The concerto

ROBIN STOWELL

The Baroque

The term 'concerto', implying an aggregation of performing forces large or small, described many musical genres in the early seventeenth century. These ranged from vocal music accompanied by instrumentalists, to purely instrumental music in which the element of contrast was prominent. The development of the *concertato* style is witnessed both in the later madrigal books of Monteverdi and in the church music and madrigals of Venetian composers such as Andrea and Giovanni Gabrieli. The Gabrielis' *Concerti per voci e stromenti musicali* (1587), comprising sacred music and madrigals in six to sixteen parts, is the earliest known publication to use the term 'concerto' in its title. The instrumental concerto emerged as an independent form towards the end of the seventeenth century and soon evolved into a genre in which virtuosity was a significant ingredient.

Italy

The earliest type of purely instrumental concerto, the concerto grosso, contrasted a large (concerto grosso) and a small group (concertino) of performers. The first essays in this genre emerged with Stradella in Rome in the 1670s,[1] but Corelli brought the form to its first peak with his collection of twelve concerti grossi for strings Op. 6 (1714).[2] These are essentially elaborations of Corelli's trio sonata ideal, the 'concertino' section consisting of two violins and a cello. Eight of the set conform to the *da chiesa* (church) slow–fast–slow–fast pattern, excluding movements of a dance character but including fugal fast movements;[3] the other four comprise largely sequences of dance-like movements in *da camera* (chamber) fashion.

The repeated-note patterns and triadic figurations of the trumpet works[4] by such Bolognese composers as Gabrielli, Perti and Torelli were prominent features of the developing concerto style. Torelli's *Concerti* musicali Op. 6 (1698) herald the emergence of the solo violin concerto, prescribing specific solo passages for violin, while the last six of his set of [12] concerti grossi . . ., published posthumously as Op. 8 (1709), specify a solo violin in the concertino role. Op. 8 No. 8 arrives at the recognised form of the Baroque solo concerto, a three-movement (fast–slow–fast) design whose outer movements are cast in ritornello form, in which varied tutti statements in different keys of a recurrent idea alternate with modulating episodes of free thematic content for the soloist with appropriate ensemble accompaniment.

In Venice, Albinoni was composing his [6] Sinfonie e [6] concerti a cinque (1700), concertos for solo violin and strings in a similar fast–slow–fast design. His Op. 5 concertos (1707) introduce fugal finales, and his Op. 7 (1715) and Op. 9 (1722) sets include works for one and two oboes as well as four for strings, those in Op. 9 as well as many in Op. 10 (c.1735) including a part for solo violin. Marcello's twelve concertos Op. 1 (1708) are essentially amalgams of the concerto grosso and solo concerto. An obbligato violin and cello make up the concertino group in a design generally of four or more movements, normally incorporating a slow introductory movement followed by a fugal Allegro.

The foremost Venetian concerto composer, however, was Vivaldi. He contributed about 230 solo violin concertos to the repertory,[5] introduced virtuosity into the genre, and was the first to make consistent use of both the fast–slow–fast concerto design and ritornello form (often elaborately treated) in the outer movements. His first printed collection, L'estro armonico Op. 3 (1711), comprising twelve concertos, arranged in four symmetrical groups, for one, two and four violins (sometimes with an obbligato cello part), proved extremely influential both in Italy and abroad. This was particularly so in Germany, where J. S. Bach transcribed six of them for keyboard (c.1714) and later arranged No. 10 for four harpsichords and orchestra. Most of these concertos are in three movements, but No. 7 comprises five, and Nos. 2 and 4 revert to the four-movement cycle of the Corellian trio sonata. Among Vivaldi's eight other published concerto collections are his experimental La stravaganza Op.4 (c.1712–13), comprising seven for solo violin, four for two violins and one for two violins and cello; his VI concerti a 5 stromenti Op. 6 (1716–17) for solo violin and strings; a similarly titled set of twelve works Op. 7 (c.1716–17), of which Nos. 1 and 7 are for oboe and strings; and the ambitious Il cimento dell'armonia e dell'inventione Op. 8 (1725), of which Nos. 1–4 form the quartet of violin concertos known as 'The Four Seasons'. Vivaldi added a 'sonetto dimostrativo' as well as some further instructions in the instrument parts as programmatic guides to each of these four works. Of the other concertos in the Op. 8 set, Nos. 9 and 12 are probably oboe concertos, and Nos. 5, 6 and 10 have descriptive titles ('La tempesta di mare', 'Il piacere' and 'La caccia' respectively).

Of Vivaldi's three subsequent concerto sets, Opp. 11 and 12 (c.1729–30) are rough and ready by comparison with the twelve concertos entitled *La cetra* Op. 9 (1727). All but one of Op. 9 are for solo violin and strings – No. 9 in B♭ major is for two violins – and Nos. 6 and 12 require the soloist to play in *scordatura*; only No. 5 deviates from the established three-movement (fast–slow–fast) design, opening with a slow introduction and running the ensuing Presto straight into the slow movement. Strangely enough, Italian composers assimilated Vivaldian precepts slowly, often combining them with earlier practices. Other contemporaries, notably Bonporti and Durante, were more indebted to Corelli.

Most important among the post-Vivaldian generation of Italian composers are Locatelli and Tartini. A pupil of Corelli, Locatelli published five sets of concertos between 1721 and 1762 (Opp. 1, 3, 4, 7 and 9) his *XII concerti grossi a 4 e a 5 con 12 fughe* Op. 1 (1721) displaying the greatest debt to his mentor (although the concertino group comprises one or even two violas as well as two violins and a cello). Like Corelli's Op. 6, the first eight works are in the church style,[6] while the final four are *da camera* concertos. Locatelli's *L'arte del violino* Op. 3 (1733) is undoubtedly his most significant and progressive set, influencing composers as diverse as Albinoni (Op. 10), Dall'Abaco (Op. 6), Leclair and Paganini in their virtuosity (especially the twenty-four *Caprices*), resourceful harmony, and skilful exploitation of the Venetian three-movement concerto plan; No. 8 comprises two movements.

Tartini's c.135 violin concertos generally conform to the Vivaldian three-movement pattern, the central movement normally adopting a contrasting tonality. Many features of the *galant* style are discernible in his works from c.1745, Brainard counting a 'peculiar blend of lyricism, pathos and virtuosity ... violinistically conceived mannerisms, frequent echo effects, occasional harmonic boldnesses and ... elaborate cadence formulae' as some of the hallmarks of his mature style.[7]

Germany

Corelli's influence was supreme in late-seventeenth-century Germany, thanks largely to Muffat, who probably studied with Corelli in Rome in the early 1680s. Muffat's *Armonico tributo* (1682) comprises five 'chamber sonatas' which are essentially concerti grossi modelled after Corelli's Op. 6, although some movements betray the influence of his other mentor, Lully. For five-part strings with solo passages for two violins and a bass, these works comprise from five to seven movements founded on a mixture of *da chiesa* and *da camera* traits. Muffat's last publication, *Ausserlesene Instrumental-Music* (1701), a collection of twelve concerti grossi, consists of six new works and six re-workings (as Nos. 2, 4, 5, 10, 11 and 12) of musical material from his *Armonico tributo*.[8]

The Dresden-based (from 1712) Pisendel, a pupil of Torelli and Vivaldi, left at least seven violin concertos modelled after Vivaldi but with hints at a more *galant* idiom, and four one-movement concerti grossi. Among others who followed Italian models but pointed towards the pre-Classical style were Graupner, Fasch, Stölzel and Heinichen, although much of Heinichen's music comprised a mixture of German, Italian and French styles in the manner of Telemann. Telemann's twenty-one surviving violin concertos comprise three or four movements but display no consistency of first-movement structure. More progressive in construction, content and realisation are Telemann's ensemble concertos for two or more soloists.[9]

The move of Telemann's contemporary and friend J. S. Bach to Cöthen (1717–23) as *Kapellmeister* to Prince Leopold changed the emphasis of Bach's compositions from church music to instrumental pieces. Bach was well acquainted with the concertos of Vivaldi and others, arranging several of the Italian composer's concertos for solo harpsichord; it is possible that he had already composed works in the genre at Weimar. The only solo concertos to survive in their original forms from the Cöthen period are the violin concertos in A minor (BWV 1041) and E major (BWV 1042), and the D minor concerto for two violins (BWV 1043). Each comprises three movements and follows the Vivaldian model, but with the interior dimensions significantly expanded and more freely treated and also with formal outlines veiled by the remarkable variety of solo writing. The slow central movements form the works' crowning achievements, each of the two solo concertos featuring a beautiful, lyrical solo cantilena over an ostinato bass.

Bach's Brandenburg Concertos (BWV 1046–51, 1721) employ largely the Venetian three-movement pattern. However, No. 1 (vn picc, 3 oboes, 2 horns) comprises seven movements, including some stylised dances and displaying some French traits in the manner of Muffat, and only a Phrygian cadence (possibly elaborated by a brief solo violin cadenza) links the two fast movements of the third concerto. No. 2 contrasts a concertino group (tpt, rec, ob, vn) of different tonal characters, while No. 3 explores the tonal and contrapuntal possibilities inherent in nine string parts (3 vn, 3 va, 3 vc) with basso continuo. No. 4 (vn, 2 rec; str, bc) gives prominence to the solo violinist, while the fifth concerto (fl, vn, hpd; str, bc) features the solo harpsichordist, notably in the opening movement's extended, written-out cadenza. The central movement of the fifth concerto is essentially a trio sonata for the solo grouping, as is also the case in the unusually scored No. 6 (2 va, 2 va da gamba, vc, bc), in which the violas and cello form the concertino group.

Great Britain

British musicians had assimilated much of the Italian and French styles from Purcell and had generally been very receptive to continental musicians and musical fashions. The music of Corelli was the prime influence, thanks doubtless to one of his pupils, Geminiani; he came to England in 1714 and, apart from visits to Dublin, lived in London. Geminiani's concerti grossi were closely modelled on those of his mentor, his earliest set of twelve (1726–7) actually comprising arrangements of Corelli's Op. 5 violin sonatas with a viola included in the concertino group. This four-part concertino became standard practice for Geminiani,[10] as did also the four-movement scheme of the trio sonata. Of the two further sets of six 'second-hand' concertos (1735 and 1743), the first consisted of arrangements of trios from Corelli's Opp. 1 and 3, and the other comprised arrangements of violin sonatas from Geminiani's own Op. 4. Of Geminiani's three original sets of six concerti grossi (Op. 2, 1732; Op. 3, 1732; Op. 7, 1746), Op. 3 and Op. 7 (wind instruments etc.) are arguably superior.

Handel, who settled in London in 1712, also assisted greatly in perpetuating the Corelli tradition. Much of his orchestral music was a by-product of his work for the theatre, and several of his concerto movements were adapted from vocal and instrumental numbers in his operas and oratorios. It is doubtful if all six Concerti Grossi Op. 3 (1734) for woodwinds and strings[11] came originally from Handel's pen, but the twelve Grand Concertos Op. 6 (1740), scored for strings and a concertino group of two violins and cello[12] are *echt* Handel. They are more dramatic and more diverse both in content and structure than their Corellian models and embody also elements of the German suite tradition. Some follow the slow–fast–slow–fast sonata scheme, while others comprise five or even six movements. Nos. 5, 9 and 11 adapt material from other works, and all but one (No. 8) include a fugue.

Of native Englishmen, only Avison, Stanley, Mudge and Bond are worthy of mention. Stanley's Six Concerto's [*sic*] in 7 Parts, Op. 2 (1742) are retrospective in their Corellian-Handelian inspiration, while Avison's sixty concerti grossi, published in seven sets between 1740 and 1769, look back to his teacher Geminiani, in both their four-movement structure and their four-part concertino grouping (2 vns, va, vc). Amongst others who published concertos in London during the mid eighteenth century were the Dutchmen de Fesch and Hellendaal, and the Italian Castrucci.

France

French composers began to write concertos only comparatively late in the period and their works followed Vivaldian precepts from the outset, notably Aubert's two sets of six violin concertos (Op. 17, 1734; Op. 26, 1739). The fast outer movements of his Op. 17 collection (the first violin concertos to be published in France) are based firmly on Venetian models, but the central movements often comprise French dances such as the gavotte or minuet. Most significant, however, was Leclair, who studied in Italy and published two sets of six Italianate concertos in Paris – Op. 7 (1737); Op. 10 (1745). Leclair follows the Vivaldian fast–slow–fast movement pattern in all but one of his concertos (Op. 7, No. 2), where he adds an introductory Adagio. His treatment of the outer movements is freer and more adventurous, with virtuosity much in evidence. As with Aubert's *opera*, the slow movements exhibit French traits, most notably in the song-like simplicity of their solo melodies and their incorporation of national dance rhythms.

The Classical period

By c.1750 the solo concerto had superseded the concerto grosso, although concerto grosso principles were later resurrected somewhat in the *symphonie concertante*, a genre especially popular in Paris in the 1770s. There was also a shift of emphasis from the violin to the keyboard concerto and the emergence, at Italy's expense, of Austria, Germany and France as centres of concerto development.

Tartini and his pupils Pietro Nardini and Maddalena Sirmen (née Lombardini) were among the first Italians to abandon Baroque practices in favour of a new, more dramatic concerto form; this was taken up by Gaetano Pugnani, Josef Mysliveček, Luigi Boccherini, Antonio Lolli and Giovanni Giornovichi. In their consistent exploitation of high position-work, double stopping and other bravura techniques, the concertos of Lolli and Giornovichi prepared the way for the virtuoso feats of Paganini and his successors.

North German composers contributed greatly to the development of the genre, particularly the keyboard concerto. However, Tartini's pupil Johann Gottlieb Graun composed at least sixty violin concertos, while the works of the Benda brothers, Franz and Georg, like those of Johann Wilhelm Hertel and Johann Friedrich Reichardt, perpetuated Baroque elements within a dramatic, expressive style.

In Mannheim, Johann Stamitz took Tartini as his model, while his sons Carl and Anton leaned more towards the ascendant French style, a model followed increasingly by such composers as Ignaz Holzbauer, Ignaz Fränzl, Christian Cannabich, Carl Joseph Toeschi, Peter Ritter and Friedrich and Franz Eck. Many of these composers contributed also to the *symphonie concertante* repertory.

In Austria, Georg Monn, Georg Wagenseil and Johann Michael Haydn were the first to absorb Classical elements in their violin concertos. However, it was not until the Mannheim composers lost much of their forward impetus – at the removal of the electoral court to Munich (1778) – that their concerto style eventually caught on in Vienna, where Leopold Hofmann, Carl Ditters von Dittersdorf and others capitalised on their work.

Concerto composition by French composers developed slowly. Parisian concert circles were dominated by the works of the Mannheim school, including *symphonies concertantes* in plenty. French *concertante* works of the period initially comprised only two movements: an Allegro in concerto-sonata form with orchestral introduction, followed by a *rondeau* (usually Allegretto) of lighter character and smaller proportions, but the three-movement concerto and *symphonie concertante* later became the norm. The most prominent French-based exponent of the *symphonie concertante* was the Italian Giuseppe Cambini, while Chevalier de Saint-Georges, Marie-Alexandre Guénin, Jean-Baptiste Davaux and Simon Leduc *l'aîné* all absorbed Mannheim influences in their *concertante* works for the violin. On the other hand, Pierre Gaviniès continued the tradition of Leclair in his Op. 4 violin concertos, but with Classical phrasing and structure and with more than a hint of Mannheim seasoning. The three violin concertos of Michel Woldemar foreshadow the technical developments of Paganini's generation. Interestingly, their slow movements are presented in both undecorated and ornamented versions.

The four violin concertos accredited to Joseph Haydn date from the 1760s. The second is lost – it is known only from an entry in Haydn's thematic catalogue – and none of the surviving three (in C, A and G; HobVIIa: 1, 3 and 4) was published until the current century. These are conservative, three-movement works written in a language characterised by numerous short sighing figures, pallid rococo triplet decorations and spirited dotted tutti rhythms.

Handel's concerti grossi inspired many native Britons to cultivate the genre, but their contributions were conservative compared with those of such foreigners as Luigi Borghi, Ignaz Pleyel and Johann Christian Bach, who 'dropped anchor' in England. J. C. Bach's concertos, largely for instruments other than the violin,[13] exerted a direct influence on Mozart and thus initiated the culminating phase of the eighteenth-century concerto, dominated by the piano.

In addition to J. C. Bach's influence, Mozart absorbed 'formal unity from Vienna, thematic sophistication from Mannheim, and rhythmic continuity from Italy',[14] but his achievement in fusing the ritornellos of the Baroque concerto with the dramatic possibilities of sonata form was accomplished principally through his piano concertos. His violin concertos number only five (all 1775).[15] K207 in Bb and K211 in D are modestly proportioned 'apprentice' works in the Austro-German tradition. Their finales appear to have caused Mozart most trouble.[16] Not so the other three concertos, whose finales display characteristics of the

Austrian serenade in their incorporation of folk-like melodies and their affinities with J. C. Bach's favoured *menuet en rondeau* form (with literal or slightly varied repetitions of the refrains, and episodes in contrasting tempos and metre). The slow movement of K216 and the modifications of the traditional form in all three movements of K219 (notably, the soloist's Adagio arioso after the very first orchestral tutti, the subtle modifications to the initial orchestral theme on its three repetitions in the ternary central Adagio, and the 'alla Turca' interruptions, with cymbals, droning horns etc., and the cellos and basses playing *coll'arco al rovescio* – i.e. *col legno* – in the final *rondeau*) testify to Mozart's experimentation and ripening craftsmanship.

By far the greatest influence in France was Viotti, who wrote nineteen of his twenty-nine violin concertos during his years in Paris. They range from those in a cosmopolitan *galant* style to those whose character, drama and expressive potential were strengthened immeasurably by operatic influences, such that the last six (Nos. 14–19) presage the Romantic concerto. But the products of Viotti's London sojourn (from 1792) surpass them in substance, drama, adventurousness, craftsmanship and solo exploitation. They represent the Classical violin concerto style in its fully evolved form.

Viotti's imaginative fusion of Italian, French and German concerto elements undoubtedly provided the main inspiration for Beethoven's Violin Concerto in D Op. 61 (1806).[17] The march-like character of Beethoven's monumental first movement (the timpani-strokes providing a rhythmic cell which pervades the whole movement) and the spirited rondo finale (ABACABA) with its striking, humorous G minor episode featuring the bassoon smack of the contemporary French concerto style. Viottian influence also extends to the shape and character of some of Beethoven's themes as well as to the technical vocabulary exploited.[18] The slow movement, in which orchestral statements of the main theme (never actually played by the soloist) are complemented by varied solo embroidery, is more individual. Apart from leading without a break into the finale, it bears little resemblance to the brief *romance*, complete with improvised embellishments, of the traditional French concerto scheme. No original cadenzas for the violin concerto have survived, but Beethoven wrote four cadenzas, including one with timpani accompaniment, for his version for solo piano.

The nineteenth century

The violin concerto developed in three main directions during the nineteenth century. One line of descent cultivated traditional musical values, while another introduced nationalistic elements; but this was also the age of the virtuoso, who contributed much to both the development and the debasement of the genre. The element of display, although omnipresent from the solo concerto's beginnings, became one of its essential ingredients.

Traditionalists and nationalists

Spohr's eighteen violin concertos (composed 1802/3–44)[19] show clear debts to Viotti and the French violin school in their lyrical, expressive slow movements, sense of drama and bravura passage-work; but their structure, texture, thematic integration and development possess a Germanic symphonic breadth suggestive of Beethoven. The four violin concertos which Spohr composed between the A major Concerto Op. 62 (1810) and the A major Concertino Op. 79 (1828) arguably represent his best work in the genre. Of these, the E minor Concerto Op. 38 (1814) is probably most characteristic of its composer, but Op. 47 in A minor (1816), subtitled 'in modo di scena cantante', confirms the operatic influence and intention already foreshadowed in the dramatic recitative in the central movement of Op. 28 (1809). Composed especially for Italian consumption, it is in one continuous movement – a dramatic, lyrical monologue with recitative, arioso and an aria in two sections.

Although Spohr's pupil David himself composed five violin concertos, he is still best known as Mendelssohn's adviser for the E minor concerto Op. 64 (1838–44). That Mendelssohn's inspiration was essentially Classical is evident from the structure and content of his initial essay in the genre, in D minor.[20] But Op. 64 also exhibits the formal experiments, some not without precedents, of a Romantic at work and initiated a new symphonic tradition for the concerto. Remarkable in its first movement are the entrance of the soloist in the second bar,[21] the central placement of the cadenza before the recapitulation, and the linking of this Allegro with the ternary Andante by a sustained bassoon note. Furthermore, a brief transition between the Andante and the sonata-rondo finale gives the impression of a through-composed form of the kind Mendelssohn had used in his two piano concertos Opp. 25 and 40.

Mendelssohn's influence on succeeding generations was made more potent through the achievements of his protégé – and David's 'pupil'[22] – Joachim. Joachim composed three violin concertos of which the Brahmsian *Concerto in the Hungarian Style* (1857–60), a nationalistic piece based upon freely invented thematic material in the spirit of Hungarian music, is by far the best.

Schumann composed two *concertante* works for Joachim in the last year of his creative life (1853) – the Concerto in D minor, published posthumously, and the single-movement *Fantasie* Op. 131.[23] Joachim had misgivings about the violin writing in the concerto and resolved[24] that it would do Schumann no service if it were included in the Breitkopf *Gesamtausgabe*. Jelly d'Arányi, Schumann's great-niece, resurrected the work for its first public performance (London, February 1938), but its structural weaknesses, uneven content and numerous miscalculations of solo writing and orchestration account for its neglect nowadays.

Bruch's Violin Concerto No. 1 in G minor (1866) also owed its inspiration to Joachim, its dedicatee. First performed in April 1866, it was later revised with Joachim's help, the new version[25] being premiered in Bremen in 1868. Bruch departs from the traditional scheme, including a large-scale Prelude ('Vorspiel') with three principal thematic elements as the first movement, punctuated by violin solo recitatives. The first and second movements are linked, and the sonata-form slow movement assumes the work's centre of gravity, dominated by a broad cantabile melody. The Hungarian characteristics of the finale's principal theme are often claimed, rightly or wrongly, as a tribute to Joachim. Here is a well-proportioned mix of noble melody and virtuoso figuration, the pace quickening in the coda for one final energetic solo burst. Of Bruch's two other violin concertos, both in D minor (1876 and 1891), the second is the more remarkable. It resembles Spohr's operatically influenced concertos, the extended Adagio and sonata-form finale being linked by a section of recitative. Bruch's *Scottish Fantasy* (1880), intended for Sarasate,[26] was inspired by the novels of Sir Walter Scott. It incorporates Scottish folk melodies in its four movements and also features a prominent part for a harp. The solemn Grave introduction proceeds via recitative-like sections for solo violin into the main Adagio cantabile section, based on 'Auld Rob Morris'. 'Hey, the dusty miller', with bagpipe effects etc., carries the second movement (Allegro) along, enhanced eventually by bravura solo writing. The recall of 'Auld Rob Morris' links the second to the third movement, a sustained Andante (based on 'I'm a-doun for lack o' Johnnie') with a contrasting middle section. The Allegro guerriero finale comprises variations on two contrasting themes – 'Scots wha hae' and a more lyrical foil – culminating in a mass of virtuoso histrionics.

Joachim also provided the inspiration behind Brahms's Violin Concerto in D major Op. 77 (1878) and became its dedicatee. He advised Brahms on technical matters[27] and premiered the work in Leipzig on New Year's Day 1879, with Brahms himself conducting. It was not well received. Hans von Bülow dubbed it 'a concerto against the violin', possibly because the solo part is not only a virtuoso showpiece encased in the wrappings of Classical concerto form but also takes its place in a totally integrated composition of symphonic breadth and character. Indeed Brahms originally planned it on a four-movement symphonic scale,[28] but he later substituted 'a feeble Adagio' for the two central movements.

The first movement keeps faith with Classical models in that nearly all the subject matter is stated in the orchestral exposition, each subject group comprising in this case three contrasted but related ideas. Less traditional is the fantasia-like process by which the soloist prepares for his statement of the principal theme, high on the E string. He even contributes a new lyrical melody to the argument[29] and invents a variety of counter-melodies to set against the orchestra, moving through an adventurous arc of keys. A fairly orthodox recapitulation precedes the cadenza, the energetic coda following only after the soloist has sung an ethereal meditation on the movement's opening idea. The central 'feeble Adagio' features a solo oboe with a ravishing, expressive melody. Curiously, this melody is never given in its entirety to the violinist, who largely extends and elaborates upon it in partnership with the oboist, particularly after the rhapsodic middle section of this ternary design. The finale, an impetuous rondo (ABACBA), has a strong dash of Hungarian flavour about it. Its two interludes are in strong contrast, one energetic, the other more tranquil and lightly scored. The pace quickens in the coda, as the main theme is transformed over the march-like tread of the orchestra.

Joachim also influenced Ferruccio Busoni in the composition of his retrospective Violin Concerto in D (1896–7), which remains faithful to the German Romantic tradition, while one of the most celebrated of David's pupils (1861–4) at Leipzig, Wilhelmj, also contributed a violin concerto to the repertory. Wilhelmj's versatile 'finishing' teacher in composition, Joachim Raff, left two violin concertos, while the two concertos of the Hungarian/'adopted Viennese' Károly Goldmark suggest the German influence of Schumann, Mendelssohn and Spohr, particularly No. 1 in A minor Op. 28. Strauss also left an early Violin Concerto in D minor (1880–2), which, though conservative in scope and lacking an opportunity for a cadenza, is pregnant with lush romantic melodies and technical challenges.

In Scandinavia, only the concertos of Franz Berwald (1820), Niels Gade (1880), Johan Svendsen (1869–70) and Christian Sinding (Opp. 45, 60 and 119) are noteworthy. Berwald's Classical sympathies are immediately apparent in his concerto, especially the influence of such contemporaries as Spohr, Hummel and Beethoven. It is remarkable for its assured craftsmanship and individuality of style, not least its imaginative harmonies, audacious modulations and striking orchestration.

Lalo and Saint-Saëns were the French nationalists/traditionalists in the genre. Of Lalo's three *concertante* works for the violin,[30] only his five-movement *Symphonie espagnole*[31] has claimed a firm place in the repertory. Displaying rhythms, orchestral colours and melodies that are part gypsy, part Moorish and wholly Spanish in suggestion while culminating in a vigorous, sparkling rondo finale, it is a virtuoso work of considerable demands. Saint-Saëns's first two violin concertos (Opp. 20 and 58) are technically demanding and of unconventional design – No. 1 is a single-movement work; the slow movement of No. 2 is linked with the finale – but the less adventurous No. 3 (Op. 61) has proved the most popular. Doubtless this is because of its richer musical content, its original scoring and its one oddity, the strange chorale contrasted with the gypsy-like main theme in the finale.

Although it initially had a rough ride from critics and performers alike, Tchaikovsky's Violin Concerto in D major, Op. 35 (1878) completely dwarfs those of his compatriots, of whom only Anton Rubinstein (1857), Arensky (the single-movement Op. 54, 1891) and Jules Conus (1896) are worthy of mention.[32] Intensely lyrical in style, it follows Mendelssohn's Op. 64 in some crucial formal aspects: these include the structure of the opening movement, the long written-out cadenza immediately preceding the reprise and the interlinking of slow movement and finale. Although the technical demands of the opening movement and the brilliant, trepak-like rondo finale are extremely challenging, virtuosity is subordinated to the musical design. The central ternary 'Canzonetta' is a second thought, Tchaikovsky publishing the original Andante as 'Méditation', in the set of three pieces entitled *Trois Souvenirs d'un lieu cher* Op. 42.

The Slavonic origins of Dvořák's Violin Concerto in A minor Op. 53 (1879–80, rev. 1882) are displayed by the first main theme of its rhapsodic, formally irregular opening movement. Of symphonic conception, the movement leaves no room for a cadenza. The melancholy ternary Adagio is interlinked with the first movement, while the lively sonata-rondo finale incorporates melodic ideas of folk derivation. Originally intended for Joachim, the work was eventually premiered by František Ondříček in Prague in October 1883.

In Britain only the violin concertos of Sir Alexander Mackenzie (1885), Coleridge-Taylor (Op. 80) and his mentor Stanford (two concertos) are worthy of passing mention, while George Enescu's Violin Concerto (1896) represents the chief Romanian interest.

Virtuosi

Musicologists are still unable to match their tally of authenticated concertos by Paganini – six are currently known to have survived – with the eight works that he (and one of his biographers, Conestabile) claimed that he had written. None of these works was published during his lifetime[33] and access to the orchestral parts was strictly controlled. The influence of the late-eighteenth-century French violin concerto is particularly evident in Paganini's opening movements, the Allegro maestoso of No. 2 and the Allegro marziale of No. 3 furnishing typical examples of Paganini's indebtedness to Viotti. Broad, intensely lyrical phrases alternate with bravura passages to form the chief hallmarks of Paganini's style in the outer movements; the central slow movements are of more simple, aria-like construction, the melodic flow occasionally being interrupted by short solo cadenzas. The finales generally incorporate popular melody. The rondos of Nos. 3 and 6, including a polonaise as their main theme and the finale of No. 2, 'La campanella', provide ample opportunity for virtuoso display.

Most notable among the violinists who imitated Paganini's approach to the violin concerto were de Bériot, Vieuxtemps, Ernst, Bull, Lipiński, and Wieniawski. De Bériot's First Violin Concerto (1827), of moderate technical demand, owes much to late-eighteenth-century French models; the second (1835) is in stark contrast, immediately betraying the influence of Paganini's virtuoso techniques. The remaining eight concertos are somewhat more restrained in their technical requirements, favouring a compromise of lyricism and melodiousness intermingled with bravura playing, rather than virtuosity for its own sake.

De Bériot's most celebrated pupil, Vieuxtemps, composed seven concertos for the instrument, all of which appeared after he had met Paganini in London in 1834. His Concerto in F♯ minor (1836), published as No. 2, combines Viottian formal principles with the enriched technical vocabulary of the early nineteenth century, setting the solo part within a full symphonic framework and subordinating technical considerations to musical ends. Nos. 1 in E (1840) and 3 in A minor (1844) continue very much in the same vein, but the four-movement Fourth Concerto in D minor (1849–50), completed in Russia with his return to Paris in mind, has been described as 'a magnificent symphony with a principal violin'.[34] Following a declamatory, impassioned introduction (with substantial cadenza) comes a rhapsodic Adagio religioso. A brilliant scherzo with brief pastoral-like trio is succeeded by an energetic, march-like finale of virtuosic demand. By contrast, the Fifth Concerto (1861), originally written as a competition piece for the Brussels Conservatoire, is in one continuous movement with a cadenza near the end. The remaining two concertos (Opp. 47 and 49), published posthumously (Paris, 1883), sustain the technical demands of the others but display no further structural experiments of note.

Lipiński's main contribution to the genre (*Concerto militaire* Op. 21 No. 2) is outshone by his compatriot Wieniawski's two concertos. Apart from the central Larghetto ('Preghiera'), Wieniawski's First Concerto in F♯ minor (1853) is a rather empty technical display piece; but the combination of rich melodic invention, nationalist inflection and extrovert bravura in No. 2 in D minor (1862), dedicated to Sarasate, has ensured for it a permanent place in the repertory. The loose structure of the first movement accommodates increasingly exuberant virtuoso passages for the soloist, concluding with a clarinet solo which acts as a bridge to the Romance, a virtually unbroken violin melody of great beauty and intensity. A brilliant cadenza heralds the ebullient gypsy-style finale.

Of Ernst's two *concertante* works, Farga claims that the Concertino in D (1839) is on 'a somewhat higher level, full of ardour and lyrical atmosphere'[35] than the *Concerto pathétique* in F♯ minor (1844), but the latter, dedicated to Ferdinand David, is undoubtedly the more genuinely inspired work. Closely resembling the concertos of Paganini in its technical demands[36] this large-scale one-movement work particularly impressed Joachim, who described Ernst as the greatest violinist-musician of his generation.

The twentieth century

The early twentieth century witnessed a consolidation of late-nineteenth-century concerto traditions, many of the more radical composers eschewing a medium with such conventional associations. Interest in the genre increased towards the middle of the century only to wane again more recently, owing partly to the lack of top-flight violinists who are willing to champion new music.

Scandinavia

Most significant of the Scandinavian contributions were the concertos of Sibelius (1903, rev. 1905), Nielsen (1911) and Lars-Erik Larsson (1952). The orchestral tuttis of Sibelius's Violin Concerto in D minor Op. 47 bear the main burden of development and are largely independent of the soloist's material; but the rhapsodic opening movement, with its unusual tonal relationships and its substitution of a cadenza (which dovetails into the reprise) for the formal development, represents a reappraisal of the traditional form. The Adagio, a lyrical ternary Romance, has a central section of sterner stuff. The finale is somewhat rondoish, its rhythmic drive, Zigeuner-like virtuosity and imaginative orchestration ensuring interest and a sense of momentum to the end. Nielsen's concerto is of unusual shape: two extensive slow introductions (Praeludium with cadenza; chromatic Intermezzo) are followed by a sonata-form Allegro, with a further cadenza, then a rondo with two contrasting episodes and a third cadenza.

Russia

Most early-twentieth-century Russian music was broadly national in spirit, but Glazunov's affinity with Western European idioms was as strong as his own native allegiances; his Concerto No. 2 (1904), a continuous work in two main divisions, with individual sections separated by solo cadenzas, demonstrates this. J. S. Bach was arguably the strongest influence on Stravinsky's neo-Classical Concerto (1931).[37] Stravinsky himself drew parallels between his finale and Bach's Concerto for two violins, especially 'the duet of the soloist with a violin from the orchestra'. Aria II, a lyrical ternary-form cantilena for solo violin and (mainly) string accompaniment, is also of Bachian stock. Thematic material is interchanged freely between soloist and orchestra, as illustrated particularly by the opening subject of the Toccata (introduced by four chords which appear in varied guise at the beginning of each movement) and the ternary Aria I. Considering the orchestral forces employed, the orchestration is surprisingly light, and the atmosphere is closer to chamber music than to the nineteenth-century 'symphonic' concerto.

Prokofiev's two violin concertos were composed or part-composed during his self-imposed exile in France. In the impressionistic No. 1 (1923), Prokofiev's motor rhythms feature briefly in the opening 'sonata' movement but play a more extensive role in the central Scherzo. The first movement's initial dreamy melody is recalled in the rhapsodic finale, firmly pulling the work into a well-proportioned circular structure. No. 2 in G minor (1935), more modestly scored than the first, was originally conceived as a concert sonata for violin and orchestra; this explains the orchestra's subsidiary role, anticipated by the soloist's presentation of the first theme unaccompanied. The ternary Andante assai incorporates two original and capricious touches towards its close: a pizzicato solo for the violin and a concluding duet for clarinet and double bass. The witty, grotesque rondo finale is of true Russian character.

By contrast, Kabalevsky's idiom originates in the same tradition as that of Russian popular song, as exemplified in the second movement of his Concerto in C (1948); and Khachaturian's Violin Concerto (1940) features Armenian folk material supported by stirring rhythms reminiscent of Gershwin. Shostakovich's two concertos represent distinct phases in his development. No. 1 in A minor (1947–8) is a complex four-movement structure of which the opening Moderato (Nocturne) is of truly symphonic cast; the energetic Scherzo includes an allusion to the composer's Tenth Symphony, and the intense third movement, a passacaglia with a solo cadenza at its climax, is the focal point. The lively rondo-like finale ('Burlesca') follows without a break, incorporating a reminiscence of the passacaglia. No. 2 in C♯ minor (1967) is a more intimate, lucid, three-movement design, with a prominent part for solo horn. The dark opening Moderato adopts a concise quasi-sonata form, while the slow movement incorporates much relaxed solo violin writing high in the register. A cadenza follows, structural in implication and incorporating previous ideas, before the rondo finale provides a riotous conclusion.

More recently, the concertos of Kara Karayev (1967) and Alfred Schnittke (1957, rev. 1962; 1966; 1982) have attracted attention; Schnittke's works juxtapose elements of atonality and diatonicism and recall somewhat the idiom of Berg.

Germany

The Romantic tradition lived on in Germany in the dominant figures of Richard Strauss, Pfitzner and Reger. Reger's large-scale symphonic

Violin Concerto in A (1907–8) is tonally, texturally and harmonically somewhat simpler than his norm, while Pfitzner's turbulent Concerto (1923) is remarkable both for its intensity of expression and for its slow movement, which omits the soloist altogether.

Hindemith revived the concerto grosso spirit in his set of seven *Kammermusiken*, using ensembles inspired by Bach's Brandenburg Concertos. The fourth *Kammermusik* Op. 36 No. 3 (1925) is a violin concerto with an opening movement in ritornello form. The Violin Concerto (1939) also looks back, this time on the symphonic concerto of the previous century. It adopts a traditional three-movement design, its lyrical central movement being framed by a fully developed 'sonata' movement and a lively finale, complete with extended cadenza. The violin concertos of Blacher (1948) and Fortner are similarly retrospective in style and content, while those of Weill and Henze are more experimental. Weill's Violin Concerto Op. 12 (1924) uses a wind ensemble in place of a full orchestra. Henze's First Violin Concerto (1947) heralds a move towards serialism, while No. 2 (1971) stands on the borders between concert music and music-theatre. It calls for bass-baritone soloist and pre-recorded tape in addition to violin soloist and thirty-three instrumentalists, and includes a setting of a propagandist poem by Hans Magnus Enzensberger.

Austria

Very much in the German Romantic concerto tradition, Schoenberg's Violin Concerto Op. 36 (1935–6) extracts remarkable lyricism from its foundations in serialism and poses severe technical challenges for the soloist. It opens with an expansive sonata movement (with a waltz-like central development section), succeeded in turn by a reflective Andante. The march-like finale incorporates a long, partly accompanied cadenza, which includes recollections of the previous two movements.

The Violin Concerto (1935) of Schoenberg's pupil, Berg, was written as a memorial for Manon Gropius, who had died of polio at the age of eighteen – it was dedicated 'to the memory of an angel'. Berg revealed that the concerto's four movements (it is in two parts, each differentiated by a pause and divided into two distinct sections) were designed as a biographical portrait – birth, teenage delight in dancing, the catastrophe of illness, death. The opening Andante, with its clear subdivisions into introduction, principal subject, subordinate subject, concluding subject and codetta, is followed by a scherzo-like movement with two trios of which the first is a waltz and the second a Carinthian ländler tune. An Allegro in the free style of a cadenza leads to a concluding Adagio based on the chorale *Es ist genug* (in Bach's own harmonisation) whose opening pitches form the first four notes of the twelve-note series on which this work is based.

France

Of 'Les Six', only Milhaud contributed to the violin concerto repertory. Of his four violin concertos, the first (1927) is remarkable for the brevity of its three-movement whole, its severe technical demands (especially in the finale's cadenza), cheerful atmosphere, monothematic central Romance, and polytonal 'Prélude'. No. 2 (1946) opens in more serious vein, passages of dramatic recitative flanking an uneasy 'animé' principal section. Not even in the lively finale, which follows the intense, sombre slow movement, are the feelings of unease lifted for good. Nos. 3 (1958) and 4 are rarely performed, but Milhaud's *Concertino de printemps* (vn, ch orch, 1934) and his three further concertinos named after the other seasons of the year (that for summer is for violin accompanied by nine instruments, mostly wind) have achieved some popularity. Other French violin concertos of note are Dutilleux's *L'Arbre des songes* (1980–5), Sauguet's *Concerto d'Orphée* (1953), and the works of Françaix (1970 and 1978–9), Jolivet (1972) and Martinon (1937 and 1960).

Italy

Italy is represented chiefly by the 'neo-Classical' works of Casella (1928), Respighi (*Concerto gregoriano*, 1921),[38] Pizzetti (1944), Zandonai (*Concerto romantico*, 1919), Rieti (1928 and 1969) and Bucchi (*Concerto lirico*, 1958). From c.1940, composers such as Riccardo Nielsen (1932), Peragallo (1954) and Malipiero (1952) turned with varying strictness to twelve-note technique; so, too, did the younger generation of Maderna (1969), Donatoni (*Divertimento*, vn, ch orch, 1954) and Clementi (1977).

The Americas

American composers cultivated a mixture of styles at the beginning of the century, ranging from French, through Austro-German dodecaphony and neo-Classicism to home-cultivated jazz and negro spirituals. The Russian-born Louis Gruenberg turned to jazz, folk and negro spirituals for his individual expression (Op. 47, 1944), while Roy Harris (1950) also exploited American idioms. Walter Piston (No. 1, 1939) favoured a neo-Classical approach, while Roger Sessions's four-movement Concerto (1935), remarkable for its exclusion of violins from the orchestral forces and the duet for soloist and basset horn (alternating with clarinet) at the beginning of the 'Romanza' (third movement), illustrates his moving towards a more chromatic and expressionistic style. Leaning towards dodecaphony was Berg's pupil Ross Lee Finney (1933, rev. 1952; 1973), whereas Menotti's (1952) and Barber's (Op. 14, 1939–40) concertos are largely lyrical and neo-Romantic – only the angular, dissonant and virtuosic Toccata finale of Barber's work does not fit such a description.

'Foreign' influences in the USA included Bloch (1938), Korngold (1945) and Krenek. Bloch described his Violin Concerto as 'pure' music, but the Jewish characteristics of his style[39] are never far from the surface of this quasi-cyclic work. Typically, Korngold's Concerto incorporates a theme from one of his finest film scores, *Juarez* (1939), and concludes with a virtuosic finale. Krenek left two concertos (1924 and 1954), the first in one continuous movement.

More recently American interest in the progress of the violin concerto has been preserved by Ben Weber (1954), Benjamin Lees (1958), Piston (No. 2, 1960), Rochberg (1974–5) and the conservative Eastman group, notably William Bergsma (1966) and Peter Mennin (1950). David Diamond (1936, 1947 and 1967) left the Eastman School after a year to seek more progressive instruction with Sessions and Boulanger. More experimental still have been Charles Wuorinen (amp vn, orch, 1972), Lou Harrison (vn, perc, 1959), Philip Glass (1987) and Gunther Schuller (1975–6), the last-named finding much inspiration in jazz.

The musical renaissance in Latin America brought to the fore several composers, many of whom were nationalistic in intent. Notable violin concerto composers include the Chilean Pedro Allende (1940), the Brazilians Oscar Fernández (1941), Camargo Guarnieri (1940 and 1953), Francisco Mignone (1961) and Radames Gnattali (1947 and 1962), the Colombian Guillermo Uribe-Holguin (Opp. 64 and 79) and the Argentinians Juan José Castro (1962), Jacobo Ficher (1942) and Alberto Ginastera (1963). Ginastera's virtuosic concerto requires six percussionists and a whole range of percussion instruments; its finale incorporates quotations from Paganini's *Caprices* Op. 1. In Mexico, the nationalistic approaches of Carlos Chávez (1948–50 and 1965), Manuel Ponce (1943) and Rodolfo Halffter (1940) have contrasted markedly with the microtonal experiments of Julián Carrillo (1963 and 1964).

Hungary

German Romanticism gripped many early-twentieth-century Hungarian composers, notably Dohnányi (1914–15 and 1949–50) and Weiner (1950 and 1957),[40] with only occasional use of folk melody. Bartók's Second Violin Concerto (1937–8), on the other hand, is symmetrically constructed around two large-scale sonata-form movements that make extensive use of variational procedures. It has as its focal point a set of six variations on a theme which incorporates the melodic and rhythmical inflexions of Magyar folk-music. The turbulent, final Allegro molto provides stark contrast with the ethereal conclusion of the Andante tranquillo. It is itself often regarded as a complex variation of the opening movement, but Bartók has skilfully manipulated its material so that it takes on a very different overall shape and character. No. 1 (1907–8)[41] adopts the two-movement (slow–fast) structure of a rhapsody and is also essentially in Romantic vein – richly chromatic, passionate, and full of lyricism and bravura. While the opening movement alternates sections of contrapuntal character with others of lyrical conception and rhapsodic treatment, the economical second movement is more savage, softened by sections of pure romanticism.

Poland

The first (1916) of Szymanowski's two violin concertos, ambiguous in tonality and complex in texture and structure, is in one continuous movement, subdivided into sections of contrasting character. Inspired by the poem *May Night* by Tadeusz Micinski, it has a marked Oriental flavour and gives the impression of an improvisation. The second (1932) is more nationalistic, incorporating Polish folk materials into its concise one-movement structure, which is clearly divisible into four sections. Other major Polish contributors to the repertory include Andrzej Panufnik (1971),[42] Grażyna Bacewicz (1937, 1946, 1948, 1951, 1954, 1957 and 1965) and Krzysztof Penderecki (1976).

Great Britain

Elgar's Concerto in B minor (1910) is in the vanguard of twentieth-century British concertos. It is especially remarkable for its thematic unity, notably the ternary Andante's naturally developed reference to the first subject of the opening movement and the reference to the Andante in the finale; and the uncontrived brilliance and unexpected formal development of this finale itself, which incorporates an accompanied cadenza and rounds off the whole work by recalling themes from the first movement. The wealth of contrasting materials in Delius's lyrical Concerto (1916), comprising three main sections played without a break, are unified by a fanfare-like motif which appears in various keys at different points throughout. Similarly, in Walton's unashamedly Romantic, symphonic Concerto (1939), the opening idea of the finale harks back to the theme of the trio; a third, broader melody is related to the concerto's opening theme, bringing unity to the whole work.[43] Unity is provided in Benjamin Britten's Concerto (1939, rev. 1950) by a motto-rhythm (timpani), which pervades the opening movement. A solo cadenza bridges the central scherzo and finale (a skilfully orchestrated passacaglia) and recalls the motto-rhythm and other principal first-movement material.

The violin concertos of Hamilton Harty (1908–9), Vaughan Williams (1925), Arnold Bax (1937–8), E. J. Moeran (1937), Roberto Gerhard (1942–3), Alan Rawsthorne (1947–8 and 1956), Iain Hamilton (1952 and

1971), Sir Arthur Bliss (1955), Lennox Berkeley (1961), Alexander Goehr (1962), Hugh Wood (1971), David Blake (1975), Richard Rodney Bennett (1975) and Peter Maxwell Davies (1985) are also worthy of passing mention, although they have never been in the forefront of the repertory.

Other countries

Other countries making notable contributions to the literature include Spain (Rodrigo: *Concierto de estio*, 1943), Switzerland (Frank Martin: 1951), the Netherlands (Henk Badings: 1928, 1933, 1944 and 1946), Greece (Skalkottas: 1937–8) and Czechoslovakia (Martinů: 1933 and 1943; and Hába: 1954–5). Martinů's concertos are in lyrical vein and comprise three movements, incorporating folk idioms in their central movements of pastoral character. Prominent Australian composers in the genre have included Arthur Benjamin (1932), Don Banks (1968) and Malcolm Williamson (1965), while Saburo Moroi (1939), Michio Mamiya (1959) and Akira Miyoshi (1965) have done much to broaden the repertory in Japan.

10 The sonata

ROBIN STOWELL

Introduction

The violin sonata took two avenues of development in the Baroque era. The seventeenth-century form, for violin and continuo, involved the violin as principal melodist. Harmonic support in the form of semi-improvised chords or the realisation of a prescribed figured bass was provided by a keyboard instrument (normally an organ or harpsichord), which could be joined or replaced by a plucked instrument (chitarrone or archlute); in addition, the bass line could be sustained, normally by a string instrument such as a cello or gamba. The sonata emerged first in Northern Italy, spreading to Austria and Germany, and later to England and France. The principal centres of sonata activity were Venice, Bologna, Vienna, Dresden, Hamburg, London and Paris, the very centres where patronage and publication were most easily attained. As the genre evolved during the seventeenth century, two different types emerged: the *sonata da camera* ('chamber sonata'), which is essentially a suite of stylised dances; and the *sonata da chiesa* ('church sonata'), the movements of which have no dance allegiances.[1]

The sonata's second avenue of development, the so-called 'accompanied sonata', involved the violinist in a subordinate role to an obbligato keyboard. This type, which challenged the dominance of the sonata with continuo and eventually superseded it, began and ended in the Classical period, giving way to the true duo sonata for two equal protagonists.

The Baroque

Italy

The earliest known sonatas for violin and bass (unfigured) appeared in Cima's *Concerti ecclesiastici* (Milan, 1610), a collection mostly of sacred works which includes six small-scale sonatas.[2] More important were Marini's adventurous essays in the genre[3] and works by Giovanni Gabrieli[4] and Monteverdi[5] which heralded the emergence of a true violin idiom. Castello published the first ever volume devoted exclusively to sonatas.[6] He added a second book (1629), his twenty-nine technically challenging essays alternating fast and slow sections, canzona-style, within one continuous movement. Fontana left six sonatas for violin (and bc) in a set of eighteen sonatas[7] of similar sectional design, some incorporating recitative-like transitional passages and complex rhythmic patterns derived from vocal declamation. More experimental were the sonatas of Uccellini[8] and Farina.[9] Particularly remarkable are Uccellini's *Tromba sordina per sonare con violino solo* Op. 5, which involves *scordatura*, and Farina's four-part *Capriccio stravagante* (1627), which incorporates such effects as *col legno*, *sul ponticello*, pizzicato and *tremolo* in its attempt to imitate the noises of various animals and musical instruments.

Among those who developed the violin's expressive qualities during the second half of the seventeenth century were Legrenzi,[10] Cazzati and G. B. Vitali. Cazzati was the first Bolognese composer to publish solo violin sonatas. His Op. 55 collection (1670) of *Sonate a 2 istromenti*, following closely after his *Varii, e diversi capricci* Op. 50 (1669) for various combinations, proved extremely influential and assisted in extending further the idiomatic language of the violin. Vitali, his most celebrated pupil, composed numerous trio and ensemble sonatas (Opp. 2, 5, 8, 9, 11, 12 and 14), but only two sonatas for violin and continuo,[11] while Vitali's son Tomaso Antonio composed a set of *[12] Concerto di sonate* Op. 4 (vn, vc, bc, Modena, 1701), chamber sonatas of which the last comprises variations on the 'folia' theme. Pietro degli Antonii, another notable Cazzati disciple, included stylised dances in his Opp. 1 (1670) and 3 (1671). Although these are significant in the evolution of the *sonata da camera*, his sonatas Opp. 4 and 5 (vn, bc, 1676 and 1686) in the church style – organ is specified as the continuo keyboard instrument – are more progressive, their four or five movements incorporating vocal inflections and instrumental recitatives or ariosos into their violin writing. Furthermore, the continuo line assumes greater importance, often developing thematic material on an equal level with the violin part.

Corelli represents an early peak in the development of the solo sonata. His twelve sonatas Op. 5 (Rome, 1700) became by far the most influential of their time, appearing in some forty-two different editions by the end of the century.[12] Arranged in two sets of six sonatas, Nos. 1–6 inclusive ostensibly adopt the slow–fast–slow–fast scheme of the *sonata da chiesa* while Nos. 7–12 represent theoretically the *da camera* kind, the twelfth comprising the famous 'Follia' variations. However, the differences between the two sets are not as clear-cut in practice. Indeed, the distinction between the church and chamber varieties gradually disappeared. Although nominally *da camera*, the two sets of twelve sonatas (Opp. 1, c.1708, and 4, 1716) for violin and cello of Evaristo Dall' Abaco, for example, comprise a mix of abstract and dance movements, mostly in the Corellian four-movement pattern. During this period, the twelve sonatas (vn, bc, 1701) of Lonati are progressive, betraying certain German characteristics in their exploitation of high position-work, double stopping and *scordatura*, while the popular instrumental works of Valentini are particularly adventurous from technical, harmonic and tonal standpoints, especially his *12 Allettamenti per camera* Op. 8 (vn, bc, 1714).

In Venice, Albinoni and Vivaldi were foremost in the development of the genre. Albinoni's output includes seventy-nine sonatas for between one and six instruments and continuo, written in church, chamber or mixed styles. Most significant here are his *12 Trattenimenti armonici per camera* Op. 6 (Amsterdam, 1711), the only set of sonatas for violin and continuo that the composer himself prepared for the press. These works display the post-Corellian mix of church and chamber varieties, adopting the four-movement sequence of the church sonata and the binary fast movements derived from the dance of the chamber type. Although three other collections of Albinoni's violin sonatas appeared during his lifetime, 'there is evidence in each case that the publisher obtained manuscripts of the sonatas at second hand'.[13]

Vivaldi's sonatas for violin and continuo are mostly in a composite church–chamber mould in which the chamber elements are predominant, although dance forms may be re-ordered. His Op. 2 collection (Amsterdam, 1712–13) is the most significant, Vivaldi acknowledging the influence of Corelli's Op. 5 by modelling the opening of Op. 2 No. 2 on that of the first of Corelli's set. Of Vivaldi's other works in the genre, his Op. 5 collection (Amsterdam, c.1716), comprising four sonatas (vn, bc) and two trio sonatas, is most significant. The vn–bc sonatas begin with a prelude and continue with two or three dance-titled movements.

As a pupil of Corelli (and possibly also Vivaldi) and teacher of Pugnani (mentor of Viotti) and some of the leading French violinist-composers of the century (Leclair, Guillemain, Guignon, etc.), Somis was a central figure in the development of the violin repertory. Only his solo and trio sonatas were published during his lifetime, among them sixty works (vn, bc) published in five sets each of twelve (c.1717; Op. 2, 1723; Op. 4, 1726; Op. 6, 1733; c.1740). The character of the chamber variety predominates, but with few dance titles, and most adopt a three-movement slow–fast–fast pattern.[14] With the reduction in the number of movements, greater emphasis appears to have been placed on the first fast movement in the scheme. Somis expanded it into a 'three-section form – a statement, a digression and an abbreviated reprise in the principal key, comparable to an incipient sonata form in the Classical sense'.[15]

The sonatas of Veracini betray a number of separate influences. These range from his Italian heritage to German models, as displayed in the elaborate contrapuntal textures of his set of twelve, Op. 1 (vn, bc, Dresden, 1721), comprising six minor-key chamber sonatas and six major-key church sonatas. A previous set of twelve (1716) is of more Italianate character, involving little counterpoint and much repetition. His most celebrated collection, the twelve so-called *Sonate accademiche* Op. 2 (1744), written probably for Italian private concerts (*accademie*) rather than being especially 'academic',[16] represents a compromise between his Italian sonata and operatic (aria) influence and an increasingly elaborate contrapuntal technique in the German manner. Some movements are given curious titles (e.g. 'Aria Schiavonna', 'Cotillion', 'Schozeze', 'Polonese') and Veracini implies in his preface that a certain flexibility is allowable in performance. He suggests that two or three movements might be selected from the four or five provided 'to comprise a sonata of just proportions'. The preface also includes a table of notation signs, by means of which Veracini specifies such interpretative details as sonority, texture, dynamics and even bowing.

Porpora's twelve sonatas (vn, bc, Vienna, 1754) were some of the latest to uphold the Baroque tradition. By contrast, some of Locatelli's later works in the genre, like those of Tartini, embrace characteristics of the *galant* style. All but one of the twelve *Sonate da camera* Op. 6 (Amsterdam, 1737) adopt an original design: a fast, contrapuntal movement in binary form being flanked by a binary slow/moderate movement and a set of variations, commonly on a minuet theme. The exception is the twelfth, a five-movement piece which culminates in a 'Capriccio, prova del intonatione'. Of Locatelli's ten sonatas Op. 8 (Amsterdam, 1744), four are trio sonatas.

Great Britain

The actual seeds of sonata growth in Britain were sown by such violinist-composers as Matteis[17] and Playford[18] and germinated by the pre-eminence of the Italian style,[19] hastened by the remarkable influx of Italian violinists in the early eighteenth century. Among those who spent much of their working lives in London were Corelli's pupils Castrucci (two sets of twelve sonatas, vn, bc), Carbonelli (*Sonate da camera*, c.1722) and, most important, Geminiani, who arrived in London in 1714 and was responsible for two collections of twelve sonatas (vn, bc; Op. 1, 1716; Op. 4, 1739) as well as numerous arrangements of his own and others' works in the genre.[20] Not surprisingly, Corelli provides the model for these works,[21] which adopt the familiar four-movement pattern. But Geminiani's Opp. 1 and 4 are more adventurous harmonically, melodically, technically, rhythmically and dramatically, and he often inserted cadenza-like passages (either written out over a continuo pedal, or merely implied by a fermata) in which the violinist might further assert his technique and musicianship.

Richard Jones is notable for two collections (vn, bc): *Chamber Air's . . . The Preludes being written (chiefly) in the Grace Manner* Op. 2 (London, c.1736) and *Six Suites of Lessons* Op. 3 (London, c.1741). These comprise full-scale, Italianate sonatas of both *da chiesa* and *da camera* types (eight in Op. 2 and six in Op. 3) in an unusually advanced technical idiom for their time and origin. His (and later Geminiani's) pupil Michael Festing also left more than thirty sonatas (vn, bc) in five collections (1730–c.1750). Most comprise four movements (slow–fast–slow–fast) and follow Geminiani's model in incorporating some elaborate ornamentation, especially in their graceful slow movements. John Stanley's two collections of *Solo's* (fl or vn, bc) Opp. 1 and 4 (London, 1740 and 1745) are also sonatas in all but name.

The Berlin-born Pepusch's sonatas are of two types: a traditional four-movement kind and one with contrasts of tempo (particularly in the first movement), a more variable overall design and titled dances, which are often subjected to variations. But the principal German influence in England was Handel, whose sonatas (vn, bc) have a complex history. Chrysander, editor of the Händel-Gesellschaft (1879), grouped together some fifteen sonatas as Handel's Op. 1, but the authenticity of many of these works has been refuted by numerous Handelians.[22] Roger of Amsterdam published twelve sonatas as Handel's Op. 1 (c.1722) in an edition highly inaccurate as regards key, instrumentation and other details, and Walsh reprinted the set with a false imprint (1730). Walsh produced a corrected edition in 1732, but the two sonatas included as Nos. 10 and 12 in Roger's and Walsh's second publication are different and neither pair is now thought to have been composed by Handel. Furthermore, three completely authentic sonatas have not, until very recently, been recognised as such, and Handelians nowadays only claim five sonatas (vn, bc), all but one in four movements, to be unquestionably by Handel: that in A major (Op. 1 No. 3, 1724–6); the D minor violin version of the E minor sonata for recorder (Op. 1 No. 1, c.1720–4); the sonata in G minor (Op. 1 No. 6, c.1720–4) described as 'oboe solo' but prescribed for violin solo in the autograph in the Fitzwilliam Museum, Cambridge (where it succeeds the D minor arrangement in the same source); the lively, three-movement G major sonata (c.1707) and the late D major sonata (Chrysander's Op. 1 No. 13, c.1750).

Germany

Early developments in the German violin repertory owed much to the efforts of immigrants from Italy (Marini from 1623; Carlo Farina, 1625), and England (Thomas Simpson, 1610; Rowe, 1614; and Brade, c.1600), who founded the Hamburg school. Brade's student Nicolaus Bleyer's set of ostinato variations on *Est-ce Mars* (c.1650) was one of the earliest German pieces for violin and continuo, while Johann Kindermann's set of *[27] Canzoni, [9] sonatae* (1653) included pieces for one to three violins, cello and continuo and exploited *scordatura* as an expressive resource. Johann Rosenmüller proved a significant figure in the dissemination of Italian styles throughout Northern Germany, particularly in his last two collections for various instrumental combinations of strings.[23] Many of Buxtehude's solo and ensemble sonatas are reminiscent of Rosenmüller's 1682 collection in the harmonic intensity of their slow, transitional homophonic sections. Buxtehude's close associate Johann Reincken's *Hortus musicus* (Hamburg, 1687) is also significant for its six sonatas (2vn, va da gamba, bc) which demonstrate characteristics of both solo sonata and suite.

Schmelzer's *Sonatae unarum fidium* ... (Nuremberg, 1664) was the first published collection devoted entirely to sonatas (vn, bc) from the German-speaking countries. A synthesis of Italian and German elements, these six sonatas are founded largely on the variation principle (notably ground bass variations) and comprise numerous sections in contrasting metres and tempos with some challenging passage-work for the violinist.

Biber was the outstanding German violin virtuoso of the seventeenth century. His eight *Sonatae violino solo* (vn, bc, Nuremberg, 1681) combine the variation principle (chaconne basses, variants of arias, or doubles of dances) with freer, more improvisatory passages such as those in the toccata-like preludes and brilliant, elaborate finales. He by far outstripped his Italian (and German) contemporaries with his technical demands (up to seventh position, double stopping, varied bowings, *scordatura* etc. *Scordatura* plays a more prominent role in Biber's sixteen 'Mystery' (or 'Rosary') Sonatas (c.1675), which depict the fifteen 'Sacred Mysteries' of Jesus and the Virgin Mary. Only two of these pieces employ the conventional violin tuning by fifths, each of the others using a different tuning and thereby offering a wide range of unusual chord combinations and sonorities. Though conceived as church music,[24] these sonatas include several stylised dance movements (gavotte, gigue, courante and sarabande) counterbalanced by movements in contrapuntal style. Some of the sonatas show programmatic tendencies[25] but musical considerations predominate. The sixteenth piece is the famous *Passacaglia* for violin solo.

Next to Biber, Johann Walther was the most adventurous and virtuosic of contemporary violinist-composers in the German-speaking countries. Most of his twelve *Scherzi* ... (vn, bc, Frankfurt and Leipzig, 1676) are in free form, with sudden changes of tempo and metre. Eight bear the title 'sonata', while two others (Nos. 5 and 12) are labelled 'aria'. Dance movements and variation sets predominate in his other published collection, *Hortulus chelicus* (Mainz, 1688), and a programmatic element occasionally provides additional interest.[26]

Johann von Westhoff also used programmatic devices in his sonatas,[27] which are of advanced technical demand. Although individual movements are repetitious and the sonatas fail to conform to any set movement plan, unity and interest are often provided by a less conventional adaptation of the variation principle, one movement sometimes comprising a variant of its predecessor.[28]

By composing a set of six sonatas for violin with obbligato keyboard[29] J. S. Bach triggered off the gradual demise of the sonata for violin and continuo, even though that genre was perpetuated well into the eighteenth century by such German composers as Kirchoff, Birkenstock, Heinichen and Pisendel. The first five of Bach's set (BWV 1014–18) adopt the regular four-movement design of the *sonata da chiesa*, the fast movements being largely fugue-like or at least highly imitative. The sixth (BWV 1019) has a complex history. Two earlier versions are at variance with that firmly established as the final form.[30] The version normally performed nowadays comprises five movements, only the first two of which remain from the earlier two versions. The overall three-part texture of these sonatas is largely akin to that of the trio sonata, the violinist and the harpsichordist's right hand taking the two upper parts and the harpsichordist's left hand contributing the bass line. However, a few brief sections remain where the harpsichordist is required to realise the figured harmonies.[31]

Bach also composed some works for violin and continuo. The G major sonata (BWV 1021), discovered in 1928, follows the *da chiesa* pattern, while the four-movement E minor sonata (BWV 1023) combines elements of the 'church sonata' and Baroque suite. The authenticity of the *da chiesa* C minor sonata (BWV 1024) is open to doubt,[32] while the F major sonata (BWV 1022) is basically an arrangement of an arrangement. Its bass line is essentially that of the G major sonata (BWV 1021), but the two upper parts derive from the G major trio sonata (BWV 1038), a reworking of BWV 1021 probably by one of Bach's pupils.

Despite the esteem in which J. S. Bach is held nowadays, Telemann was widely regarded as Germany's leading composer in the early and mid eighteenth century. Much of his instrumental music promoted the cause of music-making in the home, notably his two collections of six (vn, bc) sonatas each (Frankfurt, 1715 and 1718). More important still are his *Essercizii musici overo dodeci soli e dodeci trii* (Hamburg, 1739–40), *Solos* Op. 2 (London, c.1725), *XII Solos* (vn or fl, bc, Hamburg, 1734), and *Sonate metodiche* Op. 13 (vn or fl, bc), issued in two sets of six (Hamburg, 1728 and 1732). The 'methodical' or instructive intent of this latter collection is provided in the suggested written-out melodic elaborations of the opening movements of each sonata. Other sonatas (vn, bc) by Telemann may be found in such collections as *Der getreue Music-Meister* (Hamburg, 1728–9) and *Musique de table* (Hamburg, 1733).

Pisendel's synthesis of German and Italian traditions was taken to

Berlin by his pupils J. G. Graun and Franz Benda. Graun published a set of six sonatas (vn, bc, Merseburg, c.1726). Benda, a pupil also of Graun, claimed in his autobiography (1763) to have written eighty violin sonatas, most of them composed before 1751. Apart from a set of Six Sonatas Op. 1 (vn, bc, Paris, 1763), few of his works were published during his lifetime.

France

The violin's potential as a solo instrument remained virtually untapped in France during the seventeenth century, largely because the string orchestra was the focus of attention, especially for its role in dance music. By 1609 there were already 'Vingt-deux Violons Ordinaires de la Chambre du Roi', and in 1626 Louis XIII established the band of the Vingt-quatre Violons du Roi, some thirty years before Lully's rival ensemble, the Petits Violons (1656).

Italian instrumental music appears to have gained popularity in French musical circles during the 1690s,[33] and Corelli's music was certainly known after 1700. Significant in the development of the 'solo' sonata at this time were François Duval and Jean-Féry Rebel, both prominent members of Louis XIV's Vingt-quatre Violons du Roi. Duval was the first Frenchman to compose sonatas for violin and continuo, publishing some seven collections (1704–20)[34] which blend French dance elements with more advanced Italian instrumental techniques. The five sonatas (vn, bc) at the end of Rebel's *Recueil de douze sonates à II et III parties*,[35] are also among the earliest French examples, along with those of Elisabeth Jacquet de La Guerre and Brossard. Further sonata collections by Rebel were published in Paris in 1705[36] and 1713.[37]

The influx of Italian violinists into Paris in the early eighteenth century furthered the cause of Italian music in the French capital, which became even more attractive to foreign virtuosi with the establishment of the Concert Spirituel in 1725. Prominent among the immigrant Italians were Mascitti, Piani,[38] and Guignon.[39] Mascitti published nine collections of sonatas (vn, bc, mostly of the *da camera* variety) between 1704 and 1738 which comprise about one hundred works in the genre. Guignon published eighteen sonatas (twelve in Op. 1, 1737, six in Op. 6, after 1742), mostly in the three-movement form of the Italian opera sinfonia, while Piani's collection of twelve sonatas Op. 1 (six for vn, bc, six for vn or fl, bc), is notable both for the composer's preface, which includes detailed interpretative information, and the unusually thorough markings annotated in the works themselves.

The synthesis of French and Italian styles was also hastened by the exodus of French violinists such as Senaillé, Anet and Tremais to study in Italy. Senaillé composed at least fifty sonatas (vn, bc), published in five books between 1710 and 1727, while Tremais's sonatas (vn, bc), mostly in four movements, were published in four sets (Op. 1, 1736; Op. 4, c.1740; Op. 7, c.1740; Op. 10, c.1740), two of which (Opp. 7 and 10) have not survived. Corelli's pupil Anet's *Premier Livre de sonates* (Paris, 1724) was strongly influenced by his mentor, while the ten *Sonates* Op. 3 (Paris, 1729) pander more to French taste.

Louis and François Francœur are worthy of passing mention for their two sets each of sonatas but more significant in the development of the genre were Guillemain, Mondonville and Leclair. Guillemain composed four books of sonatas. The first three (Opp. 1, 3 and 11, 1734, 1739 and 1742) are for violin and continuo. The sonatas of Op. 1 adopt a conservative four-movement design, but some of the later works approximate the early classic sonata, with first-movement plans that include thematic contrast, formal development and recapitulation. His fourth set[40] comprises early examples of the accompanied keyboard sonata with an optional violin part.

Mondonville's Op. 1 set of sonatas (vn, bc, Paris, 1733) breaks no new ground, but his Op. 4, *Les Sons harmoniques* (Paris and Lille, 1738), is notable for its exploitation of violin harmonic effects. However, he is best known for his *Pièces de clavecin en sonates, avec accompagnement de violon* Op. 3 (Paris and Lille, 1734), in which the harpsichord predominates with its written-out part and the violinist is relegated to a secondary role.

The works of Leclair represent the culmination of the French Baroque violin school and the final reconciliation of the Italian and French styles. His forty-nine sonatas (vn, bc, although some are intended for either violin or flute), published in four books of twelve each (Paris, 1723, c.1728, 1734 and 1743) plus the posthumous F major sonata (1767), mostly follow the Corellian model (slow–fast–slow–fast), using Italian names for the movements and adding variety by including movements like the vivacious *tambourin* and *chasse*, and the old majestic *tombeau* (e.g. Op. 5 No. 6). The fast movements tend towards Italian and the slow movements towards French inspiration, and his works hold plenty of technical challenges for the violinist.

The Classical period

The Classical period was one of remarkable transition in the genre from the violin sonata with keyboard continuo to one with keyboard obbligato. But the idea of equality between violin and keyboard, suggested by J. S. Bach's sonatas, was not taken up by his immediate successors. Some composers sat very much on the fence, using the keyboard alternately as an accompanying continuo instrument and as a combination of melody instrument and supporting bass,[41] while others contributed to the decline of the violin's importance (and hence to the dominance of the keyboard) by cultivating the so-called 'accompanied' sonata.[42] Nevertheless, the demand for sonata composition, considerable in the first half of the eighteenth century, seems to have increased even more when the keyboard part was written out; and although flexibility of instrumentation persisted at the start of the period, composers later began to assign their works in the genre to a specific melody and keyboard instrument, the preferred keyboard instrument increasingly becoming the piano.

Italy

Numerous distinguished Italian composers of sonatas followed in the footsteps of Tartini, among them Campioni,[43] Ferrari, Lolli, and Tartini's most renowned pupil, Nardini. Their works display a growing awareness of the harmonic structure and ordered design of the evolving Classical style, Nardini's second-movement Allegros approximating the scheme of Classical sonata form. Furthermore, those of Ferrari and Lolli (especially Lolli's Op. 9 set) were technically demanding, requiring mastery of, for example, harmonics, *scordatura*, *sul* G playing, daring leaps and cadenza-like interpolations.

Another vital link in the continuous tradition from Corelli to Viotti was the latter's principal mentor, Gaetano Pugnani, whose sonatas (Opp. 3, 7 and 8, c.1760–74) adopt a fast–slow–fast design with the opening Allegro movements close to Classical sonata form. Viotti's sonatas are largely retrospective 'continuo' sonatas, showing an understandable preference for the violin. But Pugnani's progressive tendencies were explored further by Sammartini and especially Boccherini, who contributed a dozen or so accompanied keyboard sonatas in fast–slow–fast format with fully elaborated keyboard parts.

It is sometimes difficult to distinguish between the styles of Mozart and the Bohemian Mysliveček, who spent much of his life in Italy. Certainly, Mysliveček's six accompanied sonatas (London, 1775) display a striking resemblance to Mozart's early style; in the words of Schoenbaum: 'In Mysliveček's compositional art, Czech musicality merges with Italian influences to form an individual style, whose formal balance and harmonic variety paved the way for the Viennese Classical masters.'[44]

France

The numerous pupils of Gaviniès made their mark in Paris around the third quarter of the century, writing idiomatically for the instrument in a harmonically inventive, highly expressive style which has been called a 'French Storm and Stress'. Notable among them for their sonata compositions are Leduc, Guénin and Capron. Although Guénin bowed to the trend towards the keyboard sonata with *ad libitum* violin accompaniment, he did not make the violin totally subservient to the keyboard, occasionally using the term 'solo' to indicate sections of prominent violin writing. Saint-Georges, too, seems to have taken pains to treat violin and keyboard as equal protagonists in his three extant sonatas. L'Abbé Robineau's *Six Sonates* (Paris, 1768) also contribute to the importance of the Parisian school, whose influence on the development of the young Mozart should never be underestimated. Neither should that of a German, Johann Schobert, who settled in France and published many of his works in Paris. Schobert was one of the chief promoters of the type of sonata that was essentially a keyboard work with a simple (sometimes optional) violin part, which did little more than shadow the keyboard's melodic material in thirds or sixths or help to fill out the accompaniment.

Germany and Austria (to Mozart)

Along with his compatriot Schobert, J. C. Bach cultivated largely the 'accompanied' sonata type in which the violin plays a purely complementary role. His *Six Sonatas for Harpsichord with Accompaniment of Violin (or Flute) and Cello* Op. 2 (1764) are short two-movement works, the first movement adopting a rudimentary sonata-form design and the other comprising an Allegretto or Tempo di menuetto in da capo or rondo form. As in his Op. 10 set (1773), the violin is subservient to the keyboard. C. P. E. Bach also composed some sonatas of this type with relatively easy keyboard parts (Wq89–91, published 1776–7), but he is better known for his earlier four-movement sonatas for violin (or flute) and keyboard, which display his Baroque heritage.

Although mostly violinists, the Mannheim composers wrote little of note for solo violin. Johann Stamitz and Richter were the most prominent composers of violin sonatas. Stamitz's two collections of violin sonatas (Opp. 4 and 6, 1760–1) are somewhat conservative works with continuo, but Richter's strike a balance between the continuo and accompanied sonata types.[45]

Wagenseil left two sets of accompanied sonatas for keyboard with violin, published in London, while Haydn's oeuvre includes only one original violin sonata – No. 1 in G, also published as a trio (HXV:32). Five other works were arranged from keyboard sonatas – some of these arrangements are attributed to Dr Burney – and two further 'sonatas' are violin–keyboard arrangements of the string quartets Op. 77 Nos. 1 and 2.

Great Britain

Britain played host to many immigrant musicians of high esteem in the late eighteenth century and she provided the fertile soil on which many a progressive musical seed was sown. Among the many important sonata composers who lived for periods in London were Pugnani, J. C. Bach, and Abel, the latter composing well over one hundred sonatas of which many are of the accompanied type.

The principal sonata contributions from native Britons were largely retrospective, following the Italian basso continuo tradition. Most notable were John Collett's *Six Solos ...* Op. 1 (1755) and the Italian-trained James Lates's Op. 3 collection (1768).

Mozart, Hummel and Beethoven

Mozart brought the genre to its first peak in the Classical period. He wrote examples of sonatas for violin and keyboard throughout his creative life, his twenty-six works[46] in the genre developing from the cheerful Alberti piano basses and modest (optional) violin contributions of his childhood (K6–9, 10–15[47] and 26–31, 1763–6, in which his father probably had a hand), through the sonatas of early maturity written in Mannheim and Paris in 1778 (K296, 301/293a, 302/293b, 303/293c, 304/300c, 305/293d and 306) to the fully mature sonatas composed in Salzburg and Vienna in 1779–87 (K376/374d, 377/374e, 378/317d, 379/373a, 380/374f, 454, 481, 526 and 547) which feature the violinist as a full *concertante* duo partner.

The early works display the influence of Schobert, J. C. Bach and others in their complete subordination of the violin. Most comprise two movements and are lightweight pieces written in a language typical of the Rococo period – simple, melodic, diatonic and homophonic with foursquare phrasing. K26–31, published as Op. 4 (1766), display some progressive tendencies, notably imitative entries (K26 and 29) and greater part equality (K28), although the keyboard resumes its dominant role in K30 and 31.

In the next authenticated sonata set,[48] published in Paris (1778) confusingly as Op. 1, the violin begins to free itself from its exclusive accompanying role to introduce melodic material (e.g. in the first movement of K301 in G). Other developments include the use of a slow introduction in K303, the exploitation of a language, palette and mood anticipatory of early Romanticism in K304 in E minor,[49] and the addition of a written-out cadenza in the finale of K306 in D. Mozart's second set of six mature sonatas was published in 1781, shortly after he had moved to Vienna. Its title[50] suggests that the violin part was still optional, but although K379 and K376 would tend to support this suggestion, other sonatas such as K377 allow the violin an increasingly melodic role.

Mozart's experiments with form in the 1780s resulted in his preference for a three-movement design and his increased cultivation of polyphony, the two protagonists achieving almost equal status and being treated in more of a bravura manner. This is evident in the three sonatas which represent his major contribution to the genre: K454 in Bb, K481 in Eb and K526 in A.[51] K454 (1784), inspired by the playing of Regina

Strinasacchi, is a true concert sonata for violin and piano, introducing the spacious sonata-form opening movement with a Largo passage of great breadth. The sonata-form Andante, with its interesting elaborated reprise, and the sonata-rondo finale maintain the large-scale dimensions of the opening movement. The first movement of K481 (1785) introduces the principal theme from the finale of the 'Jupiter' Symphony into its argument and continues to develop it in the coda. The central Adagio, a rondo with two episodes and varied repeats of the main theme, includes some unusual harmonic audacities in its midst, but the final Allegretto with variations restores stability. K526 (1787) is more subtly integrated, the witty Presto finale drawing 'together the first-movement melodic material . . . and the octave writing and harmonic shifts of the Andante'.[52]

The relatively few sonatas of Hummel stand between those of Mozart and Beethoven. Their fundamentally homophonic textures, ornate Italianate melodies and clarity of harmonic and structural design were still essentially Classical, but the increased harmonic imagination, expressive intent and virtuosic brilliance of his later works looked towards a new era, as may be understood by comparing his Op. 5 sonatas (Vienna, c.1798, two for pf, vn, one for pf, va) and his D major Sonata Op. 50 (pf, vn, Vienna, c.1815).

Beethoven's ten sonatas for piano and violin further develop the legacy of Mozart and his predecessors. Although Beethoven continually emphasised the equal partnership of the two protagonists, the title-page of his three sonatas Op. 12 (written 1797–8, published 1799) reads 'Tre sonate per il clavicembalo o forte-piano con un violino composte' and they undoubtedly display vestiges of the keyboard sonata with violin obbligato. His next two sonatas were originally published together as Op. 23, but they were subsequently (1802) issued separately as Opp. 23 and 24. Op. 23 displays greater conciseness of argument, includes a cross between a slow movement and a scherzo as its centrepiece and features a large-scale rondo finale. Op. 24 in F ('Spring')[53] expands to a four-movement design with the inclusion of a witty scherzo. The Op. 30 set of three sonatas (1802, published 1803) contrasts the optimistic character of Nos. 1 and 3, in three movements, with the passionate, four-movement C minor sonata (No. 2). This latter has a terse dramatic quality, marked in the two outer movements by an abundance of short, pithy phrases. An Adagio cantabile in A♭ comes second, while the trio of the lively C major scherzo makes bold use of canon. The sonata-rondo finale reaches its climax with a Presto coda. Op. 30 No. 3 in G major reverts to a 'tempo di minuetto' as its slow movement, and its *perpetuum mobile* rondo finale incorporates a switch to E♭ which will never cease to raise the eyebrows.

Beethoven described Op. 47 (1802–3) in pidgin Italian as 'Sonata per il Pianoforte ed un violino obligato, scritta in un stilo molto concertante quasi come d'un Concerto', such a description emphasising the concerto-like brilliance of the work. He dedicated it to Kreutzer, who, according to Berlioz, declared it 'outrageously unintelligible' and never played it. Unlike any of his other sonatas, Op. 47 opens with a slow introduction[54] to an extended sonata movement of astounding energy and momentum. The central movement is an Andante with four variations, while the finale, originally intended for Op. 30 No. 1, is almost monothematic and monorhythmic, driving forward relentlessly to the witty coda, which provides a brilliant and rousing climax to this monumental sonata in the concertante style.

In his last sonata, Op. 96 (1812), Beethoven reverts to a more intimate, less vigorous treatment of the instrumental partnership, especially in the opening Allegro moderato. Nevertheless, the subsequent Adagio displays Beethoven at his most expressive, while the scherzo finds him in jocular mood. The final theme and variations is untypical among Beethoven's finales in tempo, mood and form. Each half of the binary theme is led by the piano, and all but the first of the seven variations are double variations, the seventh concluding with a brief, brilliant coda.

The nineteenth century

The sonata played a secondary role to the concerto in the nineteenth century, owing to the era's emphasis on virtuosity and brilliance.

Germany

Apart from Spohr's three *Duos concertants* (vn, pf, Op. 95) and Mendelssohn's three sonatas (1820, 1825 and 1838),[55] there were few significant German contributions to the genre until Schumann's Op. 105 in A minor and Op. 121 in D minor (both 1851). The restless melancholy of Op. 105's sonata-form opening movement contrasts strikingly with the tender happiness of the central Allegretto, a charming F major rondo with two delicate minor-mode episodes. The sonata-form finale opens in toccata fashion with bustling chromatic semiquavers over a tonic pedal and recalls the first movement's opening melody in the coda. Op. 121 is more ambitious in scope, the main theme of the sonata-form opening movement being subtly adumbrated in the detached chords of the slow introduction. The second movement is a scherzo in all but name with two trios. On its final return, the 'scherzo' broadens into a chorale-like theme which foreshadows the beginning of the slow movement – a theme with three variations on the chorale melody *Gelobt seist du Jesu Christ*. The finale uses a rather rigid sonata structure to transform the grim, turbulent opening theme into one of greater optimism.

Schumann's last completed violin work before the collapse of his mental health was the Sonata No. 3 in A minor, born out of the idea that he, his pupil Dietrich, and Brahms should collaborate on a work in honour of Joachim to be based on Joachim's motto, F. A. E.[56] Schumann contributed the second and fourth movements, while Dietrich duly provided the opening movement and Brahms the scherzo. Schumann later composed two movements to replace those of his collaborators.

Brahms had written and discarded four works in the genre before his Sonata No. 1 in G Op. 78 (1878–9), inspired by two of his own songs (*Regenlied* and *Nachklang*, Op. 59 Nos. 3 and 4), was published. The opening violin theme begins with the three-note rhythm on a monotone which opens the vocal line of *Regenlied*, while the more animated second subject also shares in this rhythmic relationship. The three reiterated notes of the song also appear in the central section of the ternary Adagio, and they usher in the actual melody of the *Regenlied*, together with its original pattering accompaniment, in the final rondo. This finale also recalls the main theme from the slow movement, and its 'più moderato' coda provides a tender, nostalgic yet fragmented summary, in the major mode, of the movement's most significant thematic material.

Brahms's Sonata No. 2 in A Op. 100 (1886) is more concise and intimate, its central movement serving as both slow movement and scherzo. However, Op. 108 in D minor (1886–8) is more dramatic and broader in design, comprising four movements of symphonic proportions. Especially remarkable are the opening movement's unique development section (built on a pedal point and featuring *bariolage* bowing), the expansive violin cavatina of the major-mode Adagio, and the way in which the pianist takes centre-stage in the playful third movement (F♯ minor). The sonata-rondo finale provides a fitting climax with its vigorous rhythms, depth of harmony and the dramatic force of its modulations. Brahms also composed a Scherzo (1853) for the collaborative 'F. A. E. Sonata' and arranged his two clarinet/viola sonatas Op. 120 for violin and piano.

Other German works in the genre include Joachim Raff's five sonatas (Opp. 73, 78, 128, 129 and 145), Weber's six *Progressive Sonatas* Op. 106, Richard Strauss's E♭ major Sonata (1887–8), and Busoni's two sonatas in E minor (1890 and 1898). Busoni's second, a three-movements-in-one structure, has achieved the more lasting success, not least because of its memorable concluding variations on the chorale melody *Wie wohl ist mir, O Freund der Seelen*. Much of Strauss's sonata was conceived in orchestral terms. A fairly orthodox sonata-form movement is succeeded by a simple ternary central movement ('Improvisation'), which enjoyed a separate existence as a salon piece, and was published separately. Most elaborate of all, however, is the impassioned finale which opens with a brief and morose introduction for piano solo from which the main theme of the movement gradually crystallises. The work incorporates a number of quotations, notably from Beethoven's 'Pathétique' Sonata Op. 13, Wagner's *Tristan* and Schubert's *Erlkönig*;

furthermore, the opening movement's second subject shows affinities with one of the leading themes of Strauss's own *Don Juan*.

France and Belgium

French composers showed little interest in the genre until comparatively late in the nineteenth century.[57] Only Lalo (Op. 12, 1853)[58] and Alkan (*Grand Duo concertant* Op. 21, 1840) made significant contributions in the first three quarters of the century. Central to Lalo's work is a set of variations (with a double cadenza towards the end) which is framed by an undistinguished essay in sonata form and a brilliant *perpetuum mobile* rondo finale. Although unevenly proportioned, Alkan's work is redeemed by its exploration of technique and its sheer inventiveness. The central movement ('L'Enfer') features some vivid descriptive writing and numerous experiments in sonority, admirably confirming Alkan's sympathies with Faustian ideas.

Saint-Saëns is believed to have composed five violin sonatas, but he published only two. The sonata-form opening movement and the lyrical ternary Adagio of No. 1 in D minor Op. 75 (1885) are linked; so, too, are the final two movements, a jovial scherzo/trio and a brilliant finale in perpetual motion which recalls a theme from the first movement. The less demanding No. 2 in E♭ Op. 102 (1896) has been described as 'a colder, more abstract, more subtle and more polyphonic work'.[59]

Fauré's Sonata in A major Op. 13 (1875–6) incorporates subtle adjustments to the conventional equilibrium of sonata-form balance in its opening Allegro molto. A melancholy ternary Andante and brilliant scherzo, with its exciting weak-beat accents and contrasting 'trio' section, precede a finale pregnant with lyrical melody. No. 2 in E minor Op. 108 (1916–17) is of different style and expression. In three movements, it is texturally less opulent and musically more concise than its predecessor, employing effective cyclical treatment of its initial motive.

In Belgium, de Bériot's numerous *Duos brillants*, written in collaboration with such renowned pianists as Osborne and Thalberg, and Vieuxtemps's single Violin Sonata Op. 12 are relatively unmemorable. The origins of Franck's A major Violin Sonata (1886) owe much to Vieuxtemps's pupil Ysaÿe.[60] Like Franck's two other chamber works of consequence,[61] this sonata is of cyclic construction, its melodic framework comprising four main recurrent themes. The first, adumbrated by the piano in four introductory bars, is announced by the violin, while the second (piano), more exuberant, is soon given a *molto dolce* restatement to conclude the exposition of the sonata-form opening movement. The tempestuous sonata-form second movement uses the same two themes among its principal melodic material. The rhapsodical slow movement begins with an oblique declamatory statement of the first theme, before introducing the third and fourth themes. The sonata-rondo finale opens with a canon. Its episodes are based largely on cyclic theme 'curtain calls', the canonic idea returning at the end in an 'animato' coda (the canon at a half-bar's distance) for a brilliant conclusion.

Lekeu, a gifted pupil of Franck and d'Indy, is remembered chiefly for his Sonata in G (1891). In the standard three-movement design, it is remarkable for its skilful application of the cyclical principle and its adoption of the advanced chromatic language of Wagner.

Austria

Schubert's three sonatas Op. 137 Nos. 1–3 (D384–5 and 408, 1816) were published posthumously as 'Sonatinas'. Displaying vestiges of Mozartian influence, these are fully developed sonatas of compact construction, the first comprising three movements, but the other two adopting a four-movement structure (with a minuet third). Schubert's Duo in A Op. posth. 162 (D574, 1817), which was not published until 1851, does not show the varied experimentation of the sonatinas but is broader in scope and surer in touch.

The Czech lands

Apart from the respective contributions of Pixis (1874) and Fibich (1875), the Czech lands are represented only by Dvořák's Sonata Op. 57 (1880) and Sonatina Op. 100 (1893). The first and second movements of Op. 57 approximate more closely the early style, textures, piano sonorities and development techniques of Brahms, but the finale, a dance-like sonata-rondo, leaves us in no doubt as to its Czech origins. Dvořák's Sonatina, composed in New York as a musical gift for his children, blends the native music of the Americas with his Czech heritage. The mournful slow movement, said to have been inspired by a visit to the Minnehaha Falls,[62] and the sonata-form finale, which contrasts dance elements with a calm E major section reminiscent of the 'New World' Symphony's slow movement, are perhaps most illustrative of this blend.

Scandinavia

Grieg claimed that his three violin sonatas represented the main periods of his stylistic development – the first, Op. 8 (1865), naive and rich in models; the second, Op. 13 (1867), nationalistic in character; and the third, Op. 45 (1886–7), more dramatic and cosmopolitan in style. The greater intensity of national feeling in Op. 13 is due largely to the dance element, which infiltrates all three movements, while thematic similarities between the 'Springdans' finale and the opening movement help towards the work's unity. Op. 45 in C minor demonstrates a type of primitive sonata-form design for which Schumann was strongly criticised. It also employs many of the chief characteristics of Schumann's harmonic style, notably the device of a chromatically falling (or sometimes rising) bass, as well as his typical four-square phrase structure. These elements coupled with Grieg's extensive use of sequence, his melodic mannerisms, particularly the lyrical folk-melody of the ternary central 'Romanza' (in the remote key of E major), and his characteristic rhythms, add up to the type of cosmopolitan style claimed by the composer.

Christian Sinding, another Norwegian graduate from the Leipzig Conservatoire, composed four sonatas (Opp. 12, 27, 73 and 99) and the popular Suite Op. 10 (c.1890). His *Sonate im alten Stil* Op. 99 is actually more of a suite in five short movements, but the other works are broadly conceived three-movement designs which betray the strong influence of Wagner, Liszt and Strauss, intermingled with elements of Norwegian nationalism. Danish interest in the sonata was represented chiefly by Johann Hartmann (Opp. 8, 39 and 83) and his son-in-law Niels Gade (Opp. 6, 21 and 59).

Other countries

Italy's contribution to the genre was meagre, comprising chiefly Paganini's duos and numerous sonatas for violin and guitar and Bazzini's various essays, notably the *Gran duo concertante*, the Sonata in E minor Op. 55 and the three *Morceaux en forme de sonate* Op. 44. The most significant Hungarian composer-performer of the period, Franz Liszt, left only a Duo on Chopin's Mazurka Op. 6 No. 2 (c.1835), a Grand Duo Concertant on Lafont's 'Le marin' (c.1837) and an *Epithalamium* (1872) for the wedding of Reményi. However, Goldmark composed a sonata (Op. 25) of some merit. Russia is represented chiefly by the sonatas of Cui (Op. 84, c.1865), Nápravník (Op. 52, 1892), Ippolitov-Ivanov (Op. 8) and Anton Rubinstein (Opp. 13, 19 and 98), the latter's Op. 98 being remarkable for its boldness in commencing with quotations from its two predecessors. Few sonatas by native Britons have reached the forefront of the repertory, only the works of Ethel Smyth (Op. 7, 1887), Coleridge-Taylor (Op. 28), Stanford (Opp. 11, 39 and 70) and Parry (1878 and c.1888–9) deserving passing mention.

The twentieth century

Scandinavia

Nielsen's Opp. 9 and 35 represent arguably the most significant Scandinavian contribution to the genre around the beginning of the twentieth century. Op. 9 (1895) comprises three movements, its ternary central movement being framed by two fairly orthodox sonata-form designs.[63] The more lyrical, expansive Op. 35 (1912) is of similar overall structure, but the sonata-form divisions of its finale are more loosely applied, development taking place more or less immediately; furthermore, its tonality is open-ended, with several transient tonal centres rather than one clearly defined key. The principal Swedish sonata composers were Emil Sjögren (Opp. 19, 24, 32, 47 and 61), Wilhelm Stenhammar (Op. 19), and Hilding Rosenberg (1926 and 1940), while Finland is represented chiefly by Sibelius's modest *Sonatine* Op. 80 (1915).

Russia

Foremost among Russian contributions to the genre in the early twentieth century was Stravinsky's *Duo concertant* (1931–2), written in collaboration with Dushkin. Its opening 'Cantilène' has only two thematic tactics – a rapid, arhythmic piano tremolo and a sharply defined, rising and falling violin fanfare. The piano later takes over this fanfare material, extending it but never developing it. This format is repeated in the subsequent 'Eglogue', which features a quick dance reminiscent of *L'Histoire du soldat*. The second 'Eglogue' recalls the Arias of Stravinsky's Violin Concerto, while, during the Gigue, the violin and piano move in parallel and the violin's left-hand pizzicatos form a bridge to the percussive piano attacks. In the final 'Dithyrambe', both instruments again share similar material and register.

Among those Soviet sonata composers who had reached a degree of maturity by the 1917 Revolution were Gnesin (1928), Myaskovsky (1946–7), Metner (Opp. 21, 44 and 57) and Prokofiev. Prokofiev's two sonatas were composed after his return to the USSR from France, No. 1 in F minor, Op. 80 (1938–46) actually coming second in the chronology. The first of its four movements 'is severe in character and is a kind of extended introduction to the second movement, a sonata allegro, which is vigorous and turbulent, but has a broad second theme'.[64] A subdued, lyrical Andante precedes the wild finale with its irregular barrings and mysterious coda, which reverts to the tempo and material of the sonata's opening. No. 2 in D major Op. 94*bis* (1946) is an arrangement[65] of the flute sonata of 1942–4. All its movements are traditional structures. The opening sonata-form Moderato, with three clearly differentiated themes, is followed by a fast ternary waltz (Presto), characterised by cross-rhythms, with a gypsy-like middle section. The subsequent Andante commences in simple vein, but its melody soon blossoms into passionate ornamentations; the finale is a jaunty, 'wrong-note' sonata-rondo march with a second subject of Bachian character.

Among Prokofiev's Russian contemporaries and immediate successors in the genre were Rakov (1951), Shebalin (1957–8), Khachaturian (1932) and Shostakovich. Shostakovich's expansive, three-movement Op. 134

(1968) is stark and uneven. Although it is based on a twelve-note idea, the first movement is not a serial piece; but its frequent juxtaposition of non-tonal and tonal writing lends ambiguity to the musical vocabulary. The energetic scherzo is percussive in character, while the finale (Largo–Andante) incorporates 'a chaconne-like theme ... but eventually the movement turns into a stylistic medley with solo cadenzas'.[66]

More recently, the work of Slonimsky (1960) and Schnittke (1963 and 1968) has come to the fore. Slonimsky's five-movement sonata incorporates third- and quarter-tones as his response to the microtonal inflections of Russian peasant vocal style. 'A tonal world with atonal means' was Schnittke's description of his First Violin Sonata (1963), later adapted for chamber orchestra. Its four movements exploit the twelve-note system and include 'citations taken from popular music and also from the Second Piano Trio by Shostakovich'.

Germany

The Romantic tradition was continued in Germany by Richard Strauss, Hans Pfitzner (Op. 27) and especially Max Reger. Reger's admiration of Bach, Beethoven and Brahms is reflected in most of his seven violin sonatas (Opp. 1, 3, 41, 72, 84, 122 and 139), while the two attractive *Kleine Sonaten* Op. 103b Nos. 1 and 2 display his talents in more concise form. Both Reger's and Brahms's influence is evident in the rather 'forced' structures of Paul Hindemith's early sonatas Op. 11 Nos. 1 and 2 (1918). His later sonatas in E (1935) and C (1939) were written largely with talented amateurs in mind, the 1939 work posing the greater challenges in its three short movements, especially its fugal finale.

Although the intellectual atmosphere in Germany was restricted by the Nazi regime in the 1930s and 1940s, composers such as Blacher (1941 and 1951), Fortner (1945) and Henze (1946) contributed to the genre, succeeded in turn by Klebe (1953) and Stockhausen (*Sonatine*, 1951).

France

France played a major part in the cultivation of chamber music in the early twentieth century, but much of it, like d'Indy's Sonata in C Op. 59 (1903–4), suffers from a somewhat stultifying intellectual approach. D'Indy's four-movement work, based on the cyclic principle of Franck, shows other parallels with his mentor's sonata, not least the 9/8 lilt of its opening movement; but it also displays more individual qualities, especially in the second movement, enhanced by a folk-like melody in 7/4 time, and the brilliant finale. D'Indy's dogmatic instruction is reflected in the long-windedness of Roussel's cyclical three-movement Sonata No. 1 Op. 11 (1907–8, rev. 1931). However, Op. 28 in A (1924), comprising a ternary Andante framed by an expansive sonata-form

movement and Presto finale, displays Roussel's mature chamber style at
its best.

The works of Koechlin, Milhaud (1911 and 1917), Poulenc (1943),
Tailleferre (1921) and Françaix (*Sonatine*, 1934) are worthy of passing
mention. But the two most significant French violin sonatas of the period
were those of Debussy and Ravel. Debussy's work (1916–17), the third to
appear of a projected set of six sonatas for various instruments,[67]
combines his impressionistic vocabulary with a rediscovered classicism
and some jazz influences in its three-movement design. The finale begins
with a reference to the melancholy opening of the first movement, before
an energetic violin improvisatory motif charts new waters.

Ravel's Violin Sonata (1923–7), actually his second essay in the
genre,[68] is also a relatively late work. It emphasises the differences in
character and technique between violin and piano and incorporates jazz
elements, especially in the central 'Blues'. This movement catches the
idiom of the blues melodically in the sad nostalgia of the flattened thirds
and sevenths, expressively in the carefully notated *glissandi* (in pizzicato towards the end) and rhythmically in the subtle syncopation; but
Ravel is never bound by the regularly recurring harmonic pattern and
strict form of the traditional blues, and the rough edges of his experiments are smoothed over by his innate lyricism. Bitonality is also
exploited here, albeit in crude form (the two instrumental parts are
notated with different key signatures), and thematic recall plays its part,
too. Much of the pianist's material in the finale is derived from the first
movement, the violin persisting with its *perpetuum mobile* figuration,
and the movement culminates very plainly in a restatement of the first
movement's principal theme.

The Americas

Charles Ives played a vital role in freeing American music from the
orthodox. He took pride in his New England heritage and followed the
experimental credo of his father. Besides two early violin sonatas, lost or
destroyed, each of Ives's four surviving works in the genre (1902–8,
1907–10, 1913–14 and 1914–16) concludes with a hymn-tune finale. In
fact, some nineteen hymns, popular tunes or dance melodies, from
'Turkey in the straw' to 'Jesus loves me', find their way into these
three-movement works, albeit with some 'alterations'. The first and third
are abstract sonatas, while the second is descriptive, incorporating
evocations of 'Autumn', a square dance ('In the Barn') and a nostalgic
view of the mounting intensity of a camp meeting ('The Revival'),
comprising variations on the old hymn tune *Nettleton*. Sonata No. 4,
entitled 'Children's Day at the Camp Meeting', is based entirely on hymn
tunes.

The naturalised American Ernest Bloch's two sonatas (1920; *Poème mystique,* 1924) make full use of a dissonant harmonic idiom. They combine elements of neo-Classicism with the more rhapsodic type of violin writing familiar from *Baal Shem.* Bloch himself described the First Sonata as a 'tormented work', while its successor is 'an expression of pure serenity' and of 'the calm conviction that all the multitudinous protean faiths of man are one'.[69] Other notable 'adopted' American composers of violin sonatas include Rathaus (Opp. 14 and 43), Korngold (Op. 6) and Krenek (1919 and 1944–5). Meanwhile, the American pupils of Nadia Boulanger were beginning to make their mark. One such was Aaron Copland, whose Violin Sonata (1942–3) uses folk idioms and much counterpoint in its three movements – a sonata-form Allegro with introduction, a modal ternary Lento and a scherzo and trio finale complete with reminiscences of previous material.[70] Other Boulanger disciples included Virgil Thomson (Sonata, 1930) and Roy Harris (1941, rev.1974), and the university-based Walter Piston (1939; Sonatina, vn, hpd, 1945) and Douglas Moore (1929). Among other sonata contributors who occupied chairs in American universities were Quincy Porter (1926 and 1929), Roger Sessions (1942) and Ross Lee Finney (three Sonatas; Duo, 1944), while Leon Kirchner (Duo, 1947; *Sonata concertante,* 1952), Benjamin Lees (1953) and Samuel Adler (three violin sonatas) are notable figures who have also been based in institutions of higher education.

Some Americans benefited from stints abroad, notably George Antheil (Sonatina, 1945; sonatas, 1923, 1923, 1924 and 1947–8), who was very much a part of the Parisian avant-garde in the 1920s. The dissonant Second Sonata contains much percussive violin writing, consistent with its inclusion of a part for tenor and bass drums.

The conservative group from the Eastman School of Music at the University of Rochester, pupils of Hanson or Rogers (Sonata, 1962), included Robert Palmer (1956), Robert Ward (1950) and Peter Mennin (1959). The contributions of David Diamond (1943–6), Henry Cowell (1945), Wallingford Riegger (Sonatina, 1947), Ben Weber (two sonatas), Charles Wuorinen (Duo, 1967) and Boulanger's pupil Elliott Carter (Duo, 1973–4) are more progressive. Carter's work contrasts the violin's sustaining qualities and enormous variety of timbre, articulation and expression against the piano's greater range of pitch and volume. The timbral contrast of common pitches is also exploited within the work's tightly-knit structure, which is given symmetry by the final recall of the expressive characteristics of the opening.

The musical renaissance in Latin America brought to the fore several composers, many of whom were nationalistic in intent. Notable sonata contributions have come from Guarnieri (six sonatas), Villa-Lobos (four sonatas), Uribe-Holguin (Opp. 7, 16, 25, 39 and 59), Castro (1914), Ficher (Opp. 15, 56 and 93), Chávez (Sonatina, 1924), Ponce (1933) and Moncayo (Sonatina, c.1936).

Czechoslovakia

Czech national elements were perpetuated in the genre by Novák (1891), Nedbal (Op. 9), and most significantly Janáček and Martinů. Janáček's four-movement Sonata in Ab minor (1914–22), technically his third work in the genre,[71] has motivic affinities with his opera *Kát'a Kabanová* (1919–21). Apart from its second movement ('Ballade'), composed separately at an earlier date, its material is skilfully integrated, most stemming from the germ announced in the opening violin solo 'improvisation'. Martinů fused national and cosmopolitan elements in his style, contributing five sonatas. The first (1930) is notable for its various cadenzas for the two protagonists. Hába's early Sonata Op. 1 (1914–15), founded on comparatively simple harmonic, structural and expressive lines, is atypical of his mature style.

Switzerland

Most Swiss composers of the period achieved a fusion of French and German influences, but Honegger's two sonatas (1916–18 and 1919) show a bias towards French idioms. No. 2 is in conventional fast–slow–fast design, but No. 1 commences with an Andante sostenuto, includes a Presto movement as its centre and concludes with a finale of mixed tempo (Adagio–Allegro assai–Adagio), in which the Allegro assai is a terse sonata-form structure.

German influence was paramount in the sonata contributions of Conrad Beck (Sonatina, 1928; 1946), Willy Burkhard (Sonatina Op. 45, 1936; Suite Op. 71 No. 2, 1944; Sonata Op. 78, 1946) and Othmar Schoeck (1908, 1909 and 1931) and it also dominated Frank Martin's early career. However, his Sonata Op. 1 (1913) betrays the influence of Franck. There followed a period of experimentation with modal harmony, folk music, Indian and Bulgarian rhythms and eventually (from the 1930s) twelve-note technique. Perhaps the most interesting movement of his Violin Sonata No. 2 (1932) is the central Chaconne.

Hungary

German Romanticism also permeates the sonatas of Hungarians Ernö Dohnányi (1912) and Leó Weiner (1911 and 1918), although some folk material was occasionally employed by both composers. Effects suggestive of cimbalom and gamelan feature in Bartók's Sonata No. 1 (1921),[72] but this is among his least folk-orientated works, except perhaps for the finale, whose driving dance rhythms and ostinatos have a characteristic Magyar *élan*. The percussive piano and the virtuosic, melodic violin parts seem to go their separate ways in this work, each protagonist flaunting his own material, figurations and even harmonies. But, ostensibly opposed, the roles of the two instruments are actually complementary.

Bartók's more compact and restrained Sonata No. 2 (1922) adopts a continuous, two-movement structure (Molto moderato and Allegretto), its opening movement unfolding in a stream of constantly changing sonorities and tempos, rather in the manner of a free improvisation. The second movement begins with extended pizzicato writing for the violin and includes several references to the melodic substance of its predecessor, each reappearance of the thematic material in this rondo-like structure being treated to ingenious variation. A 'vivacissimo' climax is followed first by a section for solo violin and then a loud statement of the work's opening material; the sonata concludes very much in the mood of the opening with the violin climbing into the heights and finally settling on a C major chord made all the more magical by much previous tonal ambiguity.

Great Britain

The structures of Elgar's Sonata in E minor (1918) are individual interpretations of Classical designs, the two outer movements adopting free sonata outlines. The first movement's argument is brief, but there is a lengthy recapitulation in which part of the development is repeated immediately prior to the coda. The finale includes a reminiscence (augmented) of the central melody from the ternary Romance, a lyrical and deeply meditative movement whose broad middle section builds to a passionate 'largamente' climax before the muted reprise.

Frank Bridge's only completed violin sonata (No. 2, 1932) is a large, dramatic piece in one movement. Its four-section sequence (sonata-allegro exposition; Andante; scherzo with two trios; and a recapitulation) relates to a conventional plan, with the material of the opening movement re-ordered, developed and intensified in the finale. The turbulent emotional climate is created by frequent changes of mood and pace and complex, dissonant harmony, but the whole is tightly constructed thanks to skilful use of motivic development.

John Ireland's style confirms how little early-twentieth-century English music was affected by the modernist trends which raged elsewhere. Ireland's music, though harmonically complex and even at times tonally ambiguous, is candidly rhapsodic and lyrical in mood, especially in the First Violin Sonata (1908–9), a three-movement piece with a central Romance. No. 2 (1915–17) is a very beautiful, melancholy work directly reflective of the years of its conception. Delius's three published violin sonatas (1905–15, 1924 and 1930) date from the years of his maturity. No. 2, in one continuous movement of varying tempi and moods, by far outstrips the prolix No. 1, but the Third Sonata, cast in three separate movements, is the most clearly and economically constructed.

Vaughan Williams's (1954) and E. J. Moeran's (1923) styles have been influenced most of all by the idioms of English folk music, whether directly through wholesale quotation of folk melodies, or indirectly in subtler matters of phrasing, rhythm and tonality. The three movements of Vaughan Williams's Sonata comprise a compressed sonata-form Fantasia in A (Aeolian) minor, a brilliant D minor scherzo, and a set of variations. A return to the material of the opening movement brings the close.

Bax's three lyrical violin sonatas are among his best chamber compositions. The three-movement First Sonata (1910) is a youthful work which underwent considerable revision (1915, 1920 and 1945), the original second and third movements being replaced by two new ones.[73] The Third Violin Sonata (1927) comprises only two movements, but the cyclic No. 2 (1915, rev. 1921) is in four continuous movements, its principal motto theme derived from Bax's own *November Woods*. Its character was certainly influenced by the war and probably by other more personal events.[74] The second movement, entitled 'The Grey Dancer in the Twilight'[75] is connected to the nocturnal Lento expressivo [*sic*] by an interlude which returns during the course of the finale. A fourth sonata in F (1928) was later arranged as the *Nonett* [*sic*] (1930).

Other significant British contributions to the genre include William Walton's two-movement Sonata (1949–50). Its first movement is an expansive sonata-form design in richly chromatic vein, while its successor, a variation movement (with a ubiquitous background ostinato), bows in the direction of serialism. Mátyás Seiber's Sonata (1960) is a true serial piece in three movements, the first two of which incorporate quasi-recitative sections,[76] while the bitonal aspects of Alan Rawsthorne's mature style are exemplified in his Sonata (1958), which focuses on the semitonal relationship D–E♭. The British contribution to the repertory also includes works by Herbert Howells (1918, 1918 and 1923), Edmund Rubbra (1925 and 1932), Lennox Berkeley (c.1934; Sonatina, 1942), Franz Reizenstein (1945), Robin Orr (Sonatina, 1946; 1956), Peter Racine Fricker (1950 and 1986–7), Arnold Cooke (No. 2 in A), Malcolm Arnold (1947 and 1953), Alun Hoddinott (Opp. 63, 73/1, 78/1 and 89) and William Mathias (1961 and 1990).

Other countries

Spain is represented chiefly by Rodrigo's nationalistic *Sonata pimpante* (1966), while Veretti (1952), Rieti (1967 and 1970), Pizzetti (1918–19), Castelnuovo-Tedesco (1929), Respighi (1916–17) and Malipiero (1956) have been amongst the most prominent Italians. Foremost among 'Young Poland' was Szymanowski, whose Romantic Sonata (1904) has close affinities with Franck's Violin Sonata.[77] Its structure, though, is relatively straightforward (apart from hints of a relationship between the sonata-form first and last movements), as is that of Grażyna Bacewicz's five violin sonatas, which are often described as neo-Baroque.

Greece's foremost contributor to the genre, Skalkottas, studied with Schoenberg (1927–c.1931), whose influence left its imprint on the Sonatina No. 2 (1929). But Skalkottas's compositional style was later to develop in isolation; as a result, Sonatinas Nos. 3 and 4 (both 1935) and the Sonata No. 2 (1940) adopt an atonal, yet non-serial style.

The three sonatas (1897, 1899 and 1926) of Romania's most versatile musician, George Enescu (Georges Enesco), provide the core of his violin output. The Second Sonata 'combines a Fauré-like sobriety with an almost excessively "cyclic" thematic structure and passages of considerable chromatic enterprise'.[78] However, the Third Sonata, composed 'dans le caractère populaire roumain', is undoubtedly the most individual. *Parlando-rubato* style abounds, and harmony, polyphony and instrumental colour all derive from folk sources, the violin part occasionally resorting to quarter-tones and music of gypsy flavouring. Enescu's contemporaries Filip Lazăr (1919), Mihail Andricu (1944), Sabin Drăgoi (1949) and Mihail Jora (1951) were also strongly influenced by folk idioms, while composers such as Paul Constantinescu (1933) and Gheorghe Dumitrescu (1939) adapted folk material more to contemporary international musical trends.

Finally, notable sonatas were composed by the Australians Margaret Sutherland (1925), Fritz Hart (Opp. 7, 42 and 142), Arthur Benjamin (Sonatina, 1925) and Don Banks (1953), while Kishio Hirao (1947) and Akira Miyoshi (1955) have flown the Japanese flag in the genre.

11 Other solo repertory

ROBIN STOWELL

In addition to the sonata and concerto, the violin repertory comprises four further principal areas: music for unaccompanied violin; variations; short genre pieces for violin with orchestra or keyboard; and transcriptions. The first examples of music for unaccompanied violin date from the late seventeenth century and the genre reached its first peak with the works of J. S. Bach. Interest in the medium then declined until it was revived in the current century by composers such as Reger, Hindemith, Bartók and Prokofiev. Among shorter genres, the variation form remained a favourite vehicle for performers from the early seventeenth century. It came to fuller flower towards the end of the eighteenth century with the popularity of the *air varié*, using a popular operatic aria or national folktune as its variation source, and became the favourite vehicle for bravura display exploited by virtuosi such as Paganini, de Bériot, Vieuxtemps, Ernst and others. The short genre piece, including romances, elegies, ballades and legends or national dances like polonaises, mazurkas or jotas, similarly found particular favour during the nineteenth century, and transcriptions of masterpieces of former times also became popular at about the same time.

Music for unaccompanied violin

Probably the earliest extended work for unaccompanied violin is Biber's *Passacaglia* (c.1675), comprising sixty-five variations on the descending tetrachord G–F–Eb–D, included as the last in the collection of sixteen 'Rosary' Sonatas. But there are also several shorter examples incorporated in John Playford's *The Division Violin* (1684)[1] and Nicola Matteis's four books of *Ayres of the Violin* (Books 1 and 2, 1676; 3 and 4, 1685). Johann Paul von Westhoff's Suite for violin 'sans basse' (1682),[2] the earliest work in this medium in more than one movement, and his six short, four-movement partitas (1696),[3] with their imaginative polyphony, are especially significant as precursors of J. S. Bach's unaccompanied sonatas and partitas. Numerous solo pieces of interest, variously described, were roughly contemporary with Bach's monumental contribution. These include Girolamo Laurenti's fantasia-like *Ricercari*,[4] a solo fantasia in C minor and a single movement in A minor by Nicola Matteis, a sonata by Francesco Montanari of which the fourth movement is a 'giga senza basso', and complete unaccompanied sonatas by Geminiani and Pisendel. Pisendel's work, heard by Bach in 1717, appears to have been especially influential. It comprises a rhapsodic Largo punctuated by chords, a binary-form Allegro and a final 'giga'.

J. S. Bach's three sonatas and three partitas (BWV 1001–6) represent the culmination of Baroque polyphonic writing for a stringed instrument. He wrote them down while in the service of Prince Leopold of Anhalt-Cöthen, and they survive in an autograph copy (dated 1720) with the title 'Sei solo. / a / Violino / senza / Basso / accompagnato. / Libro Primo'. However, they may well have been begun at Weimar, where Bach is known to have been more active as a violinist. Particularly remarkable are Bach's lavish use of multiple stopping to sustain a complete polyphonic texture and his exploitation of 'polyphonic melody', in which a single line is made to suggest a fuller texture by constantly shifting between implied voices. Such experiments in texture have caused these works to be misunderstood: Schumann and Mendelssohn, for example, each considered the sustained passages of unaccompanied melody somewhat stark and provided piano accompaniments to 'improve' the original solo texture.

Sonatas alternate with partitas in Bach's original order. Common to all three sonatas is the slow–fast–slow–fast movement-sequence of the *sonata da chiesa*. The first two movements are coupled together in the manner of an elaborate prelude, written out in improvisatory vein, and an extended fugue, the latter continually alternating between strict polyphony and single-line passagework. The fugue of the G minor sonata (BWV1001) seems to have held a special place in Bach's affections – he transcribed it for organ (BWV539) – but the massive fugue of No. 3 in C (BWV1003), based closely on a chorale melody,[5] is arguably his most resourceful in the genre. It comprises four separate sections of thematic entries, the second in stretto and the third with the theme in inverted form, and the movement culminates in a final statement of striking polyphonic density. The third movements release the tension and provide welcome tonal relief,[6] while the Allegro or Presto finales share the symmetrical plan of a typical binary suite movement.

The three partitas (entitled 'Partia' in the Ms) are of more varied and unorthodox design. Fundamentally they comprise studies of dances[7] bolstered up by more substantial, extended movements such as the opening Preludio of the E major partita (No. 3)[8] and the concluding Chaconne ('Ciaccona') of No. 2 in D minor. This latter is based upon variations (sixty-four in all) of a single open-ended four-bar phrase built around the descending tetrachord (the very phrase used by Biber in his

Passacaglia). Two sections in the minor enclose a central section in the major mode, and the movement displays almost every resource of Bach's and the violinist's art. After so many vicissitudes, it culminates in a grand restatement of the main thematic material – unadorned, but with new harmonies towards its close. The B minor partita (No. 1) is 'fattened up' by way of its scheme of four pairs of movements, the second of each pair being a simple variation (*double*) of the first main dance tune, and normally in a faster tempo.

Bach's celebrated contemporary Handel left only an Allegro in G major for unaccompanied violin, but Telemann composed twelve notable fantasias for the instrument 'senza basso' (1735). Music for solo violin appeared for the first time in Sweden and France, respectively with Johan Roman's six *Assaggi* (1739–40) and Louis-Gabriel Guillemain's *Amusement pour le violon seul* Op. 18 (1762). Among the Frenchmen who drew inspiration from Guillemain's lead were Isidore Bertheaume (*Sonate dans le style de Lolli*, 1786; [2] Sonatas Op. 4, 1786), Jean Baptiste Bédard (*Duo ... ou moyen agréable d'exercer la double corde*), Julien Mathieu (two sets of *Duos ... ou études pour la double corde*), and L'abbé le fils (*Suite de jolis airs ...*, incorporated in his *Principes ...*, 1761). The Italian contribution comprises Viotti's *Duetto per un violino*, Nardini's celebrated *Sonate énigmatique*[9] complete with *scordatura*, and Campagnoli's [6] Fugues Op. 10, [6] *Polonoises* Op. 13, [7] *Divertissements* Op. 18, [30] *Préludes ...*, Op. 12, and his *Recueil de 101 pièces faciles et progressives* Op. 20. The Czech Václav Pichl also composed [6] Fugues ... Op. 41. Apart from James Brooks's *Two Duetts for One Performer on the Violin* Op. 4, the remainder of the eighteenth-century repertory emanates from Germany, represented chiefly by Johann Stamitz's Two Divertimentos, F. W. Rust's Four Sonatas (1795)[10] and Reichardt's six *Sonate per il violino solo* (1778).

Early-nineteenth-century composers showed comparatively little interest in the possibilities for solo violin, preferring the greater expressive potential offered by the concerto, sonata and other forms. Apart from those études which found their way into the concert hall (e.g. Paganini's *Caprices* Op. 1, Vieuxtemps's [6] *Etudes de concert* Op. 16, Ernst's [6] *Mehrstimmige Studien* etc.), only Romberg's three *Etudes ou sonates* Op. 32 (1813), David's Suite in G minor, Jansa's *Sonate brillante* (1828), Ole Bull's Quartet for solo violin (1834) and the various compositions of Paganini (Introduction and Variations on 'Nel cor più non mi sento'; *Duo merveille*; Recitative and variations on 'Deh cari venite' and 'Di certi giovani'; and two further variation sets, *Tema patriotico* and *Tema variato*) are worthy of mention.

Towards the end of the century the medium was taken up again by such composers as Reger, who composed eleven three- or four-movement Sonatas (Op. 42, 1899; Op. 91, 1905) and numerous short works (Chaconne in G minor, *Praeludium* in E minor Op. posth.,

Preludes and Fugues Op. 117 Nos. 1–8 and Op. 131a Nos. 1–6) in a neo-Baroque style later imitated by Hindemith in his two solo sonatas Op. 31 (1924). Of their German successors the Spanish-born Philipp Jarnach contributed numerous works for unaccompanied violin (the sonatas Op. 8, Op. 13, Op. 31 Nos. 1 and 2 and Op. 58 No. 1; a six-movement partita 'Es steht ein Lind in jenem Tal' Op. 37 No. 1; and variations on 'Mozarts Wiegenlied' Op. 58 No. 2), his individual style being influenced by the type of neo-Classicism cultivated by Busoni. Henze's works for the medium date from his more mature years, the inspiration for his three-movement Solo Violin Sonata (1976) coming from Salvatore Accardo; the *Etude philharmonique* (1979) followed and was succeeded in turn by his *Serenade für Violine solo* (1986) written in celebration of Yehudi Menuhin's seventieth birthday. Henze's contemporary Giselher Klebe studied initially with von Wolfurt and Blacher, but his further studies with Rufer (from 1946) and his instruction in serialism were the most influential towards his stylistic development. This is demonstrated in his two solo sonatas, Opp. 8 (1950) and 20 (1955), the first of which, in two movements, was dedicated to Henze. Bernd Alois Zimmerman took the developments of Schoenberg as his point of departure for more individual creation in his three-movement Solo Sonata (1950), while a former collaborator with Stockhausen, Rolf Gehlhaar (*Naïre*, 1983), is among the members of the younger generation in Germany who have attracted international attention.

In Austria, Fritz Kreisler deserves brief mention for his Recitative and Scherzo Caprice Op. 6, composed in homage to Ysaÿe. Other notable Austrian contributors to the repertory included Josef Hauer (*7 Charakterstücke* Op. 56, 1928), who, quite independently from Schoenberg, systematised the 'law of the twelve notes' in his compositions; Hanns Jelinek (Sonata Op. 27, 1957), another serialist; the more conservative, eclectic, yet individual Gottfried von Einem (Sonata Op. 47, 1975); and H. K. Gruber, whose *Vier Stücke* Op. 11 (1963) were composed at a time when he was working with traditional serial techniques.

The works of Ysaÿe represent a further peak in the development of the genre, his imaginative and resourceful Variations on Paganini's Caprice No. 24 taking second place to his Six Sonatas Op. 27 (1924). Each sonata is dedicated to and written in a style appropriate to a celebrated violinist of his time, namely Joseph Szigeti, Jacques Thibaud, George Enescu, Fritz Kreisler, Mathieu Crickboom and Manuel Quiroga. Believed to have been inspired by Szigeti's playing of Bach's unaccompanied violin works, Ysaÿe's sonatas betray Bach's influence, not least in the complex polyphony and the tonality (G minor, the key of Bach's first unaccompanied sonata) of No. 1 and in the opening movement ('Obsession') of No. 2 in A minor, clearly inspired by the opening Preludio of Bach's E major partita. The other two movements of No. 2, 'Malinconia' and 'Danse des ombres', treat the old *Dies Irae* plainchant, the 'Danse' opening with some formidable quadruple stopping in pizzicato. Other notable features of the set include the ghostly tremolo *sul ponticello* coda of the Grave of No. 1; the rapid alternations of sixths and tenths in passage-work in the single-movement 'Ballade' (No. 3); the Sarabande of no. 4, in which different typefaces are used to indicate the voice leading and in which an inner melodic voice plays in left-hand pizzicato; the Presto finale in 5/4 metre of No. 4; the pictorial ideas and Paganiniesque effects in No. 5; and the dance characteristics and virtuosic demands of the single-movement No. 6.

Bartók's swansong for the instrument, his Sonata (1944), represents the culmination of the genre in the current century. Commissioned by Yehudi Menuhin, the work opens with a 'Tempo di ciacona' in sonata form, punctuated by a recurrent left-hand pizzicato figure. It continues with a somewhat free 'Fuga', the fugal subject being constantly modified during its unconventional course, while the ensuing ternary 'Melodia' is muted and illustrates Bartók's variation technique in its reprise. The mute remains in place for the beginning of the final Presto rondo, originally written in quarter-tones,[11] and is only removed for the contrasting, *parlando* Hungarian melody.

Prokofiev's Sonata in D Op. 115 (1947) is normally regarded as the principal twentieth-century Russian work in the medium. Intended primarily as a pedagogical work, its three movements are somewhat conservative in both technical and musical content while its language is conventionally diatonic. Other Russian contributors have included Stravinsky, who arranged *La Marseillaise* (1919) and his own *Elégie* (1944, originally for viola) for solo violin; Shebalin, whose Suite (1933) displays the influence of Russian folksong; Kabalevsky, whose one-movement *Sonata-monologue* (1975) has been included in the concert programmes of many of his compatriots; and Schnittke, whose *Canon pour deux violons* for violin and tape (violin) and *A Paganini* (1982) incorporate a variety of technical and interpretative challenges for the performer.

In France, Iannis Xenakis, of Greek parentage and Romanian birth, is worthy of inclusion here for two works written for Mica Salabert. *Mikka* (1972) is a gentle, lyrical piece to be played purely and evenly without vibrato, while *Mikka 'S'* (1976), partly written on two staves, ventures into the language of quarter tones. The late 1960s and early 1970s also proved to be an inspirational period for the medium in Italy, for it spawned Petrassi's *Elogio per un'ombra* (1971), Maderna's *Widmung* (1967) and *Pièce pour Ivry per violino* (1971), and the ninth in Berio's series of sequenzas for solo instruments (1975) – literally musical sequences by their structure – which comments on the relationship between the virtuoso and his instrument.

Hilding Rosenberg, arguably the central figure in twentieth-century Swedish music, fused the late Romantic tradition with more radical elements in his oeuvre, which includes three sonatas for solo violin (1921, rev. 1966; 1953; 1963; rev. 1967). The Norwegian contribution to the repertory comprises Sinding's Suite Op. 123 (1919) and Holmboe's challenging *Molto allegro scherzando* (1929) and Sonata (1953).

Most notable among the contributions to the medium by American immigrants were the two sonatas of Ernst Krenek (1900–87; No. 1, Op. 33, 1924–5; No. 2, Op. 115, 1948), Bloch's early *Fantasie* (1899), and his two three-movement suites (both 1958), both dedicated to Yehudi Menuhin. Bloch's pupil Roger Sessions was another significant influence on the development of American music through his composition, writings and teaching. His eventual adoption of serialism, albeit in a very individual manner, began with the four-movement solo violin Sonata (1953), dedicated to Robert Gross. Of the numerous American disciples of Nadia Boulanger, Virgil Thomson left a small legacy of violin compositions, among them *Portraits* (1928–40), eight short pieces for solo violin mostly written in France in 1928. Elliott Carter, a more progressive Boulanger pupil of a later generation, contributed his brief *Riconoscenza per Goffredo Petrassi* (1984), while Ross Lee Finney wrote his two-movement Fantasy (1958) at a time when his eclectic, international style was absorbing serial techniques. David Diamond's studies with Sessions and Boulanger are faithfully reflected in his three-movement Sonata (1959) for Isaac Stern.

One of the most progressive composers for the instrument has been John Cage, who has enjoyed a productive working relationship with the violinist Paul Zukofsky. Cage's *59½″ for Any Four-String Instrument* (1953) and *26′ 1.1499″ for a String Player* (1955) involve little conventional notation. The production of notes on each of the four strings, as well as other sounds (e.g. using the body of the instrument), is separately graphed, the intention being to indicate specific physical playing techniques rather than to annotate a performance in purely musical terms. Cage's earlier abstract of Erik Satie's *12 Petits Chorals* forms the basis of his *Chorals* (1978), which juxtaposes simple notes, unisons and 'beats', produced by playing conventional intervals microtonally 'wrong'. Microtonal inflections are also introduced in Cage's complex *Freeman Études I–XVI* (1977–80), which are very specifically annotated with interpretative information. For example, many bowings are prescribed in detail (notably the number of notes to be played in *ricochet*; and four kinds of *martellato*) and notes to be played *legato*, sometimes simulated, are connected with a beam. The two lines below the staff give both the 'measure', a constant length of time, and the appearance in time-space of the *ictus*. The performer should establish a time-length[12] for the 'measure' and then maintain that tempo from system to system and from étude to étude. Lou Harrison, a close associate of Cage during World War II, has contributed a more conventional three-movement solo Sonata (1962).

Among the numerous distinguished contributors to the medium who have been based in institutions of higher education are George Perle (two sonatas, 1959 and 1963), Vincent Persichetti (Sonata Op. 10, 1940), Leon Kirchner (*Piece*, 1985) and, more recently, Benjamin Lees (*Invenzione*, 1964–5), Samuel Adler (*Canto III*, 1975), Henri Lazarof (Lyric Suite) and George Rochberg. Rochberg's *Caprice Variations* (1970) for solo violin is a set of fifty-one variations on the theme of Paganini's twenty-fourth caprice, the variations preceding the announcement of the actual theme. More experimental have been Charles Wuorinen (*The Long and the Short*, 1969; *Variations*, 1973), Philip Glass (*Violin Solo Music from 'Einstein on the Beach'*, 1975) and Steve Reich. Reich's *Violin Phase* (1967) was inspired by the sounds produced by multiples of the same instrument, either 'live' or in a mixed 'live-recorded' context. The work is thus intended either for solo violin with a changing background of pre-recorded tape, or for a quartet of violinists. The background comprises the 'phasing'[13] of a simple repeated melodic pattern, which overlaps in a kind of 'phased canon' to produce 'still denser chords and patterns cross-hatched with slowly shifting interior lines. The soloist joins in this aural weaving to provide subtle reinforcement and connection, and is free after a while to abstract notes from the shifting background, to point out chance aural coincidences, or to propose other connections between overlapping phrases.'[14]

Noteworthy in Latin America have been the microtonal experiments of the Mexican Julián Carrillo, whose oeuvre includes six non-microtonal sonatas and numerous pieces with microtones for violin. Meanwhile, the Czech national school was being continued by Alois Hába, who paid particular attention to the use of microtones as melodic inflections in Moravian folk-songs, eventually evolving his system of quarter-tone and sixth-tone composition. This was intended to extend the possibilities of expression of the semitone system by furnishing it with more delicate sound nuances. His numerous pieces for violin, for example the *Fantasie im Vierteltonsystem* Op. 9a (1921), *Musik für Violine im Viertelton-system* Op. 9b (1922), *Suite für Violine Solo im Sechsteltonsystem* Op. 85a (1955) and the *Suite für Violine solo im Vierteltonsystem* Op. 93 (1962), admirably illustrate this initiative.

In Switzerland, Honegger's legacy includes a four-movement Sonata (1940), while the Dutchman Henk Badings composed three sonatas for the instrument (1940, 1951 and 1951). In Greece, one of Skalkottas's early works was a remarkable Sonata (1925), while the prolific Polish composer Grażyna Bacewicz left two sonatas and numerous caprices for solo violin, as well as several miscellaneous pieces, some with a pedagogical purpose. Peter Sculthorpe synthesised Australasian traditional styles with advanced Western techniques in order to create a national identity. Particularly notable is his series of pieces entitled *Irkanda*,[15] inaugurated by his solo violin piece *Irkanda I* (1955) and culminating in *Irkanda IV* (vn, str, perc, 1961). His other solo pieces *Australia Variations* (1954), Sonata (1954), and *Alone* (1976) and his numerous works for string quartet between them exploit the full gamut of technical resources – double and multiple stopping, natural and artificial harmonics, arco/pizzicato alternation, tapping the body of the instrument, etc. In Japan, composers such as Michio Mamiya (Sonata, 1970), Joji Yuasa (*My Blue Sky No. 3*, 1977), Ryohei Hirose (*Asura*, 1975), Kazuo Fukushima (*Uninterrupted Poem*, 1953), Makato Moroi (*Les Farces*, 1970), Yujiro Fukushima (Sonata, 1965), Mitsuaki Hayama (Sonata, 1964), Toshi Ichiyanagi (*Scenes III*, 1980), Yuji Takahashi (*Rosace I*, amp vn, 1967; *Sieben Rosen hat ein Strauss*, 1982) and Toshio Hosokowa (*Winter Bird*, 1978) have all played a part in broadening the solo violin repertory.

Notable among the recent generations of British composers who have been particularly attracted to writing for unaccompanied violin are Lennox Berkeley (Introduction and Allegro Op. 24, 1949; Theme and Variations Op. 33 No. 1, 1950), Elisabeth Lutyens (*Aptote*, 1948; Prelude Op. 133), Wellesz (sonatas Op. 36, 1923, and Op. 72, 1953, rev. 1959), Gerhard (Chaconne, 1959), Alan Bush (Three Raga Melodies Op. 58, 1961), Arnold Cooke (Sonata, 1976), Franz Reizenstein (Sonata Op. 46, 1968), Gordon Jacob (Sonatina, 1954), Benjamin Frankel (sonatas Op. 13, 1946, and Op. 39, 1962), David Blake (Fantasia, 1989), Richard Rodney Bennett (Four Improvisations, 1955; Sonata No. 2, 1964), Peter Dickinson (Fantasia, 1959), Cornelius Cardew (*The Worker's Song*, n.d.), John McCabe (*Maze Dances*, 1973), Edward Harper (*Solo*, 1971), Sebastian Forbes (Violin Fantasy No. 1, 1975, and No. 2, 1979), Robin Holloway (Sonata, 1982), Brian Ferneyhough (*Intermedio alla ciaccona*, 1986), Michael Finnissy (*All the Trees They Are so High*, 1977, and *Song 13*, 1971), Colin Matthews (Partita Op. 7, 1975), Giles Swayne (*Canto*, 1973), Paul Patterson (*Luslawice Variations*, 1984), Edward McGuire (*Rant*, 1977), Michael Berkeley (*Funerals and Fandangos*, 1983) and Dominic Muldowney (*One, from Arcady*, 1976).

Variations

Variation technique (whether as melodic variation, passacaglia, chaconne or in other genres) was in evidence in the violin repertory as far back as the early seventeenth century. Marini's variations on the *Romanesca* Op. 3 (1620) is a notable early landmark, followed by Biber's *Passacaglia* (c.1675), Corelli's 'Follia' variations Op. 5 No. 12 (1700), Bach's Chaconne (Partita No. 2, c.1720), Tartini's Fifty Variations on a Gavotte by Corelli (*L'arte del arco*) and a whole host of other pieces, some of dubious authenticity.[16]

Towards the end of the eighteenth century the *air varié* (commonly based on a popular operatic aria or a national folktune) became increasingly popular as a vehicle for bravura display. The French trio of Rode, Baillot and Kreutzer were significant among the numerous contributors to the medium, while Beethoven, for example, wrote [12] Variations on 'Se vuol ballare' from Mozart's *Le nozze di Figaro* (WoO40, 1792/3) and two sets of National Airs with Variations Opp. 105 and 107 (both c.1818). The nineteenth century witnessed the genre at the height of its popularity with notable contributions from composer-virtuosi such as de Bériot (twelve published *Airs variés*), Vieuxtemps (Variations on a Theme from Bellini's *Il pirata* Op. 6, *Souvenir d'Amérique [on Yankee Doodle]* Op. 17, etc.), Ernst (*Le Carnaval de Venise* Op. 18, *Airs hongrois variés* Op. 22 etc.), Wieniawski (*Souvenir de Moscou* Op. 6, *Thème original varié* Op. 15), Boehm (Variations on a Theme of Beethoven)[17] and Hubay (*Variations sur un thème hongrois* Op. 72), as well as Lipiński, Georg Hellmesberger, Pixis, Bull, Joachim and many others. Foremost among those who exploited the genre, however, was Paganini, who composed numerous sets of variations for violin and orchestra to display his own formidable technique. These range from works based on operatic themes (e.g. 'Le streghe', Variations on a Theme from Süssmayr's *Il noce di Benevento* Op. 8, Introduction and Variations on 'Non più mesta' from Rossini's *La cenerentola* Op. 12), to those founded on 'national' tunes ('God save the King' Op. 9, the Austrian national hymn[18]), and those built around dance forms or other popular melodies (*Polacca con variazioni*, Saint Patrick's Day,[19] etc.).

The term 'variation' has been interpreted in diverse ways by composers of the current century. While there has been no lack of works that exploit variation technique, the number of independent compositions for violin is comparatively few. Nathan Milstein's brilliant *Paganiniana* (1954), based on the final caprice of Paganini's Op. 1, and Szymanowski's Variations Op. 40 (1918) on three (Nos. 20, 21 and 24) of Paganini's *Caprices* Op. 1 are two of the few sets of the period modelled on the nineteenth-century bravura style. More unconventional is Messiaen's application of variation in his *Thème et variations* (vn, pf, 1932). In order to avoid any feeling of monotony inherent in the form, Messiaen builds his five mostly decorative variations on a rising slope of textural activity and dynamic vehemence, so that the whole process is felt as a unity. The theme's simple outlines (a lyrical melody, in units of seven bars, and a series of piano chords) are gradually filled in, so to speak, until the tension thus generated leads to a grandiloquent octave-transposed apotheosis in the final variation.

Short genre pieces

The nineteenth century

An explosion in the composition of short genre (or 'character') pieces (e.g. romance, nocturne, elegy, ballade, légende, or national dances like the polonaise), whether for violin and orchestra or violin and piano, widened the instrument's repertory considerably in the nineteenth century. Among the German contributions to this category were Beethoven's two Romances Opp. 40 and 50, Hummel's Nocturne (1822), Bruch's various small pieces for violin and orchestra (including Romance Op. 42, *Konzertstück* Op. 84 and *Adagio Appassionato* Op. 57) and his Swedish Dances Op. 63 for violin and piano, Raff's *La Fée d'amour* Op. 67, suites Opp. 180 and 210, [6] *Morceaux* Op. 85 (the second of which is the popular 'Cavatina') and a cyclic tone-poem *Volker* Op. 203, and Busoni's *Bagatelles* Op. 28.

In the field of the character piece, Paganini's contributions are for once less dominant in comparison with those of his compatriots, although works like the *Moto perpetuo* Op. 11 merit inclusion; but his influence extends to compatriots such as Bazzini, who composed numerous salon pieces (e.g. *La Ronde des lutins, scherzo fantastique* Op. 25, *Elégie* Op. 35 No. 1, *Le Muletier* Op. 35 No. 3) for his own concert performances.

The works of Polish and Hungarian composers tended to acknowledge their national heritage (e.g. Lipiński's *Rondos alla polacca*, Wieniawski's Polonaises Opp. 4 and 21 and Mazurkas Opp. 12 and 19, Hubay's *Szenen aus der Czarda* Opp. 12, 30 and 60 and *Hejre Kati* Op. 32), but Wieniawski, in his ternary-form *Légende* Op. 17 and *Scherzo-tarantelle* Op. 16, and Hubay, in his *Concertstück* Op. 20, have also demonstrated their expertise in abstract composition.

Smetana's *Fantaisie sur un air bohémien 'Sil jsem proso'* (1843) and *Z domoviny* (1880) also encapsulate his patriotic aims, *Z domoviny* ('From my native land'), for example, comprising two pieces, each of which identifies with Czech folk music without incorporating any direct quotations. Dvořák similarly absorbed characteristic melodic and rhythmic elements of native folksong into his own personal style, notably in his *Mazurek* Op. 49 (vn, orch, 1879). More popular nowadays, however, is the beautiful F minor Romance Op. 11, an arrangement (1877) of the slow movement of the String Quartet in F minor (1873), the Nocturne Op. 40 (vn, pf),[20] and the Four Romantic Pieces Op. 75 (vn, pf, 1887). Suk's only important works for the violin are the early Ballad Op. 3b (vn, pf, 1890), the Four Pieces Op. 17 (vn, pf, 1900) and the Fantasy Op. 24 (vn, orch, 1902–3).

Apart from Nápravník's ballades *Kazak* Op. 22, *Voyevoda* and

Tamara Op. 26 (vn, orch), few of the Russian character pieces cater for patriotic sentiments in their titles, even though Russian musical flavouring is omnipresent. More significant than his *Sérénade mélancolique* Op. 26 (vn, orch, 1875) and *Valse-scherzo* Op. 34 (vn, orch, 1877) is Tchaikovsky's *Trois Souvenirs d'un lieu cher* Op. 42,[21] which opens with the 'Méditation' rejected as the slow movement of his concerto. Other notable Russian pieces include Anton Rubinstein's Romance and Caprice Op. 86 (vn, orch, 1870) and Rimsky-Korsakov's *Souvenir de trois chants polonais* (1888).

Sarasate's four books of Spanish Dances Opp. 21–3, 26, 27 and 29 (consisting of only a couple of dances in each case) were formerly believed to be original compositions modelled on the national folk music. However, scholars have recently established the actual folk sources of some of these pieces, although at least three are believed to be entirely original: the 'Zapateado', 'Romanza Andaluza' and 'Malagueña'. Sarasate's *Zigeunerweisen* Op. 20 (1878), on the other hand, takes the Lisztian type of Hungarian rhapsody as a model and comprises a slow *lassu* followed by a brilliant *friss*.

The works of lasting significance from the nineteenth-century French and Belgian schools came from Saint-Saëns (*Introduction et rondo capriccioso* Op. 28, 1863; *Havanaise* Op. 83, 1887), de Bériot (*Scène de ballet* Op. 100), Vieuxtemps (numerous salon pieces) and Chausson (*Poème* Op. 25, 1896). Chausson's work, based on a short story by Turgenev and inspired by Ysaÿe's *Poème élégiaque* Op. 12, is a reflective one-movement piece of free form founded on two principal ideas. Berlioz's slight *Rêverie et caprice* (1841) should also be mentioned along with the numerous character pieces for violin and piano by Lalo and Saint-Saëns.

Austria is represented by Schubert's three *concertante* pieces, the Konzertstück D345 (1816) and the Rondo D438 (1816), both of which adopt a similar structure (an Adagio introduction leading to an Allegro in rondo form), and the Polonaise D580 (1817). Two later works for violin and piano, the B minor Rondo D895 (1826) and the Fantasy Op. posth. 159 D934 (1827), are in a more brilliant bravura style. The Fantasy comprises a slow introduction (which returns later), a gypsy-like Allegro, and a set of variations on the composer's own *Sei mir gegrüsst* (1822), while the Rondo is of much larger dimensions. The other most notable 'Austrian' contributor was Ernst, amongst whose oeuvre the Elégie ... Op. 10, *Boléro* Op. 16 and *Pensées fugitives* display his ingenuity in the smaller forms.

In Scandinavia, the Norwegian national interest was accommodated by Ole Bull (e.g. *Cowgirls' Sunday* and *Visit to a Farm in Summer*), while Sinding and Svendsen composed genre pieces such as the former's *Légende* Op. 46 (vn, orch), *Romanze* Op. 100 (vn, orch) and *Abendstimmung* Op. 120a (vn, orch) and the latter's popular Romance Op. 26

(1881). In Britain Sir Alexander Mackenzie's training in the German tradition was being tempered by his Scottish allegiances (*Suite: Pibroch* Op. 42, vn, orch, 1889; Highland Ballad Op. 47a, vn, orch, 1893), while the 'coloured' composer Coleridge-Taylor, infatuated with Longfellow's story of Hiawatha, modelled some of his works on negro subjects and melodies (Three Hiawathan Sketches Op. 16, Four African Dances Op. 58). He also composed three early shorter pieces for violin and orchestra (Ballade Op. 4, Légende Op. 14 and Romance Op. 39). Delius, meanwhile, contributed a Romance (1889), remembered chiefly for a motive which achieved greater significance in his *A Mass of Life* (1904–5), and the attractive Légende (vn, pf, 1892; vn, orch, 1895).

The twentieth century

In the current century the categories of 'character' piece have widened. In Scandinavia, Sibelius contributed Two Serenades Op. 69, Two Pieces Op. 77, the Romance Op. 78 No. 2 and the challenging *Humoresques* Opp. 87 and 89 (all for vn, orch), as well as numerous character pieces for violin and piano, while Stenhammar composed two sentimental Romances (vn, orch, Op. 28). In Russia, Taneyev's *Suite de concert* (vn, orch, 1908–9), Prokofiev's *Cinq Mélodies* Op. 35 bis (vn, pf, 1925; after his *Five Songs without Words* Op. 35, 1920), Lev Knipper's Concert Scherzo (vn, pf, 1964) and Kabalevsky's Concert Rhapsody (vn, orch, 1961–2) are worthy of recognition, although not in the forefront of the repertory, while Schnittke's Suite in the Old Style (vn, pf) is a pastiche in five neo-Classical movements (Pastorale, Ballet, Minuet, Fugue and Pantomime) in the manner of Stravinsky's *Suite italienne*. In Germany, Reger's Two Romances Op. 50 (vn, orch, 1900) are retrospective in style and content. By contrast, Henze's poetically inspired, symphonic *Ariosi*[22] (after Tasso, 1964) and his more recent *Il vitalino raddoppiato* (vn, ch orch, 1977) are progressive works which nonetheless fail to endorse the association of his name with the post-war avant-garde.

The composers of the Second Viennese School were in the forefront of progressive Austrian musical activity, effecting the so-called musical revolution of the century – atonality and serial composition. Schoenberg's last chamber work, the Phantasy Op. 47 (vn, pf, 1949) is in one movement, subdivided into five sections. The interval of a seventh is a common factor within the series from which the work is derived. A condensed reprise of the opening section at the end provides a convincing frame for this, one of his few chamber works not based on Classical structures. Meanwhile, the early Four Pieces Op. 7 (vn, pf, 1910, rev. 1914) of Schoenberg's pupil, Webern, are extremely concentrated and concise. They are especially remarkable for their motivic treatment, their material being further fragmented by sudden changes of tempo, metre, articulation, dynamic and instrumental colour.

One of the most significant twentieth-century French products in the genre was Ravel's highly virtuosic *Rapsodie de concert, Tzigane* (1924), composed for Jelly d'Arányi. It opens with a long, unaccompanied violin cadenza ('Lassan'), full of heavy Magyar accents, expressive *portamenti* and *rubati* before proceeding with a traditional series of gypsy improvisations, the pianist merely imitating the cimbalom. A slow, solemn gypsy-like melody and a more expressive, dance-like theme are the centres of attraction, the rhapsodic nature of the piece demonstrated by the fact that its numerous independent ideas are only lightly linked together, with improvisation on the pattern of gypsy music. Ravel's *Berceuse sur le nom de Gabriel Fauré* (1922) for violin and piano also dates from the same period, while Satie's (1866–1925) *Choses vues à droite et à gauche (sans lunettes)* (vn, pf, 1912), with its sparse textures, strange performance directions and surrealistic movement-titles, exemplifies his satirical view of Debussyian impressionism. Milhaud's *Music for Boston* Op. 414 (vn, orch, 1965) and many smaller pieces are also relevant to this category.

In Italy, Luigi Dallapiccola's (1904–75) two relevant works are progressive in language and retrospective in content, his *Due studi* (vn, pf, 1946–7) comprising a sarabande and a strongly dissonant fugue, and his two *Tartiniana* (vn, pf, 1951; vn, orch, 1955–6) being based on themes by Tartini, which provide a basis for sophisticated elaborations, canonic structures and so on. But composers like Riccardo Malipiero (*Rapsodia*, vn, orch, 1967) and Luigi Nono (*Varianti*, vn, ww, str, 1957) turned with varying strictness to twelve-note technique, while Maderna's disciples Luciano Berio (*Due pezzi*, vn, pf, 1951) and Franco Donatoni (*Divertimento*, vn, ch orch, 1954; *Recitativo e allegro*, vn, pf, 1951) were progressive in other ways.

Bloch's products of the 1920s include three separate pieces (*Nuit exotique, Abodah* and *Melody*, all vn, pf) and *Baal Shem: Three Pictures of Chassidic Life* (vn, pf, 1923; vn, orch, 1939) – a suite of three pieces, of gradually increasing liveliness and with a distinct 'Hebraic' harmonic language. 'Vidui' ('Contrition') is the most chromatic, its eloquent, pleading inflections expressed in a simple ternary form. 'Nigun' ('Improvisation') is characterised by its gypsy-like violin cadenzas while 'Simchas Torah' ('Rejoicing') is an exultant rondo. Douglas Moore's *Down East Suite* (vn, pf, 1944) smacks of his French mentor, d'Indy, while Copland's Two Pieces (vn, pf, 1926) – the blues-like 'Nocturne' and the rhythmic 'Ukelele Serenade' – were jazz-inspired, the latter piece incorporating quarter-tones for the 'blue' notes in its exciting Allegro vivo texture. Other progressive impulses came via the experiments of Henry Cowell (Suite, vn, pf, 1925; *Homage to Iran*, vn, pf, 1957; Hymn and Fuguing Tune No. 16, vn, pf, 1963) and his best-known pupil, John Cage (Nocturne, vn, pf, 1947). In his Six Melodies (vn, kb (pf), 1950), Cage concentrates on rhythmic structure and timbre, directing the violinist to play 'without vibrato and with minimum weight on the bow'. Cage's study of Eastern philosophies in the late 1940s and his discovery of the *I Ching*[23] prompted him to compose pieces in which chance played a role in the process of creation or performance. Originally for piano, *Cheap Imitation* (1969), a written-out alteration of Satie's *Socrate* prepared by use of the *I Ching*, was orchestrated in 1972 and arranged for solo violin in 1977.[24]

Bartók's two designated Rhapsodies (vn, pf or orch, 1928) clearly display his national heritage, both following the Hungarian rhapsody *csárdás* plan of an introductory *lassu* followed by a more vigorous *friss*. Furthermore, the orchestral version of No. 1 is complemented by the evocative colouring of the cimbalom.

The Swiss composer Frank Martin (1890–1974) experimented widely in matters of style, eventually adopting (from the 1930s) an individual adaptation of twelve-note technique, as exemplified in *Polyptique: 6 images de la Passion du Christ* (vn, 2 str orchs, 1972–3). The most progressive composer in 'Young Poland' was Karol Szymanowski, whose three *Mythes* Op. 30 (1915–16) were inspired by scenes from Greek mythology ('La Fontaine d'Aréthuse'; 'Narcisse'; 'Les Dryades et Pan'). The evocation of water (No. 1), the forest murmurs (No. 3) and the use of natural and artificial harmonics to depict Pan's flute (No. 3) are particularly imaginative. Szymanowski also contributed a *Notturno e tarantella* (1914), a Romance, Op. 23 (1910) and a *Kolysanka* ('Lullaby'), Op. 52 (1925), to the repertory. Also significant are Tadeusz Baird (*Espressioni varianti*, vn, orch, 1959) and Krzysztof Penderecki. The latter's scoring for strings is often adventurous and inventive, notably in his *Emanacje* for two string orchestras (1958), *Threnody* for fifty-two strings (1960) and *Polymorphia* for forty-eight strings, which exploit diverse timbres and unconventional playing techniques. His *Capriccio* (vn, orch, 1967) is based more on traditional procedures.

Vaughan Williams's poetic rhapsody (subtitled 'Romance') *The Lark Ascending* (vn, ch orch, 1921) incorporates one memorable British folk-like episode in its evocative, descriptive canvas inspired by some lines from Meredith's *Poems and Lyrics of the Joys of Earth*. Alun Hoddinott's *The Heaventree of Stars* Op. 102 (vn, orch, 1980) has a similar poetic inspiration – a quotation from James Joyce's *Ulysses* – the musical 'poem' concentrating on the ethereal quality of the quotation. By contrast, Britten's *Reveille* (1937) is a brilliant showpiece for violin, the pianist playing only a supportive role. The roles are more equitably shared in his larger-scale Suite Op. 6 (vn, pf, 1934–5), set out as a series of fantasies on a motto – the notes E, F, B and C – which heads the score. Gerhard's complex *Gemini* (vn, pf, 1966) comprises 'a series of contrasting episodes, whose sequence is more like a braiding of diverse strands than a straight linear development. Except for the concluding episodes, nearly every one recurs more than once, generally in a different context.

These recurrences are not like refrains, and do not fulfil anything remotely like the function of the classical refrain. Rather might they be compared to thought persistently on some main topic.'[25] Other notable British contributions to the category have come from Berkeley (Elegy and Toccata Op. 33 Nos. 2 and 3, 1950), Rawsthorne (*Concertante* (vn, pf, 1934, rev. 1968), Wellesz (Five Miniatures Op. 93, 1965), Seiber (Concert Piece, vn, pf, 1954), Elizabeth Maconchy (*Serenata concertante*, 1962), Thea Musgrave (*Colloquy*, vn, pf, 1960), Robin Holloway (*Romanza* Op. 31, vn, orch, 1976), Cornelius Cardew (*The East is Red*, vn, pf, 1972) and Sebastian Forbes (*Antiphony*, vn, pf, 1965).

Transcriptions and fantasias

The vogue for transcriptions started in the nineteenth century with such exemplary arrangements as Joachim's of Brahms's Hungarian Dances, the Schubert–Wilhelmj *Ave Maria*, the Schubert–Ernst *Erlkönig*, the Bach–Wilhelmj 'Air on the G String', the Wagner–Wilhelmj *Träume* (vn, orch), Wilhelmj's selections from Wagner's operas (vn, pf) and his concert paraphrases on *Siegfried* and *Parsifal*. But the genre was abused so much by so many that the fashion resulted in a glut of inferior arrangements and even falsifications by the turn of the century.

Kreisler's contribution to the genre requires particular explanation. Many of his so-called 'transcriptions' are actually pseudo-Classical pieces that he wrote or arranged himself and ascribed quite falsely to earlier masters such as Pugnani or Tartini. However, he left several *bona fide* transcriptions (e.g. *Poupée valsante*, *Chanson hindue* and *Lotus Land*, to name but a few) in addition to his numerous falsifications (e.g. Praeludium and Allegro). Like Kreisler, Dushkin made numerous arrangements of works by other composers (e.g. Albéniz, Wieniawski and Reger) for his own concert use, as well as transcriptions of Baroque and Classical works, some of which were actually his own original compositions attributed to earlier composers. More important, though, was his collaboration with Stravinsky, which spawned a transcription from *Petrouchka* (entitled *Danse russe*) as well as more substantial and significant works in other genres.[26] Among other violinists of the time, Auer's various violin transcriptions are competent but unmemorable, while Heifetz wrote about 150 transcriptions (e.g. Stephen Foster's 'The Old Folks at Home', Achron's 'Hebrew Melody', Drigo's 'Valse Bluette', Debussy's 'Golliwog's Cake-walk', items from Gershwin's *Porgy and Bess* etc.), which remind us as much of his competence as a pianist as his brilliance as a violinist.

Fantasias on operatic themes also became an indispensable part of musical entertainment in the nineteenth century. More often than not these were written by a pair of eminent virtuosos, notably Lafont and Moscheles, Vieuxtemps and Anton Rubinstein, and Ernst and George

Osborne. Other contributors to the genre were largely also of the virtuoso set, most prominent amongst these being Wieniawski (*Fantaisie brillante*, on themes from Gounod's *Faust*, Op. 20, 1868; and numerous unpublished works), Sarasate (concert fantasies on *Carmen* Op. 25, *Der Freischütz*, *Don Giovanni*, *Faust* etc.), and Ernst (*Fantaisie brillante* ... sur *Otello de Rossini* Op. 11). Rimsky-Korsakov's Fantasia on Two Russian Themes Op. 33 (1886–7) and Nápravník's Fantasia on Russian Themes Op. 30 (1878) have been described as somewhat awkward attempts at 'nationalising' the concerto.

12　The violin as ensemble instrument

PETER ALLSOP

During its history, the violin has been associated with an abundance of other instruments, not to mention its particularly close relationship with the human voice, to which it has often been compared. To chronicle this would be a formidable task, but fortunately, over a number of centuries, musical taste has favoured a quite limited range of specific groupings which quickly acquired the status of 'genre'. A Haydn string quartet suggests not just an instrumental combination but a specific mode of treatment, and it is such characteristic forms rather than any *ad hoc* instrumentation which must demand the closest attention. For the present purposes an ensemble is defined rather arbitrarily as any group of two or more instrumentalists, but excluding compositions for violin and keyboard, the main concern being that repertory categorised today by the equally arbitrary term 'chamber music'. *The New Grove Diction-ary* defines this as 'music for small ensembles of solo instruments, written for performance under domestic circumstances', but this is especially inadequate for the seventeenth century, when small ensemble music need not have been performed in 'chambers', while 'chamber ensembles' may have been used as 'orchestras' in public theatres or churches. Some flexibility has therefore seemed advisable, at least for the first two centuries of this development.

Massed bands including violins were not uncommon on grand festive occasions in the late sixteenth century, and this tradition was continued in such works as Monteverdi's *Orfeo* (1607), but they often presented extreme problems of ensemble. In Bottrigari's *Il desiderio*, Gratioso complains of the cacophony created by a great company of instruments including 'a large clavicembalo and a large spinet, three lutes of various forms, a great number of viols and a similar large group of trombones, two little rebecs and as many large flutes, straight and traverse, a large double harp and a lyre', to which his friend, Alemanno, replies, 'The explanation is that very often the instruments are not well tuned together, and can cause nothing but poor concord, and disunity'.[1] Such groupings quickly went out of vogue, but combinations of strings, cornetti and trombones survived, especially at St Mark's in Venice, where it was only in 1685 that the orchestra was finally reorganised to emphasise strings.

String-based ensembles were by then normal, as indeed they always had been in Venetian opera-houses. Five-part ensembles were not infrequent, but the smaller combination of two violins plus continuo fashionable in other spheres soon became preferred. At this period the boundaries between 'chamber' and 'orchestral' music were not so clear-cut as they are today, when the term 'orchestra' implies doubling at least of the violins.[2] Some opera 'orchestras' employed only one violin to a part, and although the courts of Mantua, Parma and Modena had string bands we again cannot automatically presume doubling. Very few Italian churches in the seventeenth century could afford the luxury of an orchestra in the modern sense and this partly explains the enormous popularity of sonatas for small instrumental ensembles.

Only after 1600 did the violin acquire a substantial repertory of free compositions, appearing under such titles – often synonymous – as 'canzona', 'sonata', and later, 'sinfonia'. The widespread sixteenth-century designation 'con ogni sorte di stromenti' ('for all types of instruments') soon lapsed, although for some years the cornetto is still mentioned as an alternative to the violin. On the evidence of surviving publications, from the 1620s the Italian public favoured combinations of violin and melodic bass, two violins, and two violins and melodic bass, each with a keyboard continuo which in the majority of cases was an organ, not a harpsichord. These combinations were precisely described on title-pages by the number of *melodic* instruments used, always discounting the continuo (the first two as *a*2 and last as *a*3). It was only in Northern Europe that such imprecise terms as 'trio sonata' were widely used. Of these groupings, easily the most popular were the last two, which far outweigh any others, including solos. While the choice of bass instrument remained flexible – trombone, bassoon and archlute as well as strings – very early on absolute supremacy was given to the violin, and until the next century no other treble instrument can muster more than a handful of sonatas.

This preoccupation with small ensembles plus continuo parallels a similar trend in vocal music, and was part of a more general rejection of polyphonic textures. Like the popular vocal duets for two sopranos, the two violins in *a*2 compositions remained predominantly imitative, but instead of the continuous web of equal-voiced counterpoint still prac-tised in *unaccompanied* duos, these preferred antiphonal exchanges in which melodic fragments, or even quite lengthy solo passages, were passed between instruments. These alternate with mellifluous passages in parallel thirds or sixths or even entire sections of homophony – all over a non-thematic continuo bass which functions as a simple harmonic

Ex. 32   from D. Castello, *Sonata quarta a 2* (1629)

support (Ex. 32). On the other hand, *a*3 sonatas frequently prefer a more conservative contrapuntal texture in which the melodic bass fully participates. Here the continuo mainly doubles the lowest melodic part, often simplifying it. Whereas the *a*2 medium was the vehicle for more radical experimentation, the *a*3 sonata preserved the fugal techniques so essential in the late seventeenth century, but only after the unprecedented success of Corelli's sonatas did the *a*3 combination supersede the other in importance.

As defined in Sébastien de Brossard's *Dictionnaire* (1710), Corelli's sonatas *a*3 fall into the well-known categories of *da chiesa* (for church) and *da camera* (for chamber),[3] but while all surviving seventeenth-century editions of the dance suites (Opp. 2 and 4) are described as *da camera* on the title pages, not one of the many editions of Opp. 1 and 3 ever mentions *da chiesa* – a term relatively rare in Italy in the seventeenth century. Corelli himself held no permanent church appointment, and the Op. 1 dedication to Queen Christina of Sweden suggests the possibility of performance at the academies (concerts) held in her palace, while Op. 3 is dedicated to Francesco II of Modena, himself a keen violinist. Suites of dances were mainly considered as chamber music but there is little reason to suppose that free sonatas were automatically intended for church use, although this was of course one possible function. The myth of a distinctive church style was perpetuated by Joachim and Chrysander, who saw fit to add *da chiesa* to Corelli's titles in their complete edition published in the nineteenth century, but at the time the accusation that instrumental music in church was far too secular was a recurrent complaint of much Papal legislation.

The new violin idiom was quickly dispersed abroad by such Italians as Valentini, Marini and Farina working at the courts of Austria and Germany. The resources of a princely environment often warranted large-scale compositions, and composers such as Antonio Bertali at the Imperial Court in Vienna produced compositions in up to eighteen parts, while the surviving output of Biber, who served the Archbishop of Salzburg, is almost equally divided between large ensembles and solos with only a modicum of 'trio' settings. Even Rosenmüller's *Sonate da camera*, published while he was in Venice, specify *a*5 with only optional 'trio' scoring.

In the northern monarchies, the Italian style met with some resistance from long-established native traditions. There is no comparable repertory of free sonatas in France until the eighteenth century, despite the violin's long pedigree as a dance instrument. Between 1560 and 1574, thirty-eight Amati instruments were commissioned by Charles IX, whose mother, the Florentine Catherine de' Medici, imported a band of Italian violinists led by Balthasar de Beaujoyeux, who took part in the important ballet *Circé* (1581), which contains dances for five-part strings. In 1626, Louis XIII established his 'Vingt-quatre Violons du Roi' described by Mersenne as 'ravishing and powerful'.[4] Under Louis XIV this band became the envy of Europe, but failed to satisfy the court composer, Lully, who acquired Louis's permission to form the small and select 'Petits Violons'. In the French orchestra the undivided violins took the melody with violas supplying three accompanying parts above the basses, and this five-part texture survived into the next century. Le Cerf's remark that the violin 'is not *noble* in France' expressed a sentiment widely held until the wave of Corelli mania swept the capital, fundamentally altering the French attitude to the sonata.[5] Thus when François Couperin championed the Italian cause at the turn of the century, he chose Corelli's works as his models ('which I shall love as long as I live'), honouring them in his 'trio' setting, *Le Parnasse ou l'apothéose de Corelli* (1724).

In England, violins are mentioned from the 1550s, and by the next century they appear as alternatives to viols on such title-pages as Dowland's *Lachrimae* (1604). The English court, ever mindful of continental practices, established the King's Violins in 1631, and after the Restoration Charles II formed a string band – 'after the French fantastical light way', as Evelyn remarked disapprovingly in his Diary. Anthony Wood mentions that the King 'did not like the viols: preferring the violins as being more airie and brisk',[6] and by 1676 Thomas Mace lamented the passing of the 'rare chests of viols'.[7] English composers such as Lawes and Jenkins had already experimented with violin 'trios', although the outcome was not necessarily Italianate. Following the influx of foreign musicians such as the violinist Nicola Matteis, English composers including Purcell set about imitating the Italian style, and as in France, the arrival of Corelli's works, which Roger North described as 'the bread of life',[8] seemed to inspire an almost fanatical devotion.

The unparalleled success of Corelli's Op. 5 heralded a fundamental shift of interest away from duos and trios in favour of the 'solo' sonata. Almost three-quarters of Vivaldi's output is solo, and 'ensemble' sonatas represent a meagre portion of Tartini's output. Locatelli (working in Amsterdam) strongly favoured the solo, and Veracini is not known to have written for any other combination. The previous century had not lacked its renowned virtuosi, but the fact remains that a considerable portion of the surviving repertory is by organists such as Merula, Cazzati and Legrenzi. French composers followed similar paths, and distinguished violinists such as Rebel, Duval and Leclair produced solo sonatas of a technical complexity to rival the Italians. By the mid-century, therefore, although the 'trio' remained by far the most popular ensemble combination, solo sonatas formed the bulk of the repertory.

Conversely, it is at this period that accounts of large orchestras become frequent, especially in Rome where the concerto grosso flourished under Corelli. One Roman work of 1689, *S. Beatrice d'Este* by Giovanni Lorenzo Lulier del Violone, is reported to have used forty violins, ten violas, seventeen cellos, seven double basses, two trumpets, one trombone and a lute. By the eighteenth century, substantial violin sections were found in the opera-houses of Milan and Naples and by then a four-part ensemble was normal. The large orchestras which performed in Roman oratorios and concertos, however, were *ad hoc* bodies formed for the demands of particular occasions, and some modification might be required for other performances. Muffat's *Ausserlesene Instrumental-Music* (1701), written, according to the composer, under Corelli's direction, and J. A. Schmierer's *Zodiacus* (1698) both sanction performance by a solo ensemble, or an orchestra. The decision related to the availability of players and to the size of the venue, and there is much evidence that chamber performance may have used one instrument per part, but that church performance required doubling. Warren Kirkendale quotes a dictionary by Johann Sulzer (1798) which clearly outlines the current church usage: 'There are trios which are set in the strict, church style and include real fugues. They consist of parts for two violins and bass, and are known also as church trios. These must be performed with more than one instrument per part; otherwise they lack strength.'[9] The Paris edition of Johann Stamitz's Op. 1 trios (1755?) specifies 'pour exécuter ou à trio, ou avec toute l'orchestre'.

If by the beginning of the eighteenth century the string section had long formed the backbone of the orchestra, the question of its direction remained unresolved. Adam Carse cites many conflicting documents, mostly from German and French sources, and comes to three main conclusions:[10]

1. Opera was directed under dual control from the keyboard and the violinist-leader, except in Paris, which followed Lully's tradition of beating time audibly with a stick.

2. Instrumental music was generally directed by the leader, less often from the keyboard,

3. In choral pieces a time beater was used.

The struggle for power underlying these documents was already present in the previous century. A particularly revealing contract of employment involved the famous violinist Biagio Marini, who was *maestro de' concerti* to the Duke of Neuburg and who clearly did not enjoy a cordial relationship with the musical director, Giacomo Negri. When Marini joined with the band the beating of time was to be left to the *Kapellmeister*, but it is also quite clear from the document that Marini hoped to 'co-ordinate the music that they normally play together nicely without his beating time'. Nor is there any suggestion that Negri directed from the harpsichord. Carse's 'dual control' may well have existed in theory, but presented serious practical problems. Keyboard players such as C. P. E. Bach of course insisted that they were in command, but the flautist Quantz considered that it mattered little which instrument led, while acknowledging that since the violin is more penetrating than any other, it would be the best choice. Among the responsibilities of the leader, who should be slightly forward and elevated in relationship to the other players, Quantz lists the keeping of 'perfect time', the tuning of the orchestra, nuances of expression such as dynamics, and the placing of the instruments, and Leopold Mozart gives much the same advice in summary form in his violin treatise: 'all the ensemble players must observe each other carefully, and especially watch the leader; not only so that they begin well together but that they may play steadily in the same tempo and with the same expression'.[11] Carse quotes extensively from one anonymous advocate of keyboard control in a booklet of 1779 entitled *Wahrheiten die Musik betreffend* (*Truths about Music*), in which the author delivers a diatribe against violinist-leaders, concluding,

when the orchestra is really playing in time and has forgotten all about the leader, it occurs to him to upset the whole thing again by means of comical grimaces, foot-stamping and so on; and where the composer is allowed to suffer all sorts of vexations; then the direction becomes not only unsafe, but also ridiculous.[12]

We know that Haydn still 'presided at the piano' for the performances of his symphonies in London, but of course ultimate victory lay in the hands of the conductor.

The tendency to treat the first violin soloistically, noticeable even in Corelli's *Sonate da camera a3*, gradually undermined an essential tenet of the 'Baroque' sonata – that of equality of the two trebles. In Playford's *Introduction to the Skill of Musick*, Purcell stresses the lack of 'predomi-

Ex. 33   from G. B. Sammartini, *Notturno* Op. 7

nacy' of one violin over the other, while Le Cerf observed with distaste their characteristic tessitura in Italian sonatas, 'The first trebles of the Italians squeak because they are too high. Their second trebles have the fault of being too close to the first, and too far from the bass, which is the third part . . . When the second treble is so high, it leaves too much of an interval and space between the first treble and the bass.'[13] Such an equality is only truly possible within an imitative fabric, and as the interest in contrapuntal forms such as fugue declined, this inevitably altered the relationship between the two violins. The second violin became more accompanimental and its range fell more consistently below that of the first, so that by the Rococo period entire sonatas by composers such as Sammartini and Wagenseil could be largely homophonic (Ex. 33). From the 1770s it became increasingly common to replace the second violin with a viola.

The trio with continuo maintained some popularity until late in the eighteenth century, but by then ensembles without keyboard had long been customary. This instrumentation is so much associated with the Classical period that it is necessary to emphasise that there was nothing new about string ensembles without keyboard. Buonamente's Book 6 (1636) consists entirely of unaccompanied string trios, and this was normal for *Sonate da camera*. There is an ingrained habit of Northerners to disbelieve the evidence of the Italians' own title-pages, but with remarkable consistency they specify two violins with 'violone' or *optional* keyboard continuo. In fact, many of the works which we now categorise as 'solos', including Corelli's Op. 5, are actually duo sonatas for violin and melodic bass with optional keyboard. It is therefore no surprise to learn that recent research by Webster and others has established that as early as 1750 a continuo instrument was not usually present in Viennese chamber music.[14]

Despite this residual interest in trios, by the end of the century the string quartet had established itself as the most characteristic medium. It is a popular musicological pastime to discover chance anticipations of a genre, and various attempts have been made to unearth the first string quartet. A four-part string ensemble was the most frequent combination in the late-sixteenth-century *Canzona francese*, and ensembles of two violins, viola and 'violone' were by no means uncommon in dance music. Giovanni Maria Bononcini included one extended free sonata in his Op. 3 collection (1669), which not only employs the string quartet scoring, but also has no continuo part! But these have little stylistic connection with the genre so clearly defined in Heinrich Koch's *Musikalisches Lexicon* (1802) under the heading 'Quatuor':

This instrumental composition for four instruments, which has been such a favourite for many years, is a special category of sonata, and in the strict sense, consists of four concerting instruments, none of which can claim exclusively the role of a leading voice ... the four voices alternate in taking the lead ... While one voice takes the leading melody (aside from the voice serving as the bass) the two others must continue with complementary melodic material that will reinforce the expression without beclouding the leading melody.[15]

Koch concludes with the inevitable references to the works of Haydn and Mozart. It was no doubt this desire to achieve some measure of equality of part-writing that led Haydn to resort to the traditional technique of fugue in the finales of his Op. 20 quartets (1772), and of course both Mozart and Beethoven had recourse to this method at one time or another. But while contrapuntal device remained an interest of all three composers, such wholesale reversion to past practices could not provide a permanent solution to the problem. Instead, greater equality is achieved through a judicious distribution of thematic material and fragments thereof throughout all the parts – a procedure already apparent in Haydn's 'Russian' Quartets Op. 33 (whether or not they were written in a 'new and special way' as he claimed) and adopted by Mozart in his 'Haydn' Quartets.

Compared with trios and quartets, the number of compositions for larger string ensembles is really quite small, with the exception of the two hundred or so quintets of Boccherini. Here, priority is given to the first violin and the first cello, both indulging in concerto-like displays accompanied by the other parts. Unaccompanied duets for two trebles became increasingly popular as the century progressed. This was the traditional medium for instruction in composition and instrumental performance, but the violin duet was particularly cultivated by composers associated with the French violin school from the middle of the eighteenth century onwards. Leclair published two sets (1730, 1747?)

while Ignaz Pleyel produced no less than eight, some of which have retained their popularity even today. This interest continued well into the nineteenth century in the hands of violinists such as Viotti, Rode and Kreutzer. Duos for dissimilar instruments were far less common, but Boismortier's Op. 51 (1734) sonatas call for transverse flute and a violin 'in chords', and violin and viola duets are represented by the incomparable works of Mozart.

Mixed combinations became increasingly popular from the beginning of the eighteenth century, especially those involving the transverse flute, but even Quantz is forced to admit that seldom was any music performed without the violin and keyboard. The combination of dissimilar treble instruments presents its own problems, and Hubert Le Blanc (1740) disparagingly remarked about the violin that it 'wishes to dominate at any price whatever, and to annihilate the flute as well as the viol'.[16] Despite the increasing number of well-known examples of chamber ensembles with wind, string trios and quartets still dominated the repertory, with mixed ensembles accounting for only about a third, and wind ensembles representing a very small percentage of the surviving output.

The challenge to the pre-eminence of the violin came not from melody instruments but from the keyboard. Both Marini and Frescobaldi included obbligato keyboard parts in compositions of the 1620s but the popularity of this genre really dates from the middle of the eighteenth century. This repertory is mainly scored for a florid keyboard with a single accompanying instrument, but Rameau's *Pièces de clavecin en concerts* (1741) includes 'un violon ou une flûte, et une viole ou un deuxième violon'. These are of secondary importance, since the composer insists that the pieces performed by the harpsichord alone give the impression of 'admitting no other treatment'. Piano-based ensembles during the Classical period seem curiously exempt from the requirement of equality of parts. In Haydn's trios the cello largely doubles the left hand of the keyboard, and although the violin is not so subordinate, it hardly equals the fortepiano in importance. Even after the example of Beethoven's Op. 1 trios (1795), which achieve admirable balance of forces, pianists such as Hummel produced works in which the keyboard almost forces the other parts into submission, while Schumann once gave his impression of the piano trio as needing 'a fiery player at the piano, and two understanding friends who accompany softly'. Most of the composers of the Austro-German tradition after Beethoven were primarily pianists (even if, like Mendelssohn, they played a string instrument), and this is reflected in the primacy now given to piano-based ensembles.

Our preoccupation with this tradition has tended to obscure other contemporary developments, particularly in respect of the violinist-composers of the period such as Spohr, Kreutzer, Rode and Viotti. The

Ex. 34   from L. Spohr, String Quartet Op. 4 No. 2, rondo finale

Parisian publishers in particular produced a considerable quantity of music which was overwhelmingly popular during their lifetimes. Naturally, these violinists favoured string ensembles. Spohr's output includes thirty-five string quartets, four double quartets, seven string quintets, and only a meagre smattering of piano-based compositions. Along with Kreutzer and Rode, he cultivated a type of composition known as the *quatuor brillant*, which is little more than a display piece for the first violin (Ex. 34). This would seem to offend against the principle of equality, but as all violinists who have ever played the second part of Haydn's 'Lark' Quartet (Op. 64 No. 5) will know, the desire to exploit the abilities of a brilliant leader is also a valid criterion.

The string quartet soon became the testing ground for composers to measure themselves against the incomparable achievements of the Classical masters. In 1842 (the year of his own quartets), Schumann reviewed a work by Julius Schapler in the *Neue Zeitschrift für Musik*:

> Who does not know the quartets of Haydn, Mozart and Beethoven, and who would wish to say anything against them? In fact it is the most telling testimony to the immortal freshness of these works that yet after half a century they gladden the hearts of everyone; but it is no good sign that the later generation, after all this time, has not been able to produce anything comparable.[17]

By the time of Brahms the medium had come to be viewed as the bulwark of traditionalism against the inroads of the new German school of Liszt and Wagner, and was cultivated by those composers such as Dvořák and Reger who felt themselves heirs to the Classical inheritance. E. T. A. Hoffmann extolled the virtues of 'pure' instrumental music thus: 'When we speak of music as an autonomous art one should think only of instrumental music, which, scorning any admixture of another art, gives pure expression to music's specific nature, recognizable in this form alone.'[18] Its very supremacy was now being challenged. Furthermore, the phenomenal increase in technical and intellectual demands from Beet-

Ex. 35   from W. Lutosławski, String Quartet (1964)

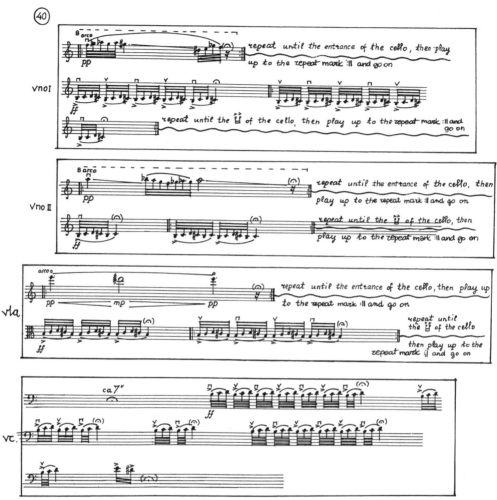

28.749

hoven to Brahms placed many works beyond the ability of most amateur players. Of course, much of the repertory of composers such as Schubert, Mendelssohn and Brahms originated in domestic performances, but 'chamber' music was increasingly becoming the domain of professional ensembles such as the Joachim Quartet, moving from its domestic environment into the concert hall. Pure instrumental chamber music was losing its *raison d'être*.

As a direct outcome of this development, much chamber music of the twentieth century is in fact concert music. Works such as Elliott Carter's Second String Quartet with its deliberately ostentatious first violin part would strain the technical resources of most professional players, let alone amateurs. Small wonder that many performers today, both amateur and professional, seek refuge in the music of the past, much of it originally written with the former's needs in mind. Attempts have been made to rectify this situation, notably by Paul Hindemith, who in *A Composer's World* (1952) proposed a 'new technical and stylistic approach ... so that music which satisfies the amateur's wishes can be created'. Despite his corpus of serviceable music for almost any combination, his goal of re-creating a stylistically and technically accessible modern chamber idiom has demonstrably failed. It is one thing to compose in a widely accepted style for an existing market, but quite another to produce works in the hope of creating a market – to convert listeners into performers, as Hindemith puts it.

Except where traditional instruments have been replaced by other methods of sound generation, the violin has been called upon to participate in almost every stylistic trend of the twentieth century from Schoenberg's atonality to the indeterminacy of Lutosławski's String Quartet of 1965 (Ex. 35), from Debussy's impressionism to the minimalism of Christian Wolff's Duo for Violins (1950) which employs only three pitches. Furthermore, the range of combinations has dramatically expanded to include multiple violin parts, as in Wallingford Riegger's *Study in Sonority* for ten violins or Xenakis's *Pithoprakta* (1956) which has independent parts for twenty-four violins, eight cellos, six double basses, two percussionists and two trombones. But it cannot always be said that violinists and audiences alike have welcomed this rich diversity of available styles. There is some degree of acceptance for the effulgent post-Romanticism of Schoenberg's *Verklärte Nacht*, and even the 'atonality' of Berg's Lyric Suite, but rather less for the dodecaphony of the former's Third and Fourth String Quartets. Despite Schoenberg's protestations of continuity from Brahms, it is not the economy and precision of the motivic working (however satisfying intellectually) in the latter's instrumental music that endears it to us as violinists, but its sustained and expressive lyricism.

Traditional instrumental groupings such as the string quartet have in fact enjoyed a revival, with outstanding contributions by Debussy, Fauré, Ravel, Janáček, Bartók, Britten, Tippett, a host of American composers such as Ives, Babbitt and Carter, and the prolific Soviet composers, Shostakovich and Myaskovsky. The medium has proven especially conducive to those composers such as Bartók and Hindemith whose mode of thought is fundamentally polyphonic. The renewal of the rapport between string ensembles and the voice is seen in such diverse settings as Schoenberg's Second String Quartet on poems by Stefan George and Vaughan Williams's song cycle *On Wenlock Edge*. The adoption of a traditional medium does not of course imply traditional treatment. Ever since Bartók's quartets, with their wide range of pizzicato effects, vibrato indications, *col legno* and microtones, composers have sought to expand the range of available sounds. This trend is taken to extremes in the 'soundscape' of Penderecki's Second String Quartet,

Ex. 36   from K. Penderecki, String Quartet No. 2

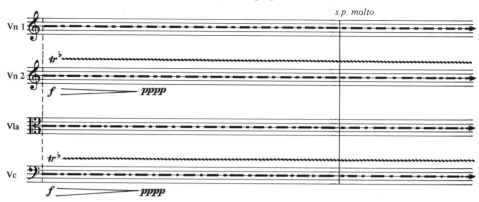

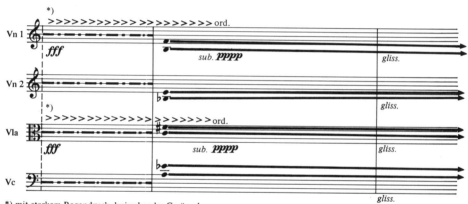

*) mit starkem Bogendruck, knirschendes Geräusch
  with strong pressure of the bow, grinding sound

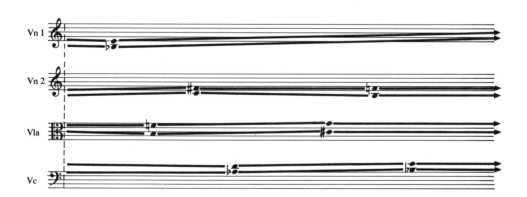

with its customised notational symbols and copious written directions such as 'tap with finger-tip on sound board', 'bow upon the tailpiece' and finally 'during the *glissando* turn down the tuning peg slowly' (Ex. 36). Such 'distortions' may be seen to herald the demise of the medium, but as long as professional quartets of an exceptionally high standard exist, one suspects that composers will write for them.

Despite this revival, it is obvious that none of the traditional ensembles (with or without the piano) can claim the pre-eminence it held in the past. Undoubtedly, the preference has been for mixed ensembles incorporating a considerable variety of tone-colours, plus a *batterie* of percussion. This desire to widen the palette is partly a by-product of the importance attached to timbre in Schoenberg's *Klangfarbenmelodie*, where changing tone-colours are used not only as a means of creating variety but as a fundamental structural element. In the programme notes for the Twentieth Birthday Gala of the Fires of London, Judith Weir remarked with some justification that 'the instrumental lineup of the Fires [flute, clarinet, violin, cello, piano and percussion] seems as indispensable to British music of our era as the string quartet was to that of Vienna a couple of centuries ago'. It seems that the violin must therefore take its place as one of an immense variety of available colours, and it is salutary to remember that a classic work of this century, Boulez's *Le Marteau sans maître* (1957), dispenses with it entirely in favour of the viola.

Much of this music strikes little accord with many players today. Violinists in general still expect their violin parts to 'sing' and are not anxious to be treated as percussion instruments, but similar objections are copiously documented from the time of Monteverdi's *Combattimento di Tancredi e Clorinda* (1624), when the string band objected to the use of measured *tremolos*. In the past, instruments have come to the end of their useful lives when they no longer seemed capable of fulfilling the composer's requirements, and the violin today does seem ill-suited to some contemporary developments. In the first place, its system of tuning in fifths by its very nature suggests a tonal context. Furthermore, the angularity so conspicuous a feature of much contemporary music presents enormous problems of intonation, since it is not, like the *bariolage* techniques of the eighteenth and nineteenth centuries, based idiomatically around the utilisation of adjacent strings. Traditional training emphasising diatonic scales and broken chords ill-equips the violinist to handle this particular difficulty. Many of these problems, however, do not really signal the decline of the violin, which is an amazingly resilient and versatile instrument, but indicate rather the basic problems of communication of much contemporary music.

13 The pedagogical literature

ROBIN STOWELL

Treatises[1]

It was not until the end of the seventeenth century that instruction books devoted exclusively to violin technique were published, John Lenton's *The Gentleman's Diversion . . .* (1693) being recognised as the first extant violin tutor. Like most of its immediate successors, it was intended for the amateur musician. Its elementary content was no substitute for oral instruction by a teacher, on whom many depended in order to learn techniques 'which may be knowne but not described'.[2] Earlier in the century some treatises had begun to reflect both the liberation of instruments from their subordination to the voice and the improved social position of the violin itself by incorporating descriptions of contemporary instruments, sometimes with some basic technical information.[3] But these were publications addressed to musicians as a whole, dealing with a wide range of instruments, and were not specialist violin texts. Among the most significant of these 'multi-purpose' volumes were Praetorius's *Syntagma musicum* (1618–20), Mersenne's *Harmonie universelle* (1636), Zanetti's *Il scolaro . . . per imparar a suonare di violino, et altri stromenti* (1645), Prinner's *Musicalischer Schlissl* (1677), Speer's *Gründ-richtiger . . . Unterricht* (1687) and Falck's *Idea boni cantoris* (1688). John Playford's *A Brief Introduction to the Skill of Musick* demonstrates the increasing popularity of the violin in amateur circles, a complete section, 'Playing on the Treble Violin', being added in a second revised edition (1658) published four years after the first.

The steady stream of unenterprising 'do-it-yourself' instruction books for the amateur continued well into the eighteenth century, whether in the form of instrumental compendia (e.g. Merck's *Compendium musicae instrumentalis chelicae*, 1695; Majer's *Museum musicum*, 1732; Eisel's *Musicus autodidaktos*, 1738; Tessarini's *Grammatica di musica*, 1741?) or tailored to specific instruments (e.g. *Nolens Volens or You shall learn to Play on the Violin whether you will or no*, 1695; *The Self-Instructor on the Violin . . .*, 1695;[4] the modest French tutors by Montéclair, Dupont and Corrette).[5] Plagiarisim was rife – for example, Majer's treatise of 1732 includes a section drawn almost entirely from Falck's of 1688; and Prelleur's section on the violin in his *The Modern Musick-Master* (1730–1) was pirated from *Nolens Volens . . .* (1695). Furthermore, much of the technical advice provided was extremely suspect; and few publications included much more than a guide-book to the fingerboard and a few simple pieces for the student to master. Nevertheless, these publications served a valuable purpose in helping the violin rapidly to gain social respectability in competition with the viol.

Although still intended for use with a teacher, the first books to reflect more advanced 'professional' practice appeared from about the middle of the eighteenth century. London was again the pioneering publishing venue, but the first significant author was an Italian, Geminiani. One of the numerous foreign violinists attracted to these shores by the expanding music-publishing industry and the flourishing concert life in London and the provinces, Geminiani disseminated the technique and style of his mentor, Corelli (but not without some French seasoning too!), through his compositions, teaching, performance and violin treatise. His *The Art of Playing on the Violin* (London, 1751) provides a concise survey of technical principles and incorporates several examples and complete compositions for their mastery. Its influence was such that plagiarised versions continued to be published well into the nineteenth century,[6] and many treatises were based firmly on its principles.[7]

Curiously, four invaluable Italian sources concerning technique and performance practice essentially postdate the period of greatest Italian influence. Tartini's 'Letter' (1760) to his pupil Maddalena Sirmen (née Lombardini) is a significant document about selected technical issues, comprising a brief violin lesson in written form. His important treatise on ornaments, first printed posthumously in French as *Traité des agrémens* (1771), was doubtless prepared for his violin pupils at the School of Nations in Padua. It may have been written soon after the School's foundation in 1728, but its manuscript was certainly in circulation by c.1750, since Leopold Mozart incorporated extracts from it into his violin treatise (1756). Galeazzi's *Elementi teorico-pratici . . .* was published in two volumes (1791 and 1796), each divided into two parts. The second part of the first volume provides a detailed, methodical survey of the main technical principles of violin playing and general performing practice, the sections on ornaments and expression constituting probably the most important source of information on improvisation published in Italy in the late eighteenth century. There are also detailed observations on orchestral playing, the duties of the concert-master, solo playing and an interesting insight into Galeazzi's own pedagogical approach, incorporating a hypothetical syllabus for the beginner. Campagnoli's *Metodo* (1797?),[8] strongly influenced by the theories of his teacher Nardini, appeared in many editions and was widely translated. Subdivided into five parts with an introduction devoted to general technical matters, it provides, in the first four sections, detailed systematic instruction regarding the application of the 250 progressive exercises incorporated in Part 5.

Although Quantz's flute treatise (1752) includes some invaluable advice (mostly about bowing) directed principally at orchestral violinists, the most important and influential eighteenth-century German instruction book for the violin was Leopold Mozart's *Versuch* ... (1756). Its significance is mirrored by its demand, for it achieved four German editions by 1800, as well as versions in Dutch (1766) and French (c.1770). Intended to lay 'the foundation of good style',[9] the parameters of this treatise far exceed that of any previous publication, its 264 pages incorporating copious examples and constituting a detailed, systematic survey of violin playing. Although inspired by Leopold Mozart's work, other late-eighteenth-century German violin treatises were generally on a much simpler level, designed more for the instruction of the orchestral violinist (*Ripienist*) than the soloist. The works of Kürzinger (1763), Petri (1767), Löhlein (1774), Reichardt (1776), Hiller (1792), Schweigl (1786 and 1795) and Fenkner (1803) come into this category, offering a sound but somewhat limited technical foundation for their readership.

L'abbé *le fils*'s *Principes du violon* (1761) confirms the ascendancy of a French violin school in the second half of the eighteenth century. It amalgamates the old French dance tradition (as manifested in the various menuets, airs and rondeaux and in the two suites of *Airs d'opéra*, which also include dances, in the form of advanced duets for two violins), the 'new' Italian sonata tradition (as represented by the numerous lessons 'in the manner of sonatas'), and a progressive attitude towards certain aspects of technique. Particularly remarkable is its instruction regarding the violin and bow holds, bow management, half position, extensions, ornamentation, double stopping and harmonics. Its limited text is supplemented by numerous examples and complete compositions for the instrument.

Corrette's *L'Art de se perfectionner dans le violon* (1782) and Cartier's *L'Art du violon* (1798) are significant principally for their musical content. Cartier's treatise incorporates in its third part an anthology of some 154 compositions by seventeenth- and eighteenth-century French, German and Italian composers. The first two parts are of less value, the text of Part 1 comprising an amalgamation of extracts from the treatises of Geminiani, Leopold Mozart, Tarade and L'abbé *le fils*, but they confirm the advent of a more uniform approach to violin playing. Michel Woldemar's *Grande Méthode* ... (c.1800) is similarly extensively endowed with musical content, including an exhaustive study of scales, a large collection of study material, examples of cadenzas in various keys and suggestions as to varying degrees of ornamentation of a given melody.

Baillot, Rode and Kreutzer's *Méthode* ... (1803) remained unchallenged as the standard French violin text for advanced performers for at least thirty years. Widely read and imitated – Fauré (c.1820) and Mazas (1830) include extracts *verbatim* in their own methods – it covers artistic, technical (though not exhaustively) and aesthetic matters (Part 2 deals exclusively with the philosophy of expression) as well as including study material. But Baillot's own *L'Art du violon* (1834), a conscious attempt to remedy the omissions of the *Méthode* ... (previously adopted by the Paris Conservatoire), easily surpasses it in content and detail. Supported by numerous musical examples, studies and compositions, Part 1 is devoted to the mechanics of violin playing and deals with most technical and stylistic matters in unprecedented detail. Part 2 concentrates on expression and is essentially a reprint of the relevant section of the *Méthode* ... with a short introduction by Baillot.

Baillot's teachings were continued by his pupils Habeneck (*Méthode* ..., c.1835), Alard (*Ecole du violon*, 1844) and Dancla (*Méthode élémentaire* ..., 1855; *Ecole de mécanisme* Op. 74, c.1882); Habeneck's treatise acknowledges the French debt to Viotti by incorporating facsimiles of extracts from the Italian's unfinished elementary method. The Belgian school was also heavily indebted to Viotti as witnessed in the contents of de Bériot's (1858) and Léonard's (1877) instruction books, both committed to 'imitating the accents of the human voice'[10] as opposed to cultivating virtuosity for its own sake.

Such virtuosity is described by Guhr in his *Ueber Paganinis Kunst* ... (1829), an informative account of Paganini's performing style. Intended not as a comprehensive violin method but 'merely as an appendix to such as already exist',[11] it focuses in particular on Paganini's tuning of the instrument, bowstrokes, combination of left-hand pizzicato with bowing, use of harmonics in single and double stopping, *una corda* playing and the extraordinary *tours de force* for which he was renowned. By contrast, Spohr's conservative *Violinschule* (1832) is a more characteristic German product, restricted somewhat by the technical and stylistic limitations that he himself imposed. Spohr objected to many of the effects employed by Paganini and other virtuosi, notably 'thrown' bowings, artificial harmonics and suchlike, preferring to cultivate a more 'classical' on-the-string bowing technique and singing tone. His pupil David, who is also notable for his anthology of seventeenth- and eighteenth-century violin works, *Die hohe Schule des Violinspiels* (1867–72), followed suit in his *Violinschule* (1864). The three-volume *Violinschule* (1902–5) published under the name of David's pupil Joachim, appears to have been written largely by Joachim's pupil Andreas Moser. Joachim's contribution apparently consisted only in making performing editions of several seventeenth- and eighteenth-century works. Otherwise, the treatise itself is notable for its concentration on matters of phrasing, dynamic expression and tuning. Among other notable Austro-German writers of violin treatises in the second half of the nineteenth century were Zimmerman (c.1842), Dont (1850), Kayser (1867), Courvoisier (1873 and 1878) and Schradieck (1875).

Flesch attributes the development of technique and teaching methods in the late nineteenth century principally to Dont, Schradieck, the Frenchman Sauret and the Czech violinist and pedagogue Otakar Ševčík.[12] Like Schradieck, whose writings are concerned chiefly with fingering technique, the majority of Ševčík's pedagogical treatises comprise mechanical exercises for the left hand. Their subordination of musical values to minute technical detail has been criticised by many celebrated teachers, but Flesch has supported Ševčík's semitone system as a time-saving method towards developing adequate technical facility, describing it as 'a medicine which, according to the size of its doses, kills or cures.'[13]

One of Dont's pupils, Leopold Auer, proved to be one of the most influential teachers of the current century, his training and career reflecting the amalgamation of German, Franco–Belgian (and thus partly Italian) and Eastern European pedagogy. He did not claim to have any particular system of teaching, but his greatest gift was his ability to inspire in each of his pupils the will to achieve his maximum potential and self-expression on the instrument. His teaching principles, which place interpretation as the last major hurdle after technique, musical intuition and good taste, are expounded in his *Violin Playing as I Teach It* (1921). Another prominent twentieth-century pedagogue was Carl Flesch, whose *Die Kunst des Violin-Spiels* (1923–8) represents a synthesis of the various schools which formed the mainstream of violin teaching in the nineteenth and early twentieth centuries. He divides the art of violin playing into three interrelated elements: technique in general, applied technique, and artistic realisation – and very much in that order, in that technique can be learnt and developed but good artistry requires a degree of inborn musical ability.

Demetrius Dounis's *Die Künstlertechnik* ... bears the lengthy subtitle 'a new scientific method for achieving absolute mastery of advanced left-hand and bowing technique in the shortest possible time'. It is essentially a guide to efficient practising, while the Dofleins' *Geigenschulwerk* (1931) is most notable for its anthology of some eight hundred violin pieces spanning a range from the Baroque through to works by Hindemith, Orff and Genzmer. Ivan Galamian's teaching method embraces the best traditions of the Russian and French violin schools. For him, the key to technical proficiency is mental control over physical movement, but his is a flexible method with no rigid rules. More important is that the teacher promotes the maximum musical and technical development in each individual. His rational, analytical approach, expounded in his *Principles of Violin Playing and Teaching* (1962) and *Contemporary Violin Technique* (1962, with Frederick

Neumann), has achieved remarkable success, judging by the number of internationally acclaimed artists that have come through his roll – Perlman, Zukerman, Laredo, Zukofsky and many others.

Kato Havas's *New Approach* ... (1964) to violin playing involves 'not so much the imparting of knowledge', but 'rather the elimination of all the existing obstacles, both physical and mental, so that through a relaxed control and co-ordination the player may be able to release the full force of his musical imagination'.[14] More recently, Paul Rolland's string research project (1966–71) at the University of Illinois has resulted in his *The Teaching of Action in String Playing*, accompanied by some seventeen colour films, which cover topics of string instruction for the first two years of study. Rolland's approach emphasises rhythmic foundation and movement free from tension and is more scientifically than technically or philosophically based. He believes that good motor skills, whether in string playing, dancing or sports, involve highly refined actions requiring coordination, timing and patient practice. He emphasises the importance of well-balanced and relaxed body movements in musical performance, and his 'Action Studies' concentrate on cultivating a correct position, free movement, healthy tone production and accurate rhythmic responses.

The Japanese educator Shinichi Suzuki started to develop his 'Talent Education' or 'Suzuki Method' when he studied in Germany. It is not so much a 'revolutionary' method as 'a classic approach to talent education'[15] aimed at young children. Suzuki concludes that everyone is born with a natural ability to learn.[16] This ability can be developed as far as the student's individual 'brain capacity' will allow, given the ideal environment, which is dependent on a triple collaboration between the child, the parent(s) and the teacher. Suzuki's teaching method is subdivided into three parts: listening, for musical sensitivity; tonalisation, for tone development; playing, for technical and artistic development. Its principal goal is to cultivate artistic appreciation in students in their formative years, allowing them, unlike Flesch's method, to develop their artistic potential simultaneously with technical skills.

Study material[17]

Early writings about violin playing were descriptive and included little of musical content. However, as violin treatises began to multiply and their texts became more detailed, their musical content generally became more copious, many incorporating short dance pieces or even substantial étude-like compositions designed to assist in the mastery of particular technical problems. Pieces in binary form were most common, but sonata, variation, fugue and other forms, including two-movement structures, were also employed. By the end of the eighteenth century, several books composed solely of studies had begun to appear independently as pedagogical works in their own right, marking the beginning of the enormous étude literature of the nineteenth century.

A wide variety of descriptive terminology for study material was employed during the eighteenth century, most notably 'étude', 'caprice',[18] 'exercice', 'matinée'. These terms generally denoted a short complete composition designed to exercise the student in certain technical procedures, sometimes specified by the composer, but rarely supplemented by detailed instructions.

Two major collections of advanced studies were published in France at the end of the eighteenth century – Gaviniès's *Les Vingt-quatre Matinées* (1794) and Kreutzer's *40 Etudes ou caprices pour le violon* (1796?).[19] Gaviniès's demanding studies are designed to promote suppleness in bowing and to perfect the left-hand action in all positions (up to and including e^4), especially the fourth, fifth, sixth and seventh positions. Many editions of Kreutzer's *Etudes* ... now comprise forty-two instead of the original forty studies. Nos. 13 and 24 were added (c.1850) by 'a French reviser, to make the work a trifle more complete'.[20] Kreutzer's sequel to this collection, *Etudes des diverses positions et démanchés pour violon*,[21] was designed chiefly to perfect position-work and shifting.

Rust's third and last *Solosonate für Violine mit Begleitung einer Zweiten* (1795–6) is often classified as a study, because it was intended to be played entirely on the E string and then transposed to the other three strings in turn. Facility in shifting and *una corda* playing was its goal, its three movements requiring an advanced technical standard, especially the final set of variations. Two posthumous publications of *Etudes de violon ou caprices* (n.d.) by Franz and Georg Benda are also worthy of note.[22]

Bruni's *Caprices et airs variés en forme d'études* (1787) and Fiorillo's *Etude pour le violon, formant 36 caprices* Op. 3 (c.1793) were among the first independent violin study collections published by Italians. Although of an advanced standard, Bruni's first set is surpassed in technical demand by his more varied and artistically satisfying *Cinquante Études pour le violon* (c.1798). Some of these are prefixed by preludes and many include an accompaniment for a second violin. Fiorillo's caprices, designed chiefly to cultivate flexibility of bowing and mastery of high position-work, are arranged so that each leads harmonically to the next. Elsewhere, the numerous pedagogical works of the Bohemian violinist Václav Pichl are particularly remarkable, notably his *Douze Caprices à violon seul* Op. 19[23] and the Andante for violin with 100 variations.[24]

The étude and related study material flourished at the beginning of the nineteenth century, prompted by the more favourable social conditions, the increasing musical interest of the amateur, the expanding music-publishing industry, the growth of the various conservatoires and the introduction of a more systematic approach to musical education. A genre known as the 'concert étude' evolved; combining technical difficulty with interpretative problems, it was exploited as both pedagogical and concert repertory.

Rode's *24 Caprices* ... (1813), comprising one caprice in each of the major and minor keys, stand out as one of the major early nineteenth-century *opera*, surpassing his later *12 Etudes* (published posthumously, c.1834) and Baillot's *12 Caprices* Op. 2 and *24 Etudes*. But Rode's achievement was soon challenged by one of Baillot's pupils, Mazas, whose *75 Études...* Op. 36 were published in three volumes and arranged in progressive order of difficulty. Indeed, the final volume of *18 Etudes d'artistes* closely resembles Rode's *24 Caprices* in its stylistic, expressive, artistic and technical aims. Among later contributors to the study literature in France were Dancla, Alard, Edouard Nadaud, Henri Marteau, Eugène Sauzay (Baillot's son-in-law), Paul Viardot and Lucien Capet. Capet's *La Technique supérieure de l'archet* (1916) has received particular acclaim. Among the pedagogues of the Franco-Belgian school, Nicolas Wéry wrote numerous studies for his pupils at the Brussels Conservatoire. De Bériot, Lambert Meerts, Prume, Léonard, Vieuxtemps, Crickboom and Sauret followed suit with similar works, including many of extremely advanced standard.

Apart from some minor works by Polledro, Puppo, Rolla and Raimondi and the posthumous publications of studies by Mestrino, Italy is represented chiefly by the works of Rovelli, Campagnoli, Saint-Lubin, Paganini and Sivori in the nineteenth century. Rovelli's twelve studies (*[6] Caprices* Op. 3 and *[6] Nouveaux caprices* Op. 5) and much of Campagnoli's pedagogical material (notably his *Sept Divertissements ...* Op. 18) focus on problems of the left hand (especially extensions and contractions, intonation and position-work), although bowing technique is by no means neglected. Attempts to locate Campagnoli's *Raccotta di 101 pezzi facili e progressivi pel violino* Op. 20[25] have failed. Paganini's *[24] Caprices* Op. 1 (published c.1818 but written c.1801) were inspired by Locatelli's caprices in the concertos of his *L'arte del violino* Op. 3. They display most of the principal ingredients of Paganini's virtuoso style of performance and composition,[26] amalgamating musical, melodic, harmonic, expressive, formal and technical considerations into a unified whole. Paganini's *Variations on Baruccaba* Op. posth. show similar musical inventiveness, each variation presenting a different challenge or special effect. The Turin-born Léon de Saint-Lubin enriched the violin repertory with several études, six of which were later edited by Jenö Hubay, while Sivori is notable chiefly for his *12 Études-caprices* Op. 25.

The first nineteenth-century German contribution of note for its pedagogical intent was Andreas Romberg's *Etudes ou trois sonates ...* Op. 32, three two-movement sonatas for solo violin. The influence of the

French violin school is evident in Anton Bohrer's *Caprices ou 18 études pour le violon* (c.1820) and Ludwig Maurer's *Neuf Études ou caprices* Op. 39, while Joseph Mayseder's *[6] Etudes* Op. 29 lean more towards the virtuoso. The publication of études in Germany later increased remarkably, prompted by numerous influential pedagogues, notably Joseph von Blumenthal, Hubert Ries, Georg Wichtl, Ferdinand David, Karl Hering, C. Böhmer, Moritz Schoen, Heinrich Praeger, Franz Schubert, Heinrich Kayser, August Casorti, Friedrich Hermann and Franz Wohlfahrt, many of whom contributed to the study repertoire.

The Polish school came well to the fore at the beginning of the nineteenth century, represented chiefly by Durand (Duranowski) (*[6] Caprices ou études . . .* Op. 15), Lipiński (*Caprices*) and Jan Nepomucen Wanski (*Caprices* and *Gymnastique des doigts de l'archet*), while Philippe Libon carried the Spanish flag, even though his *[30] Caprices . . .* Op. 15, dedicated to his mentor Viotti, are not of an especially advanced standard. Edmund Singer and Carl Flesch are representative of Hungary, Flesch's *Urstudien* (1911) breaking new ground in their approach to fundamental matters of left-hand technique. Ondříček and Hans Sitt were most prominent in Bohemia. Sitt was a renowned professor of violin at the Leipzig Conservatoire and his numerous practical studies for the instrument are the most significant of his oeuvre.

The twentieth-century étude literature for the instrument is extremely sparse in comparison with the peak of the previous century. While this may reflect a reaction against the virtuosic excesses of the concert étude, it also points both to the reluctance of contemporary composers to work in the genre and to the reliance of violinists and teachers nowadays on a comparatively small, select corpus of study material drawn principally from the 'classical' French violin school of Rode, Baillot, Kreutzer, Mazas, Habeneck and others.

The duet

The duet for two violins (the second violin initially adopting an accompanying role) became popular for pedagogical purposes during the second half of the eighteenth century. Like the étude, the duet is a child of the instrumental treatise.[27] In addition to encouraging accurate intonation and exercising students in numerous basic technical matters, it helped to add informality to the relationship between master and pupil, and the accompanying second violin part guided the student in such disciplines as rhythm, harmony, style and expression. Löhlein, amongst others, incorporates numerous duets, annotated with technical instruction, into his *Anweisung . . .*, and Spohr openly acknowledges the benefits of duet practice,[28] even using the genre to illustrate the interpretation of solo passages from Rode's Seventh and his own Ninth Concertos.[29]

Just as the étude was eventually taken into the concert hall, so various composers cultivated the duet form to similar purpose. Among the most significant contributors to the violin 'duo concertant' of the late eighteenth and nineteenth centuries were Viotti, Rode, Romberg, Spohr, Rolla, de Bériot, Kalliwoda, Krommer, Mazas and Dancla. The current century spawned violin duos by, amongst others, Toch, Reger, Ysaÿe, Honegger, Badings, Prokofiev, Hába, Milhaud, and Bartók, although the latter's 44 Duos (1930) are expressly of pedagogical intent. Duets for violin and one other instrument form another branch of the genre – for example, the violin–viola works of Mozart, Bruni, Spohr, Kalliwoda, Pleyel, Copland and Janáček and especially the violin–cello works of Ravel and Kodály – but these are essentially works for the concert hall and beyond this chapter's brief.

14 The violin – instrument of four continents

PETER COOKE

No other musical instrument has until recent years been so widely used among all classes throughout the world as the violin. One reason, of course, is quite simply the musical perfection of the instrument – its sonority and flexibility in the hands of musicians anywhere, especially, with its capacity for clean and strongly rhythmic articulation and its penetrating tone, its suitability for the performance of dance music of all styles. At the time of its invention dance musicians throughout Europe were playing a variety of bowed string instruments from the *gue* (probably a type of rectangular box zither) in Britain's northernmost islands, to the rebec-like *lira* of Greece. Such musicians, professional and amateur, looked favourably on the newcomer: first, they must have found the violin an improvement on their own instruments and, for the most part, they could readily transfer their bowing and fingering techniques to the violin. Secondly, there must have been some status attached to an instrument which found favour in courts and homes of the wealthy, even though in those *milieux* the violinist was often considered to be a professional musician of rather low rank.

Outside Europe the adoption of the violin can further be seen as an index to the expansion of European influence over the centuries. Wherever they went colonists and traders took violins with them and, as often as not, encouraged indigenous musicians to learn to make and play them. Because we know that professional violinists were seen as low-class providers of dance music compared with the more genteel amateur players of the viol family, we are not surprised to learn, for example, that the early white settlers in North America preferred to teach their musically talented black slaves to play the violin for them so that they themselves were spared the task and were free to indulge in what became at times a passion for social dancing.

Though the violin seems to have appeared in most corners of Europe by the end of the sixteenth century, its indigenous predecessors survived in use alongside it for centuries and this makes establishing a chronology for the diffusion of the violin somewhat difficult. For one thing there is often a confusion of terminology, so that when one comes across an early mention of the use of violins one often cannot tell if this is simply a rather loose reference to any kind of bowed instruments. The Romanian folklorist Tiberiu Alexandru, in discussing the adoption of the violin among Romanian peasants, quoted by way of example the account of an army officer stationed in Oltenia during the period 1718–30. The officer noted that the natives were fond of dancing to the accompaniment of violins, flutes and drum – but continued by describing the violin as being made of a half-pumpkin covered with parchment.[1]

Conversely, the names of local indigenous instruments were often transferred to the violin proper. The best known example of this is the term 'fiddle', which for centuries in the United Kingdom, Ireland and North America has been used as a synonym for the violin and is still in use today to distinguish between those 'violinists' who have learned the playing style and repertory of classical Europe and 'fiddlers' who play a local dance or dance-song repertory with a very different style. Their instruments are identical; it is the style and repertory which is different.

Alexandru also drew attention to three other important aspects concerning the diffusion of the violin: first, whenever it was taken up by the common people they usually transferred to it a playing technique learned for earlier indigenous bowed instruments. (Alexandru added that such technique was generally despised by scholarly practice no matter how suitable it might have been for the particular musical and social context in which it was used.) Secondly, he noted that, despite its very perfection of form and tone as an instrument for the classical European tradition, it was often not adopted into other musical traditions without some modifications to suit local musical preferences and techniques. Examples are the addition of sympathetic strings (as in the case of the *keman* of south-western Moldavia and the *hardingfele* (or Hardanger fiddle) of western Norway); the tying on of a fret part of the way up the fingerboard so as to raise the overall pitch of a violin to that of the instrument it was replacing or accompanying; and the making of modifications to the bridge. Thirdly, Alexandru pointed to the great variety of non-standard tunings, which was not simply a result of ignorance of any need for standardisation. Different tunings were selected to facilitate the execution of special melodies, or for reasons of sonority when playing in certain keys or modes. Some of these features will be considered in more detail when specific traditions are discussed in the sections that follow.

European popular and rural traditions

Central, Southern and Eastern Europe

In addition to providing dance music, stringed instruments in South-Eastern Europe and many parts of Asia have found much favour for accompanying the singing of epic songs, presumably for centuries, and it is one of the virtues of the violin that it can be played resting along the left arm or propped against the chest, leaving the player free to sing (if he chooses) while playing. Most epic singers accompany themselves in this manner, providing instrumental preludes, postludes and refrains which allow them to rest their vocal chords and to recall or re-compose the next set of lines. This is true for gypsy singers of southern Romania as well as for the famous *guslari* (epic singers) of Yugoslavia, Albania and Macedonia, though here the *gusle* or *lirica* (in Greece the *lira*) has co-existed alongside the violin until very recently. Birthe Traerup, writing of the music of a Muslim country wedding in Kosovo, southern Yugoslavia has described how the singers used a violin, tuned to a rather lower pitch, to provide such accompaniments as well as to play for dancing, which was interspersed among the periods of singing.

Singing to one's own playing on stringed instruments was once probably far more widespread. This is suggested by the remarks of the French historian Brantôme, who wrote most unappreciatively of the crowd of Edinburgh musicians who one night in 1561 serenaded Mary Queen of Scots during her visit to Holyrood Palace, playing on 'The nastiest of fiddles (*méchants violons*) and little rebecs, which are as vile as they can be in that country ... and accompanying them with the singing of psalms'.[2]

Unlike in Northern Europe, where it was often played on its own, in South-Eastern and Central Europe the violin has long formed part of a great variety of ensembles. In Bulgaria, southern Romania and Greece the clarinet is often the principal melody instrument, with the violinist doubling the clarinet line in a heterophonic and highly ornamental manner and continuing to accompany the clarinettist while he sings. Plucked lutes and a drum usually complete the ensemble.

In these areas, too, Alexandru reports the occasional use of the *keman*, a violin modified by adding one or more sympathetic strings. In rural Turkey itself the *keman*, the local name for the ordinary violin, is played vertically on the knees like the older *kemence* (sometimes called the 'Black Sea fiddle'), which it has been replacing. Often the violin or clarinet has replaced the shawm in the *davul zurna* (drum and shawm) duo once common in the regions of Turkish influence. The gypsy combination of violin and *gardon* is a notable example: the *gardon* resembles a small double bass (often rather ruggedly constructed), but its strings are tuned in fourths and fifths (or octaves) and, lying over a flat

Ex. 37

bridge, they are beaten rhythmically, all of them simultaneously, with a short stick. Sometimes, as in Ex. 37, pizzicato on one string alternates with the louder beaten sounds – a clear parallel to the playing of the large *davul* with a thick beater in one hand and a thin switch in the other.

Central Europe is the area where European classical traditions have had a greater influence on the dance music of both peasants and lower-class townspeople and here one finds combinations of string bands (including first and second violins), often accompanied by zithers of the plucked or hammered type and with the more recent addition of instruments such as clarinets. The clarinet seems to have been steadily replacing bagpipes throughout this region. East Central Europe, Hungary especially, is also the area where the gypsy musicians reign supreme as violinists.

Sárosi relates in detail how the violin became a favourite instrument of the professional gypsy musician during the course of the seventeenth century; as early as 1683 'nearly every Hungarian nobleman has a gypsy who is a fiddler or locksmith'. As in many other parts of Europe, this was a time when the church in Hungary looked with disfavour on the violin as no more than the instrument of the devil – 'I would have all the violins found in every town and village, and, cutting them in two, hang them up on willow trees, and the violinists who play the dances would be hung up by their legs beside them.'[3] But in spite of such strictures gypsy musicians took to the fiddle with great zest as a means of earning a living; in any case, they were often tolerated as persons somewhat outside the law as it applied to ordinary townsfolk and villagers.

During the eighteenth century gypsies formed the personnel of regular theatre orchestras in some towns of Hungary and Austria but the average dance ensemble was often little more than a quartet, with two violins (one playing the *kontra* – accompanying part), a cimbalom and a bass.

Ex. 38

etc.

Some band leaders won considerable fame: Károly Boka (1764–1827), a more classical player than most, ran a large band of twenty to twenty-four players. It was reported that 10,000 people attended his funeral and about his playing it was once remarked, 'This man does not play the violin: he speaks on the violin.'[4] The significance of such a remark only became apparent to me after listening to a Hungarian village fiddler playing a programmatic piece in which he imitated the frustrated cries and words of a shepherd who has lost his flock. Franz Liszt wrote enthusiastically about the imaginative improvising of gypsy violinists. Both Liszt and Joachim enjoyed making music with them at times, and after one such occasion Joachim remarked that 'never had his mood been so stirred by a musical performance as by this'.[5]

Gypsy bands made no use of notation – which could have inhibited the imaginative improvisations of the leader – and their harmonic idiom was not based on classical functional harmony. In central Transylvania, for example, the second instrument, the *kontra*, is often a three-stringed viola which is given a very flat bridge so that by double or triple stopping the player can bow a continual succession of consonant triads, often in root position and with the occasional seventh, while the bass player provides a root to the harmonies (Ex. 38). Because of the degree of improvisation in the performances and because the lower parts are regarded more as a kind of additional rhythmic texture (with the *kontra* player often playing between the bass player's accented beats), there are often 'discordant' and 'illogical' progressions. Their rural clients were in any case rather indifferent to harmony and, indeed, when they made their own music, the rhythmically beaten *bourdon* (or drone) of a *gardon* sufficed.

Northern Europe

In Poland, Ewa Dahlig has documented the gradual replacement of a variety of types of fiddle by the modern violin, which is now the most widely used folk instrument.[6] The *złobkoci*, similar to the rebec or kit, continued to be played in the region of the Tatra mountains until this century. Attempts have been made to revive its use recently. The *mazanki* may well have been a Polish modification of the violin and was used for playing along with a bagpipe. It was similar to (but smaller than) the violin and was generally carved out of one piece of wood; it had only three strings, tuned about a fifth or more higher than the top three strings of the violin. One leg of the bridge was longer than the other and passed through a hole in the belly to rest directly on the inside of the back. The turn of the twentieth century witnessed the gradual replacement of the *mazanki* by a violin with an artificial fret. This latter served as a nut near the middle of the fingerboard and facilitated playing in the first position but in a higher register (up to a ninth at times) required for playing with a bagpipe. The *suka* was replaced by the violin as late as the period 1920–39, but not before its shape had been considerably influenced by that of the violin. It had a bridge like that for the *mazanki* and was traditionally held vertically and its strings stopped with the finger nails (suggesting perhaps a link with older bowed-lyre playing traditions of Scandinavia). Another type, the *skrypze złobione* ('hollowed violin') is one of many instances of locally made imitations of the violin, which, like the *suka*, *mazanki* and *złobkoci*, were eventually rendered obsolete by the ready availability of cheap factory violins. Some of these predecessors of the violin have been taken up again by modern 'folk revival' groups and serve as a symbol of Polishness. One can even hear them played by Polish exiles in London.

Violins were known in many parts of Scandinavia by the early seventeenth century and, as in many other parts of Northern Europe, were to become the chief instruments of the people. The lush valleys of south-western Norway saw the flowering of a particularly beautiful refinement of the violin in the form of the *hardingfele* (Hardanger fiddle). This instrument has retained the flat bridge and fingerboard and short neck of the Baroque violin but, like the viola d'amore, has four or five sympathetic strings which are led through a hole in the bridge and under the fingerboard up to an elongated pegbox. Many of these instruments are given rich inlaid and painted decoration.

The *hardingfele* is a solo instrument *par excellence* and has a large repertory of older dance-tune types including the *springar*, *gangar* and *halling* as well as bridal marches and other listening pieces. Unlike the more four-square structures of the newer violin dance repertory, *hardingfele* pieces make use of short, frequently repeated motifs, often widely separated in pitch level, and there is much melodic ornamentation,

Ex. 39   from 'The Kivle Maidens I', *gangar* after Johannes Dale, Tinn, Telemark

double stopping and use of intermittent drones. Ex. 39 is taken from the principal five-volume collection of the repertory, which contains notated specific settings said to have been handed down (aurally, of course) from famous earlier exponents of the tradition. This piece is one of seventeen *hardingfele* tunes freely arranged for piano by Edvard Grieg (*Slåttar*, Op. 72).

The tradition, like other violin-playing traditions in Scandinavia, is full of vitality today, encouraged by fiddlers' societies and competitions. *Hardingfele* players learn specific settings of tunes originally handed down aurally, and they deliberately cultivate a more traditional type of intonation in which a 'neutral mode' (one whose third and seventh degrees are neither major nor minor, but somewhere in between) is frequently used. Over twenty different *scordatura* tunings have been identified.

In Scotland and Ireland the violin vies with the bagpipe and harp respectively to be regarded as the principal traditional instrument for each country. Both countries have large and, to some extent, overlapping repertories – they include the earlier pre-nineteenth-century dance-tune types such as reels, jigs and hornpipes and the later quadrilles, waltzes, and polkas – but the two national playing styles are relatively distinct. Within both countries there is also evidence of considerable regional differences in playing style, but the influence of radio and the recording industry are tending to produce more homogenous national styles. Fiddle playing in the Shetland Islands is still regarded as one of the most distinct and liveliest traditions. Initially it was the skill and the high degree of participation by the menfolk of the islands that earned it this reputation. With traditional fiddling now being taught in schools throughout the islands, skills and enthusiasm are as great as before, but women players outnumber the men.[7]

In both Scotland and Ireland solo playing was the norm until comparatively recently. Interest in the individual settings and playing styles of musicians forms an important part of the aesthetics of traditional fiddling, and this is even more true now that fiddlers play less for dancing and more as chamber musicians. In Scotland one style of reel playing, named after the valley of the river Spey, gave rise by the early nineteenth century to a separate genre of reel known as 'strathspey', whose sharply pointed rhythms (including much use of what is popularly known as 'Scotch snap' – that is a pair of notes the first of which is extremely short) suggest origins in the rhythms of the Scottish Gaelic language.

The violin proved popular among all classes of Scottish society (they shared essentially the same repertory), but the love of the leisured classes for dancing, especially during the eighteenth century, saw a profusion of published collections of fiddle music that included many new compositions, not all of which were dance tunes, however. Out of the strathspey dance, the slow strathspey evolved as a recital piece which, with its delicate and at times florid ornamentation, is regarded today as a true test of skill for the Scottish violinist. Ex. 40 demonstrates the highly stylised manner in which the slow strathspey 'Madam Frederick' (by William Marshall, a famous eighteenth-century fiddler-composer) was performed by Hector MacAndrew.

One of the most influential of fiddler-composers was the flamboyant James Scott Skinner (1843–1927) the son of a traditional dancing master. As a boy Skinner received classical violin training in Manchester. He then returned to Scotland to continue the family profession, but became more a recitalist, including in his repertory many of his own pieces. His playing survives on disc today, inspiring many more ordinary fiddlers to emulate him.

Fiddlers' societies are active throughout Britain, Ireland and Scandinavia and the 'folk revival' of recent decades has further seen the fiddle repertory taken up by mixed ensembles that include guitars, free reed instruments, whistles, bagpipes and drums (for example, professional folk groups such as The Boys of the Lough in Scotland and The Chieftains in Ireland).

North America

The earliest colonists of the Americas almost certainly took their musical instruments with them, and the violin has been the most prominent instrument in North America for domestic entertainment at least since

Ex. 40   Slow strathspey: 'Madam Frederick' by William Marshall, as played by Hector MacAndrew, Aberdeen. Transcribed by P. Cooke from School of Scottish Studies archive film, 1973

the early eighteenth century. By this time colonists could afford to begin to cultivate social and artistic activities, among which dancing, as in their mother countries, was one of the most favoured pastimes. The eagerness of colonists to encourage their black slaves to become competent on the fiddle so that they could play for them has already been mentioned. At times the musicianship of one's slave was highly valued – hence the appearance in local newspapers of advertisements like the following: 'RUN AWAY ... A Negro Man about 46 years of age ... plays on the violin and is a Sawyer'.[8] The violin, with the banjo (an instrument of African origin) and some type of drum or tambourine, became their prime form of instrumental music making. Black fiddlers played for their white masters and for their own kith and kin, sometimes both in the same evening: 'The negro fiddler walks in and the dance commences. After they have enjoyed their sport sufficiently, they give way to the negroes, who have already supplied themselves with torchlights and swept the yard. The fiddler walks out, and strikes up a tune: and at it they go in a regular tear-down dance; for here they are at home. The sound of the fiddle makes them crazy.'[9]

Eileen Southern's history of the music of Black Americans[10] is replete with such accounts from the eighteenth and early nineteenth centuries. Presumably the slave fiddlers learned the standard dance repertory of the white settlers – jigs, reels, waltzes, quadrilles, etc. – though we know nothing about what they might have played for their own people's dancing. Even in the North, which saw the growth of large cities during the nineteenth century, the fiddle was for a time still king of the dance. Southern reports that every hall in the notorious 'Five Points' area of New York (a ghetto slum) was 'provided with its fiddler ready to tune up his villainous squeaking for sixpence a [dance] piece'. By the 1860s, however, the piano was discovered to be less expensive to use in such halls, for it could replace fiddle, wind and bass fiddle, but in the dance halls of the South, in New Orleans for example, the so called six- or seven-piece 'string bands' that included a couple of clarinets or violins, cornet, trombone, string bass, guitar and drums, continued to flourish. Nevertheless, by the end of the century the violin was on the way out, for in the crowded and noisy city dance halls wind instruments were better heard than violins; and after the Civil War, as Southern pointed out, Blacks were free to play any instrument they wished after decades of confinement to fiddle and banjo. The violin became less and less conspicuous in the newer dance bands, though the early jazz period spawned some excellent jazz violinists. In country areas the violin continued to be valued, as recently collected oral testimony now in the Library of Congress at Washington vividly illustrates: 'One day I see Marse Thomas a twistin' de ears on a fiddle and rosinin' de bow. Den he would pull dat bow 'cross de belly of dat fiddle. Something bust loose in me and sing all thru my head and tingle in my fingers. I made up my mind right then and dere, to save and buy me a fiddle. I got one dat Christmas, bless God! I learnt and been playin' de fiddle ever since ... Who I marry? I marry Ellen Watson, as pretty as a ginger cake nigger as ever fried a batter cake or rolled her arms up in a wash tub. How I get her? I never get her; dat fiddle get her ... De beau she liked best was de beau dat could draw music out of them five strings ... '[11]

Whites did not leave all the music making to their Black slaves. In eighteenth-century Charleston, Carolina, any young gentleman was 'presumed to be acquainted with Dancing, Boxing, playing the Fiddle & Small-Sword and Cards',[12] and lively regional traditions of fiddle playing survive up to the present day in Canada and the USA. Though the violin is no longer the prime instrument for dancing, its repertory of tunes for square dances lives on amongst fiddlers who play for their own pleasure and who join together, like their counterparts in Scotland and Ireland, to hold regular competitions or group playing sessions in fiddlers' societies. These various regions have their own distinguishable styles, ultimately derived from the main ethnic groups who colonised these areas, though there was also much acculturation.

Linda Burman-Hall's study[13] suggests that greater cultural isolation in the more rural South led to the persistence of stronger traditions of fiddling there. She identified four basic sub-styles of Southern fiddling: the Blue Ridge style – to be found in an area parallel to and east of the

Appalachian mountain chain, the southern Appalachian style (along the line of the mountains), the Ozark mountain style and the western style typified by the fiddling of Texas and Oklahoma. Her descriptions of these styles read very much like descriptions of traditional Scottish and Irish fiddle playing, which perhaps only goes to show how imprecise words are for describing differences of performing style. She mentions *scordatura* tunings, neutral intonation, inflected pitches, bowings slurred over accents and much use of open strings as occasional drones. All of these features were often brilliantly demonstrated by the more virtuoso fiddlers singled out for exposure when, from the late 1920s, the popular record industry began to take an interest in hill-billy music, and styles such as that of The Bluegrass Boys became popular far outside their native areas.

There seems, however, to have developed an important difference between the fiddling of the Americans and that of the Scots and Irish 'back home'. Both sides of the Atlantic initially shared the same four-square dance repertory, but in the New World there is a strong aurally transmitted tradition of variation-making during the performance of such tunes. This is, I suggest, the result of the African influence on fiddle style. For African musicians the varied repetition of their short musical patterns within the framework of the pattern is the norm, and Black fiddlers probably have given the same kind of treatment to the short tune structures of the colonists – there is little evidence that in the eighteenth and nineteenth century the Scots or Irish practised much variation-making even though the essentially aural nature of the transmission of the repertory would have allowed for it. Since those times greater familiarity with 'standard' settings has tended to inhibit tendencies for improvisation.

Latin America

Though various types of accordions are increasingly replacing it (as is, indeed, the case throughout the world), the violin is in widespread use all over Latin America, along with guitar and harp, all three being introduced by the Hispanic colonisers from the very beginning. Among Cortes's companions who sailed from Cuba to Mexico with him in 1519 were six musicians, including one Ortiz, who was an excellent viol player and who lost no time in setting up his own music academy. In Mexico particularly, the Hispanic colonisers were amazed at the speed with which the local Indians took to learning their music and the Church was at times embarrassed by the number of competent instrumentalists and singers eager to contribute to Christian worship (so as to better themselves economically as much as spiritually). The first Bishop of Mexico had instructed his missionaries (Dominican, Franciscan and Augustinian friars mostly) to teach music wherever they went 'as an indispensable aid in the process of conversion'.

In Mexico the first cathedral orchestra was founded in 1554 and twenty years later was considerably augmented, including fifteen viols *da bracchio* among the various classes of viols used. We can assume that violins themselves were adopted equally readily. They were certainly in use in the orchestra a century later, and in Paraguay the Jesuit José Cardel reported that around 1730 every small town supported thirty to forty musicians including up to half a dozen violinists. Stevenson[14] notes that the Mexican Indians proved to be very ready to learn the skills of instrument making, so it is not surprising that a large number of locally made imitations of the violin were in use. However, Baumann considers that some of them, such as one-string fiddles, are not really debased versions of violins but of Afro-Arab origin; he further suggests that the use of the name *rabel*, for numerous three-stringed instruments in use in Chile, Guatemala and formerly in Panama, indicates Spanish-Arab provenance.

During the last two centuries the genteel, stylish salon music brought over by later colonists permeated all levels of the colonial and mestizo communities. The repertory consisted of minuets, *contradanzas*, polonaises, mazurkas (commonly called *varsovianas*), polkas and the *cotilio* – a remnant section of sets of tunes for *las cuadrillos* (the quadrilles). The ensembles also tended to be modelled on those of the salons of Spain and Portugal, with pairs of violins, playing often in parallel thirds, supported by guitars, *charangos*, other types of plucked lute and a harp or other bass instrument. Since 1900 other European instruments have joined the ensembles. For instance, the popular *mariachi* (from Fr. *mariage*) ensemble of Mexico often consists of up to three violins, two trumpets, *guitarron*, rhythm and other guitars. The violin-playing style is typified by the playing of the El Ciego Melquiades ('The Blind Magician'), who uses vibrato, some slides and occasional harmonics, backed as always by a vigorous plucked accompaniment.[15] Hispanic instruments also found their way into the ensembles of rural Indians themselves. The Yaqui for instance use violins and harps together with older instruments such as scrapers, water drums and flutes. In Inca bands the harp provides a strong string bass for the melodies of flutes and violins,[16] and the Zarabandas ensembles in the central and north-eastern highlands of Guatemala use strings in a similar way. Lastly, Belzner has reported an unusual example of syncretism among the Macunar Shuar of Ecuador, where the violin has become a shaman's instrument and important in curing rituals. It is held vertically and is not fingered – rather it is played somewhat like the musical bow it has replaced.

The Arab world, South and South-East Asia

We have read that the bow originated in the Turkish-Arab world; indeed, while the violin was evolving in Italy and Germany many different bowed instruments not only were in use in the Arabic world but had spread further east in company with Arab trade (for example, to South-East Asia, China and Japan). Trade also took the Western violin to the East and in Iran, Syria and North Africa, it was found to be ideally suited for the improvisation of *maqams*. Hormoz Farhat, writing on the music of Iran, has commented that the violin is now hardly thought of as a foreign instrument, being 'so well suited for Persian music'.[17] Until very recently in many parts of these areas, the violin was held vertically for playing in the same way as the *rebab*, often resting on or between the knees. In the classical 'Andalusian' orchestras of the Maghreb and in the more Europeanised orchestras of cities like Cairo, Arab musicians have more recently adopted the classical European hold for the violin.

Nettl considers that differences in playing style and use of the violin between musicians of the classical Iranian tradition and those of the Carnatic tradition of South India serve to exemplify basic differences of attitude towards Western influence. The violin's rapid adoption in Iran along with Western solistic tendencies suggest to him a basic compatibility with Western music, whereas in India the violin was only slowly absorbed into a strong, viable musical tradition – a case of modernisation of instrumentation rather than westernisation of style.[18]

Although reportedly introduced to the princely courts of Malabar on the west coast by followers of Vasco da Gama some three centuries earlier,[19] the violin was only accepted into the Carnatic tradition after Balasvami Dikshitar (1786–1858) and his pupil Vadivelu gave it an accompanying role in the classical music of the court of Travancore at the beginning of the nineteenth century.[20] For classical Carnatic music it is usually tuned d–a–d^1–a^1. This is nearer to viola pitch than violin and a viola is sometimes preferred, for it produces 'a deep melodious and agreeable sound perfectly suited to male musicians'.[21] Absolute pitch, however, is dependent on the preferred pitch of the soloist; as accompanists, violinists 'shadow' the soloist, echoing each phrase and following the soloist wherever he or she goes, in a kind of perpetual canon.

Originally the violinist's left-hand technique was two-fingered, modelled on the technique of the *vina* (though today, many players have explored and adopted four-finger techniques). With the violin locked firmly between the player's neck and left ankle as he/she sits cross-legged, the left hand is able to move freely around the fingerboard introducing the slides and wide shakes (*gamakas*) of many kinds which are essential to the proper performance of an Indian raga. European-style vibrato is avoided.

The violin is beginning to find favour as a solo instrument in the hands of virtuosi such as L. Subramaniam.[22] In North India, while violins have yet to be adopted into classical performance, they form an indispensable section of the modern Indian film, radio and television orchestras. Bandyopadhyaya considers the violin today to be one of the most popular and common instruments of the bowed type in India, but it occurs rarely in Indian folk ensembles except for a genre of popular rural theatre known as *jatra* in Bangladesh, and for accompanying Odissi dance, and occasionally in ensembles for genres of devotional vocal music known as *thumri* and *ghazal*. Violins are now manufactured in large quantities in the sub-continent, particularly in Bengal.

The Portuguese took violins not only to Goa, on the Indian sub-continent, but also further east to Burma, Malaysia and Indonesia, where, not surprisingly, local names for the violin (e.g. *biola*) resemble the Portuguese name for the violin – *viola*. Here also Catholic missionaries seem to have taken active steps to give training in the playing of European instruments, and as early as 1689 in Djakarta wealthy families had their slaves learn European instruments. In one instance a trio of violin, harp and bassoon is reported to have provided music at meal-times.[23]

In less European settings the violin seems to have been slowly taking over the role of the *rebab*, or the shawm, both of them an earlier importation from the Islamic world, in a variety of small *gamelan* ensembles. Earlier this century the 'Gamelan Gandrung' of the Banyu-wangi district in West Java included two violins tuned near to viola pitch, which played along with a drum and gongs of different sizes.[24] An even greater mixture of instruments is used for the Batavian theatrical dance genre called *Lenggo* in which Malay songs are heard accompanied by three *robanas* (frame drums), a couple of violins and a Chinese moon-lute.[25] Other ensembles where violins are used betray Western influence in their names, beginning with the term *orkes* (from orchestra). *Kronchong* (*keroncong*) is the name given to popular westernised Indonesian music, whose instrumentation seems to have been continuously changing. In the port of Melaka, Malaysia, the violin used to partner the accordion and indigenous gongs. Kunst reported the use of mandoline, guitar, violins and ukulele for such music in 1951,[26] and today saxophones, trumpets and electric instruments have displaced most of these.

Such a survey as this is bound to be uneven, not only because of its extreme brevity but also because studies of musical change are much rarer than those dealing with the characteristics of supposedly more stable musical traditions (and in any case can never keep pace with the rate of change). The violin music of some large and important countries, even of some continents, has been ignored completely – for instance fiddle playing in Australasia, or some of the more acculturated traditions in southern Africa, or the use of violins in the *ta-arab* music of Swahilis along the east coast of Africa.

What the future is for the violin outside the academies and concert-halls that foster our Western classical tradition is anyone's guess. As an instrument of popular Western dance its days already seem over. First came the free-reed instruments such as the accordion, and now a wide range of 'electrophones' form the core of ensembles in dance-halls throughout the world. The development of electrified violins – normal violins fitted with contact microphones – was much needed in these contexts just as the now obsolete violins-with-horns of Augustus Stroh were a necessary invention in the early days of recording. It would be wrong, however, to overlook the determination of small groups of enthusiasts (in Europe and North America especially) who continue to take up the 'fiddle'. The older traditional dance genres they perform have in many cases taken on a second existence, and with regional or national cultures under threat, their fiddling is a symbol of their identity. For many more, the fiddle is valued for sustaining an attractive repertory of much-loved melodies.

15 The violin in jazz

MAX HARRISON

It is often assumed that the violin has had only a small role in jazz and related musics, although in fact its achievement has been quite large and varied. The roots of this diversity lie in the wide range of musics that contributed to jazz and allied forms. Jazz began in the USA, whence countless immigrants travelled from Europe, plus many involuntary immigrants from Africa. They all took with them their music, which the new world changed, and it may be that the most significant aspect of jazz in particular is the extent to which it has reflected the mixture of cultures and races that characterises the country in which it emerged.

The violin's place in all this goes back a long way. In *Music in New Orleans: the Formative Years 1791–1841* (Baton Rouge, 1967) Henry Kmen writes that 'as early as 1799 fifes and fiddles were used' by the city's slaves. One line of descent from those times may be glimpsed in *Yodelling Blues* by the Buck Mt[1] Band (OKeh 45428, 1929),[2] where Van Edwards's fiddle reminds us of both country music and blues. So does the Johnson Boys' *Violin Blues* (OKeh 8708, 1928), except that Lonnie Johnson's violin, with its double-stopped imitations of train noises, anticipates the railway onomatopoeics of boogie pianists and more especially of the Quintette du Hot Club de France's *Mystery Pacific* (HMV B8606, 1937), and hence is closer to jazz.

All musics which flowed into jazz fiddling can be grouped under the usual 'vernacular' and 'cultivated' headings, and essentially there is a dialogue between the two. Most of the violinists mentioned here under-went some training in classical traditions, in certain later cases up to a high level, and this is nearly always a positive factor. European tech-niques of expression and execution both are modified by other require-ments and contribute to the latter's realisation. Thus in the quick *I've Got a Woman on Sourwood Mountain* by Earl Johnson's Clodhoppers (OKeh 45171, 1927) the leader's background in classical violin playing aids release of the music's wildness rather than weakening its stylistic integrity. This is something that can be observed repeatedly.

There was much regional variation in the country fiddle styles that were fed into jazz violin playing. Indeed, some individual traditions had considerable variety in themselves, an instance being the violin music of the Acadians, or Cajuns. They were originally French Canadians who settled in south-western Louisiana, where they remained speakers of French or of a *patois* derived from it. Guitars, banjos, *bal musette* accordions are present, but the fiddle remains the leading instrument, bringing with it suggestions of Irish reels and American hoe-downs, the latter done with a sort of European accent. There also are echoes of seventeenth- and eighteenth-century French dance tunes, cowboy songs, blues, Tin Pan Alley ditties. A good example is Wallace Reed's *Rabbit Stomp* (Arhoolie 5015), whose band includes a second violin, played by Isaac Soileau.

This was recorded c. 1956–9, which serves notice that the musics which contributed to jazz did not stop when it started, but continued alongside it, raising the question of cross-influences. Another latter-day musician, J. P. Fraley, an East Kentuckian active in the 1960s and '70s, achieved a compromise between the wildness of Georgian fiddle playing like Earl Johnson's and the gentler Cajun sounds. A piece such as his *Wild Rose of the Mountain* (Rounder 0037, c.1974) is lyrical yet with irregular rhythms which seem to echo French Baroque *notes inégales* and microtonal pitch deviations suggestive of blues.

Such is the diversity of this vein of music that one can do little more here than cite further contrasting examples. The output of Gid Tanner and His Skillet Lickers – e.g. *Back Up and Push* (Bluebird B5562, 1934) often has the wildness of Georgian string bands, while that of the North Carolina Ramblers, as in *Milwaukee Blues* (Columbia 15688D, 1930), is more controlled, purposefully shaped, although both drew their repertory from the usual wide variety of sources. Latterly such groups sustained their reputations with records and radio work rather than from just functioning in their own communities. This was even more so with subsequent developments like bluegrass, the Tex-Mex music of the Rio Grande Valley, and western swing, in which last the influence of jazz is particularly clear – e.g. *Cotton-Eyed Joe* by Bob Wills and His Texas Playboys (Columbia 37212, 1946). Inevitably the influence also travelled in the opposite direction, and Stuff Smith, an unequivocal, if overrated, jazz violinist, paralleled the country fiddler's short bowstrokes and brief phrases (*Onyx Club Spree*, Decca 1279, 1937).

For the country fiddler as for the jazz violinist playing for dancing, the instrument was an impetus to physical movement, though it was the latter who more deliberately explored its further expressive and technical potentials just as his colleagues were developing those of brass, reeds and percussion. It was this that led to most of what is most valuable and original in the music considered here, but the violin had meanwhile also entered jazz by another route. For all its syncopation, ragtime was a formally composed music, intended to be played exactly as written, and as such was an attempt at participation in the 'cultivated' tradition. Most ragtime pieces were published in orchestral form, a violin part always being included, sometimes two. Modern performances of some of these orchestrations can be heard from, for example, the New Orleans Ragtime Orchestra (Arhoolie 1058, 1971). Usually in such ensembles during the ragtime years the violinist was also the leader, and the phenomenon of the violinist bandleader lasted into the jazz period.

Typical were Charlie Elgar, who began with string groups in New Orleans, and Carroll Dickerson, whose band was fronted by Louis Armstrong in Chicago and New York. Few of these men were themselves jazz musicians, but they often exerted a significant influence. Eduardo Andreozzi, for example, was a Brazilian violinist whose band played jazz from 1919 onwards and who was one of the pioneers of this music in South America. Oivind Bergh had a similar role in Norway, Pippo Barzizza in Italy, Bernard Ette in Germany.

Also descending from the presence of violins in ragtime orchestrations is their employment in larger jazz ensembles. Here the pioneer was Paul Whiteman, who used quite varied groupings, for instance four violins and two cellos in *St Louis Blues* (Victor 20092, 1926), five violins and two violas on *Louisiana* (Victor 21438, 1928). Whiteman's arrangers, notably Bill Challis and Ferdé Grofé, showed considerable resource in fitting strings into wind-dominated jazz textures. Jelly Roll Morton added two violins to his *Someday, Sweetheart* (Victor 20405, 1926) in an amusing satire of this tendency, but it is a pity Whiteman's initiatives were not properly followed up except by a few musicians directly associated with him, such as Frankie Trumbauer (e.g. *Manhattan Rag*, OKeh 41330, 1929).

Some of the larger swing bands of the 1930s and 40s employed strings, but nearly always ineffectively because of unskilful writing. For example in *Leave Us Leap*, scored by Ed Finckel for Gene Krupa's band (Columbia 36802, 1945), the nine string instruments can be heard only during the piano solo. The exception was Artie Shaw, who built his band round a string quartet and his own clarinet. There are excellent pieces which use just these instruments plus a rhythm section (piano, guitar, double bass, percussion), such as *Streamline* (Brunswick 7852, 1936). Even when a complement of brass and reeds was added Joe Lippman managed to score so that the strings still had a prominent role in the music, a good instance being *Cream Puff* (Brunswick 7806, 1936).

Ahead of the non-jazz-playing violinist leaders musically speaking were those rank-and-file members of bands who doubled on the violin and could improvise jazz with it that approached the standard of those soloing on instruments more conventionally associated with this music. An example is Edgar Sampson, who later became a well-known arranger, and who can be heard on Fletcher Henderson's *House of David Blues* (Melotone M12216, 1931). A similar case is Darnell Howard, a clarinettist

Fig. 45   Joe Venuti (c.1930)

and saxophonist who nevertheless plays capable violin jazz on such items as Earl Hines's *Cavernism* (Decca 183, 1934). That Juice Wilson could do more is suggested by solos like the one buried amid the minstrel antics of Nobel Sissle's *Miranda* (HMV B5709, 1929), but this individual-sounding violinist spent too much time in Mediterranean countries to be recorded as he probably deserved. After working with important bands led by Andy Kirk and Alphonso Trent, Claude Williams also spent many years in obscurity, chiefly playing the guitar. But he made a convincing return to the violin later, performing, indeed, with much greater freedom and authority than before, as in *Yardbird Suite* (Sackville 3005, 1972).

Beyond such players stand the jazz musicians who specialised in the violin, foremost among these, in the earlier phases of this music, being Joe Venuti (Fig. 45). His virtuosity enabled him to emphasise just those aspects of the instrument's character which best accorded with the jazz of his time, and he removed all doubts concerning the violin's capacity as a solo voice in such music. Before the instrument could be amplified Venuti, like other violinists in jazz, had the problem of making himself heard. This was partly solved by the uncommon incisiveness of his playing but also by an unusually acute ensemble sense. In Red Nichols's *Bugle Call Rag* (Brunswick 3490, 1927), for example, Venuti can easily be followed because he threads such an individual, and essentially violinistic, path through the collective improvisation. And the quality of his solo playing was such that on Jean Goldkette's *Clementine* (Victor 20994, 1927) he could take his turn between two cornet improvisations by the great Bix Beiderbecke without letting down the music's overall tension.

The partnership of violin and guitar used to such effect by country fiddlers was also pursued by Venuti in company with Eddie Lang, the first outstanding guitarist of jazz. Their zestful *Wild Cat* (OKeh 40762, 1927) typifies the results. This basic relationship was extended into other, often adventurous, instrumentations producing the earliest examples of jazz chamber music. An instance is Venuti's Blue Four, which combined violin and guitar with bass saxophone and piano. In fact it is not possible to refer here to all aspects of his singular achievement. Venuti was still producing jazz of high quality into the 1970s and was sufficiently adaptable to work with prominent modernists such as the tenor saxophonist Zoot Sims (e.g. *Small Hotel*, Chiaroscuro 128, 1974).

Naturally Venuti had disciples, such as Matty Malneck in the USA, Stan Andrews in England, Cesare Galli in Italy, Otto Lington and Svend Asmussen in Denmark, although the last of these later pursued a more independent path. Others were doing the same, often with the violin–guitar partnership as the basis of fresh ventures. The Quintette du Hot Club de France was formed to provide a context for the work of the Belgian gypsy guitarist Django Reinhardt, the first major figure in jazz who was not American. It teamed him with two further guitars, double bass, and violin played by Stéphane Grappelli, and produced a whole range of sounds and textures that were new to jazz. On records such as *Minor Swing* (Swing 23, 1937) the invention, emotional power and originality of Reinhardt's improving makes his the dominant voice, but Grappelli's elegant playing provides an apt foil.

It is said that the violinist Reinhardt would have preferred in the Quintette was Michel Warlop, whose brilliant duets with the guitarist, such as *Christmas Swing* (Swing 15, 1937), make this theory seem plausible. Warlop ranged from exquisite tone-painting in *Taj Mahal* (Swing 28, 1937) to *Harlem Hurricane*'s fire and fantasy (Columbia DF20040, 1936). There are Gallic echoes of American string bands in his String Septet with its violins, guitars, sometimes harp – e.g. *Retour* (Swing 100, 1941) – and he undertook early 'third stream' ventures such as his *Swing Concerto* (Jazz Time 251272–2, 1942). Since his premature death in 1947 Warlop has been almost forgotten, yet he is the major European jazz violinist, at least up until the arrival of Jean-Luc Ponty.

Another who did his best work in Paris was the American Eddie South, who studied in Chicago and Budapest, where he was influenced by gypsy violinists. His earlier and later recordings are uneven, but South's 1937 performances with Reinhardt, such as *Sweet Georgia Brown* (Swing 8), are among the finest violin jazz of any period, exactly matching the instrument's resources to the needs of jazz. A special case of the violin–guitar relationship, also dating from 1937, is that of Emilio and Ernie Caceres, who added violin and clarinet doubling baritone saxophone to Johnny Gomez's guitar. Theirs is music of exceptional colour and animation, as in *Who's Sorry Now?* (Victor 25719), and it is noteworthy that Emilio Caceres, another forgotten man, was able to produce jazz of similar quality thirty-two years later (Audiophile AP101, 1969).

Attempts at amplifying the violin began with Augustus Stroh early in the century. Stuff Smith was a pioneer in the jazz use of an amplified instrument in the 1930s and he has been followed by the great majority of later players. Most employ a microphone, a transducer, or an electric violin – one that has a built-in transducer. Other electronic devices have also been adopted to improve and vary the instrument's sound: these include equalisers, wa-wa pedal, echo, time-delay and reverberation units.

Each significant jazz violinist since World War II has used this equipment to individual ends, gradually extending the resources. However, the major figure in this large group, the latter-day equivalent to Joe Venuti in the size and diversity of his achievement, is Jean-Luc Ponty. Like Warlop, he originally intended to be a classical violinist and won a Paris Conservatoire *premier prix* at seventeen. Devoting himself entirely to jazz from 1964, Ponty has performed with many distinguished musicians and groups, such as the second Mahavishnu Orchestra, led bands of his own, toured widely. Adept at an impressive range of distinct jazz styles and able to make a personal statement in each, he is an embodiment of the 'post-modernist' situation in which jazz finds itself in the closing years of the twentieth century. Illustrations of so large and richly varied an output can only be selected arbitrarily, but a start could be made with his *Upon the Wings of Music* (Atlantic 18138, 1975). From 1969 Ponty employed a violectra, an electric instrument sounding an octave below the violin, in 1977 replacing this with a five-string electric violin reaching down to c, and more recently playing both instruments plus an acoustic violin, using a synthesiser with this last to produce electronic effects.

The Polish violinist Michal Urbaniak has followed a similar course, employing additionally a six-string instrument going down to F. He is another one to work as both a classical and a jazz violinist, the latter in a wide variety of settings. Of particular interest is Urbaniak's *New York Batsa* (Columbia KC33184, 1974), which features the melodic phraseology and irregular metres of Polish folksong.

Amplification and the related electronic devices noted above have led to more jazz musicians taking to the violin than hitherto, and only brief comment is possible on a few of them. Leroy Jenkins, a pioneer of free jazz on the instrument, has claimed Heifetz and Eddie South as main influences, and of especial interest are his duos with the cellist Abdul Wadud (*Straight Ahead*, Red 147, 1979). A pupil of Jenkins, Billy Bang has followed his free jazz initiatives and says, 'Much of the time I'm playing quarter tones or eighth tones. I'm between C and C sharp a *lot*.'[3] The String Trio of New York, with Bang, James Emery (guitar) and John Lindberg (double bass), demonstrates the continuing affinity between the violin and guitar (*Rebirth of a Feeling*, Black Saint BSR0068, 1983). Bang has also produced works fusing improvisation and composition, such as *Outline No. 12* (Celluloid CEL5004, 1982) which employs three violins, three clarinets, soprano saxophone, vibraharp, double bass, percussion.

Another striking combination is Didier Lockwood's Swing Strings System, which uses violins, cellos and other instruments, as in *Paysages* (Uniteledis 131078, 1978). Lockwood is a further important violinist who has performed in many contexts and brings a virile temperament something like that of Michel Warlop to contemporary jazz. He should in particular be heard in duet with the great pianist Martial Solal in *Solar* (Stefanotis P963, 1981). Phil Wachsmann drew on a considerable variety of sources, including Webern, before turning to free improvisation and the use of electronics. He also has brought forward mixed media pieces such as *Colour Energy Reaction* for orchestra and film, but his playing is best represented by his unaccompanied *Writing on Water* (Bead 23, 1984). Several of these men have issued LPs of solo improvisation, for instance Jenkins's *Solo Concert* (India Navigation 1028, 1977), Bang's *Distinction Without a Difference* (hat Hut 1R04, 1979) and Zbigniew Seifert's *Solo Violin* (MRC 06645088, 1976). Among other contemporaries who deserve mention are Michael White, who is more influenced by avant-garde saxophonists like Ornette Coleman than by violinists, Jerry Goodman, who was in the first Mahavishnu Orchestra, Nigel Kennedy, better known as a classical player, Krzesimir Debski and Ric Sanders.

In parallel with this thorough exploitation of the violin as a vehicle for solo improvisation it has also been put to more effective use in large ensembles than formerly. Examples include André Hodeir's jazz cantata *Anna Livia Plurabelle* (Philips PHS900–255, 1966), where it is played by Jean-Luc Ponty, Martial Solal's Suite for big band (Gaumont 753804, 1981), where a cello is also employed. A string quartet is heard to fine effect in Gunther Schuller's *Abstraction* (Atlantic 1365, 1960) as are larger bodies of strings in his Concertino, Hodeir's *Around the Blues*, Werner Heider's Divertimento (all Atlantic 1359, 1960), John Lewis's *Encounter in Cagnes* (WEA 254833, 1987) and Wynton Marsalis's *Hot House Flowers* (Columbia FC39530, 1984).

Appendix

Principal violin treatises

The following pages provide bibliographical details of the principal treatises devoted specifically to the violin, arranged in chronological order by date of first edition and commencing with John Lenton's pioneering, if elementary work of 1693. It is intended to supplement the text (of Chapter 13 in particular) and is in no sense a complete bibliography of treatises for the instrument.

1693   John Lenton, *The Gentleman's Diversion, or the Violin Explained* (London, 1693; 2nd edn, 1702 as *The Useful Instructor of the Violin*)

1738   Michel Corrette, *L'École d'Orphée, méthode pour apprendre facilement à jouer du violon dans le goût françois et italien avec des principes de musique et beaucoup de leçons* Op. 18 (Paris, 1738/R1973; enlarged 2nd edn, 1779; ?3rd edn, 1790)

1751   Francesco Geminiani, *The Art of Playing on the Violin* (London, 1751; facsimile edn 1952. Fr. tr., 1752. Ger. tr., 1782)

1755(c.) Giuseppe Tartini, 'Regole per arrivare a saper ben suonare il violino' (MS, Bologna; facsimile edn as supplement to *Traité des agrémens de la musique*. Eng. tr. ed. E. R. Jacobi, Celle & New York, 1961)

1756   Leopold Mozart, *Versuch einer gründlichen Violinschule* (Augsburg, 1756/R1976; 2nd edn, 1769–70; enlarged 3rd edn, 1787/R1956; 4th edn, 1800. Dutch tr., 1766/R1965. Fr. tr., 1770. Eng. tr., 1939 [?1948]; 2nd edn. 1951/R1985)
       José Herrando, *Arte y puntual explicación del modo de tocar el violín* (Paris, 1756)

1761   L'abbé le fils [Joseph-Barnabé Saint-Sevin], *Principes du violon pour apprendre le doigté de cet instrument et les différens agrémens dont il est susceptible* (Paris, 1761/R1961; 2nd edn, 1772)

1770   Valentin Roeser, *Méthode raisonnée pour apprendre à jouer le violon* (Paris, 1770)
       Giuseppe Tartini, 'Lettera [dated 1760] del defonto Sig. Giuseppe Tartini alla Signora Maddalena Lombardini', *L'Europa letteraria*, vol. II (Venice, 1770. Eng. tr. 1771/R1967)

1774   Georg Simon Löhlein, *Anweisung zum Violinspielen mit praktischen Beyspielen und zur Uebung mit vier und zwanzig kleinen Duetten erläutert* (Leipzig & Züllichau, 1774; enlarged 3rd edn, 1797, ed. J. F. Reichardt)

1776   Johann Friedrich Reichardt, *Ueber die Pflichten des Ripien-Violinisten* (Berlin & Leipzig, 1776)

1782   Michel Corrette, *L'Art de se perfectionner dans le violon où l'on donne à étudier des leçons sur toutes les positions* (Paris, 1782/R1973)

1791   Francesco Galeazzi, *Elementi teorico-pratici di musica con un saggio l'arte di suonare il violino analizzata, ed a dimostrabili principi ridotta*, vol. I (Rome, 1791; 2nd rev. edn as *Edizione seconda ricorretta, e considerabilmente dall'autore accresciuta coll'aggiunta di molte, e nuove tavole in rame, e specialmente di quattro gran prospetti concernenti l'arte dell'arco*, Ascoli, 1817); vol. II (Rome, 1796)

1792   Johann Adam Hiller, *Anweisung zum Violinspielen, für Schulen und zum Selbstunterricht; nebst einem kurzgefaßten Lexicon der fremden Wörter und Benennungen in der Musik* (Leipzig, 1792; 2nd edn, 1795)

1797?   Bartolomeo Campagnoli, *Metodo per violino* (Milan?, 1797?. Fr. & Ger. tr., 1824. Eng. tr., c.1830; 2nd edn, 1834 and 1856)

1798   Jean-Baptiste Cartier, *L'Art du violon ou collection choisie dans les sonates des écoles italienne, françoise et allemande précédée d'un abrégé des principes pour cet instrument* (Paris, 1798; 2nd edn, [1799]/R1977, enlarged 3rd edn, c.1801)
        Michel Woldemar, *Méthode pour le violon* (Paris, 1798; 2nd rev. edn, c.1800 as *Grande Méthode ou étude élémentaire pour le violon*)

1801   Michel Woldemar, *Méthode de violon par L. Mozart rédigée par Woldemar, élève de Lolli. Nouvelle édition* (Paris, 1801)

1803   Pierre Baillot, Pierre Rode and Rodolphe Kreutzer, *Méthode de violon* (Paris, 1803/R1974)
        Giuseppe Maria Cambini, *Nouvelle Méthode théorique et pratique pour le violon* (Paris, [1803]/R1972)

1807   Johann Anton André, *Anleitung zum Violinspielen in stufenweise geordneten Uebungsstücken* Op. 30 (Offenbach, 1807)

1810–11 Franz Joseph Froehlich, *Vollständige theoretisch-praktische Musikschule für alle beym Orchester gebräuchliche wichtigere Instrumente* (Cologne & Bonn, 1810–11)

1829   Karl Guhr, *Ueber Paganinis Kunst die Violine zu spielen; ein Anhang zu jeder bis jetzt erschienen Violinschule nebst einer Abhandlung über das Flageoletspiel in einfachen und Doppeltönen* (Mainz, [1829]. Fr. tr., [1830]. It. tr., 1834. Eng. tr., [1915])

1830   Jacques-Féréol Mazas, *Méthode de violon, suivie d'un traité des sons harmoniques en simple et double corde* Op. 34 (Paris, 1830; ed. V. Bretonnière, Paris, c.1850; ed. G. Enescu, Paris, 1916)

1832   Louis Spohr, *Violinschule. In drei Abtheilungen. Mit erläuternden Kupfertafeln* (Vienna, 1832/R1960. Eng. tr., 1843)

1834   Pierre Baillot, *L'Art du violon: nouvelle méthode* (Paris, 1834)
1835(c.) François-Antoine Habeneck, *Méthode théorique et pratique de violon, précédée des principes de musique et quelques notes en facsimile de l'écriture de Viotti* (Paris, c.1835)
1844   (Jean-) Delphin Alard, *Ecole de violon: méthode complète et progressive* (Paris, 1844)
1850(c.) (Jean Baptiste) Charles Dancla, *Méthode élémentaire et progressive pour violon* Op. 52 (Paris, c.1850)
          Jakob Dont, *Theoretische und praktische Beiträge zur Ergänzung der Violinschulen und zur Erleichterung des Unterrichts* (8 vols., Vienna, 1850)
1858   Charles-Auguste de Bériot, *Méthode de violon* Op. 102 (Paris, 1858)
1864   Ferdinand David, *Violinschule* (Leipzig, 1864)
1873   Karl Courvoisier, *Die Grundlage der Violintechnik* (Berlin, 1873)
1875   Henry Schradieck, *Die Schule der Violintechnik* (Hamburg, 1875)
1877   Hubert Léonard, *Méthode de violon* (Paris, 1877)
1878   Karl Courvoisier, *Die Violintechnik* (Cologne, 1878)
1881   Otakar Ševčík, *Schule der Violintechnik* Op. 1 (Leipzig, 1881)
1887   Hermann Schröder, *Die Kunst des Violinspiels* (Cologne, 1887)
1898   August Wilhelmj and James Brown, *Modern School for the Violin* (London, 1898)
1899   Karl Courvoisier, *The Technics of Violin Playing on Joachim's Method* (London, 1899)
1902–5   Joseph Joachim and Andreas Moser, *Violinschule* (2 vols., Berlin, 1902–5; 2nd edn, 1959, ed. M. Jacobsen)
1904–8   Otakar Ševčík, *Violinschule für Anfänger* Opp. 6, 7, 8 and 9 (Leipzig, 1904–8)
1921   Leopold Auer, *Violin Playing as I Teach It* (New York, 1921)
          Demetrius C. Dounis, *Die Künstlertechnik des Violinspiels* Op. 12 (Leipzig, 1921)
1923–8   Carl Flesch, *Die Kunst des Violin-Spiels*, vol. I (Berlin, 1923; 2nd edn, 1929. Eng. tr., 1924); vol. II (Berlin, 1928. Eng. tr., 1930)
1926   Leopold Auer, *Graded Course of Violin Playing* (New York, 1926)
1931   Erich and Elma Doflein, *Geigenschulwerk* (Mainz, 1931; 2nd edn, 1951. Eng. tr., 1957)
1933   I. M. Yampolsky, *Osnovï skripichnoy applikaturï* [The principles of violin fingering] (Moscow, 1933; enlarged 3rd edn. 1955. Eng. tr., 1967)
1941   Demetrius C. Dounis, *New Aids to Technical Development* Op. 27 (London, 1941)
1960   Carl Flesch, *Alta scuola di diteggiatura violinistica* (Milan, 1960. Ed. and tr. B. Schwarz, 1966, as *Violin Fingering: its Theory and Practice*)
          William Primrose, *Technique is Memory: a Method for Violin and Viola Players Based on Finger Patterns* (Oxford, 1960)
1962   Ivan Galamian, *Principles of Violin Playing and Teaching* (Englewood Cliffs, N.J., 1962; 2nd edn, 1985 with postscript by E. A. H. Green)

1963–6   Ivan Galamian and Frederick Neumann, *Contemporary Violin Technique*: vol. I, *Scale and Arpeggio Exercises* (New York, 1963); vol. II, *Double and Multiple Stops* (New York, 1966)

1964   Kato Havas, *The Twelve Lesson Course in a New Approach to Violin Playing* (London, 1964)

1971   Yehudi Menuhin, *Six Lessons with Yehudi Menuhin* (London, 1971/R1974 as *Violin: Six Lessons with Yehudi Menuhin*)

1974   Paul Rolland, *The Teaching of Action in String Playing* (New York, 1974; 2nd edn, 1986)

1985   Robert Jacoby, *Violin Technique: a Practical Analysis for Performers* (London, 1985)

Glossary of technical terms

Acer: genus of trees, including the Norwegian maple (*acer platanoides*) and the sycamore (great maple or plane, *acer pseudoplatanus*), notable for its hardness, close grain and light colour.

Adjuster: a metal device located where the string is secured to the tailpiece; when operated by a screw mechanism, it facilitates fine tuning of strings (especially steel strings), particularly the E string.

Amplitude: the maximum displacement of a wave form.

Annular rings: red 'growth' lines of impacted resin in the wood which are crucial to an instrument's sound production.

Antinode: a point of maximum vibration.

Archings: the curved shapes of the table and back of a stringed instrument.

Arpeggio: the notes of a chord played in rapid succession, in ascending or descending order.

Atonality: a term for music in which no principal key is perceptible.

Back-plate: the strip of metal on the bow that extends along the back of the frog, ending on the underside next to the slide.

Bariolage: a slurred or separate bowstroke comprising repeated notes played alternately on two different strings, one stopped and one open.

Bass-bar: a thin, curved strip of spruce (usually about 265 mm long, 5 mm wide and 10 mm deep at the centre, tapering at both ends) set lengthways down the inside of the bass side of the instrument by the left foot of the bridge opposite the soundpost.

Basso continuo: see *Continuo.*

Bee-sting: the small projection of the black part of the purfling into the corner beyond the mitre; also, the fine cut which ends the spiral of the scroll by the eye.

Belly: the table, or top of a stringed instrument; it is normally arched and has two f-holes cut into it on either side of where the bridge is positioned.

Block: a piece of softwood glued inside the violin against the ribs where their ends meet to support them and hold them in shape. The top-block also strengthens the neck fitting and the bottom-block assists in relieving the tensions exerted on the table by the strings. See also *Corner-block.*

Blue notes: in jazz, the third and seventh notes of the key, which are often prominent and played deliberately out of tune, are known as 'blue notes'.

Bottom-block: see *Block.*

Bouts: an inward curve or bend in a rib or ribs of a violin. The curves of the waist of the violin are called 'middle bouts' or 'C-bouts'; those at the top of the violin are called 'upper bouts'; and those at its base 'lower bouts'.

Bridge: a thin piece of wood (usually maple) which supports the strings at the appropriate height above the table and fingerboard. Its two feet rest on the table, to which the vibrations are conveyed. The table acts as a soundboard and in turn transmits the vibrations through the soundpost to the back of the violin and to the column of air within.

Button: (1) the small half-round projection of the top end of the back, to which the bottom, or shoulder, of the neck is glued; (2) the round fixture let into the bottom-block. The tailgut is looped over it to secure the tailpiece.

Cadenza: a virtuosic passage in improvisatory style (normally drawing on some prominent thematic material) provided by a performer (generally a concerto soloist or soloists) near the end of a movement or composition and closing with an extended trill on the dominant chord.

Canon: a musical structure in which at least one line imitates another after a gap in time.

Chaconne: a kind of continuous variation (in moderately slow triple metre) in which the 'thematic material' comprises a harmonic sequence whose first and last chords are generally stable even though the intermediaries may be substituted.

Chin rest: a small piece of wood or vulcanite of varying size and shape clamped to the violin generally nowadays on the G string side of the tailpiece to enable the player to hold the instrument firmly with his jaw, thus allowing the left hand perfect freedom in shifting and the instrument to speak more openly without any obstruction of the vibrations by the chin.

Col legno: Italian for 'with the wood' – a direction to strike the strings with the bowstick as opposed to the hair.

Concertino: (1) the group of soloists in a concerto grosso; (2) a composition in concerto style but usually in a somewhat freer one-movement form.

Con sordino: literally, 'with the mute' – the direction to position the mute on the bridge.

Continuo: abbreviation for 'basso continuo', a bass line which may be 'figured' (hence 'figured bass') and which implies to the accompanying keyboard player (generally harpsichord, but possibly organ, fortepiano etc.; or possibly, in some contexts, a plucked instrument – lute, guitar, harp etc.) the harmonies he is expected to play above it. The bass line was normally doubled by a bass stringed instrument (cello or gamba, violone etc.).

Contraction: refers to when the fingers of the left hand are contracted to less than their normal span.

Corner-block: the wooden block at each corner of the violin to which are attached the table, back and ribs.

Counterpoint: the art of making two or more musical lines fit together satisfactorily at the same time; or a musical passage exemplifying this technique.

Crémaillère: an early bow-type with a movable frog. When the desired hair tension was attained, the frog was held in place by an iron catch or loop set into one of several indentations in the bowstick.

Curls: the waves in the veined wood.

Damping: mechanisms by which vibration energy is lost.

Détaché: literally, a 'detached', broad and vigorous bowstroke; in the eighteenth century the *détaché* was synonymous with staccato.

Double: a seventeenth- and eighteenth-century term for a simple form of variation common in certain dances of the suite or partita.

Down-bow: Drawing the bow so that its point of contact with the string moves from the frog end towards the tip.

Dynamic: loudness

Extension: refers to when the fingers of the left hand are extended beyond their normal span.

Eye: (1) the circular inset on the sides of the frog or nut of the bow, often of mother of pearl; (2) the 'ears' of the scroll, which project on either side and at which point the spiral of the volute ends.

Ferrule: the metal (commonly silver) band around the lower front of the nut which strengthens the wedge area and spreads the hair into a uniform ribbon.

F-holes: the f-shapes cut in the table.

Figured bass: see Continuo.

Fingerboard: the long piece of ebony, flat underneath but curved on top, against which the strings are pressed when the player's finger(s) contact them. It extends from the end of the pegbox over and above the table to roughly the beginning of the f-holes, and it is generally narrower at the pegbox end.

Fluting: a concave channel or groove, especially on the back of the scroll; or on numerous pre-Tourte bowsticks.

Frequency: the number of oscillations per second (Hz).

Frog: see Nut (2).

Fundamental: the lowest-order mode of a system.

Glissando: literally 'sliding'. A method of sliding up or down the string with a finger of the left hand, distinguishing in so doing each semitone of the slide.

Grain: the arrangement or direction of the fibres of the wood.

Ground bass (basso ostinato): a kind of continuous variation. A short melodic phrase is repeated continually as a bass line (but not necessarily unvaried), while one or more melody instruments exploit the principle of variation to good effect.

Harmonic: usually used to describe modes of vibration which have natural frequencies related by integer multiples of the fundamental. So-called 'natural' harmonics are produced by touching the string lightly (not pressing firmly) with a single finger at the appropriate 'nodal' point. 'Artificial harmonics' are produced by two fingers, the first finger of the left hand stopping the required note firmly (acting in effect as the nut of the fingerboard), while another finger (usually the fourth) produces the harmonic by touching the string lightly at the appropriate point.

Input admittance: amplitude of the velocity per unit excitation force.

Lapping: the protective band of leather, whalebone or silver wire that covers the bowstick at and just above the frog. It assists the fingers in gripping the bowstick and protects the stick from wear.

Linings: the thin strips of softwood glued to the side ribs and plates inside the instrument to provide sufficient glue area to hold securely the table and back to the side ribs.

Martelé: literally 'hammered'. A type of percussive bowstroke characterised by
its sharp initial accent and post-stroke articulation.

Microtone: an interval smaller than a semitone.

Mode: vibration pattern in which all points on the surface move in the same
direction or in opposite directions.

Mortice: a cavity cut into the wood into which another part fits or through which
another part passes.

Mute: a device (metal, ivory, bakelite or wood), often in the form of a two-, three-,
or five-pronged clamp which is placed on the bridge in order to absorb some
of the vibrations and thus reduce the volume and alter the timbre of the
sound produced.

Node: stationary point on a vibrating surface.

Nuances: the subtler, finer shades of expression.

Nut: (1) a small block of ebony attached to the neck of a violin and placed
between the fingerboard and the pegbox to support and separate the strings
as they are led from the tailpiece over the bridge and the nut to the pegs; (2)
the heel of the bow where the tension of the bow-hair is adjusted.

Open string: an unstopped string which sounds its full 'open' length.

Ostinato: literally 'obstinate', 'persistent'. A phrase which is repeated persistently throughout a composition or section thereof.

Passacaglia: a kind of continuous variation based on a clearly distinguishable
ostinato, normally in the bass but sometimes occasionally in an upper
voice.

Peg: one of four substantial tapered wooden (ebony or rosewood) 'pins' which
are inserted into holes in the pegbox to secure the strings and regulate their
tension, and hence pitch. Each string is threaded through a hole in the shaft
of the relevant peg, the shank of which is at right angles to the string.

Pegbox: the part of the neck extending from chin to scroll into which holes are
reamed to receive the pegs.

Period: the time lapse between identical features in a wave form.

Pizzicato: a direction to pluck the string (or strings) with the fingers, usually of
the right hand.

Plates: the table and back of the violin.

Polyphony: music in which two or more lines are sounding at the same time.

Portamento: a continuous slide between two pitches which does not distinguish
the intermediate semitones.

Portato: a bowing in which two or more notes are played in the same bow stroke,
but detached.

Position: refers to the 'position' taken by the left hand along the fingerboard. In
'first position', the first (index) finger stops the note a tone above the open
string; in 'second position' it stops the note a major or minor third above; in
'third position', a perfect fourth above, and so on.

Purfling: a narrow inlay of wood set into a channel carved around the border of
the table and back of a violin. It normally comprises three narrow strips, the
outer two of a white or yellowish wood sandwiching one of ebony. It helps
to protect the edges of the instrument and is also ornamental.

Quarter-cut: wood cut radially from a tree so that the grain (annular growth
rings) run perpendicularly through the thickness of the specimen.

Quarter-tone: interval comprising half a semitone.

Resonance: the enlarged motion which occurs when a vibrating system is excited at its natural frequency of vibration.

Ribs: the sides (generally of maple or of equivalent hardwood) that connect the table and back of the instrument.

Ricochet: involves at least two notes being played in the same 'bowstroke' (either up or down), the bow being 'thrown' onto the string and the relevant notes articulated (usually in the upper third) through the natural 'bounce' of the stick.

Ripieno: the full orchestral forces in a concerto grosso.

Ritornello 'form': a type of structure commonly employed in the first, and sometimes the last movements of Baroque concertos. It comprises an alternation of sections for tutti and soloist(s), in which the tutti sections (in a variety of closely related keys) are based for the most part on similar material (the so-called ritornello) while the content of the solo sections is freer and more varied.

Rosin: a hard, brittle material obtained from the distillation of oil of turpentine. It is applied to the bow hair, giving it the requisite 'bite' to set the string(s) in vibration.

Saddle: the small piece of hardwood (usually ebony) over which the tailgut is fitted to protect the bottom of the table edge.

Sautillé: a short, rapid bowstroke taken around the middle of the bow so that the bow rebounds lightly off the string.

Scordatura: refers to any tuning of string instruments other than the established tuning (g–d^1–a^1–e^2 in the case of the violin).

Scroll: the curved head at the end of the neck, beyond the pegbox of a violin usually carved to resemble a scroll.

Senza sordino: literally 'without the mute'; a direction to remove the mute from the bridge.

Serialism: a technique of composition in which the twelve notes of the chromatic scale are arranged in an order that is binding for the work.

Shifting: the act of moving from one left-hand finger-position to another.

Slide: the rectangular plate of mother-of-pearl that covers the bow hair on the lower face of the frog, between the ferrule and the back-plate.

Soundpost: a small piece of wood (generally of pine or spruce), about 6 mm in diameter, which fits vertically between the table and the back of the instrument, directly in line with and slightly below the right-hand foot of the bridge.

Spectrum: a graph showing the relative proportions of the different frequencies making up a wave form.

Staccato: a detached, well-articulated stroke, normally indicated by a dot (or stroke) over (or under) a note. In modern violin playing, staccato involves the playing of several *martelé* strokes taken rapidly in one bowstroke (either up or down). When the bow is allowed to spring slightly from the string, the stroke is known as 'flying staccato'.

Sul ponticello: Italian for 'on the bridge'; a direction to play with the bow very near to the bridge, in order to produce a nasal sound-quality.

Sul tasto: Italian for 'on the fingerboard'; a direction to play with the bow further up the strings than usual, over the fingerboard.

Table: the belly or top arched portion of the violin, with two f-holes cut in it and with an outline similar to the back.

Tailgut: a loop of gut, wire or nylon attached to the tailpiece, which is in turn anchored to the button.

Tailpiece: a piece of ebony (or metal for high-tension metal strings) fastened by a loop (tailgut) to the button at the lower end of a violin and to which the four strings are attached before they pass over the bridge and to the pegbox.

Transient: the initial, non-periodic part of a wave form.

Twelve-tone: see *Serialism.*

Una corda: literally 'one string'; employed when a composer/performer wishes to exploit the uniformity of timbre offered by the execution of a particular passage on one string.

Underslide: a thin metal plate attached to the upper surface of the frog. It protects the bowstick from wear from friction between the movable frog and the stick.

Up-bow: 'Pushing' the bow so that its point of contact with the string moves from the tip towards the frog.

Vibrato: an oscillation in pitch within a small range produced by 'rocking' the finger which is stopping a string.

Volutes: the spiral-shaped sections of the scroll.

Wedge: the small block of wood that secures the hair in the frog and the head of the bow.

Notes

1 The violin and bow – origins and development

1 Of the scientific research aimed at restoring the classical recipes of Cremona to general use, the work of J. Michelman and L. Condax (of Eastman–Kodak) in the USA, and Raymond White (of the National Gallery) is particularly worthy of note for its influence on *luthiers*.

2 For example, the fresco, school of Garofalo, Palazzo di Ludovico il Moro, Ferrara, c. 1505–8.

3 The origin of the soundpost is more open to conjecture. Early German violins reveal evidence of a central soundpost but no bass-bar. The soundpost was possibly introduced as a support for the bridge by makers who were unaware of the bass-bar. A post which has been cut too short can still be made to fit by drawing it across the inside of the instrument, where the ideal position may thus have been discovered.

4 There are, however, Polish violins attributed to c. 1515 in the National Museum in Warsaw.

5 His familiar title refers to the device 'I. H. S.' (= Jesus) found on his labels.

6 It is possible that Gasparo da Salò's predecessor in Brescia, the viol maker Zanetto di Montichiaro (c. 1490–1560), also made violins.

7 See Chapter 2.

2 The physics of the violin

1 For a general introductory text see M. Campbell and C. Greated, *The Musician's Guide to Acoustics* (London, 1987). References to contemporary literature on all aspects of violin acoustics are given by L. Cremer, *Physik der Geige* (Stuttgart, 1981; Eng. tr. J. S. Allen, 1984); M. E. McIntyre and J. Woodhouse, 'The Acoustics of Stringed Musical Instruments', *Interdisciplinary Science Reviews*, 3/2 (1978), pp. 157–73; and C. M. Hutchins, 'A History of Violin Research', *Journal of the Acoustical Society of America*, 73/5 (1983), pp. 1421–40.

2 Different relative resonance placement occurs in violas and cellos because these instruments are not scaled versions of the violin. Experimental sets of scaled violins have been constructed (see Hutchins, 'A History'). The 'Violin Octet' is a set of instruments ranging from a tiny violin tuned one octave above the conventional instrument to a giant bass violin with a body length of 1.3 m.

3 J. A. Moral and E. V. Jansson, 'Eigenmodes, Input Admittance, and the Function of the Violin', *Acustica*, 50 (1982), pp. 329–37.

4 K. D. Marshall, 'Modal Analysis of a Violin', *Journal of the Acoustical Society of America*, 77/2 (1985), pp. 695–709.

5 An amusing discussion of rather less subtle innovations is given by E. Heron-Allen, *Violin-Making as it Was, and Is: Being a Historical, Theoretical and Practical Treatise on the Art and Science of Violin-Making* (London, 1884), Chapter 5, pp. 104–21.

6 C. M. Hutchins, 'The Acoustics of Violin Plates', *Scientific American*, 245 (1981), pp. 170–86.

267

3 The violinists of the Baroque and Classical periods

1 T. Mace, *Musick's Monument, or a Remembrance of the Best Practical Musick* (London, 1676), p. 236.
2 Quoted in C. Burney, *A General History of Music*, ed. F. Mercer (2 vols., London, 1935), vol. II, p. 337.
3 Entry of 19 November 1674 in *The Diary of John Evelyn*, ed. E. S. de Beer (6 vols., Oxford, 1955), vol. IV, p. 48.
4 Note by translator (?J. E. Galliard) of François Raguenet, 'A Comparison between the French and Italian Music', in *Musical Quarterly*, 32 (1946), p. 419.
5 J. Hawkins, *A General History of the Science and Practice of Music* (2 vols., London, 1875), vol. II, p. 806.
6 Burney, *A General History*, vol. II, p. 990.
7 Hawkins, *A General History*, vol. II, p. 904.
8 *Dr. Burney's Musical Tours in Europe*, ed. P. A. Scholes (2 vols., London, 1959), vol. I, p. 185.
9 *Ideen zu einer Ästhetik der Tonkunst* (Vienna, 1806), pp. 61–2.
10 Diary entry of 4 February 1715 in E. Preussner, *Die musikalischen Reisen des Herrn von Uffenbach* (Kassel, 1949), p. 67.
11 G. B. Rangoni, *Saggio sul gusto della musica* (Livorno, 1790), p. 51.
12 *Public Advertiser*, 18 February 1785.
13 W. Jones, *A Treatise on the Art of Music* (Colchester, 1784), p. 54.
14 Letter of 11 July 1763 in *The Letters of Mozart and his Family*, tr. E. Anderson, 2nd edn (2 vols., London, 1966), vol. I, p. 24.
15 W. T. Parke, *Musical Memoirs* (2 vols., London, 1830), vol. I, p. 6.
16 Foreword to *Ausserlesene Instrumental-Music* (1701), tr. in O. Strunk, *Source Readings in Musical History* (New York, 1950), p. 449.
17 For detailed information on the Somis family, see the introduction by Alberto Basso to Giovanni Battista Somis, *Sonate da camera opera II*, Monumenti musicali Italiani, vol. II, (Milan, 1976).
18 B. Schwarz, *Great Masters of the Violin* (London, 1984), p. 70.
19 *Das neu-eröffnete Orchestre* (Hamburg, 1713), p. 211.
20 *Roger North on Music*, ed. J. Wilson (London, 1959), p. 359; F. A. Wendeborn, *A View of England towards the Close of the Eighteenth Century* (2 vols., London, 1791), vol. II, p. 237.
21 Burney, *A General History*, vol. II, p. 992.
22 *Ibid.*, vol. II, p. 896.
23 *Public Advertiser*, 20 February 1777. Franz Lamotte (1753–80) had a brief but illustrious career as a violinist of outstanding technical ability.
24 *Dr. Burney's Musical Tours*, vol. II, p. 206, vol. II, p. 173.
25 Letter of 9 July 1778 in *Mozart: Briefe und Aufzeichnungen*, ed. W. A. Bauer, O. E. Deutsch and J. H. Eibl (7 vols., Kassel, 1962–75), vol. II, p. 395.
26 M. Kelly, *Reminiscences*, ed. R. Fiske (London, 1975), p. 122.
27 L. de la Laurencie, *L'École française de violon de Lully à Viotti* (3 vols., Paris, 1922–4), vol. I, p. 313.
28 *Dr. Burney's Musical Tours*, vol. I, p. 28.
29 Letter of 3 July 1778 in *Mozart: Briefe*, vol. II, p. 388.
30 Parke, *Musical Memoirs*, vol. I, p. 278.
31 *Morning Chronicle*, 15 February 1793.
32 *Oracle*, 20 February 1793.

4 The nineteenth-century bravura tradition

1 A. Veinus, *The Concerto* (New York, 1944), p. 154.
2 And at its forerunner the Institut National de Musique (1793).
3 Mayseder was to take over as second violinist in Schuppanzigh's Quartet.
4 Ondříček also studied with Lambert Massart in Paris.
5 *Violin Playing as I Teach It* (New York, 1921), and *Graded Course of Violin Playing* (New York, 1926).

5 The twentieth century

1 A. Spalding, *Rise to Follow* (New York, 1943), p. 36.
2 A. Moser, *Geschichte des Violinspiels*, 2nd rev. edn (2 vols., Tutzing, 1966–7), vol. II, p. 179.
3 J. Szigeti, *With Strings Attached*, 2nd edn (New York, 1967) p. 93.
4 W. Damrosch, *My Musical Life*, (New York, 1926), p. 152.
5 C. Flesch, *The Art of Violin Playing*, Eng. tr. F. Martens (2 vols., New York, 1930), vol. II, p. 75.
6 Although Enescu is the proper Romanian form of his name, the violinist himself changed the spelling to Enesco.
7 R. Daniels, *Conversations with Menuhin* (London, 1979), p. 26.
8 Y. Menuhin, *Unfinished Journey* (London, 1977), p. 96.
9 Carl Flesch also served on the faculty at Curtis from 1924 to 1928.
10 Flesch, *The Art*, vol. II, p. 125.

6 The fundamentals of violin playing and teaching

1 Self-assessment has become more possible in recent years due to the development of lightweight compact recorder cameras. These are easy to use and offer not only instant play-back facilities, but also good sound reproduction from integral stereo microphones.
2 R. Daniels, *Conversations with Menuhin* (London, 1979), p. 140.
3 J. Szigeti, *A Violinist's Notebook* (London, 1964), 'Postscript', p. 154.
4 R. Gerle, *The Art of Practising the Violin* (London, 1983).
5 J. O'Connor, *Not Pulling Strings* (London, 1987), pp. 133–6.
6 *Improve Your Sight Reading* (London, 1987), a workbook for examinations by J. Davies and P. Harris, is a welcome addition to the teaching literature in this field.
7 K. Havas, *The Twelve Lesson Course in a New Approach to Violin Playing* (London, 1964); P. Rolland, *The Teaching of Action in String Playing* (New York, 1974; 2nd edn, 1986); Y. Menuhin, *Six Lessons with Yehudi Menuhin* (London, 1971/R1974).
8 R. Jacoby, *Violin Technique: a Practical Analysis for Performers* (London, 1985).
9 The Alexander Method has also grown in popularity over the last decade and now features in the curriculum of several music colleges.
10 E. Friedman, *The Strad*, 96 (1986), p. 792.
11 *The Strad*, 95 (1985), p. 116.
12 P. Rolland, *Basic Principles of Violin Playing*, American String Teacher's Association (1959).
13 C. Libove in *The Strad*, 99 (1987), p. 519.
14 The arm-lengths of a random cross-section of pupils can range from 45 cm to 63 cm, showing that the same full-length bow is unlikely to be appropriate for everyone.
15 Rolland, *The Teaching of Action*, pp. 164–5.
16 For further information about the history of vibrato the reader is referred to Chapter 8; G. Moens-Haenen's monumental study *Das Vibrato in der Musik des Barock* (Graz, 1988) is also highly recommended along with W. Hauck's *Vibrato on the Violin*, Eng. tr. K. Rokos (London, 1975).
17 L. Sheppard, *Tale Pieces of the Violin World*, 2nd edn (Norfolk, 1979), p. 109.
18 J. Dorner, 'Strains of Music', *The Strad*, 95 (1985), p. 760.
19 N. Brainin, in *Classical Music*, 285 (12 October 1985), p. 23.
20 Y. Menuhin in Daniels, *Conversations*, p. 63.
21 C. Flesch, 'The Musical Memory', in *The Art of Violin Playing*, Eng. tr. F. Martens (2 vols., New York, 1924–30), vol. I, p. 167; Gerle, *The Art*, p. 84.
22 Menuhin, *Six Lessons*, p. 52.
23 Except on the most formal occasion, brief introductory comments can sometimes be advantageous; they appear to relax the atmosphere and in so doing enhance communication between audience and performer.
24 *The Strad*, 95 (1985), p. 682.
25 See S. Nissel, 'Teaching Chamber Music, *ESTA Review* 13/2 (1988), p. 10; V. Orde, 'On Quartet Playing and Technique', *ESTA Review*, 11/2 (1986), p. 3.

26 See I. Bartlett, NCOS, Necessity or Luxury?', *The Strad*, 94 (1983), p. 380.

7 Technique and performing practice

1 I. Galamian, *Principles of Violin Playing and Teaching* (New Jersey, 1962), p. 12.
2 See M. Corrette, *L'École d'Orphée* (Paris, 1738). J. J. Prinner's *Musicalischer Schlissl* (1677) is well in advance of its time in suggesting a chin-braced grip.
3 Baillot, *L'Art du violon* (Paris, 1834), p. 16.
4 L'abbé *le fils, Principes du violon* (Paris, 1761), p. 1.
5 L. Mozart, *Versuch einer gründlichen Violinschule* (Augsburg, 1756), p. 54.
6 *Ibid.*, p. 148.
7 For example, B. Campagnoli, *Metodo della mecanica progressive per violino* (?Milan, 1797?); Eng. tr (1824), part 3, no. 188.
8 For example, J. Reichardt, *Ueber die Pflichten des Ripien-Violinisten* (Berlin & Leipzig, 1776), p. 35.
9 Baillot, *L'Art*, pp. 146–9.
10 *Ibid.*, pp. 152–5.
11 L. Spohr, *Violinschule* (Vienna, 1832), pp. 120–1.
12 F. Habeneck, *Méthode théorique et pratique de violon* (Paris, c.1835), p. 103; Baillot, *L'Art*, pp. 152–5.
13 C. A. de Bériot, *Méthode de violon* Op. 102 (Paris, 1858), p. 237.
14 C. Flesch, *The Art of Violin Playing*, Eng. tr. F. Martens (2 vols., New York, 1924–30), vol. I, p. 29.
15 C. Flesch, *Violin Fingering: its Theory and Practice* (London, 1966) p. 365.
16 R. Philip, in H. M. Brown and S. Sadie (eds.), *Performance Practice* (2 vols., London, 1989), vol. II, p. 463.
17 L. Auer, *Violin Playing as I Teach It* (New York, 1921), p. 63.
18 *Ibid.*, pp. 24–5.
19 Baillot, *L'Art*, p. 152.
20 Spohr, *Violinschule*, section 8, pp. 54ff.
21 Habeneck, *Méthode*, pp. 103–6.
22 Baillot, *L'Art*, pp. 140–4; Spohr, *Violinschule*, p. 195.
23 F. Geminiani, *The Art of Playing on the Violin* (London, 1751), p. 8.
24 Spohr, *Violinschule*, pp. 175–6.
25 Baillot, *L'Art*, pp. 137–9.
26 J. Joachim and A. Moser, *Violinschule* (2 vols., Berlin, 1902–5), vol. II, p. 94. According to Flesch (*The Art*, vol. I, p. 40), Joachim's vibrato was 'very close and quick', while Sarasate 'started to use broader oscillations'.
27 Flesch, *The Art*, vol. I, p. 40. Flesch here claims that it was customary in the early twentieth century to distinguish between expressive themes, which might be given a little vibrato, and 'unexpressive neutral passages', which would not. See Philip, in Brown and Sadie (eds.), *Performance Practice*, vol. II, p. 461.
28 See, for example, Mondonville's set of sonatas *Les Sons harmoniques* Op. 4 (Paris & Lille, 1738).
29 See L. Mozart, *Versuch*, p. 101.
30 L'abbé *le fils, Principes*, p. 73.
31 L. H. Berlioz, *Grand Traité de l'instrumentation et d'orchestration modernes* Op. 10 (Paris, 1843); Eng. tr. M. C. Clarke (London, 1858), p. 21.
32 Preface to his *Hortulus Chelicus* (Mainz, 1688).
33 See T. Russell, 'The Violin Scordatura', *Musical Quarterly*, 24 (1938), pp. 84–96.
34 L'abbé *le fils, Principes*, p. 1; this phrase is used by many writers on the violin from Bismantova (1677) to those of the current century.
35 J. Herrando (*Arte y puntual explicación del modo de tocar el violín*, Paris, 1756) claims that the elbow should be separated from the body by about the distance between the extended thumb and index finger.
36 Not until Corrette's *L'École d'Orphée* (1738) is the thumb-on-stick grip offered as an alternative in French tutors, and it is even then identified as an Italian practice.
37 Baillot, *L'Art*, p. 12.
38 L'abbé *le fils, Principes*, p. 1.

39 See, for example, J. B. Cartier, *L'Art du violon* (Paris, 1798), part 1, art. 6, p. 1 and Baillot, *L'Art*, p. 12.
40 For example, Baillot, *L'Art*, p. 15; J. F. Mazas, *Méthode de Violon* (Paris, 1830), p. 6.
41 Advocated especially by L'abbé *le fils*, *Principes*, p. 1.
42 Called *détaché* by many French writers, but this should not be confused with the use of the same term, from the early nineteenth century onwards, to describe a smooth, separate on-the-string stroke.
43 Baillot, *L'Art*, p. 97.
44 Habeneck, *Méthode*, p. 101. Habeneck here divides the semibreve into quaver values; the closer the quavers are placed, the slower the bow speed should be.
45 W. A. Mozart, for example, indicated dynamic markings sparingly in his early works. Only rarely were the extreme dynamics *pianissimo* and *fortissimo* and such gradations as *mezzo-forte* or *mezzo-piano* included.
46 See, for example, the prefaces to Piani's *Sonate a violino solo è violoncello col cimbalo* ... Op. 1 (Paris, 1712) or Veracini's *Sonate accademiche a violino solo* Op. 2 (London & Florence, 1744). N.B. The ability to play a long, even stroke was also vital for the cultivation of controlled bowing and variety of expression.
47 L. Mozart, *Versuch*, pp. 102–5.
48 De Bériot, *Méthode*, p. 124.
49 Phrasing was occasionally implied in the notation by the breaking of the beams.
50 Baillot (*L'Art*, 1834) adds an exception to this for very high notes, which must, on the contrary, be played softly to prevent them sounding harsh.
51 Habeneck, *Méthode*, p. 109.
52 Baillot, *L'Art*, pp. 163–4.
53 However, Quantz's comment that 'in gay and quick pieces the last quaver of each half bar must be stressed with the bow' should also be taken on board by performers in their quest for stylish performance.
54 R. Rognoni, *Passaggi per potersi essercitare nel diminuire terminatamente con ogni sorte di instrumenti* (Venice, 1592); F. Rognoni, *Selva de varii passaggi secondo l'uso moderno per cantare e suonare con ogni sorte di stromenti* (Milan, 1620/R1970); Zanetti, *Il scolaro* ... *per imparar a suonare di violino, et altri stromenti* (Milan, 1645).
55 Geminiani, *L'Art* (1751), Essempio VIII, p. 4.
56 Broadly speaking, certain keys appear to have held particular emotional meanings in Mozart's music. See R. Steblin, *A History of Key Characteristics in the 18th and Early 19th Centuries* (Ann Arbor, 1983).
57 P. Baillot, P. Rode and R. Kreutzer, *Méthode de violon* (Paris, 1803), pp. 158–65. Baillot included the survey verbatim as part 2 of his *L'Art du violon* (1834), adding only a brief introduction.
58 Baillot, *L'Art*, p. 137.
59 *The New Grove Dictionary of Musical Instruments* (London, 1984), s.v. 'Tempo and Expression Marks'.
60 See n. 26 above.
61 See J. W. Finson, 'Performing Practice in the Late Nineteenth Century, with Special Reference to the Music of Brahms', *Musical Quarterly*, 70 (1984), pp. 457–75.
62 Flesch, *Violin Fingering*, p. 365.
63 Limitations of space do not allow discussion here of the French rhythmic convention (extending roughly from the mid sixteenth to the late eighteenth century) of *notes inégales*, according to which certain divisions of the beat move in alternately long and short values, even if they are written out equally.
64 L. Mozart, *Versuch*, pp. 144–5.
65 The so-called 'Vega Bach bow' is a twentieth-century invention designed to play sustained four-note chords quite literally as such. Of very steep convex cambre, it has a mechanical lever which allows the hair tension to be altered either to accommodate sustained chordal passages or to play on individual strings.
66 P. Walls, in Brown and Sadie (eds.), *Performance Practice*, vol. II, p. 55.
67 Spohr's *Violinschule* (p. 147) includes the first known evidence of the modern practice of breaking a four-note chord upwards in twos where the lower two notes (played together before the beat) are only of short duration while the upper two notes (played together on the beat) are sustained for their full length.

68 See R. Stowell, *Violin Technique and Performance Practice in the Late Eighteenth and Early Nineteenth Centuries* (Cambridge, 1985), pp. 305–36 and pp. 375–91. See also F. Neumann, *Ornamentation in Baroque and Post-Baroque Music with Special Emphasis on J. S. Bach* (Princeton, 1978), and *Ornamentation and Improvisation in Mozart* (Princeton, 1986).

69 See Stowell, *Violin Technique*, pp. 337–67. See also F. Neumann, *Ornamentation in Baroque and Post-Baroque Music* and *Ornamentation and Improvisation in Mozart*.

70 C. P. E. Bach, *Versuch über die wahre Art das Clavier zu spielen* (2 vols., Berlin, 1753–62); Eng. tr. W. J. Mitchell (New York, 1949), pp. 79–80. Bach also argues that it was becoming customary in his circles to write out such ornamentation in full, but this approach was far from being universal at that time.

8 Aspects of contemporary technique (with comments about Cage, Feldman, Scelsi and Babbitt)

1 F. Geminiani, *The Art of Playing on the Violin* (London, 1751), Essempio XXII, pp. 30–1.

2 For a chart of most harmonics see P. Zukofsky, *An All Interval Scale Book* (New York, G. Schirmer, 1977).

3 In the interest of full disclosure, my principal violin teacher was Ivan Galamian, whom I credit not only with teaching me to *play* the violin, but far more importantly, with teaching me to think about *how to learn* to play the violin. The fact that our musical worlds and interests were so different only underscores the solidity of his foundation.

4 As an example see John Cage's *Six Melodies for Violin and Keyboard* (1950).

5 As examples see Cage's prepared piano music, or (for a group of instrumentalists) *Sixteen Dances* (1952).

6 See P. Zukofsky, 'John Cage's Recent Violin Music', in *A John Cage Reader* (New York, 1982).

7 As examples see Morton Feldman's *For John Cage* (for violin and piano), Violin Concerto, or *Piano, Violin, Viola, Cello*.

8 As the average of Pythagorean and just intonation approximations – the former used for melodic lines, the latter for beatless intervals – approaches tempered intonation, it is not clear how one could analyse the data of, as an example, a string quartet, so as to reveal which system is actually being used.

9 I admit that the line between 'opinionated' intonation and simply being 'out of tune' is a fine one. The placement of the line is primarily a function of the producer's intention, and the receiver's impression.

10 To quote Cage in regard to equal microtones: 'When the apple is rotten, cutting it in half does not help.' See Zukofsky, 'John Cage's Recent Violin Music'.

11 See his *Xnoybis* for solo violin, or his String Quartets Nos. 3 and 4.

12 Cage and Feldman both have specific injunctions against the use of vibrato. Stravinsky, as an example, does not; however, the use of a typical nineteenth-century-style vibrato in the great neo-Classic solos (such as in *Orpheus* or *Agon*) seems to me extremely incongruent.

13 'Performers there are who tremble consistently on each note as if they had the palsy.' L. Mozart, *A Treatise on the Fundamental Principles of Violin Playing*, tr. E. Knocker (London, 1948), p. 203.

14 Because of the geometry of string lengths, in order to achieve an ascending *glissando* on one string that changes pitch at a temporally equal rate, one must move the left hand quickly at the beginning of the *gliss.*, and slow down as one ascends. Descending *glissandi* require the opposite behaviour.

15 Gliding the bow lightly *through its entire length, usually at very high velocity*, due to the shortness of the duration allotted for each stroke. The sound produced is a whistling one, and is best achieved by using a stiff right elbow, thereby preventing the bow from being parallel with the bridge, and thereby adding to the 'glissez' effect.

9 The concerto

1 Stradella incorporated antiphonal effects between a trio-sonata texture and a full four-part ensemble within the instrumental sections of his serenata *Qual prodigio è ch'io miri* (1675) as well as in some of his sinfonias and oratorios.

2 Written c.1680s but published posthumously in Amsterdam. Muffat, in the preface to his *Ausserlesene Instrumental-Music* (Passau, 1701), reports that Corelli's concerti grossi were fashionable in Rome in the 1680s.

3 In theory, but not always in practice.

4 Described variously as 'sonata', 'sinfonia' or 'concerto'.

5 The published works number less than a fifth of his total.

6 The eighth is also a Christmas Concerto complete with pastorale.

7 B. Brainard in S. Sadie (ed.), *The New Grove Dictionary of Music and Musicians*, s.v. 'Tartini'.

8 These reworkings involving changes in the number, order and length of movements, textural alterations and the addition of a continuo to both concertino and ripieno groups.

9 See, for example, Telemann's anthology *Musique de table* (Hamburg, 1733) where he masters the ritornello principle, at the same time providing suggestions of the *galant* style.

10 Save for his Op. 7 collection, he dispensed with the viola part in the ripieno.

11 Commonly but misleadingly called the 'Oboe concertos'.

12 Optional oboe parts were added later to Nos. 1, 2, 5 and 6.

13 Although some of his most mature works are *symphonies concertantes* for various combinations of strings and wind.

14 J. La Rue, E. Wellesz and F. W. Sternfeld, in *The New Oxford History of Music* (14 vols., London, 1954–), vol. vii, 'The Age of Enlightenment', p. 487.

15 The *Concertone* K190 (2 vn, orch) and *Sinfonia concertante* K364 (vn, va, orch) were his other principal *concertante* works for the instrument.

16 He later substituted a rondo (K269) for his original finale of K207, and the rondo finale of the more mature K211 is somewhat lightweight.

17 By this time he had already composed his two Romances Opp. 40 and 50 (vn, orch, c.1801 and c.1798) and the Triple Concerto Op. 56 (vn, vc, pf, orch, 1803–4).

18 See B. Schwarz, 'Beethoven and the French Violin School', *Musical Quarterly*, (1958), pp. 431ff.

19 There are also two *Concertantes* for two violins, a *Concertante* for violin and cello, two *Concertantes* for violin and harp, and a Concerto for string quartet and orchestra.

20 Composed in 1822 but unpublished until Menuhin edited it for publication in 1952. Mendelssohn's Concerto for violin, piano and string orchestra (1823), also in D minor, similarly betrays Viennese Classical influence.

21 As, for example, in Mozart's Eb major Piano Concerto K2. 1.

22 David's role here appears to have been more advisory than instructional. Joachim's principal violin teachers included Hauser, Georg Hellmesberger (i) and Joseph Boehm.

23 Schumann also transcribed his A minor Cello Concerto Op. 129 for violin.

24 After trying out the work in rehearsal (Leipzig, 1858).

25 That performed nowadays.

26 Although Joachim's advice on the solo part was also sought.

27 His advice was apparently only rarely heeded.

28 Like his Second Piano Concerto, on which he was working concurrently.

29 Although this melody is related to material from the exposition.

30 The *Symphonie espagnole* Op. 21 (1874) was written specifically for Sarasate in the wake of the great Spanish virtuoso's performance of Lalo's Violin Concerto Op. 20 (1873) in 1874, and the Belgian violinist Pierre Marsick premiered the Concerto russe Op. 29 in 1879.

31 The third movement, 'Intermezzo', is sometimes omitted in performances nowadays.

32 Rimsky-Korsakov's Fantasy on Russian Folk Themes Op. 33 (1887) and Cui's *Suite concertante* Op. 25 (1884) represent the nearest they came to composing a violin concerto.

33 The only two to appear in the nineteenth century – No. 1 in Eb/D and No. 2 in B minor – were not published until 1851. No. 1 was originally intended to be heard in Eb major, with the soloist tuning his strings up a semitone and playing the work in the somewhat easier key of D (sounding Eb) major, but the work is commonly performed nowadays in a version transposed into D major.

34 As quoted in D. Gill (ed.), *The Book of the Violin* (Oxford, 1984), p. 171.

35 F. Farga, *Violins and Violinists* (London, 1950), tr. E. Larsen, p. 203.

36 Although there is no room here for harmonics or left-hand pizzicato.

37 Not only in the titles of the movements (Toccata – Aria I – Aria II – Capriccio) but also, to a certain extent, in the nature of the music.

38 The last two movements are inspired by two Gregorian melodies.

39 The rich harmonic language built on fourths and fifths as much as on thirds and sixths; the asymmetrical phrase structure; bitonality; the exotic melodic intervals and the intensely passionate, dramatic expression.

40 These concertos are in fact orchestrations of his two sonatas (vn, pf, Opp. 9 and 11, 1911 and 1918).

41 Published posthumously in 1959.

42 A naturalised Briton.

43 The soloist's accompanied cadenza clearly refers to it, as does also the ensuing 'alla marcia' immediately preceding the final flourish.

10 The sonata

1 Such is the theoretical definition. But in practice the two types are not always clearly differentiated; many 'church sonatas' conclude with one or more dance movements (not always so designated), while many 'chamber sonatas' include an opening movement which is not a dance.

2 The first is for 'violino e violone'.

3 *Affetti musicali* Op. 1 (Venice, 1617); *Arie ... Op. 3* (Venice, 1620); *Sonate, symphonie ... e retornelli, a 1, 2, 3, 4, 5, & 6 voci* Op. 8 (Venice, 1629); *Per ogni sorte di strumento musicale diversi generi di sonate, da chiesa, e da camera, a 2–4, bc* (Venice, 1655)

4 *Canzone e sonate* Op. posth. (1615).

5 *Il combattimento di Tancredi e Clorinda* (1624) and *Scherzi musicali* (Venice, 1607).

6 *Sonate concertate in stil moderno* (Venice, 1621).

7 Published posthumously (Venice, 1641).

8 Published in four sets Opp. 2–5 (1639, 1642, 1645 and 1649).

9 Ten sonatas for one or two violins and continuo.

10 Opp. 2, 4, 8, 10 (*La cetra*) and eighteen collections of instrumental music, including sonatas for various instrumental combinations.

11 Included in his *Artificii musicali ... Op. 13* (Modena, 1689).

12 Some, notably that by Estienne Roger of 1710, including examples of contemporary embellishments for many of the slow, and in a few cases, some fast movements.

13 Six *Sonate da chiesa ...* (Amsterdam, 1708); five *Sonate ...* (Amsterdam, c.1717) and six *Sonates da camera ...* (Paris, 1742).

14 Although some of op. 6 in particular are fast–slow–fast in design.

15 B. Schwarz, in S. Sadie (ed.), *The New Grove Dictionary of Music and Musicians*, s.v. 'Somis, Giovanni Battista'.

16 See J. W. Hill, 'Veracini in Italy', *Music & Letters*, 56 (1975), pp. 257–76.

17 Four books of *Ayres ...* (1685) for the violin.

18 *The Division Violin* (London, 1684), comprising dances or variation sets.

19 Purcell's trio sonatas (1683), in which he 'faithfully endevour'd a just imitation of the most fam'd Italian Masters'.

20 Interestingly, too, his Op. 1 sonatas were later revised with detailed annotations regarding ornaments and fingerings and published as *Le prime sonate* (London, 1739).

21 Op. 1 No. 1 was modelled particularly closely on the first of Corelli's Op. 5 set.

22 See T. Best, 'Handel's Solo Sonatas', *Music & Letters* 58 (1977), pp. 430–8.

23 [11] *Sonate da camera* (Venice, 1667) and [12] *Sonate* (Nuremberg, 1682).

24 They were probably intended as postludes to services in Salzburg Cathedral during October, the month specially devoted to the Rosary Mysteries.

25 For example, heavy repeated notes depict 'the Scourging of Jesus' and passages of trumpet-like writing accompany 'The Ascension' and other such joyous events.

26 In No. 28, for example, Walther sets out to imitate a 'chorus' of violins, the tremulant organ, bagpipes, trumpets, drums, the hurdy-gurdy and the guitar, while *Galli e galline, Scherzi d'augelli con il [sic] cucci* and *Leuto harpeggiante e rossignuolo* are among those works in which various birds are imitated.

27 One of the nine movements in a single sonata (vn, bc; Paris, 1682) prompted the work's nickname of 'La Guerre' from Louis XIV, and that same movement was later included as the finale of the second of a set of six sonatas (vn, bc; Dresden, 1694).

28 W. S. Newman, *The Sonata in the Baroque Era* (Chapel Hill, 1959), p. 235.

29 'a Cembalo concertato e Violino solo' (Cöthen, c.1720).

30 As found in the manuscript copied (mid 1740s) by Johann Christoph Altnikol (1719–59), a pupil and son-in-law of Bach.

31 e.g. the opening Adagio of the E major sonata (No. 3; BWV 1016)

32 Some scholars attribute it to Pisendel.

33 Sébastien de Brossard remarked (1695) that 'every composer in Paris, and above all the organists, was madly writing sonatas in the Italian manner,' and François Couperin (1668–1733), in his preface to *Les Nations: sonades et suites de simphonies en trio* (2vn, bc; Paris, 1726) claimed priority in the field.

34 His last two sets were *Amusements pour la chambre* Op. 6 (Paris, 1718) and *Les Idées musiciennes* Op. 7 (Paris, 1720).

35 Published in 1712 but completed, according to the manuscript, by 1695.

36 *Pièces de violon avec la basse continue.*

37 *[12] Sonates mellés de plusieurs récits ...*

38 Known as 'Desplanes'.

39 Originally Ghignone.

40 Six *Pièces de clavecin en sonates avec accompagnement de violon* Op. 13 (Paris, 1745).

41 For example, Giardini's *Sei sonate per cembalo con violino o flauto traverso* Op. 3 (London, c.1751), or Richter's *VI Sonate da camera a cembalo obbligato, flauto traverso o violino concertato, e violoncello* (Nuremberg, 1764).

42 Composers such as Mondonville (*Pièces de clavecin en sonates, avec accompagnement de violon* Op. 3, Paris, c.1734) and Corrette (*Sonates* Op. 25, Paris, 1742) had anticipated this sonata type, which eventually blossomed with the harpsichordist-composer Johann Schobert's keyboard sonatas with *ad libitum* accompanying instruments in Paris in the 1760s.

43 One of his keyboard sonatas has an independent obbligato part for violin.

44 See D. Dichiera, *The New Grove Dictionary*, s.v. 'Mysliveček'.

45 See note 1 above.

46 See the *Neue Mozart–Ausgabe*.

47 These sonatas also include *ad libitum* parts for cello.

48 K55–60 are now believed to be spurious.

49 Although the final Minuet is of quasi-Baroque character.

50 'Six sonates pour le clavecin ou pianoforte, avec l'accompagnement du violon'.

51 Mozart's last sonata K547 (1788), described as 'eine kleine Klavier Sonate für Anfänger mit einer Violine', represents arguably a retrogressive step when compared with the other works of the decade, despite the maturity of its language.

52 D. Carew, 'Chamber Music: Piano and Strings', in H. C. Robbins Landon (ed.), *The Mozart Compendium* (London, 1990), p. 290.

53 The title 'Spring' is not Beethoven's own; it was added by the publisher A. Cranz to a later edition of the work.

54 A major-key introduction to a minor-key main movement.

55 The F major Sonata (1838) remained unpublished until Yehudi Menuhin edited it for publication in 1953.

56 Shorthand for 'frei aber einsam' (free but alone).

57 A special society (*Société Nationale de Musique*) was formed in Paris (1871) for its cultivation.

58 Originally entitled *Grand Duo Concertant*.
59 W. S. Newman, *The Sonata since Beethoven* (Chapel Hill, 1969), pp. 526–7.
60 The length of its gestation period is arguable, its origins possibly lying in sketches made some twenty-eight years earlier.
61 The Piano Quintet and the String Quartet.
62 Arranged by Kreisler as 'Indian Lament'.
63 Although the opening movement's second theme is in a different metre from its first.
64 Cited from Prokofiev's article 'What I Am Working On', in I. S. Nestyev, *Prokofiev*, Eng. tr. F. Jones (London, 1961), p. 385.
65 Made with the help of David Oistrakh.
66 B. Schwarz, in *The New Grove Dictionary*, s.v. 'Shostakovich, Dmitry'.
67 Never completed.
68 An earlier, relatively unsuccessful violin sonata dates from 1897.
69 Quoted by D. Hall in his sleeve-note for the recording of the two sonatas by R. Druian and J. Simms, Mercury MG 50095. Bloch here refers to the fact that it incorporates a violin recitative of Jewish character as well as a Gregorian Credo (with text printed in the score) and Gloria.
70 Copland's Duo is a violin and piano version (c.1978) of his flute and piano Duo of 1971.
71 Its two predecessors are either lost or destroyed.
72 Two earlier (unnumbered) essays in the genre (in C minor and E minor) have also been preserved.
73 The new finale was inscribed with a verse from Yeats, Bax's favourite poet.
74 Bax withheld the score until 1922.
75 Bax claims it might also be called 'The Dance of Death' because it was greatly influenced by the events of 1915.
76 That in the second movement (Grazioso e danzato) is a cadenza for both players which concludes with aleatory improvisation on note-groups already presented.
77 See J. Samson, *The Music of Szymanowski* (London, 1980), p. 48.
78 J. C. G. Waterhouse, in *The New Grove Dictionary*, s.v. 'Enescu, George'.

11 Other solo repertory

1 For example, a prelude (1688; Part 1) and an allemand (1693; Part 2) by Thomas Baltzar (c. 1630?–c. 1663?). The allemand also appears in J. Hawkins, *A General History of the Science and Practice of Music* (5 vols., London, 1776), vol. IV, p. 329.
2 Published in the *Mercure galant* (January, 1683).
3 Fairly recently discovered by P. P. Várnai. See P. P. Várnai, 'Ein unbekanntes Werk von Johann Paul von Westhoff', *Die Musikforschung*, 24 (1971), p. 282.
4 Ed. F. Boghen, published by Durand, 1930.
5 *Komm, heiliger Geist, Herre Gott.*
6 The *Siciliana* of the first (G minor) sonata is in B♭ major.
7 The third partita, however, includes only one of the four dances that form the nucleus of the normal suite, incorporating instead some of the optional, lighter movements occasionally inserted after the sarabande.
8 Bach transcribed this for organ and orchestra in Cantatas 120a and 29.
9 Preserved in Cartier's *L'Art du violon* (Paris, 1798).
10 Not published until 1853.
11 The published version, edited by Menuhin, substitutes conventional semitones, a change authorised by the composer.
12 As short as his virtuosity allows – circa three seconds is suggested.
13 That is, the gradual movement in and out of synchronisation.
14 Quoted in D. Gill (ed.), *The Book of the Violin* (Oxford, 1984), p. 206.
15 Aborigine for 'a remote and lonely place'.
16 For example, the Chaconne attributed to Tomaso Vitali, rediscovered by Ferdinand David c. 1860, was almost certainly not composed by the Bolognese violinist.
17 Each variation is in the style of a well-known virtuoso (Clement, Schuppanzigh and others).
18 Paganini's so-called *Maestoso sonata sentimentale*, 1828.

19 Based on the Irish folktune.
20 Another adaptation of a movement for string quartet.
21 The *lieu cher* is Brailov, the country house near Kiev of his mysterious benefactress Nadezhda von Meck.
22 Scored for soprano, violin and orchestra.
23 The Chinese book of changes.
24 With the help of Paul Zukofsky.
25 From Gerhard's programme note for the piece's premiere.
26 For example, Stravinsky's Violin Concerto and *Duo Concertant*.

12 The violin as ensemble instrument

1 E. Bottrigari, *Il desiderio, overo de' concerti di varii strumenti* (Venice, 1594), tr. C. MacClintock, Musicological Studies and Documents, vol. IX (1962), p. 13.
2 On the definition of an 'orchestra', see N. Zaslaw, 'When is an Orchestra not an Orchestra?', *Early Music* 16 (1988), p. 483.
3 Brossard's definitions are given in W. S. Newman, *The Sonata in the Baroque Era*, 4th edn (New York, 1983), pp. 24–5.
4 M. Mersenne, *Harmonie universelle* (Paris, 1636–7) Eng. tr. R. E. Chapman (The Hague, 1957).
5 J. L. Le Cerf de la Viéville, *Comparaison de la musique italienne et de la musique française* (Brussels, 1704–6/R1972) tr. O. Strunk in *Source Readings in Music History* (New York, 1950), pp. 489–507.
6 *Life and Times of Anthony Wood*, ed. L. Powys (London, 1932), p. 212.
7 T. Mace, *Musick's Monument, or a Remembrance of the Best Practical Musick* (London, 1676); facsimile edn (Paris, 1958/R1966), p. 236. See 'The Third Part Concerning the Viol' for many intemperate remarks on the qualities of the violin.
8 *Roger North on Music*, ed. J. Wilson (London, 1955), p. 31.
9 W. Kirkendale, *Fugue and Fugato in Rococo and Classical Chamber Music* (Durham, N.C., 1979), p. 42.
10 A. Carse, *The Orchestra in the Eighteenth Century* (Cambridge, 1940), pp. 88–99.
11 L. Mozart, *A Treatise on the Fundamental Principles of Violin Playing* (1756), tr. E. Knocker (London, 1948), p. 224.
12 Carse, *The Orchestra*, p. 99.
13 Le Cerf de la Viéville, *Comparaison de la musique*.
14 J. Webster, 'Towards a History of Viennese Chamber Music in the Early Classical Period', *Journal of the American Musicological Society*, 27 (1974), pp. 212–47.
15 Quoted from L. G. Ratner, *Classic Music* (New York, 1980), p. 125.
16 H. Le Blanc, *Défense de la basse de viole contre les entreprises du violon et les prétensions du violoncel* (Amsterdam, 1740/R1975); R serially in *La Revue Musicale* 9 (1927–8).
17 Quoted from J. Gardner, 'The Chamber Music' in *Robert Schumann: The Man and His Music*, ed. A. Walker (London, 1972), p. 201.
18 E. T. A. Hoffman, *Beethoven's Instrumental Music* (1813), in Strunk, *Source Readings*, p. 775.

13 The pedagogical literature

1 The reader should note that limitations of space restrict this survey largely to those treatises of principal significance in the history and development of the violin.
2 *Roger North on Music*, ed. J. Wilson (London, 1955), p. 194.
3 If sixteenth-century treatises devoted any space at all to instruments, it was generally at the end almost as an afterthought. Jambe de Fer's disdain for the violin (*Epitome musicale* ..., Lyons, 1556) was typical of the period.
4 At least thirty works devoted to amateur violin instruction were printed in England alone between 1658 and 1731, and these works were apparently read in other countries. See D. Boyden's facsimile edition (London, 1952) of Geminiani's *The Art of Playing on the Violin* (London, 1751).

5 M. Montéclair, *Méthode facile pour aprendre [sic] à jouer du violon* (Paris, [1711–12]); P. Dupont, *Principes de violon* (Paris, 1718); M. Corrette, *L'École d'Orphée* (Paris, 1738).

6 For a comprehensive list of these pirated adaptations of Geminiani's work, see Boyden's facsimile edition of Geminiani's *The Art*, pp. x–xi.

7 e.g. Robert Bremner's *The Compleat Tutor for the Violin* (London, c.1750), Stephen Philpot's *An Introduction to the Art of Playing on the Violin* (London, 1767?), and the anonymous *An Abstract of Geminiani's Art of Playing on the Violin* (Boston, 1769); and numerous English publishers used Geminiani's name on posthumous publications, very little of whose contents was his.

8 The original date of this method is subject to disagreement, but it was in preparation, at the very least, during the 1790s. See Montanari, *Bartolomeo Campagnoli, violinistica compositore (1751–1827)* (n.p., 1969) and E. C. White in S. Sadie (ed.), *The New Grove Dictionary of Music and Musicians*, s.v. 'Campagnoli, Bartolomeo'.

9 L. Mozart, *Versuch einer gründlichen Violinschule* (Augsburg, 1756), 'Vorbericht'.

10 C. A. de Bériot, *Méthode de violon* Op. 102 (Paris, 1858), preface.

11 C. Guhr, *Ueber Paganinis Kunst die Violine zu spielen* (Mainz, 1829), preface, p. 2.

12 C. Flesch, *The Art of Violin Playing*, Eng. tr. F. Martens (2 vols., New York, 1924–30), vol. i, p. 114.

13 *Ibid.*, vol. i, p. 115.

14 K. Havas, *The Twelve Lesson Course in a New Approach to Violin Playing* (London, 1964), preface.

15 This is the subtitle of his *Nurtured by Love* (New York, 1969).

16 S. Suzuki, *Nurtured by Love*, p. 9.

17 The reader should note that limitations of space restrict this survey largely to study material of principal significance in the history and development of the violin.

18 Locatelli's twelve concertos *L'arte del violino* Op. 3 (Amsterdam, 1733), like some of Tartini's concertos, incorporate twenty-four capriccios 'ad libitum' which are in the nature of cadenzas to the concertos. But they can scarcely have been used as such, since they are almost as long as the movements they are supposed to complement.

19 This date is uncertain, since no edition of 1796 has survived. However, Vieuxtemps claimed that his edition of Kreutzer's studies (1866) was based on the original edition of 1796. See also E. Gerber, *Neues historisch-biographisches Lexikon* (4 vols., Leipzig, 1812–14/R1966), s.v. 'Kreutzer, R.'.

20 R. Kreutzer, *Forty-two Studies for the Violin* ed. Cutter (Philadelphia, 1901), preface.

21 See *Allgemeine Musikalische Zeitung*, 6 (April, 1804), no. xi, col. 48.

22 According to Moser (*Geschichte des Violinspiels*, p. 324), sixteen of these studies are by Franz Benda (vol. 1) and twelve are by Georg Benda (vol. 2). The only available edition is a modern facsimile edition by Joseph Müller-Blattau (Stuttgart, 1957), in which the works attributed to Georg Benda (vol. 2 of the original edition) are omitted and substituted by Franz Benda's *Exercices progressifs pour le violon* (Leipzig, n.d.).

23 Also published in two parts as *XII Capricii a violino solo* Op. 12.

24 Sixty-five of these variations appeared, in a different order, in a later publication, *Studies for the Violin Calculated for the Improvement of Practitioners in General*.

25 Mentioned by R. Eitner (*Biographisch-bibliographisches Quellen-lexikon* (10 vols., Leipzig, 1900–4; 2nd rev. edn, 1959–60), vol. ii, p. 296) and A. Moser (*Geschichte des Violinspiels* (Berlin, 1923; 2nd rev. edn, 1966–7), p. 277).

26 Interestingly, the caprices do not exploit harmonic effects, which appear to have been a later development in Paganini's technical equipment. In keeping with Paganini's mature style, indications of harmonics in posthumous editions were added by some editors as alternative suggestions. The possibility that Paganini played passages in harmonics which were not so notated should not, however, be ruled out.

27 It is interesting to note that several études were written in duet form with an accompanying second violin part.

28 L. Spohr, *Violinschule*, (Vienna, 1832), Preface and pp. 26 and 139.

29 Spohr, *Violinschule*, pp. 198–245.

14 The violin – instrument of four continents

1 T. Alexandru, 'Quelques repères chronologiques des violons comme instruments populaires chez les Roumains', *Studia Instrumentorum Musicae Popularis*, 8 (1985), p. 103.
2 P. de B. de Brantôme, *Oeuvres complètes*, ed. M. P. Mérimée and M. L. Lacour (13 vols., Paris, 1858–95).
3 Quoted in B. Sárosi, *Gypsy Music* (Budapest, 1978), p. 57.
4 Sárosi, *Gypsy Music*, p. 134.
5 Quoted in Sárosi, *Gypsy Music*, p. 127.
6 E. Dahlig, 'Intracultural Aspects of Violin Playing in Poland', *Studia Instrumentorum Musicae Popularis*, 7 (1981), p. 112.
7 See P. Cooke, *The Fiddle Tradition of the Shetland Isles* (Cambridge, 1986).
8 *Virginia Gazette*, 24 April 1746.
9 Quoted in E. Southern, *Readings in Black American Music* (New York, 1971), p. 91.
10 E. Southern, *The Music of Black Americans: a History* (New York & London, 1971/R1983). Southern's research forms the source for much of the information given in this section.
11 Andy Bruce, Winsboro, N.C.
12 *Journal and Letters of Philip Vickers Fithian, 1773–74: a Plantation Tutor of the Old Dominion* ed. H. D. Farish (Williamsburg, 1900), p. 161.
13 L. Burman-Hall, 'Southern American Folk Fiddling: Context and Style' (diss., University of Princeton, 1978).
14 See R. Stevenson, *Music in Mexico* (New York, 1952), and *Music in Aztec and Inca Territory* (Berkeley & Los Angeles, 1968). This section is particularly indebted to Stevenson's research.
15 See C. Strachwitz, sleeve notes to *Texas–Mexican Border Music vol. 5: The String Bands: End of a Tradition*, Folklyric 9007 (1976); and *Texas–Mexican Border Music vol. 2: Blind Fiddler Melquiades Rodriguez*, Folklyric 9018 (1978).
16 See Lyricord LLST7359, LLST7348.
17 H. Farhat, in S. Sadie (ed.), *The New Grove Dictionary of Music and Musicians*, s.v. 'Iran'.
18 B. Nettl, *The Western Impact on World Music: Change, Adaptation and Survival* (New York & London, 1985), pp. 47–50.
19 See P. Mukherjee, sleeve notes to *Le Violon de l'Inde du Sud*, Ocora 558.585–6.
20 See B. C. Deva, *Musical Instruments of India: Their History and Development* (Calcutta, 1978), pp. 171–2.
21 S. Bandyopadhyaya, *Musical Instruments of India* (Delhi, 1980).
22 See Mukherjee, sleeve notes to *Le Violon de l'Inde du Sud*.
23 C. R. Boxer, *The Portuguese Seaborne Empire: 1415–1825* (London, 1965), p. 240.
24 See J. Kunst, *Music in Java* (2 vols., The Hague, 1973), vol. I, p. 282.
25 *Ibid.*, vol. I, pp. 385 and 451.
26 *Ibid.*, vol. I, p. 375.

15 The violin in jazz

1 *sic* for Mountain.
2 Such discographical information is provided with the interested reader/listener in mind.
3 *The Wire* (November, 1988).

Select bibliography

Note: The reader is also referred to the Appendix, 'Principal violin treatises', pp. 257–60.

Abbot, D. and Segerman, E., 'Gut Strings', *Early Music*, 4 (1976), pp. 430–7

Alburger, M. A., *Scottish Fiddlers and their Music* (London, 1983)

Alexandru, T., 'Quelques repères chronologiques des violons comme instruments populaires chez les Roumains', *Studia Instrumentorum Musicae Popularis*, 8 (1985), pp. 103–4

Anthony, J. R., *French Baroque Music* (New York, 1974)

Applebaum, S. and S., *The Way They Play* (10 vols., New York, 1972)

Axelrod, H. R., *see* Sheppard, L.

Ayyangar, R. R., *History of South Indian (Carnatic) music* (Madras, 1972)

Bach, C. P. E., *Versuch über die wahre Art das Clavier zu spielen* (2 vols., Berlin, 1753–62); Eng. tr. W. J. Mitchell as *Essay on the True Art of Playing Keyboard Instruments* (New York, 1949)

Bachmann, A., *An Encyclopedia of the Violin* (New York, 1925/R New York, 1966)

Badura-Skoda, E. and P., *Mozart-Interpretation* (Vienna, 1957); tr. L. Black as *Interpreting Mozart on the Keyboard* (London, 1962/R London, 1970)

Bakker, D., 'Venuti, Lang and Friends', *Micrography*, 5 (1969), p. 3

Bandyopadhyaya, S., *Musical Instruments of India* (Delhi, 1980)

Baud, R., 'Didier Lockwood – le violon sûr de soi', *Jazz Hot*, 409 (1984), p. 16

Baumann, M. P., 'Saiteninstrumente in Lateinamerika', *Studia Instrumentorum Musicae Popularis*, 7 (1981), p. 157

Bayard, S., *Hill Country Tunes* (Philadelphia, 1944)
  Dance to the Fiddle, March to the Fife: Instrumental Folk Tunes in Pennsylvania (Philadelphia, 1982)

Beare, C., *Capolavori di Antonio Stradivari* (Milan, 1987)

Behague, G., *Music in Latin America* (Englewood Cliffs, N.J., 1979)

Berendt, J., 'Zbigniew Seifert', *Down Beat*, 44/17 (1977), p. 32
  'Didier Lockwood', *Jazz Journal*, 33/12 (1979), p. 15
  The Jazz Book: from New Orleans to Fusion and Beyond (Westport, Conn., 1982), p. 288

Berlioz, L. H., *Grand Traité de l'instrumentation et d'orchestration modernes Op. 10* (Paris, 1843); tr. M. C. Clarke as *A Treatise on Modern Instrumentation* (London, 1858)

Blumenthal, B., 'Leroy Jenkins – for the Record', *Down Beat*, 49/3 (1982), p. 20

Bonetti, C., *A Genealogy of the Amati Family of Violin Makers 1500–1740*, tr. G. G. Champe (New York, 1989)

Boomkamp, C. van L., and Meer, J. H. van der, *The Carel van Leeuwen Boomkamp Collection of Musical Instruments* (Amsterdam, 1971)

Bottrigari, E., *Il desiderio, overo de' concerti di varij strumenti musicali* (Venice, 1594), tr. C. MacClintock, Musicological Studies and Documents, vol. IX (1962)

Boxer, C. R., *The Portuguese Seaborne Empire: 1415–1825* (London, 1965)

Boyden, D. D., 'The Violin and its Technique in the Eighteenth Century', *Musical Quarterly*, 36 (1950), pp. 9–38

'Dynamics in Seventeenth- and Eighteenth-Century Music', in *Essays on Music in Honor of Archibald Thompson Davison by his Associates* (Cambridge, Mass., 1957), pp. 185–93

'Geminiani and the First Violin Tutor', *Acta Musicologica*, 31 (1959), pp. 161–70

'A Postscript to "Geminiani and the First Violin Tutor"', *Acta Musicologica*, 32 (1960), pp. 40–7

'The Missing Italian Manuscript of Tartini's *Traité des agrémens*', *Musical Quarterly*, 46 (1960), pp. 315–28

'The Violin', in A. Baines (ed.), *Musical Instruments through the Ages* (Harmondsworth, 1961)

The History of Violin Playing from its Origins to 1761 (London, 1965/R1975)

Catalogue of the Hill Collection of Musical Instruments in the Ashmolean Museum, Oxford (London, 1969)

'Violin' (1–11), *The New Grove Dictionary of Music and Musicians* (London, 1980)

'Bow' (I:2–4, 11), *The New Grove Dictionary of Music and Musicians* (London, 1980)

'The Violin Bow in the Eighteenth Century', *Early Music*, 8 (1980), pp. 199–212

Bragard, R., *Musical Instruments in Art and History* (New York, 1968)

Brantôme, P. de B. de, *Oeuvres complètes*, ed. M. P. Mérimée and M. L. Lacour (13 vols., Paris, 1858–95)

Breathnach, B., *Folk Music and Dances of Ireland* (Dublin, 1971)

Brodowski, P., 'The New World of Didier Lockwood', *Jazz Forum*, 74 (1982), p. 33

Brook, D., *Violinists of Today* (London, 1948)

Brown, H. M., and Sadie, S. (eds.), *Performance Practice* (2 vols., London, 1989)

Burman-Hall, L., 'Southern American Folk Fiddling: Context and Style' (diss., University of Princeton, 1978)

Burney, C., *A General History of Music* (4 vols., London, 1776–89/R 2 vols., New York, 1935)

Campbell, M., *The Great Violinists* (London, 1980)

Campbell, M., and Greated, C., *The Musician's Guide to Acoustics* (London, 1987)

Carse, A., *The Orchestra in the Eighteenth Century* (Cambridge, 1940)

The History of Orchestration (New York, 1964)

Condax, L. M., *Final Summary Report of Violin Varnish Research Project* (Pittsburgh, 1970)

Cooke, P., *The Fiddle Tradition of the Shetland Isles* (Cambridge, 1986)

Courcy, G. I. C. de, *Paganini the Genoese* (2 vols., Norman, Okla., 1957/R New York, 1977)

Cremer, L., *Physik der Geige* (Stuttgart, 1981); Eng. tr. J. S. Allen (Cambridge, Mass., 1984)

Dahlig, E., 'Intracultural Aspects of Violin Playing in Poland', *Studia Instrumentorum Musicae Popularis*, 7 (1981), pp. 112–17

Daniels, R., *Conversations with Menuhin* (London, 1979)

Dart, R. T., *The Interpretation of Music* (London, 1954)

Davis, F., 'Violin Madness [Billy Bang]', in *In the Moment: Jazz in the 1980s* (New York, 1986), p. 67

Dent, E. J., 'The Earliest String Quartets', *Monthly Musical Record*, 33 (1903), pp. 202–4

Deutsch, W., and Haid, D. (eds.), *Die Geige in der europäischen Volksmusik*, Schriften zur Volksmusik, vol. III (Vienna, 1975)

Deva, B. C., *Musical Instruments of India, their History and Development* (Calcutta, 1978)

Dictionnaire de musique, ed. S. de Brossard (Paris, 1703/R1964)

Dolmetsch, A., *The Interpretation of the Music of the Seventeenth and Eighteenth Centuries* (London, 1915; 2nd edn, London, 1946/R1969)

Donington, R., *The Performer's Guide to Baroque Music* (London, 1973)
  The Interpretation of Early Music (London, 1963; 3rd rev. edn, London, 1974)
  String Playing in Baroque Music (London, 1977)

Dubourg, G., *The Violin; some Account of that Leading Instrument and its most Eminent Professors, from the Earliest Date to the Present Time* (5th edn, London, 1878)

Dunning, A., *Pietro Antonio Locatelli* (Buren, 1981)

Dushkin, S., 'Working with Stravinsky', in E. Corle (ed.), *Igor Stravinsky* (New York, 1949)

Edlund, H., *Music for Solo Violin Unaccompanied: a Catalogue of Published and Unpublished Works from the Seventeenth Century to 1989* (High Wycombe, 1989)

Elschek, O., 'Die musikalische Individualität der slovakischen Primgeiger', *Studia Instrumentorum Musicae Popularis*, 7 (1981), p. 70

Emery, F. B., *The Violin Concerto* (2 vols., New York, 1969)

Falck, G., *Idea boni cantoris, das ist Getreu und gründliche Anleitung* (Nuremberg, 1688)

Farga, F., *Geigen und Geiger* (Zurich, 1940); tr. E. Larsen as *Violins and Violinists* (London, 1950; 2nd rev. edn, London, 1969)

Farhat, H., 'Iran', *The New Grove Dictionary of Music and Musicians* (London, 1980)

Farisch, M. K., *String Music in Print* (2nd edn, New York & London, 1973)

Farish, H. D., (ed.), *Journal and Letters of Philip Vickers Fithian, 1773–74: a Plantation Tutor of the Old Dominion* (Williamsburg, 1900)

Fayolle, F. J. M., *Notices sur Corelli, Tartini, Gaviniès, Pugnani et Viotti* (Paris, 1810)

Feintuch, B., 'Examining Musical Motivations: Why Does Sammy Play the Fiddle?', *Western Folklore*, 42 (1983), p. 208

Fétis, F. J., *Notice sur Paganini* (Paris, 1851)
  Antoine Stradivari, luthier célèbre (Paris, 1856; tr. J. Bishop, London, 1864/R1964)
Finson, J. W., 'Performing Practice in the Late Nineteenth Century, with Special Reference to the Music of Brahms', *Musical Quarterly*, 70 (1984), pp. 457–75
Flesch, C., *Alta scuola di diteggiatura violinistica* (Milan, 1960); tr. B. Schwarz as *Violin Fingering: its Theory and Practice* (London, 1966)
  The Memoirs of Carl Flesch, tr. H. Keller (London, 1957)
Forster, S. A., see Sandys, W.
Fry, G., *The Varnishes of the Italian Violin-Makers* (London, 1904)
Garztecki, M., 'Krzesimir Debski – String Connection', *Jazz Forum*, 73 (1981), p. 46
Gerle, R., *The Art of Practising the Violin* (London, 1983)
Giazotto, R., *Giovan Battista Viotti* (Milan, 1956)
Giddins, G., 'A Penchant for Mayhem [Joe Venuti]', in *Riding on a Blue Note* (New York, 1981), p. 79
Gill, D. (ed.), *The Book of the Violin* (Oxford, 1984)
Ginsburg, L., *Giuseppe Tartini* (Zurich, 1976)
Glaser, M., and Grappelli, S., *Jazz Violin* (New York, 1981)
Grappelli, S., see Glaser, M.
Greated, C., see Campbell, M.
Gruenberg, E., *The Violinist's Manual: a Progressive Classification of Technical Material, Etudes, Solo Pieces and the Most Important Chamber Works* (New York, 1896)
Gruenberg, M. P. E., *Führer durch die Literatur der Streichinstrumente* (Leipzig, 1913)
Gurvin, O., *Norskfolkemusikk: Serie 1 Hardingfeleslåttar* (5 vols., Oslo, 1958–67)
Haid, D., see Deutsch, W.
Hamma, F., *Meisterwerke italienischer Geigenbaukunst* (Stuttgart, 1931)
  Meister deutscher Geigenbaukunst (Stuttgart, 1948)
Harrison, M., 'Eddie South', *Jazz Journal*, 15/6 (1962), p. 5
  'Joe Venuti', *The Strad*, 97 (1986), p. 408
Hart, G., *The Violin: its Famous Makers and their Imitators* (London, 1875)
  The Violin and its Music (London, 1881)
Hauck, W., *Vibrato on the Violin*, Eng. tr. K. Rokos (London, 1975)
Havas, K., *Stage Fright: its Causes and Curses with Special Reference to Violin Playing* (London, n.d.)
Hawkins, J., *A General History of the Science and Practice of Music* (5 vols., London, 1776)
Heim, E., *Neuer Führer durch die Violin-Literatur* (Hanover, 1889)
Henley, W., *Universal Dictionary of Violin and Bow Makers*, vols. I–V (Brighton, 1959–60); vol. VI ed. C. Woodcock as *Dictionary of Contemporary Violin and Bow Makers* (Brighton, 1965)
Hennessey, M., 'French cooking – Jean-Luc Ponty', *Down Beat* 33/22 (1966), p. 24
Heron-Allen, E., *Violin-Making, as it Was and Is: Being a Historical, Theoretical, and Practical Treatise on the Art and Science of Violin-Making* (London, 1884; 2nd edn, 1885/R1984)

De Fidiculis Bibliographia: Being an Attempt towards a Bibliography of the Violin and All Other Instruments Played with a Bow (2 vols., London, 1890–4/R1961)

Hill, J. W., *The Life and Works of Francesco Maria Veracini* (Ann Arbor, 1979)

Hill, R. (ed.), *The Concerto* (Harmondsworth, 1952)

Hill, W. H., A. F. and A. E., *Antonio Stradivari: his Life and Work* (London, 1902; 2nd edn, 1909/R1963)

   The Violin Makers of the Guarneri Family (London, 1931; rev. edn, London, 1965)

Hofmann, R., *Führer durch die Violin-Literatur* (Leipzig, 1904)

Hogwood, C., *The Trio Sonata* (London, 1979)

Hopkins, P., *Aural Thinking in Norway: the Transmission of History through the Musical Codes of the Hardingfele* (New York, 1985)

Huggins, M. L., *Gio. Paolo Maggini: his Life and Work* (London, 1892)

Hull, E. H., 'The Earliest Known String Quartet', *Musical Quarterly*, 15 (1929), pp. 72–6

Hutchins, C. M., 'Founding a Family of Fiddles', *Physics Today*, 20 (1967), p. 23

   'The Acoustics of Violin Plates', *Scientific American*, 245 (1981), pp. 170–86

   'A History of Violin Research', *Journal of the Acoustical Society of America*, 73/5 (1983), pp. 1421–40

Hutchings, A., *The Baroque Concerto* (London, 1959)

Hyman, D., 'Bix Beiderbecke and Joe Venuti', *Keyboard*, 11/6 (1985), p. 76

Jambe de Fer, P., *Epitome musical des tons, sons et accords, es voix humaines, fleustes d'Alleman, fleustes à neuf trous, violes & violons* (Lyons, 1556)

Jansson, E. V., see Moral, J. A.

Jazz String Newsletter [Joe Venuti issue], 2/1 (1983)

Jensen, N. M., 'Solo, Duo and Trio Sonata', *Festskrift Jens Peter Larsen* (Copenhagen, 1972)

Johnson, D., *Scottish Fiddle Music in the Eighteenth Century: a Music Collection and Historical Study* (Edinburgh, 1984)

Kahn, E. H., 'Hilly Billy Music', *Journal of American Folklore*, 78 (1965), p. 309

Kirkendale, W., *Fugue and Fugato in Rococo and Classical Chamber Music* (Durham, N.C., 1979)

Kolneder, W., *Antonio Vivaldi* (London, 1970)

   Das Buch der Violine (Zurich, 1972)

Kowal, R., 'Zbigniew Seifert – Rapid Ascent', *Jazz Forum*, 34 (1975), p. 53

   'Zbigniew Seifert – a Musical Legacy', *Jazz Forum*, 59 (1979), p. 42

Kunst, J., *Music in Java* (2 vols., The Hague, 1973)

Laurencie, L. de la, *L'École française de violon de Lully à Viotti* (3 vols., Paris, 1922–4/R Geneva, 1971)

Le Blanc, H., *Défense de la basse de viole contre les entreprises du violon et les prétensions du violoncel* (Amsterdam, 1740/R1975); R serially in *La Revue Musicale*, 9 (1927–8)

Leipp, E., *Le Violon, historique, esthétique, facture et acoustique* (Paris, 1965)

Lington, O., *Jazz skal der til* [Jazz is what we need] (Copenhagen, 1941)

Lochner, L. P., *Fritz Kreisler* (London, 1951)

Loft, A., *Violin and Keyboard: the Duo Repertoire* (2 vols., New York, 1973)

Lotz, R., 'Eduardo Andreozzi – the Jazz Pioneer from Brazil', *Storyville*, 122 (1985–6), p. 62.

Loupien, S., 'Voix nouvelles – Didier Lockwood', *Jazz Magazine*, 281 (1979), p. 40

Lütgendorff, W. L. F. von, *Die Geigen- und Lautenmacher vom Mittelalter bis zur Gegenwart* (6th edn, Frankfurt am Main, 1922/R1968)

Mace, T., *Musick's Monument, or A Remembrance of the Best Practical Musick* (London, 1676; facsimile edn, Paris, 1958/R1966)

Magee, L., 'The Jazz-Rock Violin of Jean-Luc Ponty', *The Instrumentalist*, 30/6 (1976), p. 62

Magidoff, R., *Yehudi Menuhin* (New York, 1955)

Mandel, M., 'Jean-Luc Ponty's Electronic Muse', *Down Beat*, 51/1 (1984), p. 20

Marcan, P., *Music for Solo Violin Unaccompanied: a Performer's Guide to the Published Literature of the 17th, 18th, 19th and 20th Centuries* (High Wycombe, 1983)

Marshall, K. D., 'Modal Analysis of a Violin', *Journal of the Acoustical Society of America*, 77 (1985), pp. 695–709

McArtor, M., 'Francesco Geminiani: Composer and Theorist' (diss., University of Michigan, 1951)

McIntyre, M. E., and Woodhouse, J., 'The Acoustics of Stringed Musical Instruments', *Interdisciplinary Science Reviews*, 3 (1978), pp. 157–73

McVeigh, S., *The Violinist in London's Concert Life, 1750–1784: Felice Giardini and his Contemporaries* (New York, 1989)

Meer, J. H. van der, *see* Boomkamp, C. van L.

Menuhin, Y., *Unfinished Journey* (London, 1977)

Menuhin, Y., and Primrose, W., *Violin and Viola* (London, 1976)

Merck, D., *Compendium musicae instrumentalis chelicae, das ist: kurtzer Begriff welcher Gestalten die Instrumental-Music auf der Violin, Pratschen, Viola da Gamba, und Bass gründlich und leicht zu erlernen seye* (Augsburg, 1695)

Mersenne, M., *Harmonie universelle* (Paris, 1636–7/R1963; Eng. tr. (of the book re instruments) R. E. Chapman, The Hague, 1957)

Meyer, E. H., *Early English Chamber Music* (London, 1946; rev. edn, London, 1982)

Millant, R., *J. B. Vuillaume: sa vie et son œuvre* (London, 1972)

Moens-Haenen, G., *Das Vibrato in der Musik des Barock* (Graz, 1988)

Monosoff, S., 'Violin Fingering', *Early Music*, 13 (1985), pp. 76–9

Moral, J. A., and Jansson, E. V., 'Eigenmodes, Input Admittance, and the Function of the Violin', *Acustica*, 50 (1982), pp. 329–37

Morgenstern, D., 'Jazz Fiddle', *Down Beat*, 34/3 (1967), p. 16

Morris, W. M., *British Violin Makers* (London, 1904; 2nd rev. edn, London, 1920)

Moser, A., *Joseph Joachim: a Biography*, tr. L. Durham (London, 1901)
 Geschichte des Violinspiels (2 vols., Berlin, 1923; 2nd rev. edn, Tutzing, 1966–7)

Nelson, S. M., *The Violin and Viola* (London, 1972)

Nettl, B., *The Western Impact on World Music: Change, Adaptation and Survival* (New York & London, 1985), pp. 47–50

Neumann, F., *Ornamentation in Baroque and Post-Baroque Music, with Special Emphasis on J. S. Bach* (Princeton, 1978)
 Ornamentation and Improvisation in Mozart (Princeton, 1986)

Newman, W. S., *The Sonata in the Baroque Era* (Chapel Hill, 1959)
  The Sonata in the Classic Era (Chapel Hill, 1963; rev. edn, 1972)
  The Sonata since Beethoven (Chapel Hill, 1969)
Nolens Volens, or You shall learn to play on the violin whether you will or no (London, 1695)
Nunamaker, N., 'The Virtuoso Violin Concerto before Paganini: the Concertos of Lolli, Giornovichi, and Woldemar' (diss., Indiana University, 1968)
O'Connor, J., *Not Pulling Strings: an Exploration of Music and Instrumental Teaching Using Neuro-Linguistic Programming* (London, 1987)
Palmer, R., 'Soaring with the Frenchman [Jean-Luc Ponty]', *Down Beat*, 42/20 (1975), p. 17
Peyser, J., (ed.), *The Orchestra: Origins and Transformations* (New York, 1986)
Pfäfflin, C., *Pietro Nardini: seine Werke und sein Leben* (Stuttgart, 1930)
Pincherle, M., *Jean-Marie Leclair l'aîné* (Paris, 1952)
  Corelli: his Life, his Work, Eng. tr. H. Russell (New York, 1956)
  Vivaldi, Genius of the Baroque, Eng. tr. C. Hatch (London, 1958)
  The World of the Virtuoso, tr. L. H. Brockway (London, 1964)
Playford, H., *Introduction to the Skill of Musick for Song and Violl* (London, 1654; 7th rev. edn, 1674/R1966; 12th rev. edn. 1694/R1973; 19th rev. edn, 1730)
Praetorius, M., *Syntagma musicum*, vol. I (Wittenberg and Wolfenbüttel, 1614–15/R1959, 1968); vol. II (Wolfenbüttel, 1618; 2nd edn, 1619/R1958, 1980; Eng. tr. 1962, 1986); vol. III (Wolfenbüttel, 1618; 2nd edn, 1619/R1958, 1976)
Previn, A., *Orchestra* (London, 1979)
Primrose, W., see Menuhin, Y.
Pulver, J., 'Violin Methods Old and New', *Proceedings of the Royal Musical Association*, 50 (1923–4), pp. 101–27
  Paganini the Romantic Virtuoso (London, 1936/R New York, 1970)
Quantz, J. J., *Versuch einer Anweisung die Flöte traversiere zu spielen* (Berlin, 1752; 3rd edn, 1789/R1953); tr. E. R. Reilly as *On Playing the Flute* (London & New York, 1966)
Ratner, L. G., *Classic Music* (New York, 1980)
Retford, W. C., *Bows and Bowmakers* (London, 1964)
Reuter, F. von, *Führer durch die Solo Violinmusik* (Berlin, 1926)
Roda, J., *Bows for Musical Instruments of the Violin Family* (Chicago, 1959)
Rognoni, F., *Selva di varii passaggi secondo l'uso moderno per cantare e suonare con ogni sorte di stromenti* (Milan, 1620/R1970)
Roth, H., *Master Violinists in Performance* (Neptune City, 1982)
Rouda, R., 'The fourth way – Michael White', *Coda*, 9/12 (1979), p. 32
Rowen, R. H., *Early Chamber Music* (New York, 1949)
Russell, T., 'The Violin Scordatura', *Musical Quarterly*, 24 (1938), pp. 84–96
Sacconi, S. F., *I 'segreti' di Stradivari* (Cremona, 1979)
Sadie, S., see Brown, H. M.
Sadler, M., *The Retford Centenary Exhibition* (London, 1975)
Sagawe, H., 'Elgar's Creole Orchestra', *Storyville*, 52 (1974), p. 150
Saint-George, H., *The Bow: its History, Manufacture and Use* (London, 1896; 2nd edn, 1909)
Sandys, W., and Forster, S. A., *History of the Violin* (London, 1864)

Sárosi, B., *Gypsy Music* (Budapest, 1978)
  'Geigenspezifische Melodiegestaltung', *Studia Instrumentorum Musicae Popularis*, 6 (1979), p. 63
  'Eine "mehrsprachige" Zigeuner-Kapelle in Transsilvanien', *Studia Instrumentorum Musicae Popularis*, 8 (1985), p. 94
Schaffer, J., 'An innermost vision [Mahavishnu Orchestra, Jerry Goodman]', *Down Beat*, 40/8 (1973), p. 11
Schenk, J., 'Darnell Howard', *Jazz Session*, 6 (1945), p. 2
Scholes, P., (ed.), *Dr Burney's Musical Tours in Europe* (London, 1959)
Schreckloth, T., 'Jean-Luc Ponty – Synthesis for the Strings', *Down Beat*, 44/20 (1977), p. 12
Schroeder, C., *Guide through Violin Literature* (London, 1903)
Schwarz, B., 'Beethoven and the French Violin School', *Musical Quarterly*, 44 (1958), pp. 431–47
  Great Masters of the Violin (London, 1984)
  French Instrumental Music between the Revolutions (1789–1830) (New York, 1987)
Segerman, E., see Abbot, D.
  'Strings through the Ages', *The Strad*, 99 (1988), pp. 52–5
Selfridge-Field, E., *Venetian Instrumental Music from Gabrieli to Vivaldi* (Oxford, 1975)
Senoff, P., 'Jean-Luc Ponty', *Jazz & Pop*, 9/3 (1970), p. 26
Sevåg, R., 'Die Hardingfele: Instrument, Spieltechnik, Musik', *Studia Instrumentorum Musicae Popularis*, 6 (1979), p. 71
Shankar, L., 'The Art of Violin Accompaniment in South Indian Classical Vocal Music', (diss., Wesleyan University, 1974)
Sheppard, L., and Axelrod, H. R., *Paganini* (New Jersey, 1979)
Smith, G., *Stéphane Grappelli: a Biography* (London, 1987)
Southern, E., *Readings in Black American Music* (New York, 1971)
  The Music of Black Americans: a History (New York & London, 1971/R1983)
Speer, D., *Gründrichtiger ... Unterricht der musicalischen Kunst oder Vierfaches musicalisches Kleeblatt* (Ulm, 1697/R1974)
Stevenson, R., *Music in Mexico* (New York, 1952)
  Music in Aztec and Inca Territory (Berkeley & Los Angeles, 1968)
Stolba, K. M., *A History of the Violin Etude to about 1800* (Fort Hayes, 1968–9/R1979)
Stowell, R., 'Violin Bowing in Transition: a Survey of Technique as related in Instruction Books c.1790–c.1830', *Early Music*, 12 (1984), pp. 317–27
  Violin Technique and Performance Practice in the Late Eighteenth and Early Nineteenth Centuries (Cambridge, 1985)
Straeten, E. S. J. van der, *The Romance of the Fiddle* (London, 1911)
  The History of the Violin (2 vols., London, 1933/R New York, 1968)
Strunk, O., *Source Readings in Music History* (New York, 1950)
Swalin, B. F., *The Violin Concerto: a Study in German Romanticism* (Chapel Hill, 1941)
Szigeti, J., *A Violinist's Notebook* (London, 1964)
  With Strings Attached (2nd edn, New York, 1967)
  Szigeti on the Violin (London, 1969)
Talbot, M., *Vivaldi* (London, 1978)

Tartini, G., *Traité des agrémens de la musique* (Fr. tr. P. Denis, 1771; Eng. tr. ed. E. R. Jacobi, Celle & New York, 1961)

Taylor, C., 'The New Violin Family and its Scientific Background', *Soundings* 7 (1978), pp. 101–16

Thede, M. V., *The Fiddle Book* (New York, 1967)

The New Grove Dictionary of Music and Musicians (London, 1980)

The New Grove Violin Family (London, 1989)

The Self-Instructor on the Violin (London, 1695; 2nd edn, 1697 as *Instructor on the Violin*)

Toskey, B. R., *Concertos for Violin and Viola: a Comprehensive Encyclopedia* (Seattle, 1983)

Tottmann, A. K., *Führer durch den Violinunterricht* (Leipzig, 1873; 4th rev. edn, Leipzig, 1935, as *Führer durch die Violinliteratur: ein kritisches, systematisches und nach den Schwierigkeitsgraden geordnetes Verzeichnis*

Townley, R., 'Michal Urbaniak', *Down Beat*, 41/17 (1974), p. 38

Townley Worsthorne, S., *Venetian Opera in the Seventeenth Century* (rev. edn, London, 1968)

Traerup, B., 'Albanian Singers in Kosovo', *Studia Instrumentorum Musicae Popularis*, 3 (1974), p. 244

Tronchot, J., 'Jean-Luc Ponty', *Jazz Hot*, 198 (1964), p. 8

Ulrich, H., *Chamber Music: the Growth and Practice of an Intimate Art* (2nd edn, New York, 1953)

Vannes, R., *Dictionnaire universel des luthiers* (2nd edn, 2 vols., Brussels, 1951–9/R1972)

Vatelot, E., *Les Archets français* (Nancy, 1976)

Veinus, A., *The Concerto* (New York, 1944)

Vidal, L. A., *Les Instruments à archet, les faiseurs, les joueurs d'instruments, leur histoire* (Paris 1876–8/R1961)

Violinspiel und Violinmusik in Geschichte und Gegenwart: Internationaler Kongress am Institut für Aufführungspraxis der Hochschule für Musik und darstellende Kunst: Graz 1972 (Vienna, 1975)

Walls, P., 'Violin Fingering in the Eighteenth Century', *Early Music*, 12 (1984), pp. 300–15

Wasielewski, W. J., *Die Violine und ihre Meister* (8th edn, Leipzig, 1927)

Webster, J., 'Towards a History of Viennese Chamber Music in the Early Classical Period', *Journal of the American Musicological Society*, 27 (1974), pp. 212–47

Wechsberg, J., *The Violin* (London & New York, 1973)

White, E. C., 'G. B. Viotti and his Violin Concertos' (diss., University of Princeton, 1957)

White, R., 'Eighteenth-Century Instruments Examined', *The Strad*, 95 (1985), pp. 258–9

Whitehead, K., 'The String Trio of New York', *Down Beat*, 54/11 (1987), p. 26

Wilson, J., (ed.), *Roger North on Music* (London, 1959)

Winternitz, E., *Gaudenzio Ferrari, His School and the Early History of the Violin* (Milan, 1967)

   Musical Instruments and their Symbolism in Western Art (Yale, 1979)

Woodhouse, J., see McIntyre, M. E.

Yampolsky, I. M., *The Principles of Violin Fingering*, tr. A. Lumsden (London, 1967)

Ysaÿe, A., *Eugène Ysaÿe* (Brussels, 1974)

Zanetti, G., *Il scolaro ... per imparar a suonare di violino, et altri stromenti* (Milan, 1645)

Zschinsky-Troxler, E. M. von., *Gaetano Pugnani* (Berlin, 1939)

Index